Black African Cinema

Nwachukwu Frank Ukadike

UNIVERSITY OF CALIFORNIA PRESS
Berkeley / Los Angeles / London

This book is a print-on-demand volume. It is manufactured using toner in place of ink. Type and images may be less sharp than the same material seen in traditionally printed University of California Press editions.

.

University of California Press
Berkeley and Los Angeles, California

University of California Press
London, England

Copyright © 1994 by The Regents of the
University of California

Library of Congress Cataloging-in-Publication
Data

Ukadike, Nwachukwu Frank.
    Black African cinema / Nwachukwu Frank
Ukadike.
        p.   cm.
    Includes bibliographical references (p.   )
    and index.
    ISBN 0-520-07747-4 (cloth).—ISBN 0-520-
    07748-2 (paper)
        1. Motion pictures—Africa, Sub-Saharan.
    I. Title.
    PN1993.5.A35U4   1994
    791.43'0967—dc20   92-26076
                                        CIP

Printed in the United States of America

The paper used in this publication meets the
minimum requirements of ANSI/NISO Z39.48-1992
(R 1997) (Permanence of Paper).

At the beginning of my graduate studies, which ultimately led to this book, I experienced two breaks in family continuity: the deaths of my mother, Mary Ukadike, and my only brother, Patrick Nordi Ukadike. I dedicate this book to them.

Contents

Acknowledgments

This book would not have been possible without the numerous encouragements that sustained my effort. I thank the following institutions and persons for their contribution. The University of Ibadan, Ibadan, Nigeria, graciously granted me leave of absence to pursue research. I am indebted also to Mypheduh Films, Washington, D.C., and its proprietor, film director Haile Gerima, for access to the collection of African films, critical reviews, and production notes. Med Hondo, Kwaw Ansah, Gaston Kaboré, Ngangura Mweze, and many other African filmmakers shared their thoughts and feelings with me. I would also like to thank June I. Givanni of the British Film Institute, California Newsreel, and the University of Michigan (the Office of Vice President for Research).

I am grateful to the following journals for granting me permission to use previously published materials: *The Black Scholar* for "Western Film Images of Africa: Genealogy of an Ideological Formulation"; *Film Quarterly* for "Yaaba"; *Jump Cut* for "Anglophone Media"; and *UFAHAMU* and *Afterimage* for portions that appeared in these publications. I am humbly grateful to the late Professor Jay Leyda, who was supportive of my ambition to pursue this project. He was able to read only the proposal, the introduction to this work, on his hospital bed and was hoping to read the book before he was called to his final resting place. His concern for clarity and creativity sustained the completion of this study. I am deeply grateful to friends and colleagues for their support: Richard Porton for his invaluable suggestions and perceptive comments; Françoise Pfaff for her generosity; and Joan Rayfield for her cross-cultural awareness and incisive comments that rectified some lapses. I would like to express my gratitude to my friend Andrew Bryant, a linguist, for his immensely helpful translations of French, Italian, and Portuguese articles and for his frequent research trips on my behalf to the British Film Institute and London public libraries. I would also like to acknowledge my cousin, Martin Egun, for the many problems he encountered while trying to obtain articles from Nigerian newspapers and magazines.

Finally, inexpressible gratitude goes to my wife, Penelope, who, from the beginning of the project, endured my moods, and without whom this manuscript would never have been completed, and to the Ukadike family of Umunede, Nigeria, for their cherished, indefatigable, moral and spiritual support.

Introduction

Black African cinema did not develop under the same circumstances as European or American cinema. Besieged by European colonizers, African cinema was not controlled by Africans until the 1960s, when Africans began to achieve independence and make their own feature films. Nonetheless, since political independence in black Africa has not been followed by economic and cultural independence, film production, even when under the control of Africans in independent countries, has mimicked the general uneven pattern of Africa's overall development. This dilemma, created by a colonial past and cemented by a neocolonial present, has prevented the emergence of a real national cinema capable of speaking for and to Africans. In the United States, Britain, or France, for example, the audiovisual mass media is a complex organizational and bureaucratic technical system, formed by the political economy of advanced capitalism. In most of Africa, the electronic media has become an instrument for the consolidation of power. Instead of being utilized as an integral arm of the sociopolitical and economic infrastructure, serving useful developmental purposes, its function has been that of an ordinary bureaucratic propaganda machine, helping to perpetuate the leadership of powerful oligarchs. This type of situation and attitude is a contributing factor to the lack of real cinematic development in black Africa, except in the case of some independent filmmakers' work. It is this very personal cinema that has given luster, meaning, and purpose to African film language.

The aim of this study is to examine black Africa's cinematic practices which, in conjunction with traditional forms of communication and representation, offer a cultural means of expression—a coherent system-atic definition of social life, politics, and conflict—spanning the colonial and neocolonial periods. I will trace Africa's historical past, particularly the oral traditions (hereby referred to as Africa's traditional media) which have been instrumental to the development and understanding of black Africa's cinema and its forms of entertainment and information media. I will also trace the dismantling of these traditional media by European colonialists who for almost a century manipulated the politi-cal, economic, and social life of African people. I will outline the broad movement of African cinema, beginning at the turn of the century, when in 1897 Lumière's film titles first stigmatized Africa with exoti-cism (marking the beginning of the portrayal of Africa in European movies), continuing through the twenties, thirties, forties, and fifties, and on to the emergence of a true black African cinema in the sixties. Since its inception, black African cinema has been struggling to reverse the demeaning portrayals presented by the dominant colonial and com-mercial cinemas which blatantly distorted African life and culture, as, for example, the Tarzan jungle melodramas and, more recently, *The Wild Geese* (1978), *The Gods Must Be Crazy* (1984), and the so-called ethnographic films of Jean Rouch, David MacDougall, and Trinh T. Minh-ha.

It was not until some African countries liberated themselves from European colonialism (notably in the mid-fifties and sixties) that black Africans began to participate in film production. It was at this time that film was first used meaningfully as a voice of and for the people. This account of three decades of black African cinema—from the sixties to the present—will focus on feature films, shorts, and documentary productions as well as on some aspects of coproductions and television programs exchanged within sub-Saharan Africa. This will lay the groundwork for examining the "alternative" means by which black African cinema has moved beyond a chronic domination to espouse its own position within a decolonizing process. Intrinsic to contemporary Third World cinema, and to black African cinema in particular, are films aimed at addressing these new situations, which in turn demand that filmmakers formulate an approach to filmmaking that is in syn-chrony with their own cultural environments. Though psychological pressures and cultural differences abound among black African film-makers, they are united in their opposition to what they see as escapist tendencies in Western cinema.

This book does not propose once again to summarize the history of black Africa's film production; rather, it seeks to explore the history, theory, and practices of black African cinema from an interdisciplinary perspective, at once geopolitical, socioeconomic, and ideological. My discussion of cinematic trends will emphasize some sociocultural factors previously ignored in other works. It is hoped that this examination will herald new strategies and assert new critical criteria and grounds for appraising the accomplishments of this burgeoning cinema.

From the beginning, the major concern of African filmmakers has been to provide a more realistic image of Africa as opposed to the distorted artistic and ideological expressions of the dominant film medium reflecting (to borrow from Erik Barnouw's terminology) "the attitudes that made up the colonial rationale." Colonial films such as *Sanders of the River* (1935), *King Solomon's Mines* (1937), and *Congorilla* (1932), which excluded African participation in their making, gave no priority to African interests. Instead, they provided a distorted view of "natives," portraying them as ingenuous, outlandish, somewhat mysterious beings who were nevertheless loyal and grateful to the Europeans for coming to "guide and protect them."

The new black African cinema concerns itself with the role film can play in building African society. Black African filmmakers contend that traditional ways of filmic representation—old ideas and attitudes—must give way to new ones, especially in portraying African cultures. The interest, participation, and collaboration of the people must be secured, stimulated, and maintained. Toward this goal, the majority of black African filmmakers are united by their art and ideology. Despite differences in their backgrounds, it is evident that these filmmakers have worked to establish certain criteria that might serve as the basis for black African cinema.

Although black African governments have recognized the cinema as a strong vehicle for the promotion of traditional culture, they have failed to promote it internationally. Nor have they nurtured the idea of cinema as a viable and competitive industry worthy of investing their meager resources, hardly surprising in a situation in which hard-pressed governments must do battle against drought and famine, wars and interethnic strife, ignorance, and disease. The African filmmaker is inundated by conflicts relating to the complexities of economic, political, and psychological subordination. But despite these limitations and other shortcomings (for instance, the absence of material resources), the cineastes have not succumbed to failure. Inadequate financing has prevented many of them from completing their films on schedule: Med Hondo, the exiled Mauritanian filmmaker, took seven years to complete his epic thriller *West Indies* (1979); Désiré Ecaré devoted twelve years to making an exuberant raucous comedy, *Visages de femmes* (Faces of women, 1985); and Moyo Ogundipe, a Nigerian newcomer, has completed *The Song Bird* four years after production began.

These films appear as vibrant as they are ambitious. Aesthetically and artistically, *West Indies* and *Visages de femmes* are remarkable and have been internationally applauded. (Reviews indicate that *The Song Bird* is equally ambitious.) This inestimable achievement, emanating from a body of films broad in scope, superb in talent, yet limited in material resources, exemplifies strengthened traditional structures aimed at the (decolonization and reaffirmation) of all aspects of black life, particularly black African life. This study asserts, but not without some reservations, that black African cinema has attained aesthetic and artistic maturity, and although a wide variety of Hollywood and European cinematic practices are evident in these films, black African filmmakers have used these practices to forge their own cinematic language and style.

I will assess black African films from the pioneering years which tend to constitute what might be called "national consciousness" films: films of French-speaking (francophone) African countries (Senegal, Mauritania, Upper Volta, now Burkina Faso, and Côte d'Ivoire (Ivory Coast), which concerned themselves with the denunciation of colonialism, and films with the commercial tendencies of English-speaking (anglophone) Africa,[1] notably Ghana and Nigeria. I will examine new developments and explore other trends that have, through experimentation, achieved a cinematic language that could be called African—notably the Mozambican and Angolan revolutionary cinema resembling that of Cuba and the half-Western, half-African *Visages de femmes,* which mixes pulsating African music and dance with steamy eroticism. I will also explore why *Visages de femmes* is seen as subverting moral codes in black Africa, where sexual explicitness is taboo in the cinema, whereas it is highly acclaimed in the United States.

This book does not pretend to provide a comprehensive study of all black African films. The list of films I will be drawing from, however, is representative of three decades of black African cinema. My purpose will be to evaluate the accomplishments of these films by taking significant steps in a critical discussion that I hope will provide new insight into this developing cinema. In outlining the historical perspective of black African cinema my main aim will be to accommodate the larger thematic issues emanating from political and cultural experiences as manifested by colonialism and neocolonialism. My analysis will be strongly influenced by the notion of "culture," "self-affirmation," and "recognition" as reflected in the thoughts of Amilcar Cabral, Frantz Fanon, and Kwame Nkrumah.[2] The cultural concepts propagated by these thinkers suggest that if there is to be meaningful development, African states must be independent of the monopolistic international, sociocultural, and economic order, which, as the brainchild of colonialism and imperialism, (perpetuates underdevelopment) In essence,

Fanon's views, as well as those of Cabral, Nkrumah, and other exponents of African cultural identity, reflect the idea that "this cultural renaissance represents a change in consciousness, a turning point in the liberation of the self and of one's society."[3] This is the position the pioneers of black African cinema have also adopted—that cinema should be regarded as a powerful instrument in developing the cultural ethos of a people. Toward this end, African filmmakers have begun to examine the psychological dimensions of oppression and underdevelopment, and to explain them in cultural terms through the cinema, thus advancing the struggle for liberation in contemporary Africa.

For many African filmmakers cinema is a revolution. African filmmakers perceive film as a stimulating medium that the Third World must use for social, political, and artistic enlightenment in order to achieve what Fanon has called "a new revolutionary humanism." Under this theory, the need to break completely with the patterns of colonialism, the need for colonized people to reeducate themselves in order to achieve revolutionary objectives, and the need to build a new revolutionary culture become imperative. Even though many Third World filmmakers are heavily influenced by the theories propagated by Fanon, they find that the winds of change necessary for their full realization are controlled by the very forces that Fanon has attacked. Fanon and, subsequently, most Third World filmmakers see political education as the means for a transformation of consciousness. And, for this new way to succeed, an educational program must be initiated whose task is to raise the level of political consciousness of the masses.

In neocolonial Africa, any effort to intervene at the ideological level, as well as to transform the material base, implies that the education and full participation of the masses is necessary. But the fact that this concept of mobilization has failed in the black African system of leadership also illustrates the complexity of that transition within a society, or from one mode of production to another. How has the shift from colonialism to neocolonialism or from direct domination by Europe to indirect domination by Europe and the United States enhanced or stifled the material resources necessary for the growth of an indigenous film industry?

Corresponding with the various patterns in which Britain, Belgium, France, and Portugal carved out and shared Africa, the cinema in the ex-colonies followed different patterns of development. For example, the films of French West and Equatorial Africa share similarities not seen in the films of ex-British colonies. Moreover, both groups are distinct from the representative styles adapted by Angola and Mozambique, both ex-Portuguese colonies whose independence came only in the mid-seventies. All three groups differ in their approach to and execution of narrative, methods of representation, and definition of documentary.

The dominant black cinema of Nigeria takes the form of theatrical adaptations originating from Yoruba traveling theater (whose main exponents are Hubert Ogunde, Moses Olaiya, and Ade Love). Nigerian cinema owes little to Western models, nor does it derive its style from any known national cinema, East or West. Capable of fascinating a popular audience, especially among the Yoruba, these films make invigorating use of popular traditions such as those found in Yoruba fairy tales, magic, and superstition. Set within the confines of oral tradition, mixing traditional songs and dances, folklore and farce, the films are highly satirical. In such films as *Aiye* (1980), directed by Ola Balogun, and *Jaiyesimi* (1980), directed by Hubert Ogunde, traditional communication merges with "modern" cinematic representation, and any effort to analyze these films must recognize the constituents of their unconventional structures. These films also draw our attention to the problem of the search for(a genuine African film language.)

Perhaps the best way to start considering cinema in the sub-Saharan continent is to establish first what is accepted as black African cinema. Focusing this inquiry on Africa south of the Sahara and separating it from culturally Arabic-inclined North Africa, this study will cover the areas from the western Sudan and countries on the West Coast of the Atlantic (Mauritania to Nigeria and Cameroon) to the Congo, East Africa, South-East Africa, and Madagascar. From this breakdown, it is apparent that there is no justification for positing a single African cinema. In black Africa, cinema depicts the stories and cultures of the people it represents, just as traditional African art (sculpture, body painting, murals, and so on) portrays the area from which it comes. A similar problem occurs when historians attempt to classify any art object from any part of Africa as "African art." Is it possible to posit any stylistic criteria with which to unite all the trends in African art—be that art a Bambara sculpture from Mali, a Nok or Ife head from Nigeria, an Ashanti "Akuaba" fertility doll from Ghana, or a Baluba sculpture from Zaire? Even if we reduced black Africa to an area comparable in size to Nigeria, we still would notice a range of styles. For example, in comparing the classical naturalism of Ife art from Oyo State with the abstract geometric pattern of the Kalabari water spirit masks from Cross River State, one can see that they have relatively little or nothing in common, and Oron figures, also from Cross River State, do not look very much like the Nok heads found in the northern region.

Rather than propose one stylistic entity in African art, the illustrations given here demand that we begin to understand African art as "a collection of art forms" ranging from the "classical naturalistic to the purely abstract'' whose patterns and styles of execution may be different from art forms found elsewhere.[4] In the cinema one is also dealing with a substantial body of work from diverse geopolitical and sociocultural perspectives whose ideologies and themes are different, though inflected by, cinematic styles borrowed elsewhere. Thus we can see elements of Italian neorealism and French new wave in Paulin Soumanou Vieyra's *Afrique sur Seine* (Africa on the Seine, 1955) and in Ousmane Sembene's films such as *Borom Sarret* (1963).

For the purpose of this study I will posit black African filmmaking as emerging out of the excitement of nation-building and a quest for the revivification of Africa's lost cultural heritage and identity, a quest that has inspired innovative and creative diversification in the cinema and the arts. In black African cinema we find a profuse selection of films: from Senegal the biting satirical drama *Xala* by Ousmane Sembene; from Burkina Faso *Wend Kuuni* (The gift of God, 1982) by Gaston Kaboré, a film imbued with oral tradition and filmic poetry; from Mozambique the revolutionary folk epic *Mueda: Memória e massacre* (Mueda: Memory and massacre, 1979) by Ruy Guerra of Cinema Novo fame; and from Mauritania Med Hondo's musical drama *West Indies*.

These contrasts do not, however, represent a broad thematic and stylistic sampling of black African cinema. A close examination of this cinema reveals that colonialism, neocolonialism, and their social and political issues dominate its themes. Such trends derive from the Third World cinema's seeking to: ''(1) decolonize the mind; (2) contribute to the development of a radical consciousness; (3) lead to a revolutionary transformation of society; and (4) develop new film language with which to accomplish these tasks.''[5] Elements of ''cinematic Third Worldism'' found in black African cinema can be compared to elements in Latin America cinema, particularly to Cinema Novo, in which Glauber Rocha played an important role, to the ''Third Cinema'' proposed by Fernando Solanas and Octavio Getino, and to the revolutionary cinema of Jorge Sanjines and other Cuban directors. The unifying element between black African filmmakers and their Third World counterparts is perhaps the basic concept of film as an artistic tool with which to counter the hegemony of imperialism.

The earliest black African films—*Afrique sur Seine* and *Borom Sarret*—were undeniably studies of Africans from an African point of view. While the theme of *Afrique sur Seine* suggests ''existentialist alienation,'' *Borom Sarret* depicts cultural alienation, social and economic exploitation, and, as Françoise Pfaff has remarked in her *The Cinema of Ousmane Sembene*, ''the tragedy of misplaced expectation.'' A blend of semidocumentary and fictional narrative forms combines to expose colonialism and the forces that are (or should be) at war with that system, directly or indirectly stimulating the audience to reflect on the issues affecting them. Films in this category also include Ousmane Sembene's *La noire de. . .* (Black Girl, 1966), Eddie Ugbomah's *The Mask* (1979), Sarah Maldoror's *Sambizanga* (1972), Haile Gerima's *Harvest: 3,000 Years* (1978), and films by the Mozambican National Institute of Cinema such as *Estas são as armas* (These are the weapons, 1979), *Mueda: Memória e massacre*, and José Cardoso's *Abaixo—o apartheid* (They dare cross our borders, 1981).

The emergence of the neocolonial elite after the granting of independence compounded the continent's problems, and filmmakers found themselves confronting new societal issues. Cinema became introspective. It is interesting that the vivid portrayal of postindependent Africa is informed by both Marxist and non-Marxist analyses that filmmakers have incorporated into their films. The language of these films also echoes the training and experience of individual directors. Some of black Africa's directors received their training in eastern and in western European capitals. For example, Souleymane Cissé of Mali and Ousmane Sembene of Senegal trained in Moscow and then later lived and worked in France, acquiring a firsthand knowledge of French society. Safi Faye of Senegal and Ola Balogun of Nigeria studied in France, and Med Hondo of Mauritania (who claims to be self-taught and who infuses Marxist philosophy with African socialism) still lives as an expatriate in France, where he has established a base for his filmmaking career. Haile Gerima (who told me he claims no political affiliation but whose film *Harvest: 3,000 Years* is highly political) is a product of the University of California. And Ababacar Samb-Makharam of Senegal, who for several years served as the General Secretary of the Fedération Panafricaine des Cinéastes (FEPACI), trained in Rome. These filmmakers' education and experience culminate in their individual creativity. Whether it be Souleymane Cissé's *Baara* (Work; Mali, 1978), Med Hondo's *Soleil O* (Mauritania, 1969), Kwaw Paintsil Ansah's play adaptation *Love Brewed in the African Pot* (Ghana, 1981), Ola Balogun's *Cry Freedom* (Nigeria, 1981), or Sembene's *Ceddo* (Senegal, 1977), virtually all these films have one thing in common—the depiction of situations as they exist and the identification of the struggling masses as undisputed heroes who have undertaken as their task to "right the wrongs" in their societies.

Shifting toward commercialization (that is, cinema functioning as an industry rather than a didactic tool), the new generation of African filmmakers are now focusing on broad-based contemporary issues. Portraying Africa's transition from traditional life to contemporary life, and vice versa, their films tend to focus on the sociopolitical and economic forces at work among a particular group of people in different geographic locations. In most cases, these forces are either the focus of intense investigation in the depiction of social changes or the subject of allegories of culture which intertwine with breaks and continuities within history. Appropriately, this corollary structure constitutes the scenario for the recurring theme of black African cinema: the conflict between old and new. Clyde Taylor observes that "this is never a conflict between symmetrical opposites, but rather the choice from among the modern, individualistic and industrialized, Marxist socialism, and some form of African socialism."[6] I will explore these issues as they relate to such films as *Poko* by Idrissa Ouedraogo (Burkina Faso, 1981); *Lettre paysanne* (Peasant letter) by Safi Faye (Senegal, 1975); *Jom, ou l'histoire d'un peuple* (Jom, or The story of a people) by Ababacar Samb-Makharam (Senegal, 1981); *Wend Kuuni* by Gaston Kaboré (Burkina Faso, 1982); and *Heritage . . . Africa* by Kwaw Ansah (Ghana, 1988).

Black African cinema is infused with an infinite variety of subjects and styles, as diverse as the lives of the people it portrays; therefore, the continent cannot be completely understood or wholly evaluated by the screen image alone. Hence the social, cultural, and historical analysis here will draw from a broad spectrum of ideas: the notion of Africa's triple heritage (Ali Mazrui, Ngugi wa Thiong'o); the critique of cultural colonialism and underdevelopment (Walter Rodney, Basil Davidson, D. K. Fieldhouse); and work on traditional culture (Amadou Hampaté Bâ, Cheikh Anta Diop, Joseph Ki-Zerbo) and decolonization (Aimé Césaire). This discussion will also draw on Marxism as elaborated and disseminated by Louis Althusser's view of "ideology" (especially the concept of ideology as a total phenomenon identified with culture or the symbolic as a whole), Raymond Williams's notion of "realism" as a "conscious movement towards social extensions," and Antonio Gramsci's work on "hegemony."

In a broader light, African cinema must be understood from the point of view of historical experiences spanning colonialism to neocolonialism. That the formal independence of African states has not been followed by economic independence shows a new form of economic and cultural strangulation emerging in the form of dependence on former colonial governments, with the latecomer—the United States—playing an even larger role in Third World dominance. How has economic dependence and political impotence harmed African culture? Films like *Xala* have addressed this question, but to detail the full ramifications, this analysis will draw enormously on "dependency" theorists (André Gunder Frank, Eduardo Galeano, Samir Amin, and Aguibou Yansane). Aware of certain limitations and constraints of Marxist theories, and cultural theories in general, I will use Gramsci's *Prison Notebooks,*

Amin's critique of the theory of underdevelopment, and L. Adele Jinadu's "Some African Theorists of Culture and Modernization: Fanon,
Cabral, and Some Others."[7]

The classic texts of anticolonialism are indispensable to this study:
Edward Said's *Orientalism*; Albert Memmi's *The Colonizer and the
Colonized* and *Dominated Man*; Frantz Fanon's *The Wretched of the
Earth* and *Black Skin, White Masks*; and Ngugi wa Thiong'o's *Decolonizing the Mind: The Politics of Language in African Literature*. Although the sources mentioned are not directly concerned with film,
they reflect important Third World aspirations, delineating how cultural
history informs contemporary events and why past and present events
are depicted in films as a useful communication process in black Africa's development.

The above summation of concerns patterns the shape of the overall
discussion. On specific applications to film, I shall contrast the topics
presented in these works with numerous previous studies of stereotyp-
ing, racism, and colonialism in dominant cinema. These include Donald
Bogle's *Toms, Coons, Mulattoes, Mammies, and Bucks,* Thomas
Cripp's *Slow Fade to Black* (on stereotyping black Americans), Richard
Maynard's *Africa on Film: Myth and Reality,* and David S. Wiley's
Africa on Film and Videotape 1960–81. I will also draw on studies of
Third World cinema by such critics and scholars as Roy Armes, Ferid
Boughedir, Julianne Burton, Teshome Gabriel, Guy Hennebelle, Ran-
dal Johnson, Françoise Pfaff, Robert Stam, and J. Koyinde Vaughan.
Finally, I shall conclude by asking where black African cinema fits
within this context. It is here that we can link past and present circumstances with black African film production, exhibition, and distribution
so as to best illustrate, for example, the social, political, and artistic
concerns of the times.

My intention is also to expose questionable cinematic strategies
wherever necessary, whether in relation to the noncinematic qualities
of some films, to the misdirected policies of Africa's military oligarchs,
to an assimilated elite who disdains nationalistic patriotism, or to a
populace that, out of a colonial mentality, prefers foreign goods to
locally manufactured ones. I shall be looking at black African films
with a critical eye (an insider's eye), focusing on the realities and contradictions of contemporary Africa. To place the directorial work, major
themes, and styles of black African cinema in perspective, three main
questions will have to orient the discussion. First, even if this cinema
is derived from Western technological invention, isn't it also necessary
to have a working definition that incorporates the meaning of the nature
of black African cinema? In other words, is this cinema purely a re-
hashing of Hollywood or European film? Second, how might we dis-

cover the way in which cultural identity is pursued in the film medium? Third and finally, how do we compare and contrast aspects of black African cinema's militancy with those of some other Third World cinemas? Ferid Boughedir identified some of the principal tendencies of African cinema in his thesis *Cinéma Africain et décolonisation* (1974), and the classification he proposes remains germane to this discussion. But since 1974 new directions and new developments have surfaced, and for this reason I will modify or expand on his classifications.

Cinema, like literature, storytelling, religion, and other aspects of culture, reflects the natural world of things, including the human community. How these things are perceived profoundly affects their interpretation. But like the artist and the interpreter, ideological determinants combine class sympathies and beliefs to affect the production of art as well as the evaluation of the work itself. My emphasis will not only center on basic choices of subject matter but also on the ideological assumptions behind such choices, utterances, and evaluations.[8]

In methodological terms, this book presents a comparative analysis of films from black Africa, considering these films as a diachronic series that synthesizes the motivational and ideological forces that structure each film. The films are evaluated within the framework of the communal role of art in traditional African societies, as well as within the context of the historical, political, social, and economic contingencies that govern the production process. Because cinema in Africa reflects African belief systems, these films incorporate symbolic, cultural, and ideological details that render them difficult for the uninformed viewer to decipher. They defy the critical methods used to analyze Western cinema, which, when applied to films from the Third World, impair their understanding and domesticate the subversive elements of their cultural traditions. Cinematic representation entails storytelling or interpretation that uses such specific cinematic conventions and codes as camera movement, lighting, editing, image and sound relationship, and mise-en-scène. How black African filmmakers infuse these codes with their own oral narrative patterns (also considered an indispensable artistic code) demands thorough scrutiny. In light of this, black African films will be viewed through a relevant theoretical framework deeply rooted in African cultural traditions and social texts and a comprehensive methodology that attends to the intervening mediations between community life and representation. Using cultural sources as a vital prerequisite for reaching the ''real'' meaning of films helps us to determine the differences and transformations that have occurred in black Africa, from film to film, thematically and diachronically. I will approach each film, each individual case, on the basis of how the production materialized—negative or favorable inferences will best be understood from that angle. For the above reasons, some aspects of this study will be metacritical.

My analytical method for this project is also syncretic. By employing social, political, cultural, and economic history, I will take into account, on the one hand, the historical situation in Africa to date and, on the other hand, the ideological differences among the various filmmakers (reflecting the diverse ideological perspectives operating in today's neo-colonial Africa). The filmmakers' intentions closely align with their concern for an African form of vision, so that the specific organization of codes and subcodes may not correspond with the conventions typical of the dominant Western cinemas. An understanding of the filmmakers' intentions can assist us in coming to terms with the specificities of black African cinema. The "Africanness" of such intentionality will be a central point of focus.

In black Africa, where many ethnic subcultures coexist, filmic representation is replete with numerous cultural symbols. The application of an ethnocentric reading of such films is at best useless. In order to get to the meaning of a text, the approach must also be *intertextual*. Of particular importance in this study is the exploration of the relation between cinema and the traditional arts—folklore, dance, and music. Until now, only a few studies have examined how films' narrative structures have been influenced by or interwoven with African oral traditions. Using African oral tradition as a creative matrix, filmmakers focus on social issues that address, among other things, the transition from village to city, how the "new" (Western values) impinges on the "old" (traditional values), and pastoral settings. From the perspective of creating narratives imbued with originality and filmic poetry, *Sey Seyeti* (One man, several wives; Senegal, 1980) by Ben Diogoye Beye, *Jom,* and *Wend Kuuni* are appreciated for audaciously blending cinematic conventions with oral narrative patterns.

My summation of oral tradition in these and other films will examine black African film as a medium of expression and communication, and assess how and to what degree the films are indebted to oral traditions. I will also examine two major approaches that characterize black African cinema—one following Western cinematic tradition, the other modeled on African traditional culture. I will explore how the colonial, British, French, American, Italian, Indian, Egyptian, and Cuban cinemas have influenced black African film production. And I will examine the relationship between the film text and other texts (both filmic and non-filmic), looking particularly at such source material as plays and novels adapted for the screen. In addition, I shall focus on other arts that have influenced black African cinema, such as the impact of music on *Naitou* (1982), *West Indies,* and *Visages de femmes.*

Because African audience expectations have been formed by foreign cinematic and cultural conventions (prior to the advent of African film), I shall explore audience consumption and reception patterns in African society. My approach will therefore also address *the reception of films by spectators*. This critical orientation will be useful not only in terms of the analysis of what makes imported foreign films fascinating but also in helping understand African film of the eighties, when the younger generation of African filmmakers began to challenge the filmic paradigms initiated by film's pioneers.

Although I have emphasized ideological and intertextual analysis, as well as metapsychological analysis, all of these do not form an exhaustive interpretation of a film's meaning. For this reason, my approach will also be *contextual*. All those forces bearing on the cinematic industry will be considered, such as the changes and challenges that have occurred in production, distribution, and exhibition, as well as the social institutions and production practices that construct the image of the continent. It is important to posit black African cinema within multiple contexts: historical, economic, political, and cultural. African existence is punctuated by such events as internecine conflicts, internationally inspired wars, coups d'état, and unstable economies (caused both by Western financial supergiants who regulate the prices of Third World exports and Africa's own internal mismanagement). I shall also concern myself with the contradictions inherent in the evolution of technology and cinematic practices and with the tension between government agencies and independent filmmakers. I shall investigate the cooperation between theater groups and film production groups and between film industries inside and outside Africa. Addressing these issues, I will draw from relevant resources in other disciplines—sociology, anthropology, politics, and economic history—linking these references with the development of cinema. It is here that this study becomes fully interdisciplinary.

A considerable amount of work has been done by scholars of Africa's economic history. Recent works on this subject provide a platform on which to base the study of African film's economic history. Cultural historian Ali Mazrui, in his book *The Africans: A Triple Heritage,* for example, offers illuminating insights into Africa's sociocultural and political problems. But owing to some limitations, especially his obsession with Islam and his bias against other religions, his socialistic views lack the cultural foundations on which to base my analysis. For Ali Mazrui, the most serious form of decay in African society is deeply rooted "in the institutions inherited from the Western world, rather than those bequeathed by Islam."[9] His view of Islam contradicts those expressed by the film director Ousmane Sembene in *Xala* (1974) and *Ceddo* (1976), in which Muslim imperialism is condemned for its role in the breakdown of African spirituality. (Both Mazrui and Sembene were brought up as Muslims by parents who were ardent and loyal followers of Islam.) In *Soleil O,* Med Hondo reverses the Christian meaning of the symbol of a cross into a sword. In doing so, he dichotomizes the cultural polarities signified by the white man's symbol of ideology (the cross and Christianity) and Africa's adoption of the Christian religion, which he sees as a "violent" and unwelcome intrusion into Africa's social fabric. However, this type of contradiction reflects Africa's sociopolitical structures and helps to explain how the issue of "Africanness" in this study relates to the proclamations of filmmakers, individual films, and writings on African cinema in general. Reality is perceived on so many levels that what is factually accurate for one may become propaganda for another; "one man's meat is another man's poison." To deal with these discrepancies, Edward Berman's critical analysis "African Responses to Christian Missionary Education"[10] will be used in conjunction with the examination of other films about religion, for example, *Njangaan* (The Koranic school student, 1975) and *Shaihu Umar* (1976).

In the past, international organizations such as UNESCO and the Paris-based Agence de Coopération Culturelle et Technique have made positive contributions by supporting organizations and events that allowed African filmmakers to meet, exchange views, see one another's films, and debate issues affecting African film production. Also, Africa has several long-established biennial film festivals such as JCC (Journées Cinématographiques de Carthage) and FESPACO (Festival Panafricaine du Cinéma de Ouagadougou), the proceedings of which will provide valuable primary information and have been published in Guy Hennebelle's *Cinémas d'Afrique noire* series, *Cinémaction,* and *Colloques des journées cinématographiques de Carthage: Bilan et perspectives.* Moreover, reports about African cinema have been published in the gazettes of African governments that have attempted to develop film production in their countries.

There is little secondary literature in English on black African cinema. Recently, however, some international English-language film journals have devoted whole issues or published articles on Third World cinema: *Jump Cut, Screen, Sight and Sound, Film Quarterly, Présence Africaine, UFAHAMU, African Studies Review, Thirdworld Affairs, Frame Work, BFI Dossiers,* and *Cineaste.* Generally, in discussing black African films and filmmakers, writers seem to prefer Western critical criteria to judgments reflecting African cultural traditions. This study will abide by the fact that the historical complexity of black Africa's cinema is not to be approached with a method that reduces the

problem to a mere simplistic economic determinism as most writings
on Africa have done in the past.

Since the mid-1950s, when African filmmakers started to produce
films, literature on African cinema has consisted primarily of articles
written in French and published in African and European magazines,
journals, and newspapers. Gradually, a growing number of articles in
English by scholars, critics, and historians (in America and Britain as
well as in anglophone Africa) also began to emerge in a wide variety
of periodicals. Diverse in scope, some of these works have coalesced
into a series of new, short books that focus on filmmaking in specific
African countries. In this category are five books that have been published in the *Cinémas d'Afrique noire* series: Victor Bachy's *Le cinéma
au Mali, Le cinéma en Côte d'Ivoire,* and *La Haute-Volta et le cinéma*;
Rik Otten's *Le cinéma dans les pays des grands lacs Zaire, Rwanda,
Burundi*; and Paulin Soumanou Vieyra's *Le cinéma au Sénégal.*
(Vieyra's other books on African cinema include *Le cinéma Africain:
Des origines à 1973* and *Sembene Ousmane cinéaste.*) The books in
these series deal with the diverse origins and development of filmmaking in a number of African countries, cataloging the problems of African
filmmaking from preindependence to the neocolonial era and focusing
most notably on the lack of capital for film production, foreign domina- *literature*
tion of exhibition and distribution channels, lukewarm government support for filmmaking, absence of infrastructure to support a film industry,
inadequate training facilities, and misplaced government priorities for
using film. These books are generally brief, and, as a result, their discussions of filmmakers and the chronology of their works, concerned as
they are with themes and content analysis, are devoid of details.)

Vieyra's ambitious project *Le cinéma Africain des origines à 1973*
chronicles African cinema from country to country, while Françoise
Pfaff's *The Cinema of Ousmane Sembene: A Pioneer of African Film,*
as the title suggests, is an in-depth study of Sembene's work. *The Development and Growth of the Film Industry in Nigeria,* edited by Alfred
Opubor and Onuora Nwuneli, is a collection of seminar papers in which
various contributors discuss Nigeria's Indigenization Decree which attempted (but failed) to implement the transfer of the distribution and
exhibition of feature films into the hands of Nigerians from the hands
of foreigners, who own and control American Motion Pictures Exporters and Cinema Association (AMPECA), specializing in American and
European films, and NDO Films and CINE Films, owned by the Lebanese, specializing in Indian, Egyptian, and Asian films. These books
cite the origins and multiformity of African film production. However,
none of them, except Vieyra's *Le cinéma Africain,* attempts to bring
together into one source information pertaining to the entire continent's

film production. Important developments since 1973 have yet to be compiled into one single source.

Françoise Pfaff's *The Cinema of Ousmane Sembene* is an exception to the other books mentioned because of the quality of its in-depth analysis of Sembene's films. Pfaff uses Sembene's biographical data as a blueprint for her interpretations of his films, which makes this work, despite a wealth of detailed analysis, seem somewhat hagiographical. Despite this observation, the book is highly informative. Pfaff's second book, *Twenty-five Black African Filmmakers: A Critical Study with Filmography and Bio-Bibliography,* attempts a broader documentation of black African film practice and is a valuable research source for scholars concentrating on francophonic films.[11]

The shortcomings of the published writings about African cinema illustrate the limitation not only of French, British, and American perspectives on black African cinema but also that of the new emerging critics of Franco-African descent. As of this writing, Vieyra is the only African author who has published books on African cinema. As an experienced filmmaker who is also regarded as one of the "fathers" of African cinema, his in-depth knowledge of African cinema separates his work from that of foreigners who have written about African cinema. He asserts an authoritative voice that divorces him from the pedestrian view characterizing other works.

The list of writings on black African cinema indicates that the majority are in French, perhaps evidencing France's lead in encouraging the development of cinema in Africa. However, many of these books emphasize context more than the text. They ignore, for example, the emerging trends and styles of this new cinema. When these books discuss the films, their coverage is not extensive enough to incorporate the wider issues treated in African historiographies, such as the influence of both Eastern- and Western-style education; Marxist method and historical process in contemporary African studies; the implications of mortgaging African countries to the International Monetary Fund (IMF) as a prescription for reviving degenerating Third World economies; and the uses of oral tradition, music, and art in African culture. All these, in one way or another, are vital attributes that should inform our understanding of the cinema of black Africa. The process of studying black African cinema demands sociopolitically informed methodology, one that measures up to the demands of its cultural range and ideological complexity. Such will be my guiding principle and the challenge of this book.

It is my contention that any study of black African cinema should start with an introduction to some cultural dynamics of African tradition. This will give the reader a broader picture of why this cinema is informed not only by the cultural preferences and ideological needs of the people it represents but also by the oral tradition that precedes the grapplings of black African cinema.

The first chapter of this book will survey Africa's earliest contacts with the cinema: the evolution of colonial cinema and the era of exoticism and the various forms of travesty, the ambiguities of ethnographic films, and the origins of the quest for seeing Africa through African lenses. I shall argue that prior to the colonialist invasion of Africa and the introduction of the photographic image as a medium of communication by Christian missionary groups there already existed sophisticated systems of communication that will be referred to as "Africa's traditional media." I will explore the ways in which these traditional media, operating within the auspices of cultural norms, function informationally, educationally, and as entertainment. Given these facts, I shall demonstrate that the cinematic codes in black African movies are not completely foreign, only the ways in which they are presented. I will explore the methods by which this traditional system was dismantled by colonialism and investigate how the West provided its own account of African history and culture leading to the still uniformly accepted external view of Africa as the "dark continent" propounded by the romance-adventure stories of H. Rider Haggard, Edgar Rice Burroughs, and Elspeth Huxley, among others. Films following this same exotic path not only gave us neosafari films but also perniciously distorted the history and culture of Africa.

Chapter 2 will survey the origins of black African cinema in the "francophone" region from the mid-fifties to 1970 within the context of the domination of foreign films in Africa. This study accounts for the introspective and "engaged" characteristics of black African cinema during this period. Nearly all the films reflect a collective malaise caused by sociopolitical problems. Actually, their overall theme reflects the conflict that has permeated their existence: traditional African culture versus Western ways. Thus we have films dealing with varying subjects: on alienation, *Afrique sur Seine*; on the transition to neocolonialism, *Et vint la liberté* (And then freedom came; Guinea, 1969); on the recapture of Africa's distorted past, *L'Empire Songhai* (The Songhai empire; Senegal, 1963); on ancestral African dances, *Sindiély* (Senegal, 1963) and *Tam tam à Paris* (African drums in Paris; Cameroon, 1963). Other topics include illiteracy—*Mandabi* (The money order; Senegal, 1968)—and indigenous bourgeoisie and corruption, nepotism, and mismanagement—*F.V.V.A.—Femmes, voiture, villa, argent* (Women, car, villa, money; Niger, 1970). I will examine the Marxist stance of filmmakers and its effect on film style, as well as the use of film as a pedagogical tool, so important to Africa given its high rates of illiteracy.

Chapter 3 deals with the battle of frames between television and film as it relates to the development of film production in the "anglophone" region. I will explore the documentary pattern of the British tradition in government-sponsored educational films for television in Ghana, Kenya, and Nigeria. I will also survey commercial tendencies in films such as Nigeria's *Money Power* (1980), *Aiye* (1980), *The Mask, The Death of a Black President* (1983), and Ghana's *Love Brewed in an African Pot*, plus examples of coproductions, such as *Kongi's Harvest* (Nigeria, 1970) and *Kukurantumi* (Ghana, 1983).

Of particular importance here are the narrative patterns of Nigeria's Yoruba films. Although I shall be dealing with both theme and structure in these films, this investigation of narrative will draw us into a detailed analysis of films that might be called "theater on the screen," leading us to ask if an African film style actually exists. The question of cinematic narrative structure will be contrasted with theater conventions, filmic structures of the francophone region, and dominant styles of Hollywood and other national cinemas.

The fourth chapter provides a critical assessment of post-1970 phases of diversification. In this period, when cinema became truly introspective, I will focus on the neocolonial circumstances that provided the scenario for the dominant theme of this cinema—the conflict between old and new, or, as some have put it, tradition versus modernity. This dominant theme will be examined and contrasted with aesthetic innovation stemming from individual experimentation, enabling us to conceptualize what constitutes African film language.

Since some of the films have incorporated oral tradition, it is important to show, through close reading, why such films are markedly different from those of other cultures, even when certain Western and Eastern European cinematic styles are evident. Films in this category include *Jom, Wend Kuuni, West Indies, Visages de femmes,* and Segun Oyekunle's *Parcel Post* (Nigeria, 1982). It is here that the cultural contexts of African cinema will be fully explored. And to illuminate fully the cultural codes and ideology regulating African film practice, this chapter also explores the militant liberationist tendencies of the lusophone (Angolan, Guinean, and Mozambican) cinema, in which the film medium serves as a revolutionary tool. These militant documentary films will be examined and compared to those of a similar vein that evolved in Latin America.

Chapter 5 explores the trends launched by the "new breed" of African filmmakers of the late eighties whose "rebellious" structures can be seen as promoting aesthetic competition and inquiry in diverse filmic applications. Although my intention is to focus on innovative styles and ideological orientations, I shall also be deconstructive. The shifts and transgressions in modes of address in Souleymane Cissé's *Yeelen* (Brightness; Mali, 1987) in conjunction with Cheick Oumar Sissoko's *Finzan* (Mali, 1989), Idrissa Ouedraogo's *Yaaba* (Burkina Faso, 1987), Ngangura Mweze and Benoît Lamy's *La vie est belle* (Life is rosy; Zaire, 1987) and Henri Duparc's *Bal poussière* (Dancing in the dust; Côte d'Ivoire, 1988) is contrasted with the traditional structures exemplified by Med Hondo's *Sarraounia* (Mauritania, 1987), Ousmane Sembene's *Camp de Thiaroye* (Senegal, 1987) and Kwaw Ansah's *Heritage . . . Africa* (Ghana, 1988). In considering the emerging trends in terms of the conventions and the strategies they deploy, this chapter probes the concepts of the "traditional" and the "hybrid" in African cinema, and the notion of "rejuvenated" African film language, particularly in the manner in which African films create an authentic or "positive" portrayal of African reality.

Chapter 6 concludes this study by focusing on the question, "Whither black African cinema?" (As funding for black African films continues to come from foreign sources, and as black African filmmakers continue to rely on overseas distribution as the only way of recouping finances (owing to a lack of audience interest and the distribu- tion and exhibition problems in Africa), one must ask whether filmmakers' style of execution conforms to their sponsors' dictates.) It is hoped that this analysis will serve as a case study on how distribution affects African film style and how this cinema, if set in a supportive atmosphere, might draw on its rich cultural heritage and sophisticated oral tradition to thrive economically, instructively, and internationally.

* "we are being colonized by media"
   — control → mental
         control how people perceived themselves
         and their relationship to the world

1

Africa and the Cinema

Information and Entertainment Media in Black Africa before the Arrival of Cinema

Ngugi wa Thiong'o, a disenchanted critic of colonialism, indicates in his book *Homecoming* that in any society there is a way of life which, through time, reflects the sum of a people's collective endeavor. In discussing the constituents of a society's unique material and spiritual values, Ngugi reminds us that ("no living culture is ever static."[1]) Ngugi's contention implies a connection between living in an environment and coming to terms with that environment. He notes, however, that a society's "art, science, and all social institutions, including [the] system of beliefs and rituals" that derives from the people's way of life, change as that way of life is modified or developed through the ages. Some developments and changes are more radical than others, and the adverse effects can be awesome (as in the case of the colonization of Africa).

Though Africa's traditional life was never static, its social transformation was more gradual than modern change.[2] Frantz Fanon was acutely aware of this dynamic and urged a revitalization of abandoned African traditions, while always aware of the conflicts between African and European culture as well as the alienation from tradition wrought by colonialism.[3] Fanon's analysis of changes in tradition is culturally oriented with liberation as its goal; his observation points to the need for the reestablishment of the "nation" to rekindle national culture

from the remnants of the past. These remnants remind one that, before
Europeans came to colonize Africa and impose their culture and ideologies on the people (a process dating back to the fifteenth century
when "discovery" of the African coastlines by Portuguese explorers
also ushered in slave traders), Africans had already developed a system
of sophisticated communication—the traditional media or oral tradition, including song, dance, folklore, drawing, sculpture, rites, and ceremonies. These activities covered all information, education, and entertainment needs.

Under colonial domination, new values initiated by Western ideologies were introduced into African life, and under neocolonialism, Africa struggled—and is still struggling—to develop distinct national cultures. This study considers the impact of these new values as they
apply to each of the three phases of Africa's development: Africa before
white conquest; Africa under colonial domination; and Africa since
independence. The issues considered within each phase of development
are information and entertainment media before white conquest, cinema as a form of cultural and ideological domination in Africa under
colonial rule, and the quest for independent African film production in
the dying stages of colonialism.

With the exception of Ethiopia and the Bamum and Vai people (including the Akan people,[4] as recent discoveries have shown), black
Africa, until recently, had no written records. This does not mean, of
course, that Africa had no culture or history. Rather, wisdom, knowledge, and national history were conveyed orally from generation to
generation.

But with the European colonization of Africa and the subsequent
introduction of the slave trade, the oral tradition was threatened. The
European presence brought with it an onslaught of alien influences
from industrial nations, that is, the "Western way of life," yet this and
endemic natural disasters such as drought, famine, and disease never
entirely destroyed the tenacity of the old order. In various forms, old
traditions, which hovered on the brink of extinction, can still be found
today, preserved in various domains of African society. The peasants
of black Africa, described as a group that has seen "no contradiction
between speaking their mother tongue and belonging to a larger national
or continental geography,"[5] have upheld national pride by keeping their
traditions alive. Even under colonialism and neocolonialism, the peasants have shown an unlimited ability to unite in pursuit of one goal—to
gather together and keep reactivating the remnants of the old culture
emblematic of the rich store of "orature" found in their stories, proverbs, poems, riddles, and jokes. Thus, "orature," dynamic and genera-
tive, is omnipresent; it permeates every aspect of life, and the word

itself, in Africanist terms, broadly refers to the entire oral tradition of Africa, the whole oral discourse on every subject and in every form of expression initiated by people of African descent.[6] Naturally, such indigenous traditions are meticulously depicted in African films.

Relying heavily on the cultural codes of the people, vis-à-vis the value of the word for meaning and nuances, oral narrative serves as the genesis of communication influencing all aspects of community concern, or what Harold Scheub calls "readily retrievable images of broad applicability."[7] Some items are sung, others are spoken in narrative form, and others are left for special occasions. It is here that the nucleus for rapid and effective dissemination of important community information, attitudes, norms, and ideas is distilled and maximized to evoke emotional response.

To appreciate the effectiveness of the spoken word consider, for example, the traditional evening gathering. Most storytelling takes place in the evenings when friends and relatives gather, which provides mutual cooperation and a mellow atmosphere in which to hear tales and fables, some of them initiating a deeper understanding of the community, the society, and the universe as perceived by the elders. In many communities, moonlight provides the natural floodlight for open-air gatherings—the *théâtre naturel*. An important aspect illustrating the effectiveness of the gathering is that the children who participate will, in the course of their daily activities, retell the stories they heard from the elders.

Once a member of the peasant community and now a leading expert on African oral literature, Ngugi wa Thiong'o, as a child, listened to the elders tell stories at the fireside. He writes how stories are then retold to other laborers working together in the fields picking the pyrethrum flowers, tea leaves, or coffee beans of the European and African landlords:

> There were good and bad storytellers. A good one could tell the same story over and over again, and it would always be fresh to us, the listeners. He or she could tell a story told by someone else and make it more alive and dramatic. The differences really were in the use of words and images and the inflexion of voices to effect different tones. Our appreciation of the suggestive magical power of language was reinforced by the games we played with words through riddles, proverbs, transpositions of syllables. . . . So we learned the music of our language on top of the content. The language, through images and symbols, gives us a view of the world, but it had a beauty of its own. The home and the field were then our preprimary school but what is important . . . is that the language of our evening teach-ins, and the language of our immediate and wider community, and the language of our work in the fields were one.[8]

The viability of storytelling is enhanced by the heterogeneity of its
mediating elements; in the narrative structure, there is, for example,
the use of truth and fiction in the depiction of circumstances, plot and
dramatization, continuity and discontinuity of time, and the relationship between image and sound. In comparing this ancient traditional
medium with the modern-day cinema, the similarity of method of execution is apparent. In cinematic storytelling, the heterogenous nature
of the cinematic signifier is tied to the multileveled process of narrative
construction, the combination of diverse codes. Some examples of
these cinematic procedures are camera work, image organization (editing), dialogue, voice-over or off-screen narration, image sound relationship, and mise-en-scène. These similarities are not usually appreciated,
however, since the cinema is technologically based in contrast to oral
storytelling, which is derived from everyday language and culture.[9]

In broader terms, oral tradition is cherished for its ritual, performance, enactment, and event. Conveyed by the arrangement of imagery or recontextualization of cultural images by performers or artists
who, in the words of Ruth Finnegan, "formulate in words," the oral
tradition is presented in one or a combination of genres: the proverb,
the riddle, the lyric poem, the tale, heroic poetry, epic. It is beyond
our scope here to elaborate upon these genres; however, their functions
in oral tradition have been thoroughly documented in Africanist writings.[10] Oral traditions, national or regional, are entrenched in endogenous cultural values—a collective will of existence bound by national
identity. In the Malian traditionalist Hampaté Bâ's terms, oral tradition
is "the great school of life," the sculptor of the African soul. Its grand
and omnipotent characteristics serve the unlimited goal of encompassing "at once religion, knowledge, natural science, apprenticeship in a
craft, history, entertainment, recreation, since any point of detail can
always take us all the way back to primordial unity."[11]

If the storytelling includes riddles, proverbs, dance, or song, it is
because they are necessary punctuations that highlight the dramatization of the inevitable coexistence within the universe. Song, chorus,
music, and dance from this perspective are often misunderstood by an
outsider. In Eurocentric interpretations, for instance, they are simply
a cultural explosion of rhythm, joyful call-and-response singing and
vivacity, gorgeously attired native dancers. But for the African initiates, every chant, drumbeat, song, chorus, and dance replicates nuances that serve as part of a ritual as stringent and resonant with tradition and symbolism as "air is vital to life" (in traditional African adage).
The subject matter of folktales is sometimes determined by historical
circumstances, but the "drama," observes Ngugi, "has origins in
human struggles with nature and with others."[12]

Stories, told extemporaneously or professionally, are adapted to suit all occasions. The invocation of ancestral gods through traditional rhythms, songs, and dances preserves the communality of cultural bonds and historical past. Significantly, the unifying element in this communitarian ethos is the story. This is the reason, often inferred many times, that the story is probably the most common and the most appreciated literary genre in black Africa.

Oral tradition is used to confront the difficulties, complications, and achievements of this unique autochthonous society in what amounts to a defiant process of signification, a demystification of occurrences, and thus such expressions are likely to assume allegorical posture. Before colonialism, oral tradition did not necessarily project a political dimension in the form of national allegory (to reverse Fredric Jameson). The textual resonances of its allegorical structure at first seemed more anthropological than ideological, more inclined to cling to traditional imperatives than to impose new political systems. Colonialism reversed this position. With the clamor for freedom and subsequent ushering in of postindependent structures, which in turn created ineptitude and lack of discipline (resulting in mismanagement and corruption), individual stories become synonymous and indicative of "national character," or as Jameson contends, "the story of the private individual destiny [becomes] an allegory of the embattled situation of the public Third World culture and society."[13]

From this perspective of the individual being implicated in the collective destiny, the allegorical tradition (at least, in the African sensibility) is deeply rooted in a pedagogical process to which expression and interpretation are coded in a special or sacred language as a "fragmentary discourse" (Angus Fletcher) utilizing cultural models in which meanings must derive from hermeneutic deciphering of known symbolic values. To this effect, cultural productions, literature of protest, and cinematic practices, for example, take the form of deliberate fragmentation and are suffused with a particular authorial voice. Allegory forms the basis for the indelible register of social concerns: here political, historical, and thus, literary and cinematic teleology coalesce into ideological discourse. (Hence, the majority of the activist films of black Africa provoke action rather than complacency.) The very notion of black Africa's problematic emancipation demands a cultural practice expressed in forms commensurate with the cultural specificities of the producing nations. In this regard, applying this principle to black Africa's film practice, I shall show how this inevitable allegorical juxtapositioning is used to subvert the dominant mode of production and aimed at acquiring a sense of identity and national transformation.

The function of oral literature is as diverse as African languages.[14]

As the expanding society requires continuous carriers of tradition, continuity of interaction between artists and the masses assures meaningful artistic appreciation of life's complexities, zeroing in on specific traditional values. In this regard, storytelling is an appropriate form of personal expression whose appeal depends on individual stylistic performance techniques. To inspire an indoctrinating message of irresistible appeal, the actual execution process depends on how these ancient images are reconstructed. Significantly, the creative matrices involved (and hence the reception of that art) depend on selectivity (narrative choices) as it correlates with the historical and cultural process. Here the transformations and creative interpretations of subject matter rely, by and large, on the prowess of a gifted individual (the artist) to weave through the literary traditions and conventions.[15] In like manner, as the following chapters will show, black African film practice exhibits stylistic and thematic diversity in defining regional, national, and, thus, the continent's experience.

If, on the one hand, the level of the artist's imagination elevates the effectiveness of the folktale as a tool for communication, on the other hand, the native language enhances the communication of that folktale as well as the entertainment it provides. Because the language is indigenous, intimate, and personal, the folktale maximizes interaction among the receivers—the collective—who are, in the phrase of Frantz Fanon, "fixed on the same pedestal." Contact with new creative ideals also gives rise to new rhythms of thought that develop the audience's imagination. "Everytime the storyteller relates a fresh episode to his public," observes Fanon, "he presides over real invocation. . . . The storyteller replies to the expectant people by successive approximations, and makes his way, apparently alone but in fact helped on by his public, toward the seeking out of new patterns, that is to say national patterns."[16] Flourishing under its language systems and boosted by its artists' creative impulses, black Africa's oral patterns have developed irresistible appeal. They are effective because they make use of established and well-coordinated communication and reception codes. Here I must draw attention to Africa's diverse linguistic and translinguistic practices. Although this diversity is inflected by what has been characterized by Mikhail Bakhtin as "polyglossia" (boundaries separating natural languages) and "heteroglossia," or "many languagedness" (and in our case many dialects), this system is indebted to heterogeneous phenomena typifying what Bakhtin refers to as "open unity." The impact of these intralinguistic differences upon intercultural film reception and interpretation might as well be posited within the signifying elements in the African film. The purpose is to examine how cultural and lingustic differences impact on the production, exhibition, and reception of films, all of which shall become apparent in the following chapters dealing with black African film practice.

I have tried to demonstrate that oral literature, in its various ways or styles, imparts knowledge to the indigenous society and that the long-term impact of these messages depends on the skill of the carriers of that tradition (the storytellers) in manipulating the primary materials available to them. That material was replete with valuable information, historical and otherwise, and artists would creatively turn it into entertainment for maximum audience appeal. The level of imagination which inspired this extraordinary creative prowess of traditional African societies was believed to have begun from time immemorial, descended from lessons in history and civic virtue to encompass astronomy, metaphysics, philosophy, and theology. Ivan Van Sertima's book *Blacks in Science: Ancient and Modern* and his article "The Lost Sciences of Africa"[17] vividly explain African involvement in these fields.

The internal (indigenous) and external (foreign) dynamics of the struggles within these societies came to a sudden halt when the Europeans arrived and declared that the African's vision of the universe was uncivilized. Colonial powers had failed to respect what Jorge Sanjinés called the "internal rhythms of our people" reflecting the organizing principles of African society—the origins and status of the primacy of national allegory embedded in tradition. In colonial eyes, Africa was a vast continent of savage peoples, riddled with superstition and fanaticism.[18] In addition to this portrayal, the white conquest of Africa brought shame and degradation to the human race when trading in human cargo, otherwise known as the slave trade, was legitimized. Slavery undermined ethics and respect for human beings, separated families, disrupted settled agriculture, and forced mass migration movements. This is best explained in Ivan Van Sertima's words:

> No human disaster, with the exception of the flood (if that biblical legend is true) can equal in dimension of destructiveness the cataclysm that shook Africa. We are all familiar with the slave trade and the traumatic effect of this on the transplanted black but few of us realize what horrors were wrought on Africa itself. Vast populations were uprooted and displaced, whole generations disappeared, European diseases descended like the plague, decimating both cattle and people, cities and towns were abandoned, family networks disintegrated, kingdoms crumbled, the threads of cultural and historical continuity were so savagely torn asunder that henceforward one would have to think of two Africas: the one before and the one after the Holocaust.[19]

The awakening of consciousness that would allow for a liberated popular voice was hampered by Africans' loss of control over their own destiny. Africa's natural development was dealt a catastrophic blow, and the architect of this destruction was imperialism.

Imperialism, through the missionaries of its ideology, attacked and condemned ancient rites, the dances and the graven images of tradition, as satanic. In *The Wretched of the Earth,* Frantz Fanon aptly observed the logic of the European "choke hold" on Africa's emancipation: "Colonialism is not satisfied merely with holding a people in its grip and emptying the native's brain of all form and content. By a kind of perverted logic, it turns to the past of the oppressed people, and distorts, disfigures, and destroys it."[20] European explorers, travelers, slave traders, missionaries, and scholars of all kinds have projected or extrapolated the lies that Africa was a continent of no history, no culture, no political structure.

Imperialism came to Africa armed with Western science and technology. One would have expected a meaningful and equitable sharing of this new development to ensure maximum efficiency of Africa's economic growth. Instead, technology was used to ensure the continuation of the political, cultural, and economic domination that imperialism had established. As a result, when the cinema came to Africa, little did the natives know that the forces of imperialism were once again "adopting new and more subtle and diversified ways, forms, and themes to disseminate its ideology."[21]

There is no faster way to change a people's culture or impose a model of behavior and system of values than through new technologies of communication: books, radio, photographs, newspapers, magazines, television, and the cinema. For example, the contents of publications mass produced by missionary printing presses were carefully chosen so that only the moral messages the authorities considered suitable were allowed to reach the Africans. Retelling of old fables and tales was permitted only if they did not contain political messages. Similarly, special films designated "for Africans only" were produced or screened for the natives by, for example, the British Colonial Film Unit.[22] Films imported from overseas were censored and reedited to suit the colonizer's purpose. (One reason for reediting imported films from Europe and America was to delete any portion that might teach Africans to agitate for independence through self-determination) The traditional evening gatherings, at which children listened to the words of wisdom from generations of forefathers, gradually faded into the dim light of the missionary slide projection of portraits of their holy saints. Bible stories, such as the Gospel According to St. John or St. Mark (but not St. Nordi), replaced the familiar stories of oral tradition. Nordi is an African name, but to the missionary it was heathenism! Everything that symbolized African culture was discredited as primitive, ungodly, and unchristian. Missionaries, the colonial administrators, and their agents superimposed a Western ideology upon Africans by convincing them that "they had no culture worth preserving; the European culture was promoted as superior and anybody who wanted to succeed in the society had to adopt the European culture."[23] The audiovisual medium expedited this philosophy by showing Africans how Europeans lived. The natives, given no other choice, came to grips with European culture.

We must bear in mind that "the most crucial aspect of precolonial African education was its relevance to Africans" compared to the European type that was used for "subordination and exploitation, [and] the creation of mental confusion,"[24] through alienation. If the major preoccupation of colonial power was to cut the natives off from autochthonous traditions (which it was), then the introduction of both secular or religious schools and the technologies of communication (notably print and cinema) fostered that process. In the advent of this so-called civilization, what has happened to Africa's traditional media? And how has African culture survived the onslaught of European cultural and ideological views imposed by the cinema? In other words, have the bonds of unity been torn asunder?

Some Early Contacts with the Cinema

In the second half of the nineteenth century, the European colonizing powers began to show interest in the exploration of interior Africa for potential economic and commercial exploitation. It therefore became expedient that the European slavers, in what constituted a major policy change, abandon their old trading habits of waiting on the coastlines while their African cohorts raided the interior. This time the Europeans embarked upon the task of discovering the African heartland—a move aimed at consolidating their "effective" occupation of the continent. This proposition was enticing, and so European and American explorers swarmed through Africa. But the actual scramble for the partitioning of Africa into colonies was done by four major European powers—Britain, France, Portugal, and Belgium.

The abolition of the slave trade in the nineteenth century necessitated the reversal of policy. (We might note here that Britain, the biggest shipping nation in the slave trade in the eighteenth century, became the leading abolitionist power in the nineteenth century.) During the infamous Berlin Conference of 1884–1885, in which Western powers deliberated their future engagement in Africa, the European colonizers agreed both to end slavery and facilitate free-market imperialism. This meant that while emphasis was to shift to "lawful" trade from trading in human cargo, it was justifiable to colonize in order to exercise the freedom to search for new sources of raw material for Western markets. The Berlin Conference was a double-edged sword that, ironically, shamelessly exhibited a perfect example of the contradictions of imperial exploitation.[25]

The Europeans feared that venturing into the communities of African villagers might provoke hostility, and thus jeopardize their commercial ventures. For this reason they sought and obtained the services of missionaries—to neutralize African antagonism with their preaching—pressing upon the natives the acceptance of the European presence. In many respects Christianity served as an adjunct to the economic and political objectives of imperial governments that sponsored explorers. It is not surprising that missionary groups participated in the dividing and sharing of Africa. They too sponsored their own explorers to open up and widen new routes for Christendom. As a result, common interests shared between the missionary explorers and large commercial conglomerates in partnership with exploitative governments necessitated reciprocity of benefits. For example, in exchange for winning over the Africans, and in fulfillment of one of the resolutions reached at the Berlin Conference, the missionaries received money and protection from European commercial concerns (exactly the same type of treatment exploitative governments accorded their commercial agents). It was agreed that Christian missionaries would be allowed to indoctrinate Africans under the full protection of the European powers occupying the territories in which the missionaries operated. In theory, missionary involvement with Christianity and the work of God as opposed to imperial governments and their fostering of colonialism and exploitation may seem diametrically opposed. In practice, however, Christianity in Africa became allied with European colonialism, involving two aspects of the same process: the destruction or deliberate undervaluing of a people's culture and colonial subjugation of the continent.

In West Africa, for example, missionaries seeking to convert Africans were armed not only with copies of the Holy Bible but also with film and slide projectors, which were used to facilitate the understanding of their evangelical crusade.[26] According to Edward Horatio-Jones, the first "film shows" in West Africa, known as the "Magic Lantern," were brought to Sierra Leone by missionaries,[27] who showed slide projections depicting the birth and death of Christ. The missionaries accomplished two objectives by using these visual means: first, they were able to draw and convert a larger and more curious audience; and second, in what amounts to a "cultural rupture" with Africa's past, they were able to infiltrate Africa's culture.

Cinema came to Africa as a potent organ of colonialism. Because film is a powerful visual medium with an extraordinary ability to inordinately influence the thinking and behavior of its audience (as the missionaries proved), films proved to be a powerful tool for indoctrinating Africans into foreign cultures, including their ideals and aesthetics.

It is not quite clear when cinema came to black Africa. In his article "The Awakening African Cinema," Jean Rouch states that "the cinema made its debut in Africa in the very first years after its invention," citing 1896 as the year that a vaudeville magician stole a "theatregraph" projector from the Alhambra Palace Theater in London and used it to "introduce motion pictures into South Africa."[28] While Rouch contends that the first motion picture projection in West Africa dates not as far back, in 1905 mobile cinemas started showing animated cartoons in Dakar, Senegal, and its suburbs. In that same year, a French circus group and filmmakers exhibited the Lumière brothers' films *L'arrivée d'un train en gare de Ciotat* and *L'arroseur arrosé* in Dakar. Meanwhile, George Méliès made some short films there—*La marche de Dakar* and *Le cake-walk des négres du nouveau Cirque* are known examples.[29] And according to Edward Horatio-Jones, although missionary slide projections were in Sierra Leone by 1923, "to the African countries [south of the Sahara] cinema never arrived until 1925."[30]

From the beginning of cinema, the film business has shown an interest in Africa. Developments in the Maghreb indicate that not only were films projected in that region as early as 1896 but in actual fact, Felix Mesguich from Algiers, working as camera operator for the Lumière brothers, made some films in that region in 1905.[31] However, owing to the fact that Africa-as-producer came late to the cinematographic business (genuine African film production did not start until independence was won), [the continent's image ultimately was presented and interpreted by foreigners.] It was only two years after that first remarkable projection of the famous Lumière film *The Workers Leaving the Factory* (1895) that George Méliès made *The Comic Moslem* (1897), followed by *Ali Barbouyou* and *Ali Bouf in Oil* (1903). Although copies of the Méliès's films are no longer available, "it is not hard to guess from their titles alone, that they marked the beginning of the subsequent questionable treatment of the subject."[32]

Two formats initiated by Lumière and Méliès, among the earliest filmmakers, have left a permanent mark on film and the film industry. First was the Lumière documentary or "actualité" film, followed by Méliès's invention of the fiction film in 1897. The implications of these formats, as we have witnessed through the various stages and genres of the cinema, is that filmmakers, and also the audience, have preferred one format over the other. It has been stated that it was Méliès's fictional approach rather than the Lumières' documentary genre that triumphed in the representation of colonial Africa. As one writer has put it, "This is quite understandable since it was the exoticism of the African continent which interested the European filmmakers, producers, and audiences. In these circumstances it was natural that the documentary should be supplemented by fiction."[33] Emilie de Brigard has also remarked that "the distinction" between the tendencies "is often blurred to take advantage of both."[34]

By 1897 the motion picture was already giving audiences an unprecedented sense of capturing the world, and Africa was in the forefront of this experiment, which was later to be turned into exploitation by its colonizers. Along with colonialist tendencies, the original film (from the inception of motion pictures, called variously documentary, actualité, interest films, educational films, or travel films) became inextricably linked with ideology, thus promoting increased divergence from reality. With the story film set in exotic backgrounds becoming visible on a commercial scale, Africa again became center stage.

Since film production, exhibition, and distribution were in the hands of the colonial powers, Western aesthetic and ideological concepts prevailed. African influence was only superficial, limited to the utilization of the continent as background, sometimes exotic and with action alien to African culture based on the preconceptions of the people who made the films. Where the action is played by blacks or when whites acted out black roles in such films as *The Birth of a Nation* (1915), the black image was presented as either demeaned or stereotyped. Such misrepresentation, it was reported, contributed to the reason why African soldiers from Senegal fighting alongside their colonizers in World War I, though pleased with their first contact with cinema, began to lose interest in the motion picture after the novelty wore off, at least in films that debased their race and dignity or had nothing to do with their culture.[35]

An interesting development that should not escape the film scholar's attention occurred in 1915, with the release of D. W. Griffith's *The Birth of a Nation*. When the film was shown in France it was banned by the government for fear its volatile contents might incite French racists or offend Africans and thus induce discontent among African soldiers. Although the French were boosting their war effort and protecting their interests, this measure is the epitome of "respect and dignity" toward the colonized, whom they could have easily dehumanized if they had so desired—as in the American example, when, during World War II, German prisoners were treated better than African-

American soldiers.[36] However, this does not mean that French films portrayed blacks or Africans in a positive light.

In the British East African territory of Tanganyika (now Tanzania), some of the earliest contacts with cinema were with the films of Martin Johnson, including *On the Borderland of Civilization* (1920), *Simba* (1924–1928), and *Congorilla* (1929–1932). These were, notably, explorer films. Africans contributed to the production of these films by acting or appearing before Johnson's camera, albeit as victims of exploitation. Since the postproduction work was reportedly done outside the African continent and the films were not commercially exhibited in Africa, it is doubtful if the African participants ever saw the finished films. However, East and Central Africans' first full-scale contact with cinema was with the experiment conducted by the British Colonial Office between 1935 and 1937. Known as the Bantu Educational Kinema Experiment (BEKE), its assignment was to make and show instructional films, especially health films, to Africans. Tanzania was the production center, and educational films were then taken on lorry tours to East and Central Africa. The leading organizers of BEKE were L. A. Notcutt and G. C. Latham, authors of *The African and the Cinema* (1937), in which they note that BEKE was a project of the International Missionary Council largely financed by American philanthropic organizations such as the Carnegie Corporation of New York. The British Colonial Office played a direct advisory role, and at the end of the experiment Notcutt and Latham were unable to set up a permanent film production unit. The British and East African governments were either unwilling or unable to make the financial contribution needed to sustain a permanent production center. The overall initiative of BEKE and the colonial context in which the films were set were often controversial. Critics attacking the condescending portrayal of Africans saw in the films a depiction of the European way of life as exemplary, giving Africans the impression that their culture and traditions were inferior to those of the Europeans. These early contacts were not meant to show Africans how to produce films or manufacture the cinematic apparatus; rather, cinema was used as an extension of imperialism.

Some modest breakthroughs that occurred in North Africa must be accounted for. Albert Shemama Chikly of Tunisia shot *Ain el Ghazel* (Gazelle's eye) in 1924, but this ambitious start died because no other Tunisian film was made for another three decades. In Egypt, it was the embargo caused by World War I, halting the importation of foreign films, that engendered local film production. By 1927 Egypt already had a quarter of a million Europeans living in its territory, playing visible roles in its industrialization. It was from this perspective that the filmmaking initiative was launched under the auspices of European entrepreneurship, notably the Frenchman De Lagarne, under whose direction a series of short actualité films on Alexandria were realized, and the Italo-Egyptian cinematographic company that had the financial backing of Banco di Roma and that produced Italian-directed short dramas. It was not until 1925 that serious indigenous participation in film production was initiated. Under the leadership of a notable aristocrat, Widād 'Urfi, this involvement, which was not without the help of foreign cooperation, resulted in the making of four films after two years of preparation.[37] *Lailā* (1927), directed by Istephane Rosti and Widād 'Urfi, and produced by and starring the stage actress Aziza Amir, is regarded as the first feature-length film produced entirely by Egyptians.

Lailā, a rather crude production appreciated for its pioneering status, indicates a rising spirit of public interest in locally made films. Shot in the streets of Cairo, this film is divided into acts similar to the format of a theatrical play rather than following conventional film structure. In the same year, the Lāma brothers, Ibrahim and Badr, both Chilean emigrés of Lebanese origin, made *Qubla fi' l-Ṣaḥrā'* (A kiss in the desert). The public's embrace of these two films propelled actor Yūsuf Wahbī, a popular stage actor, to launch his own experiment in sound film when he took a film in which he starred—*Aulād al-dhawāt* (The children of the upper class)—to Paris for "synchronization."[38] Arabic-speaking films were thus given a special significance—generating interest and enthusiasm in the Arab world—at a time when Western "innovations in studio equipment" and the exploitation of North Africa's climate for film production were making an impact.[39]

Other Egyptian and Arab films followed soon after these productions. Regretfully, this encouraging beginning did not inspire a competitive film industry in sub-Saharan Africa. The reasons for this are two-fold: first, Europeans were not interested in sharing film technological know-how with black Africans; second, Arabs in North Africa, who were privileged to learn from European technologists and from their Muslim "brothers" north of the Mediterranean, did not cooperate with other African neighbors outside the Maghreb, nor did they advocate a renaissance of technological and industrial revolution reminiscent of the Euro-American initiative. Although northern Africa and sub-Saharan Africa are geographically mapped as belonging to the continent of Africa, its peoples are distinct—the Arab-inclined North Africans and the blacks of sub-Saharan Africa. As it stands today, this dichotomy of existence makes no secret of North Africans' permanent attachment to the Arabic norms and culture which, arguably, they prefer. Rooted in multiple identities stemming from what Ali A. Mazrui identifies as "cultural countervailing forces," the birth of Islam and its subsequent expansion into North Africa from the seventh century A.D. onwards promoted assimilation and acculturation—Islamization (a religious conversion to the creed of Muhammad) and Arabization (a linguistic assimilation into the language of the Arabs). This religious and linguistic bind reinforced the North African communion with Arab heritage, a tenacious claim they believe makes them no less Arab than the inhabitants of the Arabian peninsula.[40] However, after the independence of most African countries and the formation of African filmmakers' organizations, the presence of North African filmmakers in African film festivals and their pronouncements of solidarity for African unity and the advancement of African cinema indicate their attachment to the African cause.

Western Images of Africa: Genealogy of an Ideological Formulation

"The real aim of colonialism," Ngugi writes, "was to control . . . the entire realm of the language of real life. . . . But its most important area of domination was the mental universe of the colonized, the control, through culture, of how people perceived themselves and their relationship to the world."[41] We have seen that in West Africa, for example, Christian missionaries used audiovisual images to influence Africans—as an educational and informational tool, as a weapon for propaganda, as a hegemonic device for ideological expansionism, or, as exemplified by Méliès's early film titles, as an instrument for the questionable treatment of subjects. Since the simultaneous inventions of the motion picture in Europe and America coincided with the height of European imperialism, it is not surprising that for many years the dominant image of Africa seen on Western screens was that of condescension and paternalism. Western filmmakers began to film in Africa, taking advantage of the beauty of the landscape, the so-called exoticism of its customs, relegating the African to the background. The cinematographic invasion of North Africa by foreign filmmakers was inspired by the rush for exotic backdrops to meet the escapist needs of European investors and the Western audiences for whom the films were intended. These movies inverted African values by imposing the language and culture of the colonizer on the colonized. They also served to justify "military escapades" and white mans' "civilizing mission." Thus the African countryside offered natural scenery for fiction, which, for a long time, kept the whole world from African reality, providing a false perspective through which the continent was to be viewed.

Since the inception of the motion picture, it is probable that almost every people of the world has had, at one time or another, cameras

human ecology

photographing them. It is also true that some groups have been filmed by foreign cinematographers more "repeatedly," more "intensively," and sometimes "brilliantly," and have had their privacy violated more often than others.[42] Africans are a typical example of this. Because the inhabitants of this vast continent were seen only in terms of "objects of spectacle" for Western voyeuristic gaze, to use Robert Stam's phrase, European and American moviemakers, through their lenses, caricatured Africa as a "dark continent" whose inhabitants were nothing but savages or docile primitives doing funny things in the jungles to amuse white thrill seekers.

For purposes of entertainment and "fast-buck" results, the local landscape of the film-producing countries was too familiar, too banal; hence the search for sensation, excitement, and fascination. To this day, the unfamiliar image of the so-called primitive peoples of faraway regions of the world still delivers the much needed unconventional themes. Some of the films that bore the trademark of colonial clichés—for example, *Tarzan, the Ape Man* and *Trader Horn,* made in the thirties, and *King Solomon's Mines* (the remake of an earlier British success), *The Snows of Kilimanjaro, Mogambo,* and *Safari,* made in the fifties taking full advantage of technological achievements of the period, notably sound and color—were, admittedly, sometimes brilliantly contrived, beautifully photographed, and visually seductive. However, "the norm, as recent studies have indicated, is to use the selectively photographed or fictionally created exotica of Africa to create sensation, to titillate the imagination, to transport the . . . consumer to the wild, weird, and either wonderful or terrifying Africa."[43]

This image the filmmakers projected of Africa was to have a lasting effect, haunting not only the black people of Africa but also all blacks in the diaspora. Perhaps there is no country that exhibits motion pictures in which audiences have not seen a film of Hollywood origin, or a Hollywood-inspired film, that caricatures the African as a "savage" or a jungle "cannibal," or that depicts the African-American as a second-class citizen who is inferior to his white American counterpart. "Indeed," Robert Stam and Louise Spence write, "many of the misconceptions concerning Third World peoples derive from the long parade [in films] of lazy Mexicans, shifty Arabs, savage Africans and exotic Asiatics."[44] They recount the numerous safari films that have presented Africa "as the land of 'lions in the jungle,' " when in fact the areas that fit the definition of "jungle" constitute only a tiny portion of African land acreage. (This writer, for example, did not see lions throughout his twenty-some years in Africa until 1978, and saw them only when he visited London's Kensington Zoo during his undergraduate days in England.) There are profound reasons for being wary of

these films: cultural and historical inaccuracies, clichés, and the condescending attitude with which black characters are treated. This overt
misrepresentation, entrenched in the dehumanizing spirit of slavery,
became even more pronounced with the increase in production of fictional films, in which blacks played cooks, agricultural laborers,
scrubwomen, and docile servants of varying sorts. There was also the
image of the "threatening black native" in jungle melodramatic settings, in which blacks were portrayed as "brutal," "vicious," and "superstitious." Moreover, black characters were used as a vital plot en-
hancer (to create suspense and excitement) and, as critics have
repeatedly pointed out, would be shown achieving a momentary bravery in their encounters with whites, but never to the point of defeating
them, as in *Voodoo Vengeance.*

Typifying the ideological governance of the period, films such as *The
Wooing and Wedding of a Coon* (1905), *The Kings of the Cannibal
Islands* (1908), *The Slave* (1909), *The Sambo Series* (1911), *Missionaries
in Darkest Africa* (1912), *Voodoo Vengeance* (1913), and *The Terrors
of the Jungle* (1913) are among the numerous others that reassert the
established notion of white superiority over nonwhites, whose deeds
provided laughable comic relief for the amusement of Western spectators. In assessing the all-time height of black stereotype in movies,
Daniel Leab notes that "between 1890 and 1915 the movie black,
whether played by a white or not, and whether presented as an uneasy
menace, a dancing machine, a comic stooge, a faithful retainer, a cheer-
ful flunky, a tainted unfortunate, or an ignorant savage, was presented
as a composite of qualities that were the opposite of values treasured
by white American society."[45]

Colonialist representation of Africans began long before the invention of motion pictures. In various forms, vicious misrepresentations
aimed at tumbling authentic traditional African values existed in the
literary works of Henry Rider Haggard and other European writers and
scholars. The European colonizers were hell-bent on telling the world
that colonialism was a valuable philanthropic "civilizing mission" inspired by the necessity of stamping out ignorance, disease, and tyranny
and ushering in the "best" cultural patterns (European cultural forms).
British writers indefatigably reinforced this claim by publishing adventure literature and history books that were widely read in America. In
Robinson Crusoe (1719), for instance, Daniel Defoe glorified colonialism when his protagonist, a wealthy slave merchant, shipwrecked and
after many years alone on an uninhabited island, sees footprints in the
sand. His first thoughts are not of having a companion but of at last
finding a slave.

Accordingly, other writers undermined African traditional values and customs, including Joseph Conrad (*Heart of Darkness,* 1902), whose books simply depict Africa as a continent waiting to be colonized. Operating as conduits where distortions were intentionally manufactured and distributed for public misinformation and entertainment, some of these colonial texts were adapted for the screen. So, for most Americans, knowledge and perception of Africa came from movies.

Stories by nineteenth-century writers like Henry Rider Haggard, author of *King Solomon's Mines,* Etherelda Lewis, whose work Hollywood turned into the movie *Trader Horn* (1931), Elspeth Huxley, Robert Ruark, and Nicholas Monsarrat, to mention a few, have, according to J. Koyinde Vaughan, "clothed Africa with a mantle of mystery."[46] In the ludicrous fabrications found in the works of these writers, Vaughan notes that Africa was portrayed as peopled by savage tribes living "behind inaccessible forests," or as a bizarre, miserable, vast land inhabited by unintelligent and barbaric people. In this way the reader's sympathy was directed against the Africans, who were viewed as a miserable people needing to be saved. The only God-sent initiative capable of this rescue operation was none other than white man's wisdom. Reinforcing this myth, the literary world of "genuises of racism," as Ngugi wa Thiong'o has described them, involved two aspects of the same process: the deliberate and conscious domination of a people, and the elimination of possibilities for self-definition in relation to other people. So Africa was suffused with the language and racist ideology of the colonizer, and it is not surprising then that racism "has historically been both an ally and product of the colonization process."[47]

Racist tales did not mesmerize only black Africans but anybody of African descent. Recently, two eminent black personalities, one from the United States and the other from Africa, told how unsettling it is to confront memories of persistent fears, eerily evocative of the dangerous misinformation about Africa and its people. In her article "Written Literature and Black Images," the Kenyan writer and scholar Micere Mugo recalls reading the description of Gagool, the old woman character in Henry Rider Haggard's *King Solomon's Mines,* who "had for a long time made her feel mortal terror whenever she encountered old African women."[48] In his autobiography *This Life,* Sidney Poitier states that the Haggardian literature he read as a youth made him identify Africa with a continent infested with snakes. So when he visited Africa, although he was accommodated in a modern hotel in a modern city, his fear of being besieged by snakes was not allayed. He could not sleep, for he constantly kept looking for snakes to appear at any time, anywhere in his hotel room.[49]

These experiences quickly remind one that the images of this world once implanted in our memories can take a long time to eradicate. "The subtlest and most pervasive of all influences," writes Walter Lippmann, "are those which create and maintain the repertory of stereotypes. We are told about the world before we see it. We imagine most things before we experience them. And those perceptions . . . govern deeply the whole process of perception."[50] Joseph Boskin echoes this contention that many common myths are based on stereotypes, not facts:

> A stereotype is . . . staggeringly tenacious in its hold over . . . rational thinking [and gains] its force by repetitive play. . . . Once implanted in popular lore, an image attached to a group, an issue, or event tends to pervade the deepest senses and profoundly affects behavioral action.[51]

The statements by Mugo and Poitier illustrate how fabricated tales can instill fears in a people, and hurt Africans and the black race. Such information has also perpetrated deception of and disservice to the Western audiences such tales were meant to "educate" and entertain. Even when the truth is discovered, contends Jack Shaheen, a "stereotype may endure in defiance of all evidence."[52] Racism and colonialism in cinema, in fact the whole gamut of the black images on film, have been the subject of many books and essays.[53]

In the colonial era, few scholars had made African affairs their major area of concern, and in most cases their writings were riddled with patronizing attitudes. From bastions of intellectualism to gigantic political establishments, external views of Africa were a slipshod ratification of the original colonial mentality propounded as absolute. David Hume is credited with the ridiculous statement that "the negro is naturally inferior to the white."[54] Thomas Jefferson commented that "the blacks are . . . inferior to the whites on the endowments of both body and mind."[55] And in what constitutes the racist core of Jungian psychology, to be black is to be "primitive" and "savage."[56] Consider Hegel's prescription for Africa's emancipation. He wrote that "slavery is in and for itself injustice, for the essence of humanity and freedom; but for this man must be matured. The gradual abolition of slavery is therefore wiser and more equitable than its sudden removal."[57] This, according to Ngugi wa Thiong'o, makes Hegel "the nineteenth-century Hitler of the intellect,"[58] because his ideas and conceptions are directly interwoven with colonial doctrines. In the visual arts, Albert Boime's review recalling Hugh Honor's seminal work cited below, notes that the racist overtones in the work of mainstream artists stem from their depiction of "otherness"—images of black people functioning in most cases as signifiers of opulence in relation to white social status, colonialist desire, and exotic decor. To Paul Gauguin, whose notion of work in Martinique "consists of supervising Negroes while they pick fruit," women in his paintings were examined not only from a condescending vantage point but were also stripped of their individuality. Edouard Manet, "experimenting with tone" in *Olympia*, was said to have contrasted a black maid and an ivory-skinned courtesan. Despite the fact that Eugène Delacroix, like Manet, is considered a renowned nineteenth-century romantic painter, his racism is no less virulent than that of a "minor" genre painter such as Auguste-François Biard.[59] With these kinds of writings, paintings, and pronouncements, Africa fell victim to the atrocities, abuse, and discrimination that have incarcerated its inhabitants. In this process, access to early forms of mass communication—the printing press, for example—facilitated the dissemination of colonial and racist ideologies. By contrast, Africa, stripped of its dynamic self-expression, was not equipped with the means to falsify information about other people. The Western media, in print and in cinema, was an ideological propaganda machine that could be transported with relative ease to every part of the globe while Africa's traditional media were unfortunately restricted.

In America, European racist texts found a new haven. Influenced by such writings, Edgar Rice Burroughs exploited the condescending romance-adventure stories to new commercial heights. In his "dime novels," he created fictional images of Africa and, although he never set foot on African soil, his legendary character Tarzan was to fascinate generations of Americans and audiences everywhere. Burroughs's romance stories were so popular that they inspired a series of Hollywood films. This new commercial Hollywood cinema exploited the popular misconceptions already embedded in the African romance-adventure stories of nineteenth-century writers by creating its own jungle and safari melodramas. Here the tradition of Hollywood films exhibiting disproportionate interest in Tarzan/animal characters as opposed to the depiction of the human life of Africa was firmly established. *Tarzan of the Apes* (1918), directed by Scott Sidney, a film classic that glorified the animal and the jungle and reduced Africa to a mere landscape, was the forerunner of numerous Tarzan escapades. Hollywood's fictional adventure movies such as the *Tarzan* series, *King Solomon's Mines*, *Hatari!*, and many others show fascination with African wildlife, more so than with its human inhabitants, whom they do not portray in a positive light. Paralleling this tendency is the reportage of the American and European news media, which have focused on the negative aspects of events—political and economic upheaval, famine, and diseases of epidemic proportions.

Hollywood's predictable yet dubious ambition, the profit motive, led to the portrayal of Africa as a reservoir of wild animals and impenetrable jungle, reducing Africans to wild natives, all part of an attempt to appeal to and satisfy the taste of cinema audiences for exoticism. At the expense of exploiting others, *Tarzan of the Apes,* a film created from an imaginary Africa based on the misconceptions inherent in Burroughs's fantasies, made a mark in the history of cinema as one of the first films to gross one million dollars. Burroughs, who was a cattle driver, gold digger, and railroad policeman, was so poor during one period of his life that "the only recreation he could afford was a habit of daydreaming wild adventures on other planets or in wild places of the earth."[60] However, his story became highly successful, selling over three million copies in 1914.

An examination of Hollywood cartoons of this period also shows that black characters were caricatured in the same contexts and narratives as in live action films. They were portrayed either as good-humored servants, a parallel to the Uncle Tom figure; as the comedian-buffoon and minstrel; or as knife-carrying savages.[61] These general stereotypes, however, can be traced to early filmmaking when "blackface" actors "within usually rudimentary narratives" were used "to display mythical qualities attributed to the race, such as a love of music and dance, religious fervor and superstition, large appetites, and primitive simplicity."[62]

In the portrayal of animals or natives, stereotypes were in effect in creating scenarios for, Hollywood movies. In this case, since African authenticity is not striven for, African landscape was used as background for scenes shot in New York. Interestingly, during the filming of Metro-Goldwyn-Mayer (MGM) epics and similar extravaganzas

animals were flown from New York City into East Africa to liven the action, and an assortment of gaudily dressed tribes provided the decor for a melodrama between two popular American stars. In these grandiose epics, the African people play either scenery props (picturesque crowds with spears) or curiously unintelligent menials.[63]

It is not surprising that the background footage for *Tarzan of the Apes* was shot in Brazil using Brazilian blacks as natives while some location scenes were shot in Louisiana. The corpulent young men wearing ape skins who swing tree-to-tree like monkeys were reportedly recruited from the New Orleans Athletic Club, and the canoes used were replicas of American Indian canoes. Yet, from the plot of this film we are told that "Lord and Lady Greystoke are set down on the African Coast."[64]

Setting the stage for many African safari melodramas that were to follow, especially in the 1950s, is the singularly offensive classical African melodrama, MGM's *Trader Horn* (1931), directed by W. S. Van

Dyke. Some segments of this film were actually shot on location in Africa, which was unusual at that time; nevertheless, *Trader Horn* depicts blacks as ignorant savages who brandish spears for their frantic dances in contrast to the white civilized characters. The only African exempt from this degrading stereotype is, of course, the faithful white master's servant. When the white goddess goes to rescue Horn (who is surrounded by fierce-looking natives), this trusted servant's death, as far as the enslaver is concerned, is a respectable death, in the service of a white master. (This servant's death for the white cause reminds one of the Africans who died fighting for the European colonizers during the First and Second World Wars, a theme well dramatized in Ousmane Sembene's *Camp de Thiaroye* [1987].) When the whites finally escape to the civilized world, the blacks are left to roam about, languishing in the merciless savagery of Africa's primeval wilderness.

By the 1950s, with the making of such safari melodramas as Compton Bennett and Andrew Marton's *King Solomon's Mines* (1950), a remake of the 1937 British film, John Ford's *Mogambo* (1953), John Huston's *Roots of Heaven* (1958), and jungle melodramas like Terrence Young's *Safari* (1956), John Huston's *The African Queen* (1951), and Richard Brooks's *Something of Value* (1957), Hollywood reached new heights in the adventure-melodrama film. In spite of the yearning of such coalitions as the National Association for the Advancement of Colored People (NAACP) for the positive portrayal of Africa and the diaspora of blacks in America, as well as many voices for change in Africa, the movie industry still applauded the demeaning caricatures of past decades. Not only did films of the 1950s reinforce stereotypes of previous decades but they were also betrayed by numerous inaccuracies. For audience intrigue, whether it was safari or jungle melodrama, the animals provided the spectacle and excitement or a great white hunter put into a precarious African environment heroically triumphed over vicious African natives and the menace of ferocious lions, buffaloes, crocodiles, and snakes. Although set in the African landscape, in structure and design these films are, as Françoise Pfaff put it, more "a reflection of America rather than Africa." It is no coincidence that many of the discrepancies the films display provide escapism intended for audience appeal. In this vein, distortion of geographical, cultural, human, and environmental facts is a deliberate practice designed to create a hostile environment wherein only a white hero who applies excessive violence is allowed to trespass. This white hero, like the cowboy of the American western, is dexterous. He is skillful at gunslinging and surmounting all odds; he is the embodiment of the good Hollywood western character who must triumph over evil. (Not surprising, as many of the directors of safari and jungle melodrama films were filmmakers who had made American westerns.) Within this trend, and in most films, Africans were treated as objects rather than as people.

For the British, justification for occupying Africa becomes a more important concern than cinematic exploitation of exotic decor. This accounts for the fact that British films about Africa reflect the ideology of the British Imperial Government, providing also a precedent that had influenced protagonists whose roles, in J. Koyinde Vaughan's term, "differed from the individualistic law-defying hunter or lover of her American film rivals."[65] That the African should be patronized, uplifted, and governed provided a good rationale for continuing British occupation of African countries. This imperial philosophy was advanced through the condescending attitudes of the white heroes in British colonial films. The general tendency was to project the British way of life as desirable and that of the African as foolish, in order to instill in the minds of Africans feelings of inferiority about their own tradition, culture, and, indeed, their whole being. While the Briton, or white male character, is adorned with intrepid heroic candor, the African is superstitious and backward, his culture presented as no match for that of the European. Thus, in *Sanders of the River* (1935), *King Solomon's Mines* (1937 and 1950), *Men of Two Worlds* (1946), and *Daybreak in Udi* (1949), Africa becomes the locus for the European civilizing mission by rendering the African as ignoble.

Sanders of the River, directed by Zoltan Korda, encompasses all the characteristics of dehumanization, running the gamut of historical stereotypes of Hollywood and European colonial films. But for Paul Robeson, the star of this film, the result was devastating; he had hoped that by crossing the Atlantic to England he would find a nonstereotypical role to play. The role of Bosambo, however, is that of the enlightened native chief who is subservient to Sanders, a powerful representative of the British government. This film's significance derives notoriety from two crucial factors: as colonial propaganda, the exotic production reaffirmed the superiority of whites over the savage African "native" along with perpetuating Western naïveté of Africa's history and culture; and in Africa itself, this film blinded spectators to the realities of colonial occupation and cultural assimilation. *Sanders of the River* was warmly received in Africa, although it was detested by intellectuals who understood Robeson to be a leading campaigner for both liberated art and a liberated Africa, a militant who was betrayed by the dubious director and producers of the film. The Africans were fascinated by the black actor Paul Robeson, whose presence on the screen overshadowed the film's intense colonialist and racist content. Ironically, when the film premiered in London in 1935, Robeson left the theater in disgust after seeing, for the first time, how anti-African the final version was.[66]

Men of Two Worlds and *Daybreak in Udi* fall under the category of what the British called "instructional films." Supposedly made to educate the natives, African characters are never developed or given a chance to express their feelings but are structured to further the fabricated notion that Africa needs British help to control its own affairs. Instructional filmmaking was founded after the Second World War under the auspices of the British Colonial Film Unit (CFU), a permanent film unit of the film division of the newly created Ministry of Information. Established during the war, the CFU's primary assignment was the making of films "for Africans and other unsophisticated colonial audiences" to explain the war for the purpose of enlisting their cooperation in the war effort. To this primary concern was added the making of instructional films, which became the main function of the CFU after the war, until it was disbanded in 1955.

To institutionalize fundamental colonial ideologies the CFU made films for screening in British African colonies. These films extolled colonialism by showing the British way of life, to "brainwash" the African psyche into accepting that progress was only attainable through colonial rule. *Mister English at Home* (1940) and *An African in London* (1941) attempted to teach British etiquette to Africans; *Lusaka Calling* (1951) was made to divert African attention to Western-made goods such as transistor radios; and *Leprosy* (1952) demonstrated the superiority of Western medicine over the traditional ways of healing in Africa in the same manner that *Men of Two Worlds* ridiculed African witch doctors. The best-known film of the colonial film unit is *Daybreak in Udi*, produced by the London Crown Film Unit in Nigeria. This film praises the progress made by colonial officials in the implementation of community projects in eastern Nigeria, winning that year's Academy Award for documentary film.

This unit, condemned by African critics for its paternalistic tendencies, was also derided for being contemptuous of African culture. For instance, in contrasting the condescending portrayal of the natives (usually looked down upon as dirty, lazy, and foolish) with the white hero in British colonial films (shown as the "embodiment of civilization" or simply "the friend of the black man") African critics charged that the films extolled the virtues of African colonizers, police officers, district commissioners, civil servants, and settlers.[67] As in the film *Daybreak in Udi*, which deals with an Igbo self-help community project and was berated by the nationalist press as "yet another film unit come out to our country to depict us as naked savages and unfit to rule ourselves,"[68] this colonial tendency was most apparent. Although Nigerians in this film are seen effectively conducting some of the projects, the real power is centered around British-delegated officers. Here the importance of the British presence, as is always asserted, implies that without the help of the colonial masters none of these projects would have been accomplished, even though communal self-help projects had been going on in Igbo land before the arrival of the British.[69]

Likewise, *Men of Two Worlds,* a film that discredits African traditional medicine and healing processes, presents the British way of life as a symbol of progress, one that must be emulated, the ultimate replacement for Africa's "antiquated" cultural forms. Most Africans found this film offensive, especially its portrayal of the witch doctor. In many feature films made by the British colonial film units, witch doctors are often objects of ridicule, portrayed as representing the forces of darkness and the epitome of evil, which only British rule is capable of eradicating. *Men of Two Worlds* indulged in distortion, taking a superficial view of traditional medicine and choosing to ignore its beneficial aspects. The fact that an organized system of curing disease existed in Africa well before the arrival of the white man was ignored. The British had vehemently argued that it was morally justifiable to colonize Africa in order to civilize its people. In the 1950s, *Salute to the Queen* was made to show how everything was going well with the colonized people, depicting Africans as dutifully obedient to the British crown. Valorizing the Europeans and downgrading the Africans, the British also demonstrated their total lack of understanding of African life and tradition. Such misrepresentations were part of a deliberate attempt to hide the manner in which colonialism functioned.

Hollywood, British, and French cinematographic involvement in Africa also raised awareness of the indirect use of film for ethnic portrayal. Although, as we have seen, cinema in Africa began as a phenomenon of colonialism and as an organ of capitalism, it also quickly developed into an instrument for ethnographic studies of the patterns of human behavior. In 1918, when *Tarzan of the Apes* was released, the *New York Times* film critic praised it and encouraged readers to see it, because "the picture as a whole, in addition to being interesting, also has a touch of educational value."[70] Before Hollywood movie moguls became fascinated with Africa as decor, British and French explorers were already making travelogues, signaling the use of film for anthropology. In this direction, as Emilie de Brigard's article "The History of Ethnographic Film" indicates, it was the French involvement, exemplified by the works of Felix-Louis Regnault (the first practitioner of ethnographic filmmaking), that was more profound and directed toward educational research, because it opened up new aspects of inquiry that lead to a better understanding of diverse cultures. Regnault's works, as they pertain to Africa and its sentiments, remain a genuine and well-intentioned endeavor, at least in comparison with other foreign explorers who have pointed their lenses on Africa and Africans for mere exotic reasons.

Film, according to Regnault, the French pathologist turned anthropologist, "preserves forever all human behaviors for the needs of our studies."[71] Regnault was advocating the need for developing photography from its then "fragmentary and idiosyncratic" stage to a purposeful, "systematic, and thorough" usage. After seeing the inventor of "chromatography," Jules-Étienne Marey, demonstrate his new camera, which used a celluloid roll of film, to the French Académie des Sciences in 1888, Regnault discovered that photography had immense potential. Motivated by the task of championing new systematic use of motion pictures in anthropology, Regnault, aided by Marey's associate Charles Comte, filmed in the spring of 1895 a "Wolof woman making pots at the Exposition Ethnographique de l'Afrique Occidentale." Regnault's experiment involved two significant developments. First, educational content in this film represented not only the accurate portrayal of the Wolof method of making pottery but also compared this method to that of other ancient civilizations, including those of Egypt, India, and Greece. Second, in 1895, the same year that saw the first public projection of Lumière's "cinématographe" films, Africans were used in another kind of motion picture that was to flourish—ethnographic documentary film. It has been noted that Regnault's subsequent films used Africans for "the cross-cultural study of movement," including Wolof, Fulani, and Diola men and women climbing trees, squatting, and walking.[72] It is unfortunate that Regnault's genuine scientific exposition was to turn against the values he envisioned for his film. Africa, which he used to pioneer his ethnographic experiment, was also to be used as superficial decor, misrepresented cinematically with aberrant interpretations derisive of traditional values.

After critically evaluating Western films and some racist literature that dealt with Africa, J. Koyinde Vaughan remarked, "It is in the anthropological films that the people of Africa spring suddenly to life on the screen. Here human activity is starkly recorded, free of distortions of colonial propaganda or the sensationalism of the motion picture industry."[73] However, in most of these ethnographic films, it was clear that the camera "seeks out the primitive, and shows a marked predilection for the past. The new, urban life in Africa—throbbing with vitality—finds little place in these films."[74]

In the time period between the two world wars, "explorer films" and "fiction films set in exotic locations" outgrossed other films, enjoying immense popularity, profitability, and visibility.[75] Unfortunately, the documentary films of this period imitated the characteristics of feature films, despite their "honest" beginnings. Filmmakers were more interested in packing their films with exotic clichés than in showing the real life of the people of Africa. The most blatant abuse in the explorer-as-documentarist tradition is found in the work of Martin and Osa Johnson, the makers of the faddish film *Congorilla*. This film, as noted in Erik Barnouw's *Documentary: A History of Non-Fiction Film*, is about "big apes and little people"—the life and habits of gorillas in Central Africa, including many scenes of Pygmy tribes. Production began during the transition from silent to sound cinema. Since the Johnsons, by their own account,[76] managed to surmount the technical difficulties of using sound equipment, they included sound sequences and added commentary proclaiming *Congorilla* "the first sound film from darkest Africa." The Johnsons' attitude toward the natives was one of condescension and disrespect for their culture and tradition. Not only did they present deprecatory images of the Africans they worked with but their own exhibitionist tendencies epitomized arrogance, "master race" narcissism, and self-glorification. In order to create amusement and laughter for the audience, the Johnsons appeared frequently on camera not only to valorize their work but, in what amounts to a vivid example of sadistic behavior, to poke fun at the coarse, unattractive image of Africa they had created. Here is how Erik Barnouw describes their attitude:

> In a forest clearing we see them [the Johnsons] recruiting forth "black boys" as carriers. When one gives his name, it sounds like "coffee pot" to Mrs. Osa Johnson, so his name is written down as Coffee Pot. Johnson's narration speaks of funny little savages, happiest little savages on earth. His idea of humor was to give a pygmy a cigar and wait for him to get sick; to give another a balloon to blow up and watch his reaction when it burst; to give a monkey beer and watch the result. During a shot of a crocodile opening its mouth, Johnson's narration comments: "Gee, what a place to throw old razor-blades." To catch two baby gorillas, seven huge trees are chopped down, isolating the gorillas in a tree in the middle; then it is chopped down.[77]

The explorer-anthropological genre went beyond the jurisdiction of independent filmmaking and scientific inquiry to influence the approaches and techniques of commercial films made on the African continent. The genre had enormous impact on the French box office hit of the period *La croisière noire* (The black cruise, 1926) directed by Léon Poirier. Sponsored by the car manufacturing company Citröen, *La croisière noire* is reminiscent of Robert Flaherty's *Nanook of the North* (1922). The latter film did a much better job of advertising fur coats

manufactured by Revillon Frères than filming the "sympathy and understanding" of the Eskimos, which Flaherty claimed was his main
motive. Léon Poirier's film recorded an extraordinary automobile rally
across Africa, from north to south, and on to the French African island
of Madagascar (now independent). This film did very well in advertising
the ruggedness of Citroen trucks under adverse conditions on Africa's
rough roads. Released in a sound version in 1933, *La croisière noire*,
in its long journey across Africa, provided its spectators with glimpses
of ethnic village life in a series of vignettes, but the images were inadequate in substance and not in agreement with Rouch's contention that
these fragments of life "showed the most representative aspects of the
people encountered en route."[78] Devoid of detailed individual character traits, this film would be best remembered for the contribution it
makes to documentary film history and aspects of documentary values
that it confronted in much the same way as Flaherty's *Nanook of the
North*. And like Flaherty, whose interest in expedition exhibited strong
evidence of paternalism and prejudice, Léon Poirier's jaundiced expedition to Africa appears superficial, if only for the mockery of the art
of filmmaking; his ax-grinding technique only serves to stress his pre-
conceived bizarre image of Africa.

   La croisière noire traveled Africa's rough roads promoting French
automobile technology, but it never showed the oppressive logic of
colonialism, the ignored welfare of Africans, the underdevelopment of
the continent—from which raw materials are confiscated and siphoned
off to the West for the manufacture of goods for the nourishment and
comfort of the affluent. Too many Western producers have refused to
portray Africa in the best light by not using film to draw the public's
attention to the need for liberation of a continent ensnared by slavery
and oppression. Only a few courageous films treated Africans as normal
human beings.

Banishing the Exotic: Toward a
Positive Image?

Finally, some early steps toward a courageous portrayal of African
reality were made, especially of the colonial reality. Marc Allegret's
Voyage au Congo (Voyage to the Congo, 1927), a cinematic record of
André Gide's travels in the Congo, although criticized for its noncinematic quality, is regarded as the first French "anticolonial" film. Efforts
toward meaningful documentation of Africa's sociopolitical reality by
French filmmakers denouncing European colonial African policies were
chided by colonial administrations. While making *Afrique 50* (1950), a
film about political uprisings in Côte d'Ivoire and Upper Volta (Burkina

Faso), a young student from the Institut des Hautes Etudes Cinématographiques (IDHEC) in Paris, René Vauthier, was asked to discontinue
filming because he had not obtained the proper permit. But the real
reason for this banning order was the film's virulent attack on colonial
rule by the colonial administrators, who saw it as a threat to the survival
of their regime. *Afrique 50* was suppressed and banned in Africa and
France.[79]

Chris Marker and Alain Resnais are two other non-African filmmakers whose documentaries about Africa were banned. Both were
commissioned in 1952 by *Presénce Africaine* to make a film called *Les
statues meurent aussi* (Statues also die, 1953); the completed film was
prohibited from being shown for ten years. Finally, when the prohibition was lifted, it was only to be shown in truncated form. Together
with the extraordinary editing that juxtaposes sequences of African art
filmed in European museums with archival footage dealing with Africa,
the voice-over narration explains the reasons that led the colonial nerve
to twitch:

> The subject is the black man cut off from his own culture and not in
> contact with ours. His work no longer has either spiritual or social conse-
> quences. It has no prospects, it leads to nothing but a derisory wage. In
> these countries of gift and barter, we introduced money. And so the
> black's work is bought and his art degraded. Religious dance becomes
> a spectacle. We pay the Negro to give us the amusing spectacle of his
> joy and enthusiasm. And in this way there appears, alongside the Negro
> as slave, a second figure—the Negro Punch.[80]

This powerful statement from non-Africans no doubt shamed the colonialists. The film so much impressed Ousmane Sembene, a veteran
critic of the foreign lens view of Africa and one of the pioneers of black
African filmmaking, that he described it as "the best film ever made
on Africa, colonization, and traditional art objects."[81] In her keen observation of colonialism's double standard, Pfaff, comparing *Les statues meurent aussi* with Rouch's African ethnographic films, states that
"Rouch's earliest documentaries could be 'safely' released because
they were Western inquiries into Africa's traditions rather than solely
investigations of contemporary issues."[82]

Rouch and his ethnographic film expedition to Africa have called
into question the whole tradition of ethnographic filmmaking. As he
practiced it, ethnographic filmmaking represented a stage in the evolution of the colonial cinema, and this method has raised unsettling questions about the ambiguities of this type of cinema. As a major force in
French cinema for many years, Rouch has made about sixty or so films
(including shorts and features) with the majority focusing on Africa.

Infuriated by Rouch's wrongful portrayal of Africa, Africans and critics alike contend that his films perpetuate the exoticism and exploitation initiated by colonialism. It is here that his cinema, as an anthropological study of humans, ran into trouble, and his method helped increase the debate on the problems of the relationship between ethnographic film and reality, anthropology and imperialism, the ideal nature of ethnography, and the very question of ethics and reflexivity—or as J. R. Rayfield puts it, "the nature of film as a medium."[83]

Rouch has spent many years filming in Africa, and his use of African collaborators has contributed to the development of African cinema. Indeed, this recognition is deeply expressed in Manthia Diawara's Ph.D. dissertation more than by any other African writer. As a result of this collaboration, some Africans who worked with him as actors became important filmmakers. Among them are the late Oumarou Ganda of Niger, who starred in the documentary psychodrama *Moi, un noir* (I, a black man, 1958), his first feature film, which depicts problems faced by stevedores in the Treichville district of Abidjan, and Safi Faye of Senegal in *Petit à petit ou Les lettres Persanes 1968* (Little by little or the 1968 Persian letters, 1969), a loosely structured film about the experiences of a young man from Niger sent to Paris to discover contemporary French life. Scripts for both films were jointly produced by Rouch and the actors. With this collaboration, Rouch transcends other Western filmmakers concerned with exotic travelogues. For its spontaneity and innovation, *Moi, un noir,* for instance, won the 1959 Louis Dulluc Prize. However, Ganda's reaction to Rouch's work was less than enthusiastic. For him, this film should have been "made in an entirely different way." He claimed he disliked it because some points were falsified.[84] On the positive side, Ganda acknowledged that through working with Rouch he was able to discover from his "direct cinema" the potential of cinema as an effective means of expression, one that can reflect reality as opposed to distorting it in the fashion in which the medium has been used by foreign filmmakers against Africa.[85] Faye also openly acknowledges Rouch's part in spurring her serious interest in filmmaking, particularly referring to his cinéma vérité technique in which unobstrusive camera movement, spontaneous shooting, nonprofessional acting, and long and single takes are main features—all of which are common in her own films. However, Faye disliked *Petit à petit,* and like Ganda, questioned its significance.[86]

Rouch's *Les maîtres fous* is the most objectionable to Africans and the most controversial of his African films for the polemical discussions it has generated. Rouch was invited to Africa to document the spiritual cult of the Hauka sect in Ghana. But instead of concentrating on the images of "spirituality" or the "essence" of Hauka ritual, he focused on the Haukas as a sect that slaughters dogs, cooks and eats them, marches back and forth, dances violently and foams at the mouth when possessed by the spirit of the generals, doctors, and truck drivers from the British colonial power structure. Rouch has been accused of wrongly superimposing the Haukas' normal daily routine on the cult's religious rituals to deliberately distort facts. The point of the film, according to Rouch, is "that the ritual plays a therapeutic role in the lives of the marginalized and oppressed people, allowing them to accommodate to the psychological disjunctions caused by colonialism."[87] *Les maîtres fous* provoked antithetical responses among its initial audiences. European audiences, on the one hand, viewed the Hauka ritual, with its seemingly ironic assimilation of colonialist practices, as inherently subversive. (The film in fact served as the inspiration for Jean Genet's absurdist drama *The Blacks*.) African audiences, on the other hand, thought that Rouch's prolonged use of the camera for the psychological study of the Hauka members' gory ritual revealed an intractable racist perspective. (This film also marks Rouch's diversion from conventional documentary film practice to what he and Edgar Morin, reminiscent of Dziga Vertov's *Kino-Pravda*, describe as cinéma vérité.) These polarities of audience response reinforce the idea that cinéma vérité is a culturally specific (perhaps even Eurocentric) documentary approach, despite its avowed stance of detachment and neutrality. *Les maîtres fous* functioned as an anticolonialist allegory for Europeans, who were actually ignorant of African reality and insensitive to African sensibilities.

In his assessment of Rouch's methodology, Teshome Gabriel charges that "obsession with 'penetrating' the African mind reached its climax with *Les maîtres fous,* but most of his films in Africa, other than *Moi, un noir,* have studied Africans by employing 'psychological essays' in the human interior."[88] He refers to Rouch's later films and points out the "growing tendency to personalize and fictionalize" a process dictated by Rouch's training as an anthropologist; however, he abused its ethics, making African people look like "scientific specimens" and "laboratory subjects."[89] Ousmane Sembene has also accused Rouch of "treating Africans like insects." On photographic reality, Rouch is quoted as saying, "I don't think it's possible to be a witness to the things happening around you and not take a stand."[90] Cinematographically, Rouch is highly acclaimed for outstanding filmic innovations, but to critics who saw his work as racially motivated, this method was too debasing. Despite some altruistic intentions, Rouch's *Les maîtres fous* unwittingly reinforces racist stereotypes, and his vérité aesthetic incorporates imperialist myth, despite its pose of liberalism and anthropological inquiry. Under intense criticism he admitted that ethnology is "the daughter of Western Imperialism."[9]

The subtle condescension of Rouch's portrayals might be usefully contrasted with the more conventionally degrading modernist tendencies of the 1970s, exemplified in the work of David and Judith MacDougall. In 1976 the MacDougalls went to the Turkana District of northwestern Kenya to study that society's way of life. The filmmakers lived for one year with the Turkanas, during which time they mastered and came to understand the Turkana way of life sufficiently enough to start a psychological study of the people. Thus, they became self-appointed sociologists studying another culture. In actuality, their methodology is perfunctory and comparable to "spot reporting," in that it is journalistic rather than anthropological or sociological; interrogation of one family in one exercise is surely an inadequate and unacceptable procedure for explaining to the outside world a complex culture like the Turkanas'. This is the major flaw in the MacDougalls' African cinematic work.

The MacDougalls have made more than a dozen films, all of which pierce through the private lives of powerless people such as the "primitive" peoples of Africa and Australian Aboriginals. As has been the tradition, these filmmakers, wherever they went, found similar objects of study: poorest of the poor, misery, backwardness, naked people. One of their films about Africa, now circulating in American colleges and museums, is *Lorang's Way* (1977). The film opens with a close-up of Lorang, the old man MacDougall tormented in marathon question and answer sessions. We see his eyes, blinking as he talks to the camera. The left one is infected, and we see the big, whitish secretion stuck there like an ornament, which the MacDougalls never bothered to ask him to clean. It is ironic to see the filmmakers treat Lorang in this way, as he was to yield them hundreds of thousands of dollars through exploitation. Moreover, the MacDougalls came from a society where presidential and gubernatorial aspirants wear makeup before facing the camera to say "vote for me." For this writer, photographing Lorang in this way implies that they did not care if the old man dropped dead the next day. As this tradition had been dictated from colonial days, the victim is always subjugated, too powerless to know he is being violated. One of the problems with this film, even though the makers claimed they lived with the Turkanas, thus enabling them to understand their way of life, is that they only succeeded in distorting the authentic values, history, and culture of these people for the outside world.

In Africa some nomadic herdsmen are employed by rich cattle owners to take care of their herds, and some possess their own animals, which they take out every day to feed wherever they can find pasture.

While the animals graze, the herdsmen remain in their huts or home-steads, waiting for the animals to feed and return home to the villages whenever they want. This aspect of Turkana life is haphazardly pre-sented. In the film nothing is mentioned about Lorang's home in the village, nor is there any sign of life existing outside the homesteads. Worse still, important questions remain unanswered. Why would Lo-rang and his family live in abject poverty if they owned such a well-nourished herd of cattle and camels? Why don't they have good houses? Are the animals grazed for food or for sale? In the presence of these well-nourished animals, why would there be famine?

From this writer's point of view, any anthropological inquiry into a culture which negates crucial ways of life relevant to the understanding of that culture (such as the meaning of cattle rearing in pastoral Tur-kana) would amount to a distortion of facts of the highest order. Ali Mazrui, a native Kenyan and one of Africa's leading cultural historians and theorists, explains why the Turkana people are very resistant to Western influences and choose to remain loyal to the tenets of their own culture:

> The rural world of Africa is divided between lovers of land and lovers of animals. Lovers of land in this context are those Africans who have responded to the challenge of cultivation and agriculture, and have learnt to take advantage of the soil and seeds as a means of production. These are the Africans who plant, tend their farms, and harvest their corn or yams.
>
> Lovers of animals, on the other hand, are those Africans whose entire way of life is bound by a cattle complex or a camel imperative, or a concern for sheep and goats. Land is important to these Africans, but primarily for the sake of pasture for their beasts. Nor do they necessarily cultivate the pasture. They accept it as nature's bounty, very much as the ancient gatherers accepted the wild fruit and wild roots.[92]

Mazrui notes that "on a pure pragmatic basis" one of the immediate solutions to combatting famine in Africa would be to commercialize "cattle breeding and the life-styles of cattle societies such as the Masai and the Turkana," which hitherto have been adamant against "selec- tive capitalism and profit motive." As much as this will amount to "engendering some economic value for the cattle instead of almost pure cultural value," Mazrui concludes that "most efforts towards replacing a cattle culture with a cattle economy have so far failed. The pastoral people have remained defiantly idealistic in their attachment to both their ancestors and their animals."[93] These are salient characteristics at the forefront of Turkana life, and yet *Lorang's Way* ignores them all, choosing instead to show us homesteads and other superficialities.

As disjointed and informatively sterile about the Turkana life as this film is, it is hailed as resourceful and remains one of the best films for anthropological study of Africa in American classrooms.[94]

It is amazing how, when such films with exotic images reach the Western screens, their hollow content does nothing to diminish their anthropological value or rating. Nor is the audience inclined to seek detailed and accurate information for a true anthropological rendition of the culture. Leroi-Gourhan warned about the dangers of the "exotic" travel film, stating that this type of film "produced with no scientific aim [only derives] an ethnological value from its exportation."[95]

In the 1980s, the MacDougalls' tradition of devaluing the history and culture of Africa was revitalized in a subtle way by such films as those of the misassemblage of Trinh T. Minh-ha's *Reassemblage* (1982) and *Naked Space: Living is Round* (1985), and Jamie Uys's *The Gods Must Be Crazy* (1984). It will not further our purpose to put these films into the same category; rather they will be examined individually, their methodologies contrasted where relevant, based on the ideological assumption of their creators. This may also furnish the reader with valuable information from an African perspective on why these films provide a limited anthropological basis for understanding Africa and its cultures. In this context, if it is pertinent to expose Uys's unacknowledged prejudices and lies, the same procedure would also seek to untangle the unacknowledged contradictions responsible for the taxidermic but fuzzy images of Minh-ha's Africa. In this regard, while Jamie Uys's sly artistry makes a comic mockery of Africa (understandably, in defense of apartheid), Trinh T. Minh-ha's professed argument for the Third World, in what has been described as her condemnation of the First World's false anthropological view of Africa, is undercut by the stereotypical images she promotes. In the flier distributed by the Whitney Museum of American Art, Minh-ha has defended her work as challenging "the ethnocentricism underlying Western anthropological studies of 'other' cultures." Anthropological films, she says, are marred by "colorful images, exotic dances, and fearful rites—the unusual." Yet an examination of her two films by anyone who is conversant with African history and culture, with or without filmmaking experience, will clearly reveal that this filmmaker fails to make a convincing case against First World misrepresentation of Third World people. Instead, she has chosen to expand the perpetuation of the reductionist romantic and paternalistic treatment of Africa, much in the tradition of Rouch and the MacDougalls. In *Reassemblage,* Minh-ha, who is a Third World feminist of Vietnamese origin and a naturalized American, incorporates all of the cinematic misappropriations of Western ethnographic films on Africa which she sees as distortive and insensitive in respect to African culture.

The irony here is that Minh-ha, Rouch, and the MacDougalls wield the same commonality of interests. They focus on the lives of the same types of people—people who can easily be manipulated and their privacy violated without their knowledge. Despite their disparities, the three filmmakers are animated by a similar desire—a yearning to be hailed as cultural "discoverers" and "demystifiers." This compulsion inspires them to focus on low-life details and similar modes of filmic representation (framing, image selection, and close-up) that conspicuously highlight African "exotica." These predilections have certainly not promoted the decolonization process in modern Africa.

Reassemblage uses close-ups and repetition of shots to highlight specific points. Consider the close-ups (extreme close-ups, in some cases) of conspicuous features of her victims, such as blistered mouths, overstretched earlobes, sagging breasts, tattered clothing; her methods of framing and selection of details; and the composition of shots, which indicates that her fixation is to draw the audience into African exotica, knowingly or unknowingly pandering to the basest instincts of her Western viewers. But Minh-ha attributes this philosophy of her observation (point of view) to the camera's observational role, forgetting that when a camera photographs something in close-up, the implication is that the viewer is asked to see the detail as the camera has seen it. But this camera position implicates the filmmaker as well because (proximity of the camera to the subject also indicates the filmmaker's position. Point of view shifts the deception of the image receiver and no doubt affirms the perspective of the producer.)Indeed, the filmmaker directs the viewer to see and reflect upon an important element of an image from a certain viewpoint. *Reassemblage* is inundated with stereotypes and misrepresentations. As pieces of collage, the so-called African culture which this film haphazardly assembles gives an indistinct view of life in traditional and modern Africa. Similar to the First World's view of Africa, Minh-ha's exotic clichés also result in a romanticized image of Africa in which cultural specificities are taken for granted.

Interweaving exoticism with nudity in a semipornographic blend, Minh-ha reaches Western audiences in a facile manner, a measure which also has sacrificed her Third World values for First World capitalistic taste. This strategy seems to have worked to her advantage in the same way it did for Rouch and the MacDougalls in that she attained international recognition with her films' circulation in museums, classrooms, women filmmakers' conferences, and critical reviews in literary quarterlies. But why Africa? Trinh T. Minh-ha would have found simi-

lar subjects of study in her native Vietnam. Yusuf Grillo, my former
teacher, commenting on how fast African products sell in the United
States and Europe, especially African art, notes that "the view has
been expressed that some buyers would buy a carving of Abraham
Lincoln if someone would just say it is African." I have never seen so
many close-ups of naked breasts in any other film, fifty-one shots in a
forty-minute film. Perhaps *Reassemblage* is admired by its promoters
for its pornography rather than ethnography; hence reviewers continue
to praise it.[96] Needless to say, the reviews are based on Eurocentric
assumptions rather than African sensibility. This is also why my observations here regarding Rouch, the MacDougalls, and Minh-ha are no
doubt difficult to get across in the Western media, no matter how convincing.[97]

In fact, Minh-ha's filmmaking is amateurish, bracketed by opportunism. Some of the major flaws of her films (*Reassemblage* and *Naked
Spaces: Living Is Round*) are lack of continuity emanating from unclear
structure, incorrect exposure, out-of-focus shots, bad editing, and disconcerting voice-overs, which make one wonder if anybody would have
looked at these films, let alone distribute them, if Minh-ha had made
them outside of Africa. Although she argues that these obvious flaws
are deliberate (and some of her admirers agree with her), *Reassemblage*
is structurally and aesthetically sloppy and is a failed experiment that
should not be commercialized.

From inside Africa comes the South African farce *The Gods Must
Be Crazy*. Uys's view of the Bushman (and Africa in general) is that
of slapstick comedy, but like some other documentaries about exotic
cultures, this film constitutes a distorted microcosm of the clash of
peoples and ideologies. *The Gods Must Be Crazy* is the story of a Bushman in the Kalahari Desert who is nearly struck by an empty Coke
bottle tossed from a passing airplane by a careless white pilot. Reminiscent of anthropological filmmaking where interests center on poor,
sometimes unclothed, helpless people, the star of *Gods* is a loincloth-
clad South African Bushman named N!xau. He is the leader of a tribe
disrupted by contact with the modern world. Watching this film, the
ordinary viewer might not suspect that there is political antagonism,
which tends to stigmatize one culture (the blacks) while glorifying another (the whites) as "God's Almighty People." In fact Uys is a white
South African, though he presented *Gods* as a Botswana film.

Most of the scenes did not take place in South Africa but in Botswana, the independent African republic where blacks and whites work
and live in harmony. No reference is made to apartheid (in fact some
sequences showed blacks and whites working or dining together) or to
the infamous Immorality Act of South Africa (which prohibited sexual

relationships among whites and blacks). This immensely popular comedy is wittily crafted so that its inventive slapstick comedy is well paced and the audience keeps laughing, devoid of the thought that the injustices of apartheid or racial problems exist anywhere in that region.

The beginning of this film is malicious and particularly offensive because it paints an ugly picture of the Khoisan people ("Bushmen") by distorting their history. Uys tells his viewers through his facetious sound track narration, "The Bushman are sweet, little, noble savages who spend their days gamboling about in the desert; their existence is idyllic, despite the barren earth." The film, reminiscent of John Marshall's *N!ai: The Story of a !Kung Woman* (1953–1980) in which a white South African refers to "Bushmen" as lazy people, blames the tribe for its inherent misfortune of being backward. What it does not tell us is that this ancient culture has been driven to near extinction by centuries of colonialism and demoralization by the forces of imperialism that have stripped it of any genuine advancement resulting from modern development. These people depend upon South African government handouts for subsistence.

In this pseudodocumentary, where the rhino is proclaimed a fire prevention officer, Uys's camera follows N!xau from his primitive enclave to the mythical Gaborone/Johannesburg civilization, encountering a pretty white schoolteacher, a band of black guerrillas who are armed to the teeth but cannot differentiate between the butt of a gun or the barrel and mistake a bunch of bananas for an attacking helicopter, and an ingenuous slapstick white scientist who studies elephant manure for his doctoral dissertation.

Provoking laughter through the mockery of human frailty, this film makes its journey into the absurd. Jamie Uys tries to change the course of history, society, and politics to the advantage of the white South African government. However, "sly artistry may not be the point here," as Caryn James has pointed out, since the "film is just . . . silly."[98] Although this film epitomizes degradation and exploitation, its numerous ugly features did not prevent it from becoming the longest running first-run feature film in New York's history.

Since most ethnographic films are sponsored by or come from independent filmmakers who prefer to use images of a so-called strange society in order to gain recognition, profit may be the main goal. But where do the profits go? The poor people whom these filmmakers utilize do not profit from the films they star in. When these filmmakers leave the areas they have exploited, they are gone forever! For example, Oumarou Ganda, star of Jean Rouch's *Moi, un noir,* after reading in the newspaper *Abidjan Matin* that Eddie Constantine earns eight hundred million francs to make a single film, took the newspaper as evidence and approached Rouch for enhanced remuneration. Rouch's reply was, "It's not possible, you can't have eight hundred million like Eddie. Besides, you're not an actor."[99] The most Rouch did for his African crew was to offer them beer and token change. How about those young bare-breasted girls jumping up and down for Minh-ha's camera? Have they received a penny now that *Reassemblage* is circulating in America, Britain, and other countries, probably making money for Minh-ha? This writer has already explained how MacDougall would not have cared if Lorang were to drop dead after those marathon interviews. The marvel of ethnographic deceit and exploitation is exhibited by Jamie Uys in *The Gods Must Be Crazy*. It has been said that Uys, becoming increasingly worried about N!xau's health, the man he "loved" so much, "put a radio mike around the man's neck, told him it was 'special medicine' and proceeded to monitor N!xau's personal conversations."[100]

The films mentioned thus far have been attempts by foreigners to bring Africa to the screen—from their point of view, of course. Some film historians have argued that it was from ethnographic films that serious steps were taken to banish the exotic and to portray Africa in a more positive light. The previous discussion has indicated that partial or falsified images of Africa have not ceased and that the desire to make a profit continues to be the basic motivation for this endless exploitation. This probably explains the renewed interest in the serialization of Tarzan movies, and in wild animal and adventure programs, which still depict Africa on American television as evil, primitive, and a wild world of terror. These include television programs such as "Daktari," "Mission Impossible," the mini-series "Shaka Zulu," and feature films such as *Zulu, The African Queen, Nun's Story, Zulu Dawn, Greystoke: The Legend of Tarzan, Lord of the Apes, The Wild Geese, Out of Africa,* and *Gorillas in the Mist*.

If the objective of anthropology is to gather information to increase understanding rather than to support the situation of the colonizer judging the colonized, these foreign views of Africa have not been inspired by the desire to assist Africa's emancipation. By all indications, these instances have provided neither a positive nor as true an image as have African stories told from the inside—those that show the continent with its problems and the forces at play as it tries to gain international influence. It is within this context, in chapter 2, that we shall examine the development of black African cinema, the exploration of Africa through the African lens, the telling of African stories or, perhaps, the African side of the story.

Francophone Origins

*Sixty-five years after the invention of the
cinema, not one truly African feature length
film has been produced to my knowledge. By
that I mean a film acted, photographed,
written, conceived and edited by Africans and
filmed in an African language.*
—Georges Sadoul

General Trends and Problems of Development: An Overview

Judged by the level of world industrialization, Africa is constantly referred to as "Third World," and in fact some analysts call it "Last
World" because many of the world's poorest nations, which came late
into the age of industrialization, are in black Africa. In the case of
cinema, the industrial foundation of the African film industry, seen in its
entirety, is still a mirage. This situation is not alien to other dependent
economies where basic production capabilities are restricted, largely
due to the inability to manufacture essential components locally. However, India, the world's largest film producer, Brazil, Cuba, and some
other Latin American countries with dependent economies were able
to effectively bring film production to the level of industry. In postindependence black Africa, colonial and neocolonial emphasis has not given
cinema the development status shared by other sectors of the economy,
considered essential, such as rural electrification projects, education,
or assembly plants.

Clyde Taylor's description of African cinema as the "Last Cinema"[1] is indeed appropriate considering its thorny road to evolution. It echoes the frustration expressed in the epigraph above by film historian Georges Sadoul. Both Sadoul and Taylor call attention not only to the factors hindering the growth of African film industry but to the entire problematical emancipation of that continent. In this vein, the question persistently asked is: Why did this happen? Why would it take so long for cinema to develop in black Africa?

Several factors account for Africa's economic desperation. Colonial rule established institutional structures that would perpetuate Western domination for decades following colonialism's formal demise. Postcolonial economic exploitation forced Africa further into the European system of capitalism, which discourages the indigenous control of African economies, since export and import commodity prices are determined by First World economic developments. And since independence, the nations of black Africa have not been able to acquire the technological capability needed to break loose from the economic orbit of the West. The neocolonial period has been an era of greed in which the unmistakable scent of public and private corruption infests the political atmosphere of the continent.

Black African cinema emerged with the independent movements to liberate African states and coincided with the black consciousness movement of the diaspora. In their protest literature African writers were already launching their own attacks on colonialism. With the emergence of African cinema, a quasi-connubial rapport was established between the cinema and the literature of protest. A mutual understanding of the cultural situation urged independent African cinema toward a protest designed to inspire political awareness in the African public, a protest directed not only toward the condemnation of imperialism as the cause of Africa's predicament but also toward the contradictions of independent, postcolonial Africa. It is here that we begin to trace the situation in each of these stages as they affected the development and growth of national film industries in black Africa.

The current economies of black African states have been molded by the legacy of the colonial era. When Africa and other Third World countries were being colonized, Europe and the United States were advancing technologically, politically, and economically into the industrial age. Thus a gap in material development was created that made the African states dependent on the industrial nations. Walter Rodney describes this disparity between the economic status of the First and Third Worlds as an "integral part of underdevelopment in the contemporary sense."[2] He notes that in one way or another, all the countries of the world generally referred to as "underdeveloped" have been exploited by others, notably the colonialist powers. Africa and Asia were already developing independently until their economies were disrupted and taken over. "When that happened," according to Rodney, "exploitation increased and the export of surplus ensued, depriving the societies of the benefit of their natural resources and labor."[3] For this reason, theories of underdevelopment have generally blamed the capitalist, imperialist, and colonialist exploitation for instigating much of the economic retardation in the Third World.

In another important study of this situation, Edward P. Skinner has stated that "what the Europeans attempted to do to the psyche of Africa's peoples, they also tried to do to its economies."[4] By replacing Africa's traditional economic structures with Western capitalist paradigms, Europeans turned ignorance into advantage. Thus protracted economic control of the colonies was effected, and the means with which to ensure that control, even after the colonized nations became independent, was consolidated. As there was no policy to transform Africa's economy to reflect the industrial revolution going on in Europe, its economy was limited to the production of export crops and extractive industries such as mining and timber felling. If this had been coordinated with Africa's progress in mind, the mining industries would have provided much-needed technological know-how, but the processing and refinement of the minerals was done outside of Africa. Commercial dealings were effectively controlled by multinational holding companies such as Unilever, Union Minière, United African Company (UAC), John Holt, LOHNRO, Société Commerciale de l'Afrique Occidentale, and others who had infiltrated every sector of the economy. These companies, needless to say, are European-owned and ideologically aligned with the policies of Western governments, which had forced their colonies into monoculture.[5]

Africans were not trained in commercial and entrepreneurial skills. The British colonialists, for example, never encouraged Africans to participate in such professions. Instead, middlemen were called in to fill the void—notably, Indians, Lebanese, and Syrians.[6] The outcome of this situation is that Africa is still far removed from the benefits of its minerals and other economic resources. Most of the daily output of its natural wealth is siphoned off into the coffers of developed countries rather than remaining in Africa for the benefit of Africans. Even in postindependent Africa, the situation remains the same. Zambia and Congo produce vast quantities of copper; Ghana, gold; Nigeria, tin, oil, and bauxite—all of which benefit Europe, North America, and Japan. The same can be said of uranium produced in Chad and Namibia (the latter forcefully annexed by apartheid South Africa, until March 21, 1990, when it became independent), which continues to enrich European, American, South African, and Israeli nuclear facilities, plus other innumerable mineral and export crops.

In the case of the cinema, exploitation by foreign-owned distribution companies exemplified colonial ideologies. Distribution of films was entirely controlled by powerful and highly profitable European-owned companies that suppressed the emergence of African cinema. To them, African cinema would bring competition and a change in audience taste that might challenge their exclusive hold on the African market. In the francophone regions two powerful French companies, COMACICO (Compagnie Africaine Cinématographique Industrielle et Commerciele) and SECMA (Société d' Exploitation Cinématographique Africaine), both subsidiaries of Monaco-based holding companies,[7] dominated the film distribution and exhibition business covering African countries, in what was formerly French Western and Equatorial Africa (Senegal, Côte d'Ivoire, Mali, Niger, Burkina Faso, Benin, Chad, Central African Republic, Gabon, Congo, Mauritania, Cameroon, and Togo). COMA-CICO and SECMA controlled about 80 percent of the cinema in this region; the remaining 20 percent was in the hands of other nationals, notably the Lebanese who depended on supplies regulated by this French "duopoly."

In his excellent study of foreign distribution patterns, Ferid Boughedir, denouncing the methods used by these cartels, charged that the films imported into Africa from all sources (westerns, Italian and French thrillers and spy films, Indian melodramas) were trashy and excessively loaded with sex and violence.[8] As there was no native competition against imported films, the cartels' policy was to flood the African market with mostly "B" movies already rejected by the metropolises which could thus be obtained at relatively low prices. The African market was prosperous for the cartels, yet this operation failed to promote domestic capital accumulation, or the creation of local manpower. In effect, what they did was to institutionalize the depletion of real resources. Deliberately refusing to invest even part of the profit on African film production, their overseas headquarters were instead the beneficiaries. Worse still, they prevented easy passage, through their own exhibition circuits, of films made by black Africans. For many years this monopoly prohibited African audiences from ever knowing another form of cinema.

In the anglophone region, the film business was primarily dominated by America. This position, rather than constituting a colonial venture, followed the same pattern of domination by the United States from World War I onward. America had no colony in Africa, but by arrangement with its overseas allies such as Rank (London) and Gaumont (France), Hollywood was able to extend its operations to Africa through an organization established in 1961 known as the America Motion Picture Export Company (AMPEC-Africa), which was soon to bring under its domination the market controlled by the British Colonial Film Unit. Later, in 1969, Afro-American Films Inc. (AFRAM)—representing MGM, Paramount, 20th Century-Fox, Columbia, United Artists, Buena Vista, and Warner Brothers—was created specifically to fight the monopoly enjoyed by SECMA and COMACICO in the francophone zone. It did not take long for the American companies to monopolize the African market. They became so powerful that not only did they determine which exhibitor to rent films to and which to deny such a request but they also controlled the number of films allowed in the market. As Thomas Guback observes in his book *The International Film Industries,* American companies were free to "turn the flow on, or off, as conditions warrant."[9] Transition to the neocolonial era has done nothing to rectify this one-sided situation, and the business of film distribution and exhibition in black Africa is still an empire controlled by foreign companies to the detriment of the African film industry.

African filmmakers consistently maintain that breaking this monopoly over film distribution and exhibition is a necessary prerequisite to boosting Africa's own film production. Certain measures have taken place at the national level aimed at establishing indigenous control. But these measures were either circumvented by the powerful European conglomerates or neglected and abandoned by Africa's lawmakers, who, even though they publicly acknowledged the importance of cinema in nation building, have continued to adopt a lukewarm attitude toward its development and growth.

In 1970, when Burkina Faso (then Upper Volta) nationalized its cinemas and created a national distribution organization, Société National Voltaique de Cinéma (SONAVOCI), the French-controlled SECMA and COMACICO responded by shutting down their distribution network in that country, which resulted in the closing of theaters. Although the compromise that was negotiated gave COMACICO the right to continue supplying films to Burkina Faso under modified terms approved by the government, "the principle of nationalization was preserved and SONAVOCI had total control over importing and distributing of films within the territory."[10]

Kenya's state organization, the Kenyan Film Corporation (KFC), formed in 1967 to oversee the importation and distribution of films, came into serious conflict with American companies that imposed a six-month boycott of the Kenyan market, forcing theaters to shut down. This was not nationalization per se, for theaters in Kenya are still owned by foreigners.

Nigeria's "Indigenization Decree" of 1972 did nothing to bring distribution and exhibition of films under the control of Nigerians, as originally ordered, owing to lack of enforcement by the authorities. Instead, the Asians, Syrians, and Lebanese who own the theaters and most of the businesses affected by the "Indigenization Decree" became naturalized citizens through the conniving of powerful and unscrupulous Nigerians. Those who did not naturalize, however, crept back into their businesses under the shadow of business partnerships with a Nigerian as the figurehead on the board of directors. Asian, Syrian, and Lebanese contributions to Africa's economy are best summarized in Edward B. Horatio-Jones's apt observation: the motto of their African entrepreneurship was, and still is, to "get [their] hands into anything that will turn to gold. When they were not busy smuggling gold from Liberia or exploiting the diamond trade on the Guinea Coast, they were somehow in legitimate deals such as the cinema."[11] They too did not invest their profits in the countries they exploited.

With the exception of Guinea, which successfully broke with foreign distributors and established its own national cinema (Sily Cinema), no other black African country had autonomous distribution cartels. This development followed the successful mass mobilization that inspired the electorate to give an emphatic "no" to General De Gaulle's referendum of 1958 (the year of Guinea's independence), which would have kept Guinea subservient to France, like other African colonies that voted to remain under French rule. France responded with punitive measures, and Guinea could not rely on French assistance to improve its audiovisual media. Instead, with the help of the Soviet Union, Yugoslavia, and Poland, Guinea established its own 16mm black and white filmmaking facilities.

The reader might assume that in emphasizing preindependence structures I am suggesting that postindependence economic stagnation was fated and that black Africa's colonial inheritance predetermined its later economic development. But this is not entirely the case. In fact, African governments must begin to accept responsibility for the economic decay and the lack of cultural initiative of the decades during which they assumed control. The general assumption when independence euphoria was sweeping through Africa in the late 1950s and 1960s was that political freedom would lead automatically to rapid economic development and social growth. Kwame Nkrumah's prophecy that "if we get self-government we'll transform the Gold Coast (now Ghana) into a paradise in ten years"[12] attests to this widely held belief. Why, then, has African self-determination resulted in economic decline? D. K. Fieldhouse's statement that "African governments have never been, despite their protestations, primarily concerned with economic growth but rather with maintenance of political power and the distribution of wealth to themselves and their supporters"[13] echoes the contention of African critics of postindependence maladministration.[14] For example, during Nigeria's indigenization process, a cabinet member who served in the defunct, corrupt military government of Yakubu Gowon had his chain of theaters, "The Bendel Cinemas," confiscated by the Murtala Muhammed's "corrective" regime. These theaters were not only illegally acquired through misuse of an official position but also through misappropriation of public funds.[15]

Analysts of Africa's economic stagnation have based their explanation of limited African development as deriving from badly managed policies. It is true that some of the development strategies aimed at modernization have been counterproductive and that growth has been limited simply because governments have adopted the wrong policy. But this assessment may prove to be simplistic if we recognize that cause and effect work to reinforce each other.

The inappropriate development of strategies which we have witnessed in the postcolonial period demonstrates the underutilization of Africa's mental resources and the waste of what should have become their constructive use. It is the contention of some analysts that the African dilemma of today transcends that of natural resources or manpower capability, with future hope cast on "mental change, a sense of responsibility and direction."[16] In this regard, if all the monies that have been hidden in Swiss and foreign banks by Africa's past and present rulers were channeled to productive developmental purposes, black Africa would have advanced technologically, to a much greater degree than is apparent today.

In the thriving cocoa years of Ghana, or in the oil boom years of Nigeria, rapid changes in the form of the acquisition of technological know-how, such as the establishment of manufacturing plants, could have been initiated, rather than the building of assembly plants (as in Nigeria) for French Peugeot and German Volkswagen cars. Similarly, why and how did President Mobutu Sese Sekou acquire such enormous wealth (estimated to be worth over five billion dollars by the U.S. State Department, some sources ranking him the fourth richest individual in the world), while his country, Zaire, ranks among the world's poorest? (By comparison, Mobutu's enormous wealth is token change considering the huge sums of African money locked up in foreign banks or buried in the ashes of Lebanon.) Since independence, Africa's wealth has been at the disposal of the elite and the urban rich. The initiation of prestigious development projects has, over the years, proven to be the easiest avenue to drain resources, since projects are left unfinished or abandoned after millions of dollars have been squandered. This, in turn, forces governments to seek international financial assistance and, in fact, nearly three-quarters of black African countries have mortgaged themselves to the International Monetary Fund (IMF). Given the incalculable ineptitude of Africa's political and management agencies, the sustainability of economic reform, even under heavy borrowing, is still questionable. Because the decision making and implementation must conform with the dictates of industrial nations, and because the political and social uses of aid in tropical Africa make it an instrument of corruption, foreign aid and IMF loans have not provided any long-term bailout for black African economies. In fact, the countries that have mortgaged their economies to the IMF use more than two-thirds of their individual GNPs to service the loans obtained from the World Bank.

The so-called aid meant to bail out African economies has also turned out to be a factor in recolonizing Africa since one of the requirements for such loans or aid allows for the management of local African companies by international capitalist experts. A classic example is Liberia. General Samuel K. Doe, the deposed president of Liberia (one of Africa's most egregious examples of economic mismanagement), said before his death that "there is nothing wrong with Liberia's economy, it is the people who are bad."[17] In actual fact, Liberia's economy is so badly battered that it had to rely on U.S. economic aid. And to check the recklessness that squandered previous aid, the U.S. State Department and the Liberian government devised a plan that allowed American financiers to play "financial diet doctor" to that country's economy. Under this measure (which Doe's government heartily approved because it was a prerequisite that guarantees future U.S. aid), seventeen American finance experts would take charge of Liberia's finance ministry, including the Central Bank, and control the highest level decision-making posts in departments of import and export, computer operations, procurement, customs and excise tax collection, budget, and foreign exchange.[18] That Liberia is unable to sustain itself economically 140 years after independence is a pathetic case that signifies a bad omen for black Africa. This leaves "Africa watchers" gasping and wondering if there is a future for black Africa in view of the fact that the level of economic and political corruption and indiscipline in Liberia is the same elsewhere. From the lowest strata to the highest echelon, corruption has become a way of life that continues to punch holes in state treasuries.

Apart from the complication created by humans, other factors hinder Africa's economic development and social growth. Black Africa's tropical climate (in opposition to the temperate regions) is hostile to many aspects of economic growth. Rainfall, for example, is one of Africa's major problems. Variable in geographical belts, too much rain results in outbreaks of pestilence and disease; too little makes the soil infertile for sufficient crop yield. Drought has continued to have a detrimental impact on black Africa's economy. From 1960 to 1986, each zone of Africa suffered through serious drought conditions. From the Savannah-Sahel regions of West Africa to East Africa and Ethiopia, the catastrophic holocaust it brought upon the inhabitants was climaxed by the Ethiopian famine of 1984 and 1985—a living misery of modern times. There is no question as to whether tropical heat reduces efficiency. Prone to endemic diseases such as malaria, river blindness, parasitic worms, leprosy, and more—much of which modern medicine could contain—the enormous drain of financial resources that goes into the provision of medicine and other preventive measures provides no antidote for black Africa's economic illness. This predicament is now complicated by the AIDS epidemic that is ravaging Africa's population.

In areas in which famine has not threatened to wipe out entire populations, the population increase is outpacing Africa's ability to feed itself. Significantly, since independence, most African countries have seen no peace. Characterized by political upheavals, young men in military uniforms are changing governments through coups d'état only to discover that economic recovery does not reside in the barrel of a gun. Alongside war, tyranny, hunger, and disease are Africa's tragedies.

Pan-Africanism and negritude are the two great philosophies invoked by African leaders. But today these movements have proven inadequate to the profound challenges of independence.[19] Similarly, Marxism and capitalism as "imperfect systems," to use the papal phrase, have failed to erase Africa's underdevelopment. In other words, these latter two philosophies have been considered by many Africans as sinister forces that continue to interfere with the affairs of weaker nations in order to further Marxist and capitalist strategies. For example, the world before the demise of communism was divided into rival ideological blocs and Africa was used by the superpowers to play out their competition. Dragged into this East-West ideological power play, African states are still inundated with regional squabbles and internal conflicts that lock them into civil and interstate wars. While this is also true of other Third World countries, the massive weapons of destruction from capitalist and formerly Communist countries used to sustain Africa's wars have over the years proven a major obstacle in the transformation of the abysmal conditions of underdevelopment.

These are the problems that Africa must contend with which do not provide a conducive atmosphere for all phases of economic development, including the cinema. The purpose, however, is to show how African cinema evolved out of unique circumstances (a situation that will also affect our analysis) and that, despite all the problems and the general lack of an immediate solution to some of the crises, filmmakers' coordinated efforts continue to produce films of political, cultural, and aesthetic significance.

The Indigenous African Film Production

In some parts of Africa, especially in West Africa, cinema evolved from varied disciplines of learning. In a keen assessment of West African cineastes, Edward B. Horatio-Jones identifies two categories of the pioneers of black African cinema: self-taught filmmakers who were writers with no formal training in film production or screenwriting for film or television; and those who, after spending considerable time in apprenticeship performing menial roles, were trained overseas in the humanities—in schools of fine arts—or in photography or film departments and in European theaters.[20]

The education of Africans in the cinematographic art is an important development in the history of black African cinema. In the 1950s, Africans who managed to enter film schools in Europe, East Berlin, and Moscow were from French-speaking West African countries. Francophone African countries thus took the lead in developing cinema in Africa partly because no film schools in Britain offered admission to African colonial students and partly because the British were less interested in promoting education in the field of cinematography.

Aspiring black African filmmakers wanted to make their perceptions of Africa (from centuries of colonial oppression to neocolonial repression) the themes of their work. More than this, they also learned from colonial examples that the film medium had enormous potential and that in the postcolonial African situation its potential for communication and the opportunities it could offer for projecting a new self-image, especially to a society predominantly illiterate, was indeed a blessing.[21] It is from this perspective that black African filmmakers, since independence, have striven for the need to work for African culture on African terms.

Starting in the francophone regions, black African cinema first appeared in 1955 when a group of African students in Paris led by Senegal's Paulin Soumanou Vieyra, along with Mamadou Saar, Robert Cristan, and Jacques Melo Kane, made the short film *Afrique sur Seine* (Africa on the Seine). This film, conceived and made by Africans, is also the first African fiction film. It dealt with emigration, alienation, and racial discrimination; from a humanist perspective, it depicted African youths who had left their countries to study in France as they walked "thoughtfully," as Clyde Taylor puts it, along Paris boulevards. In the same year, Mamadou Touré, a Guinean, produced a film called *Mouramani*. Although these two films, by today's standards, may not represent typical examples of advanced cinematography, they do set an important precedent for black African cinema.

It was not until seven years later that other films made by black Africans appeared—a development that also marked the arrival of independence for a significant number of African countries in the early 1960s. Paulin Soumanou Vieyra directed *Une nation est née* (A nation is born, 1961), a twenty-minute documentary film commemorating Senegal's first independence anniversary. Yves Diagne produced *L'Afrique en piste* (Africa gets on the track, 1961), a twenty-minute film dignifying the Senegalese official entry into the hierarchy of international sports competition at the Tokyo Olympics. This was followed by Blaise Senghor's *Grand magal à Touba* (The great pilgrimage to Touba, 1962), a twenty-five-minute documentary about African religious customs, including the depiction of the pilgrimage to the great Mosque of Touba, performed annually by the Islamic sect of the Mourides. This is the only film made by Blaise Senghor, who, like Vieyra, graduated from the French Institut des Hautes Études Cinématographiques (IDHEC). In Cameroon, Jean Paul N'Gassa's *Aventure en France* (Adventure in France, 1962) echoed *Afrique sur Seine*'s theme of alienation in a foreign country. While Niger's Mustapha Alassane focused on traditional life with his film *Aouré* (Wedding, 1962), which dealt with the subject of African marriage, his next-door counterpart, Mali's Djibril Kouyate, made *Le retour de Tiéman* (Tiéman's return, 1962), a thirty-minute study of new agricultural methods. In francophone countries, this decade was marked by the production of short films,[22] mainly educational documentaries and newsreels supervised by respective ministries of information. Among independent francophone countries, Côte d'Ivoire, Mali, and Senegal had production centers.

French-speaking African countries have a longer production history than the rest of black Africa. In the forefront is Senegal, which has more filmmakers than all other African countries in the sub-Saharan region, although Burkina Faso is now closing the gap. Owing largely to French government intervention to assist the newly independent colonies in developing their own audiovisual media, Senegal was the first francophone country to sign a newsreel production agreement with Consortium Audiovisual International (CAI), created in Paris in 1961.[23] Under this arrangement, France provided Senegal with equipment and cameramen-reporters who filmed newsreels in Senegal. The postproduction work was done in Paris and the completed film sent back to Senegal, CAI and Senegal splitting the production costs. This led to the birth of Les Actualités Sénégalaises and the department within it, Service de Cinéma, which was responsible for the production of documentaries for government departments—marking also an African government's involvement with the financing and production of films.

Another important move highlighting the development of cinema in black Africa was the creation of Bureau du Cinéma, which functioned under the auspices of the French Ministère de la Coopération. Under the CAI, the director and film technicians were mainly French nationals whose job was to oversee the improvement of communication while Bureau du Cinéma encouraged African participation in all phases of filmmaking. Two options were available for African filmmakers: the Coopération could produce films directed by Africans, providing the financial and technical support; or the African director could opt to complete his film, at which point the Coopération could pay for the cost of production in exchange for some rights to distribute the film noncommercially. This agreement has been heavily criticized by African filmmakers, in light of the Coopération's demand that scripts conform to so-called acceptable French cinematographic standards and its insistence on control of distribution (by way of acquiring the right to distribute the films noncommercially for a period of up to five years).

French aid for the production of African films is problematic. Though useful, it is regarded as paternalistic at best and imperialistic at worst. Considering that African filmmakers have lacked the material resources to make films, that their own governments have been apprehensive about the film medium (for fear of it being used against them), and that many years of oppression have left exhibition and distribution of films monopolized by foreigners who were indifferent to indigenous production, the argument that the Coopération's demand to acquire the rights to African films hindered distribution and slowed down its purpose seems plausible. It was the neocolonialist aspects of this otherwise rather munificent aid package that critics found unappealing.

France's interest in the development of cinema in most of its West African ex-colonies—Gabon, Congo, Niger, Mali, Senegal, Benin, Madagascar, Cameroon, and Burkina Faso—is certainly linked to the educational and cultural patterns that it adopted in colonial days, otherwise known as the policy of assimilation. This policy sought to "detribalize" the Africans by bringing them to the threshold of French culture. The French government, rather than regarding Africans as colonized people, preferred to call them "overseas Frenchmen."[24] However, since the French did not recognize or respect local African cultures, and since they considered culture the basis on which French citizenship was determined, they resolutely embarked on a program of turning the elite of their African wards into Frenchmen. The historical impetus for discrediting the African way of life, in other words, lay in the ideology of imperialism, enshrined in this case in the principles of assimilation. Thus assimilation resulted in the creation of an elitist class of Africans crowned with what Bernard Magubane aptly termed "the accoutrements of Western civilization."[25] This class of a few selected Africans was accorded certain privileges enjoyed by French citizens. More than any other benefit, their French education alienated them from their own culture.

Although directing films was one such privilege, some of the assimilated pioneers of African cinema did not cooperate with this policy,[26] demonstrating that cinema in Africa transcends the ideological motivations rooted in a specific dogmatic interest. The experiences marking each production confirmed the vitality of this cinema geared toward multinational development. As Hannes Kamphausen explained, "The range of themes, styles, temperaments, and formations among the different artists on the lively African film scene underlines the importance of taking idiosyncrasies into consideration."[27] However, without the type of aid made available by the Ministère de la Coopération it would have taken longer to complete some of the well-crafted films of black Africa or, more likely, some of them may not have been made at all.

Between 1962 and the end of 1980, a great majority of films made in the francophone region were partially financed through the assistance programs provided by the Coopération. Some of the first directors who benefitted from this scheme between 1962 and 1970 were the following: Niger's Mustapha Alassane, *Aouré*, *La bague du roi Koda* (King Koda's ring, 1964), *Le retour de l'adventurier* (The adventurer's return, 1966), and Oumarou Ganda, *Cabascado* (1969); Senegal's Ousmane Sembene, *Borom Sarret* (1963), *Niaye* (1964), *La noire de . . .* (Black girl, 1966), and Mahama Johnson Traoré, *Diankha-bi* (The young girl, 1969); Côte d'Ivoire's Timité Bassori, *Sur la dune de la solitude* (On the dune of solitude, 1966), *La femme au couteau* (The woman with a knife, 1968), and Désiré Ecaré, *Concerto pour un exil* (Concerto for an exile, 1967); and Cameroon's Urbain Dia Mokouri, *Point de vue* (Point of view, 1965).

The best known among the French-aided films are Ousmane Sembene's *Borom Sarret* and *Black Girl*. With the release of *Borom Sarret*, the impact of a serious indigenous African film production was felt. When it was exhibited at the 1963 Tours International Festival in France, it not only made history as the first black African film seen internationally by a paying audience but it also made an impression on the international scene by winning a prize—the second African film to do so after *Aouré*. Since then, recognition has accorded it the status of the first professional film ever made by a black African. Shot in

Dakar, *Borom Sarret,* only nineteen minutes long, is unquestionably an African masterpiece. It dealt, in embryonic form, with important issues that later became dominant themes of black African cinema and which Sembene and other filmmakers since then have emphasized in greater detail. In the filmic treatment of microcosmic situations, *Borom Sarret* is deliberately allegorical, structured to evoke national (and by implication continental) specificities, through the introduction of "fragmentary discourse" that reveals coded political messages. The contrast between the urban poor and the urban rich of Dakar served as the basic subject, but Sembene interweaves a series of vignettes to present African life in a neocolonial setting. But this neocolonial setting reflects, in the first place, the disappointment of being colonized. Here we see a poignant attack on the African elite who have replaced the white colonial administrator, on cultural alienation, and on social and economic exploitation, all pointing to the mantle of misery that was to prevail under neocolonial African governments—civilian or military.

Borom Sarret is Sembene's first film, which perhaps explains why it is photographically and technically somewhat deficient. His camera was not in perfect control of the subject matter, and the film's pace of editing is slow, at times lacking rhythm and continuity. There are a few slow-moving ponderous scenes, but what Sembene loses in technique and style he gains in theme and in his sensitive use of music. When the cart driver travels between the European quarters and the medina, Sembene switches back and forth between the native indigenous music (Wolof guitar) and European classical music (Mozart). Sembene, in offering an explanation regarding his choice of music for this film, admitted he probably would have used a different approach had his experience in filmmaking been more mature. His primary motive was to

> show the European area and the Africans who live in the European lifestyle. The only music I could relate to them was the classical music, the minuets of the eighteenth century, because they're still at that mentality.[28]

The universe Sembene described in this short fictional piece is a reflection of specific Senegalese and African history. Before he started to make films, he served in the French colonial army, the Tirailleurs Sénégalais. Following this military service, he worked in the southern port city of Marseille as a fisherman, bricklayer, automobile mechanic, and dockworker. His working experience gave him a thorough knowledge of French society and he became directly involved in French political life. As a militant trade unionist—as a migrant worker and as a shop steward—his experience culminated in the feeling, the need, to express himself.[29] As a result, in the late 1950s Sembene came out with a series of three novels: *The Black Docker* (1956), which reflects his varied experiences as an African worker in France; *Oh My Country, My Beautiful People* (1957), which depicts the return of a Senegalese war veteran to his native village and his desire to modernize the farming techniques of the peasants; and *God's Bits of Wood* (1960), his most successful novel and an offshoot of his involvement with unionization, which vividly portrays what A. Adu Boahen describes as the "glimpses of [traditional] culture as it existed beneath the yoke of colonization."[30]

Sembene is a committed writer, and as their titles suggest, his novels are works of a revolutionary in the making. But to Sembene, the role of a committed writer transcends that of simply using the text to inform. He believes the text should also evoke an individual's political awareness. But as he continued with his writing he became increasingly dissatisfied with literature as a forum for his ideas and began to question the effectiveness of the written word on a continent where the majority of people cannot read or write. This prompted him to divert his interests to cinema, believing that film "could become the vehicle 'par excellence' for the creation of a modern form of African culture—able to transcend artificial frontiers and language barriers."[31]

Ironically, when *Borom Sarret* was released, its sound track was in French, with English subtitles for prints distributed in the United States. Did this language barrier further stymie Sembene's zeal to reach the illiterate mass audience whom he was determined to inform and educate? The impact of *Borom Sarret* on the supposedly "illiterate" masses could be glossed with a distinction François Sourou Okioh, a filmmaker and critic from Benin, has made regarding the strengths and weaknesses of language versus pictures. Echoing Sembene's reason for turning to cinema, Okioh writes:

Pictures are more eloquent than an ideographic language or natural signs. They represent the object itself with such perfection that the viewer feels in contact with reality. While languages are particular to the people, the language of pictures is universal. Words are abstract. Pictures are concrete. Words evoke a corresponding intellectual scheme, limited by lexicographical definition. Pictures are concrete, a reality registered by the camera. Words are much deprived of substance, pictures have the savour and complexity of reality—they are the presence of the object itself. Words have richer intellectual contents, pictures an emotional charge that is more important.[32]

If these remarks can be said to be applicable to *Borom Sarret* in particular, it is due to the film's simple structure. Although the story or stories are short and familiar, it is plausible to argue that the absence of indigenous language in a complicated feature-length film, irrespective of how African the theme, would entail using the techniques of silent cinema where pictures clarify the unspoken word. It is through what Okioh terms "intensive expressiveness of style" that *Borom Sarret* manages to conquer this problem. This creative process entails character delineation and masterful use of monologue and is intended to encourage the audience to participate in the experiences of the cart driver. The film's open-endedness is also a strong appeal to the viewer to think about the ironies of this society in transition. Many critics would agree that these are the elements of a stylistic combination that make "this film a masterpiece by which black African cinema clearly" expresses what was to become the composition of its main itinerary: "the placing of pictures and sounds in the service of awakening and raising awareness of the realities of . . . Africa"[33] and the creation of filmic works by and for Africans.

In 1963 Sembene also made for the government of Mali a somewhat obscure documentary, *L'Empire Songhai,* which attempted to recapture the events of the old Songhai empire in precolonial Africa. This historical survey depicts the Islamized inhabitants who occupied the areas now known as Mali—the Songhai's struggle against foreign invasion, French colonialism, and the dissension within, all of which contributed to the deterioration and fall of the empire. Similarly, recapturing the past was the subject of Momar Thiam's *Sarzan* (Senegal, 1963), a film partly financed by the director with financial and technical support from Senegal's Ministry of Information which portrayed a colonial army officer returning to his village after being used by France to fight its war. Here, the issue of acculturation was also dealt with forcefully. After fifteen years of military service, Moussa, a sergeant, now Westernized and alienated, could not fit into the traditional setting of his society. He decided to embark on a mission to "civilize" his people. This prompted him to destroy sacred altars as well as himself eventually. The film acknowledges the alienation from tradition wrought by modernism as inevitable but suggests that gradual rather than abrupt transformation is necessary in order to protect society from the social and psychological trauma associated with sudden changes. *Sarzan* is indifferently directed and shot, but its historical significance lies not only in its pioneer status as one of the very first fiction films conceived of and produced by an African but also in the African filmmakers' understanding of the film medium as venerable palimpsest and document for posterity. To preserve on film cultural forms of expression in *Sindiély* (Senegal, 1963), which depicts traditional dances of the society, Vieyra used ancestral African ballet to tell the story of forced marriage. And Cameroon's Thérèsa Sita Bella, the only African woman filmmaker at this time, made *Tam tam à Paris* (African drums in Paris, 1963). This theme was later echoed in *Les ballets de la forêt sacrée* (Dances from the sacred forest; Senegal, 1970) by Abdou Fary Faye.

In Côte d'Ivoire, Timité Bassori directed *Sur la dune de la solitude* (On the dune of solitude), which dealt with traditional culture in its exploration of Africa's legends, traditionally transmitted orally. The film told the story, a famous West African myth, of the river goddess (Mamy Watta, or in Yoruba, Yemoja) who takes men into captivity to seduce them in her deep-water abode. This film is actually quite experimental. In the street scenes, black, white, and shadow contrasts display elements of film noir, which, together with surrealistic composition, suggest Bassori's potential for creativity and innovation.

Significantly, this creative zeal emerged in 1962 from Côte d'Ivoire's remarkably early establishment of the national film production organization Societé Ivoirienne de Cinéma (SIC), part of its television production center. (It is unfortunate, though, that this encouragement had, in the 1970s and 1980s, turned out to be a great disappointment and "one of the most frustrating in Africa."")[34] SIC had 16mm and 35mm laboratory facilities, and although this organization produced documentaries and newsreels until 1979, no significant achievement had been made through its feature film production unit, despite the presence of a host of Ivorian talents and coproductions involving France.[35] Television, which enjoyed larger support from the government, proved to be an effective challenger to SIC with its debut of the two-hour feature production *Korogo* (1964) directed by Georges Keita. Timité Bassori, Désiré Ecaré, and Henri Duparc are among the pioneers of Côte d'Ivoire cinema—all studied at IDHEC in Paris—and their works will be discussed in the following chapters.

The examination of Africa's traditions through its legends was also important to Niger's rather unique cinematographic establishment, where most of its prolific filmmakers, Mustapha Alassane, Oumarou Ganda, and Inoussa Ousseini, were self-taught. Many of the filmmakers of Senegal, Mali, and Côte d'Ivoire were formally educated outside Africa, in such places as Paris and Moscow, while those of Niger received no formal film training; they learned from personal experiences while working with French filmmakers in Niger or in neighboring African countries.[36]

One of the most innovative and respected filmmakers in Niger is Mustapha Alassane. His extreme talent for drawing and his quest for invention prompted him, before he even knew what cinema was, to organize a one-man exhibition in which he projected his color drawings for his audience by using transparent cellophane wrappers from cigarette packets.[37] His first film, *Aouré,* was made in 1962. His second,

La bague du roi Koda (King Koda's ring, 1964), drawing from the African oral tradition and fictional narrative structure, tells the popular legend of a king who tries to seduce the wife of one of his subjects, a fisherman. But the king finds out that luck can turn evil machination to triumph. In the drama that unfolds, the magic of oral tradition enables the fisherman to outwit the king. Rather than being killed by the mischievous king, the fisherman becomes the beneficiary of half the king's property. (This topic, set in a traditional, rural environment, was also the theme of Sembene's little-known second film, *Niaye* [1964], a moralistic tale depicting sex and the taboo subject of incest.)

In 1965, after working briefly with Jean Rouch, Alassane proceeded to Montreal, Canada, where he studied animation for nine months under Norman Maclaren at the National Film Board of Canada. Upon returning to Niger, he made two animated social-satire films, *La mort de Gandji* (The death of Gandji, 1965) and *Bon voyage, Sim* (1966), the first two African animated films. *La mort de Gandji*, a political commentary, depicts courtesan toads in the court of a king toad competing for attention; and *Bon voyage, Sim*, a film that mocks official state visits performed by Africa's heads of state, portrays a king toad, returning from an overseas trip, who finds he has been dethroned. When Alassane's interest shifted to narrative filmmaking, this astute director discovered that Western narrative structure could blend with traditional folktale to effectively deliver a devastating political punch. The result of this switch is *Le retour de l'aventurier* (The adventurer's return, 1966), about the dangers of cultural pollution resulting from the impact of westerns (cowboy movies) on traditional life. *F.V.V.A.-Femmes, villa, voiture, argent* (Women, villa, car, money, 1972), his first feature, is a satiric study of African male chauvinism which will be discussed later in this work.

From 1965 to 1970, diaries of individual adventures to foreign lands (either by Africans trained abroad or by African veterans of the world wars) continued to preoccupy filmmakers. While some of the films actually detail personal or group experiences, some depict the adjustment problems these people faced when they returned home. In Cameroon, adjustment was the subject of N'Gassa's *Aventure en France* (1962) and the focus of *Point de vue* (Point of view, 1965), by Urbain Dia Mokouri, and in Senegal, Ababacar Samb's *Et la neige n'était plus* (There was no longer snow, 1965) echoed the alienation theme of Vieyra's *Afrique sur Seine* while also dealing with readjustment problems. And most important, there was Ousmane Sembene's *La noire de . . .* (Black girl, 1966). This film was adapted from one of the short stories in his novel *Voltaique* (published in English under the title *Tribal Scars*).[38] If *Borom Sarret* was executed with lucidity, *Black Girl* demonstrated with eloquence a remarkable narrative ingenuity. The native quarters of Dakar are again exploited here, but this time Sembene uses a female principal character, Diouna, and the psychological essay he makes of her parallels his own antiestablishment stance. The political imperatives of this film are historical in latitude as well as sociological in depth. Its obvious binary structure makes it a key study of black-white conflicts.

Black Girl explores the maltreatment of a Senegalese woman who is taken out of Africa to work as a maid for a French family. In a scene widely regarded as reminiscent of a slave auction, a young black girl is hired as a domestic servant. When the white family takes her to France, her life is no less than a slave in captivity. Cut off from all social standing, she is constantly subjected to inhumane treatment by the Madame. Even letters to her mother in Senegal must be dictated by the white French couple. As Henry Morgenthau points out, she is no longer a person, she is simply "the black girl."[39] Diouna's disenchantment with her position leads to despondency. This sense of deprivation and isolation ultimately drive her to suicide. Considered Africa's first dramatic fiction feature, *Black Girl* won the 1966 Jean Vigo prize for best director, the Golden Tanit in Carthage, and first prize at the Festival of Negro Arts in Dakar.

The year 1966 was important for black African cinema. It was a period of exceptional productivity which heralded the emergence of African fiction film. It also brought to the limelight other filmmakers like Oumarou Ganda, Mustapha Alassane, and Désiré Ecaré. *Mandabi* (The money order; Senegal, 1968) by Ousmane Sembene, and *Cabascado* (Tough nut; Niger, 1969) by Oumarou Ganda are among the African films of this period which were distributed internationally, attaining world recognition and popularizing African film practice.

From all the francophone regions came films that pursued similar themes. Côte d'Ivoire's Désiré Ecaré, a former student of IDHEC, demonstrated a considerable directorial talent in the two films he made in Paris, *Concerto pour un exil* (Concerto for an exile, 1967) and *A nous deux, France* (Take care, France, 1970), renamed *Femme noire, femme nue* (Black woman, naked woman) by the distributors. Set in the Parisian exile community of which he was a member, the first film extends the study Vieyra made in 1955 of the Africans on the Seine while the second depicts the sexual acculturation of the immigrant community. In *La femme au couteau* (The woman with the knife; Côte d'Ivoire, 1968), Timité Bassori in an engagingly provocative and highly personalized style (but reportedly with little impact on its African audience), tells his friends how this author-actor discovered Europe. In Cameroon, Thomas Makoulet Manga offered the account of his own

Ousmane Sembene: La noire de . . . (*Black Girl*); *Senegal, 1966.* Courtesy of New Yorker Films.

training experience in *Mon stage en France* (My training in France, 1968). Other films in this category include *Ame perdue* (Lost soul; Guinea, 1969) by Amadou S. Camara, *Cabascado* by Oumarou Ganda, and *Soleil O* (O Sun, 1969) by Med Hondo of Mauritania.

Oumarou Ganda, whose untimely death occurred in 1981 at the age of forty, was the second pioneer of Niger cinema. His first film experience dates back to Jean Rouch's *Moi, un noir* (Me, a black man), a film shot in 1957 in which he played a major role. He also worked as an assistant director in the film division of the French Cultural Center in Niamey. He was one of the few Africans to benefit from the French

Coopération, which made it possible, according to him, to "set out to 'correct' the image of Africa offered by Rouch."[40] *Cabascado,* his first film, is based on his own experience as a soldier returning home to be welcomed by everyone after fighting for four years for France in Indochina. But when his money runs out, his friends, including the girls, desert him. Finally, he goes to the countryside, with an axe over his shoulder, to seek solace. In some respects, *Cabascado* echoes the theme and performances of Sembene's *Borom Sarret* and *Mandabi,* which are colonial and neocolonial perspicacious portraits of African individuality, executed with sincerity, simplicity, and neatly detailed characterization. His other works extend into the late 1970s, but it was not until 1980, the year before his death, that he was able to make his second feature *L'exilé* (The exiled), a full-length feature and probably the most important film of his career.

The oppression and exploitation described in Oumarou Ganda's *Cabascado* are similar (in colonial and neocolonial contexts) to the problems portrayed in Med Hondo's *Soleil O.* But unlike Oumarou Ganda, Med Hondo explores the predicament of the people of Africa with an innovative style and theoretical orientation. His films are total portraits, a reflection of his anger at a decadent society he would like to see changed. Med Hondo (his full name, Mohamed Abid Hondo) has lived in France since 1958. He worked at many menial jobs to finance his acting classes and had originally wanted to use theater acting or stage directing to showcase black performers in France, where, according to him, racism had relegated them to relative obscurity. In 1966 he established his own theater group called *Shango* which performed in cultural centers and small theaters in France. His aim was to use this forum to draw attention to work by playwrights of the black diaspora: Martinique's Aimé Césaire, Afro-American authors such as Imamu Baraka, and unknown African and South American playwrights.[41] To his disappointment, his efforts had little impact on the French indifference to black theatrical involvement. Like Sembene, he then turned to filmmaking in the hopes of reaching a larger audience.

While Med Hondo was acting, he also learned to make films. *Balade aux sources* (Ballad to the sources, 1969), a reflection of an African immigrant disenchanted with his living conditions, and *Partout ou peut-être nulle part* (Everywhere, or maybe nowhere, 1969), about two white couples seen through the eyes of an African, were both made in 1968 while he was preparing for the filming of *Soleil O.*

Soleil O, a title that owes allegiance to the old song of African slaves en route to the West Indies, sung to express indignation over their abrupt disengagement from their native land, is Med Hondo's first feature-length film. Described by the maker in the opening sequence as a "pamphlet," this film meticulously attacks foreign imperialism in Africa from slavery to the present. It is this colonial-neocolonial paradox that provides the core of *Soleil O*'s complex structure. In it we see a tapestry of history fashioned as an avant-garde essay on racism and the intense sense of estrangement and alienation to which Med Hondo and entire black immigrant communities in France are subjected.

"I make films," Hondo said, "to show people the problems they face everyday and to help them fight those problems."[42] *Soleil O* begins with an animated sequence of an African puppet ruler being catapulted to power by foreign military intervention only to have his reign terminated by the same people who installed him. From here, the film's subsequent episodes revolve around a young African immigrant, an accountant, whose experience Hondo uses to dramatize the frustrating existence of numerous other black immigrant workers (Africans and West Indians) living in France. The accountant goes through unprecedented humiliation as he faces racially motivated rejection looking for a job and accommodations; even when he does menial jobs, cold attitudes greet him. As he meanders through dehumanizing settings, indicative of living conditions for blacks in France, Hondo synthesizes contradictory vignettes of colonial and neocolonial life suggestive of Africa's relationship with France. Subjected to anguish, mental torment, and internal conflict, the accountant is forced to reflect on his conscience, seeking solace in a hospitable enclave where social and political actions for self-determination and liberation are preferably contemplated. The last segment is a meditative sequence with glimpses of superimposed images of martyred revolutionaries (Patrice Lumumba, Che Guevara, Malcolm X) shown as cultural metaphors reminiscent of Fanon's concept of returning to one's roots.

The theme and style of *Soleil O,* as Clyde Taylor has rightly indicated, is estrangement.[43] Hondo's carefully chosen images, starkly presented on screen as a visual dramatization of African history, no doubt reflect his rage over the injustices he considers devastating to the Arab and African community. Throughout the film Hondo's panoramic lens spans a spectrum of colonial and neocolonial landscapes comprehensive enough to capture the structural duality (Western and traditional) of African emancipation. From this film the viewer learns that the educational, civil, and religious dogmas inculcated by French colonialists are more or less superficial, especially when the French system of hierarchical bias keeps benefactors at bay. The ambiguous character of the film's protagonist, the accountant, makes this point explicit. Just as Ousmane Sembene's *Black Girl* protagonist, Diouana, is only identified by her colonial masters as black girl, maid, or African, so too is the accountant in *Soleil O* identified only by his color. This character, representing waves of Africans from ex-colonies seeking a better life in France, is nameless, symbolizing France's marginalization of its black community. As a symbolic figure, who by virtue of his education is the bridge between the past and the present, he is also a chronicler who understands colonial and neocolonial traits. Moving through a succession of episodes from intellectual and proletarian standpoints, beginning with his appearance in a classroom, to his impressive discussion of capitalism with a French executive, to becoming a Parisian street-sweeper, to his identifying with his black compatriots and even being shunned by some of them, Hondo aggressively frames a complicated cross-cultural and timeless vision of societal conflict and inequality. In this regard, the role of the accountant, reminiscent of Dieng in *Mandabi*, fulfills a collective experience. *Soleil O* vividly defines the existential rejection and alienation pertinent to the black community, reaffirming the fact that regardless of individual status, the situation remains unchanged as long as one is black.

In the film, Hondo's elliptical use of symbolism, juxtaposed with a cinéma vérité approach and self-reflexivity, draws attention to the uncompromising style of this enterprising young Marxist director. *Soleil O* is perhaps the least understood of African films and has been grossly misinterpreted by Western critics. Nonsequential and disregarding continuity editing, it favored what has been described as a "modular and metaphoric" mode of representation that is distinctly non-Western in narrative pattern. This is probably why the film (in non-African circles) has received mixed reviews. While *Soleil O* has been hailed by many as the most significant African expatriate film,[44] some Western critics have described it as too didactic,[45] too experimental, too arty, and too disjointed.[46] Its style has been termed reminiscent of Godard's political antiestablishment films and the European avant-garde theater—assumptions rejected by Hondo.

Soleil O engages in a kind of filmic didacticism and hyperbolic virtuoso display of cinematic ingenuity. If the film is viewed as too pedagogical, it is because it presents the viewer with protagonists who become symbolic vehicles for expressing the film's analysis of cultural specificity in a style that is quasi-Brechtian and uncompromisingly anti-realist. This style incorporates accelerated camera movement, repetition of shots (deriving from oral storytelling technique), disruption of the "natural" harmony and coherence of images and icons, and ironic contrasts. Rather than maintaining what would be regarded as the traditional or conventional narrative homogeneity, the film induces a clash of codes; its disjointed structure, united by an evocative sound track, involves a mixture of real and fictive images ultimately geared toward audience attention and participation. Invoking the spectator's atten-

Med Hondo: Soleil O (*O Sun*); *Mauritania, 1969.* Courtesy of Med Hondo Films.

tion, for example, to the severance of Africa's culture by the French policy of assimilation described earlier, Hondo's protagonist (who by implication fits into this term) is a symbol of alienation, his role later reversing to that of revolutionary who for salvation seeks his roots. Reflecting Hondo's personal view, the narrator, at one point in the film, aware of his African identity and the marvelous achievements credited to African ingenuity in science, politics, and government prior to colonialism and seldom acknowledged in Western circles, says, "We had our own civilization. We forged iron, we had our own judicial and educational systems." In extending its criticism of the policy of assimilation and cultural colonialism, in another sequence the film attacks European-induced collective baptism. In this scene one of the Africans being baptized says to the officiating priest, "Forgive me, Father, I have spoken Bambara." (Bambara is a Malian language, and in such baptismal ceremonies only French is spoken.) The priest, of course, baptizes him as John and not by his native name.

The reflexive qualities of *Soleil O* also call attention to its own status as an evocative construct and, more generally, to the status of the film as political and ideological artifact. In this vein, the above qualities extend to other dimensions; the utilization of familiar and unfamiliar cultural symbols hereby function as a decoding device with which to scrutinize the immanent meaning of implied reality. In deconstructing the teleological norms of representation and storytelling technique, *Soleil O* subverts the concept of realism, using the inverted image to reveal an instrument of oppression. In one sequence, for example, the Christian symbol of the cross is turned into a sword, an instrument of violence, which some Africans will later use to kill themselves as a white colonial officer looks on. This is a typical example of Hondo's use of a signifier to reverse the meaning of the signified.

In all episodes, "narrative and reportage, dream or nightmare and actuality," as observed by Roy Armes, coalesce into a dialectical organization, the pivotal sustenance of the thematic richness and stylistic inventiveness of this film.[47] This dialectical concern draws him closer in principle to the political context envisaged for African cinema by Ousmane Sembene, whose work is also heavily inundated with Marxist dialectic. But *Soleil O* is neither a documentary nor a narrative feature film. It does not necessarily tell a story; instead, the film is segmented, and each scene gives Med Hondo the creative opportunity to slam his audience with a political point in a stylistic amalgam accompanied by an intense, imaginative, and eerie musical score. As an allegory of national consciousness, this film, which indicts Western imperialism and racism as well as neocolonial attitudes, remains a valuable example of African political cinema. Even though Med Hondo may not have been consciously influenced by the Russian filmmakers of the twenties and thirties, in many respects *Soleil O* typifies some of the stylistic, if not the thematic, concerns of that period. But, unlike Eisenstein, whose films center around a carefully chosen central thematic object in what amounts to the "celebration" and "glorification" of the past, Med Hondo has a closer affinity to Vertov, whose films, in breaking with conventional rules, explained or tried to elucidate the struggles of the present moment.

Hondo is black Africa's Dziga Vertov, and *Soleil O* is Africa's *The Man with a Movie Camera* in its attempt to synthesize the contradictions of neocolonial African reality in much the same way Vertov did with the Soviet Revolution. In his search for authentic African film language, Hondo has stressed theme; thus, for him, the content dictates the style. His films are songs of experience and indignation. Paris remains the gray place that inspired his "tropical" lens, the grimy, racist universe where he felt estranged and outcast. The series of styles he weaves is a testimony to personal reflection and the search for creative autonomy. Med Hondo sees this style, more than any other filmmaking tradition, as deriving from Africa's oral tradition.

In the late 1960s, when the concept of pan-Africanism was increasingly politicized and permeated the African social fabric, filmmakers also turned to a deeper exploration of social issues and contemporary problems: traditional culture versus Western influence, the dichotomy between urban and rural life, unemployment, corruption, the position of women in a male-dominated society, and polygamy. As early as 1957, Vieyra had started to explore the relationship between African traditional ways of life and Western ways, focusing on the impact of Western technology. The motorization of a fishing boat serves as the subject of *Mol* (Fishermen). This film, a didactic documentary emphasizing the need for industrialization, was not completed until ten years later owing to a lack of adequate funding. In a satiric study of Dakar's imposing cosmopolitanism, Djibril Diop Mambety, a famous Senegalese actor, directed *Contras' City* (A city of contrasts, 1968). To summarize his distress over the prevailing lack of administrative foresight, he said, "I find it strange that we had a Sudanese-style cathedral, a chamber of commerce building looking like a theater, while the theater resembles a block of council flats."[48] The degradation of African art examined in *Les statues meurent aussi* (1953) by Chris Marker and Alain Resnais (earlier described in chapter 1 as the most serious European film to examine the effects of colonialism on Africa and African art) is taken up again in *Mouna ou le rêve d'un artiste* (Mouna, an artist's dream; Côte d'Ivoire, 1969) by Henri Duparc, but this time questioning the wisdom of reproducing "old" African masks and artifacts in series. Subsequently, Ousmane Sembene gave African cinema a new dimension. He examined social injustice more forcefully, critically, and at greater length in *Mandabi* (The money order, 1968), focusing on the exploitation of illiterates by the smart, corrupt, and self-centered literate (usually overseas educated, but not entirely in all cases). Illiteracy was also the theme of Yaya Kossoko's *La réussite de Meithèbre* (Meithèbre's success; Niger, 1970), and by this time, Mustapha Alassane used his improved cinematic skill to dramatize in *F.V.V.A.* the issues of the corruption, nepotism, and mismanagement permeating the indigenous bourgeoisie.

In Africa, a woman's position in relation to her male counterpart has always been a function of the particular rules of the social circle to which she belongs. For example, while a woman's activity is severely restricted and closed in the Muslim community, in Christian or more traditional homes, a woman's role is more open and expanded. In this rapidly changing African environment, where traditional cultures blend with imported ones, filmmakers began examining the role of women in a realistic manner rather than the usual Western cinematic portrayal of African women as sensuous, bare-breasted sexual objects, submissive to male demands and having a minute role or no role at all in societal matters. Mahama Johnson Traoré's *Diankha-bi* (The young girl; Senegal, 1969) and its sequel *Diègue-bi* (The young woman, 1970) initiated studies in this area which received greater attention throughout the seventies and eighties in films like Sembene's *Ceddo,* Ecaré's *Visages de femmes* (Faces of women), and Hondo's *Sarraounia.*

Likewise, sociologically oriented films touched sensitive nerves, causing African leaders to try to restrict dissemination of audiovisual materials. Criticism of such practices as polygamy, for instance, which existed from time immemorial and which the elders would say is the bondage of communal existence, would be antitraditional.[49] As one traditionalist of African culture pointed out to me, "Which artist would have addressed this issue publicly if not for the changing African world?" Oumarou Ganda did so in his film *Le wazou du polygame* (The polygamist's moral; Niger, 1970), and since then, African traditions concerning marriage, excessive dowry, circumcision, the question of illegitimate children, and other related issues have been addressed by numerous filmmakers.

Returning to *Mandabi,* this study will deal with some of the important issues it raises concerning black African cinema. This film, made without the assistance of the much criticized French Coopération, is the first black African full-length feature to be filmed in color.[50] It was partly financed by the famous Centre National de la Cinématographie Française (CNC). Up until this time, the center had only awarded grants to French nationals such as Godard, Truffaut, and others, but on the recommendation of the French minister of culture, André Malraux, Sembene competed and won. A French producer, Robert Nesle, was assigned to oversee the budget for *Mandabi,* and their working relationship was no better than the control exerted by administrators of the Coopération funds.[51]

Mandabi is a comedy, a simple story whose chronological plot depicts the social ironies of Senegal. The film revolves around a central character, Ibrahima Dieng, who lives peacefully in his village until a money order arrives from his nephew working in Paris. His struggle to have it cashed marks the long road to misadventure and humiliation by an uncompromising government bureaucracy that has ground Africa's economic establishment to a halt. The news of his additional income induces Dieng's two wives (who have seven children between them) to celebrate by purchasing some food items on credit. Neighbors and friends anticipate a share. His creditors expect to be paid. The Imam, a Muslim minister, who expects some donations, meets with Dieng's flamboyant sister (also part beneficiary of the money order). Even before the arrival of the money order, Dieng has established his character in the community as lovable and benevolent, and the poor women of the village who have heard the story of his wealth seize the opportunity to move closer to him for their own share.

This communal love, the spirit of sharing, is still a normal and natural expectation associated with African life. In the events that follow, however, Sembene's carefully laid out theme shows the viewer that the natural order of things, such as this communality of existence, or give and take (call it traditional socialism), is gradually becoming rarer in the face of modern-day African realities such as the monetary economy. Sembene's theme and narrative structure are shaped by the influences informing the present sociocultural dynamics of the African people, notably the vestiges of colonial oppression and domination now operating in full gear as neocolonial repression—or what Okey Onyejekwe has aptly termed "recolonization."[52]

Mandabi's themes emphasize abhorrence of ineptitude, inefficiency, and inhumanity. It is here that Sembene finds the environment for impugning the petite bourgeoisie and the neocolonial bureaucracy that has stratified African society as an insidious reversion to the hierarchical bias of the French colonial administration. His method is undiluted realism. The central character is an individual who identifies with traditional values, the representative of an "underclass" with self-respect who is most likely to be less privileged in the new society. (Indeed, Dieng is an illiterate who probably would trust anybody who can read and write and naively accept any figure given as the face value of European currency or a money order, much to his detriment.)

For Sembene, "professional actors are simply not convincing as laborers, as ordinary human beings." However, he does not rule out the use of professional actors when "the story is right." Reminiscent of the Italian neorealist films of the 1940s noted for their "universal power and appeal," *Mandabi* has been called by one critic no less than an African rendering of *The Bicycle Thief* (1948):

> A simple story of a simple, uneducated man in the city (a nonactor, as in the De Sica film) who is reduced to hopelessness in his circular confrontation with the bureaucracy, and brought to despair when stolen from by a younger generation made corrupt by a society which has lost its human values.[53]

Unlike *The Bicycle Thief,* however, *Mandabi* remains for Sembene a political tool. Sembene himself, ironically, fell victim to both French and Senegalese bureaucracies. While this film was circulating in American and European film festivals, it was banned in Senegal. Even after independence, the French exerted enormous pressure and maintained vigilance over their ex-colonies. A similar case was that of *Soleil O*. The Mauritanian government would not even acknowledge it as that country's official entry for international film festivals.

After *Black Girl, Mandabi* (the first black African film distributed commercially outside Africa) reignited the flame of black African film in international arenas. It was shown at the Venice Film Festival in 1968, the New York, San Francisco, and London film festivals in 1969, and at the Second African Film Festival held in Ouagadougou, the capital of Burkina Faso[54] in 1970, winning several awards. Here is how Jay Leyda saw *Mandabi*:

> What we saw went far beyond anyone's expectations—a wonderful, handsome, and real comedy. . . . We had seen what we were always looking for—a new film master and a new kind of film. It lifted the whole festival [New York]—here was the masterpiece that could justify any film festival. . . . None of Sembene's three films could have been made by any visitor to Senegal. Nor could they have been made in any other African country. But they teach that continent a lesson of vital importance: do it yourself and in your own way. Filmmakers in the black communities . . . should study the deep individuality of Sembene's films.[55]

Rather than focusing on detailed analysis of this film, which most studies have already done,[56] I will point to another aspect of the contribution this film has made toward the development and growth of African cinema. At the Ouagadougou Second African Film Festival of February 1970, *Mandabi* and Mustapha Alassane's *Deela* (Niger, 1969) instigated the debate by African filmmakers on one of the major problems of African films—that of language. Long before Sembene made *Mandabi*, his intention had been to use film to address the largely illiterate peasant community in a language it would understand. But owing to the restrictions imposed by French agencies that provided the money to back African film production, Sembene's films shot in French had not met that obligation. Although this restriction was still in effect when he made *Mandabi*, he was able to shoot two versions—one in French and one in Wolof. (After *Mandabi* came Sembene's not too well known twenty-four-minute film, *Tauw*, 1970.)

If *Mandabi's* contemporary social themes struck a responsive chord with the public, *Deela* found it necessary to recapture old African traditions still present in contemporary African societies but also found that the universality of the message is impeded by the problem of language. In *Deela*, which was commissioned by the Centre des Traditions Or-

Ousmane Sembene: Tauw; *Senegal, 1970.* Courtesy of New Yorker Films.

ales, Mustapha Alassane used a well-known storyteller (the griot, or itinerant minstrel singer) to illustrate the power of proverbs. But Alassane is not as insightful as Sembene. Despite the interesting subject, he lacked the technical dexterity to put the story together visually on screen. As Marie Claire Le Roy observed, the visual treatment of *Deela* is "static, its composition is insufficiently thought out and the narrative is poorly coordinated."[57] But we are not evaluating the artistic achievements of *Mandabi* and *Deela*. Although they may be miles apart stylistically and thematically, they both share a sensitivity to the independent black African cinema's concern with the specific needs and desires of its audience.

In Senegal, the Wolof language is spoken by 85 percent of the population. Thus there remains a fraction of the population unable to understand films made in Wolof (the situation is much more severe in other African countries where diversity of dialects abound). However, the use of French is inhibitive, reducing the impact of the film's message. In *Deela,* where the minstrel speaks in the local dialect, French is used in the commentary, which poses a problem. Some critics of this system think that the solution will perhaps be found only through general political development; perhaps a continental lingua franca, or government subsidy should be provided to help dub films into different languages—an uphill task!

Since the late 1960s, films dealing with the theme of a changing Africa have been made in practically every black African country. The inspiration for this commitment resulted from the complications of the colonial and neocolonial systems, with their attendant ideological mystifications. The films of this period present themselves not as aesthetic artifacts but as an impetus for political dialogue. The images, styles, structure, and motives explore the multiple political and cultural responses that these films evoke. More important is the attempt to fashion a style of purposeful cinema, capable of addressing various African political and cultural patterns. In this respect, their cinematic approaches are stylistically and thematically varied, freed in many respects from Hollywood's glamour and escapism.

The chronology of events, analysis, and interpretations offered here concerning francophone African film production cannot claim to be totally exhaustive. For example, owing to the inconsistency of the colonial administration and sponsorship of African cinema,[58] this study does not deal with the contribution made by Chad in terms of the short films produced in the 1960s by Edouard Sailly, trained in Paris at the Actualités Françaises. Thematically similar films that pursue the same African objectives have also been excluded if they are not especially inventive cinematically. These African objectives are what this study has tried to establish, that is, to show the structural coordinates of African cinema in its attempt to define African history by examining African cinema's patterns and configurations, its thematic structures, contradictions, meanings, and specifications. By delineating the historical and cultural significance of this development, it is the intention of this writer to establish some guidelines for understanding this cinema, and also to suggest some appropriate directions for criticism as well.

From this difficult beginning, as we have already stated, films were often misunderstood and at times misinterpreted when judged by Hollywood or Western standards. Some see Sembene's style as influenced by Italian neorealism, Med Hondo's as influenced by Godard, while others view them simply as crude Hollywood or Western imitations. While the extent of these influences is debatable, the various experimentations involved emerged from the search for an enduring conceptual base on which a coherent African cinema could be established. By articulating national cultural patterns, a conglomeration of diverse themes and approaches culminate in patterns of treatment. These periods mark an exploration of the patterns of expression and ideological formulation firmly rooted in the spirit of pan-Africanism, calling for the rearticulation of Africa's history distorted by colonial ideologies.

One such protest of significant historical and ethical value was registered by Inoussa Ousseini in his first film, *La sangsue* (The leech; Niger, 1970). This little film (which deals with an African's interpretation of Western sexual relations) explains why Nigerois filmmakers, even though they learned filmmaking by working with French filmmakers, did not hide their contempt for films made about Africa by Europeans, such as the ethnographic films of Jean Rouch in particular. Ousseini made it clear that for him *The Leech*

> is a sociological essay on the sexuality of the French as seen by an African. . . . I was trying to shock people in order to draw a reaction. . . . Jean Rouch was to play a role: I wanted to show him naked in the same way as he shows naked Africans in *Jaguar,* for example. My idea was to create a psychological shock. But he didn't turn up for the shoot.[59]

Mandabi, as Sembene has stated, also does not present a beautiful, glowing picture of neocolonial Africa,[60] as with so many other films of this period. Out of the ideologically, sometimes diverse political and cultural national contexts a tradition is being established linking this overall determination to what one would call an African cinematic tradition that recognizes the need to embellish conventional narrative structures with African oral narrative modes. With this, black African cinema established a structure that links traditional culture with western technology (typified by the technologically dominant mode of production). This structure is exemplified in the innovative work of two men whose theories and film practices have greatly influenced the younger generation of black African filmmakers, Ousmane Sembene and Med Hondo.

Med Hondo and Ousmane Sembene: The Schism between Theory and Practice

Typifying the mood of the 1960s, when national consciousness and revolutionary awareness were sweeping through all the world, some artistic expressions, political manifestations, and the fully formed strategies of the structures and concrete practices of some committed individuals were directed toward anticolonial and anti-imperialist struggles. During this decade there emerged the black consiousness movement in America, armed guerrilla struggles in Latin America, student revolts, and the intensification of national liberation struggles that led to the freedom of most African states, with the exception of the Portuguese-held territories and white minority-ruled states of Rhodesia (Zimbabwe), apartheid South Africa, and South West Africa (Namibia).

From the first decade of African cinema, nowhere else did the philosophies expounded by these movements become more apparent than in the writings, speeches, and film practices of Senegal's Ousmane Sembene and Mauritania's Med Hondo. As this study has demonstrated, there were many films produced during these years that developed out of various traditions and an assortment of themes and styles. Characterized by social and domestic concerns, films simply reflected the tensions and contradictions of African experience which the filmmakers tackled with individual approaches. Some filmmakers were explicitly apolitical, but others found being so inadequate to address Africa's problematic emancipation and politically diverse contemporary events.

The coalition of all African filmmakers, Federation Panafricaine des Cinéastes (FEPACI), accorded full political observer status at the Organization of African Unity (OAU), has devoted its doctrinal efforts to the advocacy of pan-African aspirations. For example, during the FEPACI conference in Algiers in 1975, filmmakers, concerning themselves with the future of Africa and African cinema, debated the role of cinema in political, economic, and cultural developments. Arguing to make consciousness-raising a priority, they suggested a bold design that would eventually free the continent from imperialism's economic and ideological domination by politically reeducating the masses. The aim of these measures was to encourage an African film style, which in its process of decolonizing, would also "question the images of Africa" and challenge the received narrative structure of the dominant cinema. As a model for Africa's "new" informative cinema, the films of Ousmane Sembene, Med Hondo, and Mahama Johnson Traoré met the standards envisioned for African film by emphasizing instructional values while opposing the "sensational" and "commercial" aspects of dominant cinemas.[61]

Hondo's and Sembene's work is set apart from that of other filmmakers of this period. The ideological orientations of these two men gave direction to the creativity embodying the exposition, revivification, and solidification of Africa's national cultural systems, which should be attributed to the revolutionary pan-African awareness of this period. Although these filmmakers differ in both their approach to and style of filmmaking, their goals were the same—to facilitate the freedom of the oppressed with social justice and equality in every area of life.

Hondo and Sembene, as major artists of this period, introduced many of the thematic concerns and stylistic characteristics that permeate much of black African cinema. Their endeavors include the exploration of cultural imperatives and the infusion of African oral narrative patterns into Western, technologically inspired cinematic narrative forms, thus establishing an African cinematographic language with which to analyze traditional and modern cultures. This unique combination, both filmmakers maintain, stresses African cultural forms and ancient African representational patterns, but it also dilutes the potency of the dominant representational forms that have not and cannot be completely eliminated from their films. However, the major aesthetic significance of this undertaking should not be underrated. In the aftermath of continuing foreign cultural influences, especially Western, Africans are looking more and more at indigenous African traditions, and contemporary African film practice is shifting its focus to the potentials of African oral traditions as the quintessence of its creative autonomy.

This portion of our discussion examines the theoretical and artistic motivations, politics, and ideology manifested in the work of these great innovators in the first one-and-a-half decades of the evolution of black African cinema. As already indicated, it was the ideology and the philosophy of pan-Africanism that illuminated the structure of African political thought and the artistic development of certain individuals such as Hondo and Sembene. It is necessary at this juncture to pause briefly and examine the nature of the intellectual stimulation that structured this pan-African movement.

Since the pan-African movement was initiated, the patterns of African political thought[62] have extended far beyond national boundaries and assumed international ramifications. The pioneers are intellectuals of various nationalities representing several generations emerging at specific historical periods. They were motivated by the same course of action—principally to advance the need to seek out the structures and coordinates of African history. Among the intellectuals who developed the theoretical concepts that strengthened this position as we know it today are Frantz Fanon, Amilcar Cabral, Eduardo Mondlane, Kwame Nkrumah, Julius Nyerere, and Leopold Sédar Senghor. The various schools of thought they expounded were negritude, Marxism, African socialism, African nationalism, and pan-Africanism, the last being the most influential in the development of various African intellectual systems, politically and artistically.

This important political philosophy was born, paradoxically, outside Africa, a creation of African descendants living in America and the West Indies, committed intellectuals who, although living many thousands of miles from their African motherland, never lost faith in their identification with the culture slavery had forced them to abandon. As an intellectual process aimed at demystifying the ideological distortions of the colonial historiography of Africa and African cultures, the explication of the nature and structure of the history of the African continent and its people in the diaspora could assist in bringing to fruition the liberation of Africa.[63] The exponents of this philosophy included Edward Wilmot Blyden, W. E. B. Dubois, Marcus Garvey, and C. L. R. James, among others.

Between the late nineteenth century and approximately the middle of the twentieth, this movement was at the peak of its influence. However, its importance began to wane with the attainment of independence by many African countries; other political-intellectual systems developed and expanded the original pan-African agenda to deal with contemporary realities. But in terms of the revolutionary orientation given to the anti-imperialist and antineocolonial struggles in Africa, the political philosophies of Fanon, Cabral, Nkrumah, and Nyerere undoubtedly illuminated African national liberation struggles.

As a mobilizing effort destined to give direction to a growing cultural consciousness, liberation movements sometimes stagnated, owing to the fact that the culture and nationalism that it set out to revive had disintegrated in the face of colonialism. In black Africa, centuries of European occupation had, through force or ideological distortions, eclipsed African ethnic cultural and national histories. It is vital to point out that this debilitating condition also retarded the intellectual and artistic maturity that would have inspired its opposition. The colonial process infiltrated the psyches of some of Africa's intellectuals and artists, denying the continent, in its early stages of formation, the intellectual vigor necessary for orderly growth. The result was that this deficiency engendered complacency for what Chinua Achebe has befittingly termed "a tendency to pious materialistic wooliness and self-centered pedestrianism,"[64] with no deeply ingrained sense of nationalism. This was indeed disastrous since a well-planned agenda of social and economic reorganization or at least a well-conceived and consistent program of reform (which Africa was and still is in desperate need of) is critical in effecting productive change. Since it is within the dawn of the neocolonial era that the production of cinema started, and since the pioneers of black African cinema are among the neocolonial elite (people who came to prominence by virtue of their education in Eastern and Western European colleges and film schools), it is also vital that we briefly explore the position of the African intellectual in relation to African development. This will also clarify the status of black African filmmakers and their ideological, political, and aesthetic pursuits.

Fanon, in an intensely critical evaluation of Africa's rather complex social, political, and economic process, viewed the evolution of Africa's intellectuals as traversing three phases of development: assimilation; questioning or rediscovery; and revolutionary identification with national liberation struggles—national identification.[65]

In the assimilation phase, intellectuals maintain complete loyalty to colonial doctrines and care less about Africa's cultural heritage and its history. In fact, they make European culture their own, preferring to be thought of as European rather than African. (It is in this vein that Senegal's Blaise Diagne,[66] before the Second World War, and Niger's Hamani Diori, between 1946 and 1958, served as deputies in the French Parliament—becoming classic examples of assimilated intellectuals.) Many scholars have argued that in this period, there was no real intellectually significant work of monumental value.

The second phase marks the period of rediscovery when the intellectual, identifying with his roots, begins to question colonialist assumptions about African societies, or in broader terms, the black culture. Césaire (of the West Indies) and Senghor (of black Africa) are the leading exponents of this tradition. Their well-known but often controversial negritude philosophies[67] did inspire noteworthy intellectual thought and responses of lasting value. Césaire's work, situated within the framework of culture and politics, stimulated innovative practices, and in fact, his brand of negritude influenced Fanon, the dominant figure of African political thought, whose work and influence is more encompassing.

In the third phase of national liberation, the intellectual, attaining maturity, teams up with the masses to form a combative liberation force and develops "a fighting literature, a revolutionary literature, and national literature."[68] The political philosophies of Fanon, Cabral, and Nkrumah make this direction concrete, and it is here that the maturity and impact of African political thought is most formidable. It is also here that we can find the level of inspiration that these political thoughts have imparted to Hondo and Sembene. But before we do that, and to provide further ground for understanding these filmmakers, it is vital that we relate Fanon's phases to Antonio Gramsci's categorizations of intellectuals and Teshome H. Gabriel's connection of these phases with the general patterns of Third World filmmaking.

Writing on European cultures, Antonio Gramsci, the Italian political theorist, identified in his *Prison Notebooks* "two conceptual categories of intellectuals": the traditional and the organic.[69] Whereas the traditional intellectual identifies himself with the main organ of the ruling class (as in the assimilationist phase, for example), the organic intellectual sees himself as an integral element in the strings that hold together the aspirations and the nationalistic ideals of an emerging "new" society as well as those of oppressed social ethnic groups. This phenomenon, which Gramsci defined as a "universal process," is relevant to

the African context. Here, in the fight against colonialism and imperialism, most intellectuals could be grouped in the category of organic
intellectuals.[70] But in the postindependence era this tradition has split
into two important traditions that we shall call the bourgeois tradition
of narcissism and the service tradition. Here the importance of the new
frontiers of human development, intellectual-cum-spiritual maturity,
and how it is to function for the well-being of the society, is tested.
In any society, there are people who cultivate intellectual and moral
richness, making them more socially dependable and less prone to devi-
ance; and even if they do deviate from cultural norms, they are still
useful to society because they are inclined to work for the betterment
of that society. It is in these terms that the principal tendencies of
African cinema begin to manifest themselves.

Ferid Boughedir, in his examination of the thematic and formal concerns of African cinema, identified categories of African filmmakers.
One of these categories is "those who make films in order (before anything else) to be of service to their people."[71] There is no question that
this reason dominates Hondo's and Sembene's desire to make films.
They both defied the postindependence, neocolonial lure. They relentlessly spoke for the common people; they committed their art to the
people in a pan-Africanist spirit. It is this writer's contention that during
this period both filmmakers belonged to the service tradition as opposed
to the bourgeois tradition of narcissism and materialism.[72]

Film theorist Teshome H. Gabriel states that "the three stages Fanon
traces alternatively mark and compose the genealogy of Third World
film style,"[73] of which black African cinema must be located within the
same social space. Gabriel identifies the first phase with the tendency to
imitate Hollywood film style, "submitting both to the concepts and
propositions of commercial cinema"; the second with the championing
of the establishment of national cinemas, with filmmakers still retaining
aspects of conventional film languages; and the third with intentional
radicalization of modes of representation. Applied to black African
cinema, the second and third categories are most appropriate.

Hondo and Sembene believe that cinema contributes to the struggle
for national liberation through demystification of the distortions of colonial ideology. In other words, film must be explicitly ideological. How
then has this assumption propelled the search for the authentic, or as
Clyde Taylor puts it, "undominated African film language," which both
filmmakers have relentlessly pursued?

Even before Sembene started making films, he had already vividly
portrayed the relationship between Africa and Western cinema in his
novel *God's Bits of Wood* in the character of N'Deye, a teacher training
college student:

She lived in a kind of separate world; the reading she did, the films she saw, made her part of the universe in which her people had no place, and by the same token she no longer had a place in theirs. . . . When N'Deye came out of a theater where she had seen visions of mountain chalets deep in snow, of beaches where the great of the world lay in the sun, of cities where the nights flashed with many colored lights, and walked from this world back into her own, she would be seized with a kind of nausea, a mixture of hate and shame. . . . N'Deye herself knew far more about Europe than she did about Africa; she had won the prize in geography several times in the years when she was going to school. But she had never read a book by an African author—she was quite sure that they could teach her nothing.[74]

The ability of film to build and change people's consciousness was also greatly elaborated in Hondo's article "What Is Cinema for Us?" Referring to what he calls "Euro-American Cinema," Hondo wrote:

Film plays a major role in building people's consciousness. Cinema is the mechanism *par excellence* for penetrating the minds of our peoples, influencing their everyday social behavior, directing them, and diverting them from their historic national responsibilities. It imposes alien and insidious models and references and without apparent constraint encourages our people to adopt modes of behavior and communication based on the dominant ideology. This damages our own cultural development.[75]

In a tone reminiscent of other Third World theorists of ideology, both Sembene and Hondo called for the establishment of a national cultural and political force capable of inspiring the development of national liberation and therefore social transformation, echoing Fanon's ideological position that "an authentic national liberation exists only to the precise degree to which the individual has irreversibly begun his own liberation."[76] Fanon's theory of ideology puts great emphasis on the importance of restructuring African society in order to create an emancipatory force formidable enough to take Africa back to its true national culture. In Hondo's and Sembene's films, we see a conscious recapitulation of the multilayeredness of African cultural-historical formations. And reminiscent of Fanon's views, this position is situated and posited within the threatening currents that inform the complex interconnections between traditional African culture and imposing international forces. At the beginning of black African cinema, Fanon's philosophy of culture and ideology seems to have had the most commanding influence, more so than in later films where sociohistorical aesthetic meanings exhibit formulations similar in construction to Cabral's philosophy of history.[77]

Med Hondo and Ousmane Sembene both discovered their creative vocation in Europe (in Hondo's case France, in Sembene's both France and the U.S.S.R.). While Sembene returned to his native Senegal to pursue his career, Hondo is still exiled in France where he has become a formidable expatriate filmmaker. The film practices of both directors exemplify a meticulous examination of concrete problems within the society. Aware of the intimate relations between the cultural and the social, they convey the sense of the situation which they address. Above all, their work emphasizes the right to speak in one's own cultural idioms. As in the tradition of the African storyteller, their cinematographic language reveals their distinctive view of African reality mingling narrative, reflection, didacticism, and information in a haunting audiovisual flow of imagery. Hondo's experience in France of the confinement of Arab and black African immigrant workers in subhuman conditions has been the driving force behind his filmic approach. He, like Sembene, is an activist, and both filmmakers apply Marxist dialectical organization (and pan-African structures) to address various African issues.

For Hondo and Sembene, there is a bond that connects the artist to his audience. The audience, which both filmmakers aspire to educate and entertain, are the peasants. Like Fanon and other Third World national liberation theorists, the peasants are the force behind successful revolutions. In *The Wretched of the Earth,* for instance, Fanon calls for absolute political education, stating that "to educate the masses politically is to try, relentlessly and passionately, to teach the masses that everything depends on them; that if we stagnate it is their responsibility and that if we go forward, it is due to them too."[78] Correspondingly, in the films, writings, and speeches of Hondo and Sembene, similar emphasis is placed on the educational role of the cinema among the "proletariat" (Hondo), or as a "night school of my people" (Sembene), for the benefit of the peasantry. As Fanon's position concerning Africa and the Third World is similar to the views of other liberation theorists such as Cabral, Guevara, and Mao, to mention a few, so do Hondo's and Sembene's cinematic practices bear close affinity to those of other practitioners of Third World/Third Cinema. The connotations of the term "Third World" have already been briefly stated. For the purpose of this study, the term used in relation to film simply means those made by filmmakers who come from peripheralized countries (generally referred to as the Third World) as well as by filmmakers of Third World origin living in the so-called First World (developed countries) and whose films meet the Third Cinema criteria.[79]

The notion of Third Cinema began in Latin America in the 1960s, partially inspired by the Cuban Revolution in 1959 and by Brazil's Cinema Novo. Glauber Rocha's article "The Aesthetics of Hunger" (also known as "The Aesthetic of Violence")[80] became the driving force that accelerated its polemical significance. The term "Third Cinema" and its relevance to film history was actually launched and given prominence by Octavio Getino and Fernando Solanas, two veteran filmmakers and theorists from Argentina who made *La hora de los hornos* (The hour of the furnaces, 1968) and wrote a manifesto entitled "Toward a Third Cinema,"[81] followed by Cuba's Julio García Espinosa who published an avant-gardist manifesto in 1969 entitled "For an Imperfect Cinema."[82]

Getino and Solanas's manifesto addresses two major concerns, calling for the rejection of the cinematic model imposed by the Hollywood tradition and the need to create a new cinema that would fulfill ideological and revolutionary purposes. The new form of cinema they advocated was to be used for "the development of a worldwide liberation movement whose moving force is to be found in the Third World countries."[83] Its purpose was to assist the decolonization process by transforming the unchanged individual to the "new man" exemplified by revolutionary objectives and revolutionary culture.[84] In tones that correspond with Fanon's third phase, where militant literature is likened to a weapon, Solanas and Getino liken the film image to guerrilla tactics: the camera is "a rifle"; the film, "a detonator"; and the projector, "a gun that can shoot twenty-four frames per second"; while the filmmaker is the guerrilla fighter who "travels along paths that he himself opens up with machete blows."[85]

Getino and Solanas's manifesto attacks two existing forms of cinema, namely, "First Cinema" and "Second Cinema." While the former, Hollywood cinema, is seen as expressing imperialistic, capitalistic, bourgeois ideas, the latter is dubbed "author's cinema" and ranges from the French Nouvelle Vague to the Brazilian Cinema Novo. Although, in many respects the Second Cinema does not actually belong to the dominant cinema, since it attempts cultural decolonization, under the terms by which the Third Cinema was to function, it still "expresses the aspirations of the middle strata, the petit bourgeoisie."[86] Clarifying the demarcation line between Third Cinema and First and Second Cinema some years later, Solanas put it this way:

> For us, Third Cinema is the expression of a new culture and of social change. . . . Third Cinema gives an account of reality and history. It is linked with national culture. . . . It is the way Third World is conceptualized and not the genre nor the explicit political character of a film which makes it belong to Third Cinema.[87]

Also, Solanas reminds us that there are many categories of filmmakers in the Third World as well as good and bad authors in any of the categories.

Julio García Espinosa's argument in his manifesto emphasizes the relationship between "art" and "life." According to him, the purpose was not to create a minority of intellectual full-time artistic filmmakers but to question the division existing between filmmakers or critics and the masses. His main concern was how the cinema was to maintain an effective permanent function in cementing the relationship between culture and society. The technical or aesthetic perfection of the mainstream ("perfect") cinema which he said "is almost always reactionary" came under attack. For him, aesthetic quality or the valorization of technique was of less importance to his notion of imperfect cinema, which "finds its audience in those who struggle" and "its themes in their problems."[88] But their aspiration must be shown in a different way. Distinct from Western cinema, which celebrates in results and outcome, imperfect cinema concerns itself with the processes that cause the problem. And because much emphasis is placed on process rather than on technique or quality, imperfect cinema could be created "equally well with a Mitchell or with an 8mm camera, in a studio or in a guerrilla camp in the middle of the jungle."[89] Ideally, the filmic results are stylistically varied, and for the interpretation of Third World sociohistorical circumstances in cinematic language the approach has been anti-Hollywood.

Primarily, Third Cinema and the black African cinema exemplified by the political films of Hondo and Sembene attempt to divorce themselves from the cinematic traditions created by Hollywood. The extent to which this occurs in relation to the actual filmic practice is debatable. The audience's perceptions are transformed by making them aware of the underlying causes of their societal reality, and the relationship between their own lives and the "reality" encoded in film becomes a matter of paramount importance. This cinema is antitraditional in the sense that it goes against the universally accepted classical Hollywood narrative film style regnant since the twenties. But as film historians Robert C. Allen and Douglas Gomery note, "The stylistic transparency of the Hollywood style prevented films from raising the issue of their own status as cultural or aesthetic objects, for to do so would have been to undermine the primacy of the narrative."[90] Such exponents of the cinema of the Third World as Fernando Solanas, Octavio Getino, Miguel Littin, Ousmane Sembene, Med Hondo, and others have criticized Hollywood films for not encouraging their audiences "to think of them as films or to question their relationship to the events on the screen."[91] Third World film practice seeks to develop an aesthetic

deemed relevant or appropriate to its own cultural environment. Meaningful theorizing of ideological and artistic significance is the goal toward which African cinema should strive.

In theme, theory, or practice, what these theorists and filmmakers
are in effect saying is that the masses should mobilize or be mobilized
for action toward the total liberation of oppressed peoples and transformation of society, through political activity, violent revolt, or by any
other means. In fact, most of Fanon's theory of ideology emphasized
violence as the only language that the colonizer understands. The villages he depicts are riddled with suffering masses, implying that suffering causes violence, and violence, in turn, can cause more suffering.
But "for the native," according to Fanon, "violence represents the
absolute line of action."[92] This aspect of Fanon's position on revolution
and violence is the least understood, his critics charging that it is too
simplistic and deterministic.[93] Although Fanon's strong emphasis on
the liberating role of violence does provide room for aberrant interpretations, Paul Nursey-Bray has observed that Fanon also "anticipated a
number of contemporary positions in his recognition that a liberated
consciousness is not an automatic response to social change. Indeed,
[Fanon] also asserts that being directly engaged in the struggle to
achieve that change may, in itself, be insufficient."[94]

Similarly, Sembene's position echoes this observation. Agreeing that
all work marks "a point of reference in history," this filmmaker is
specific about the relationship between film and revolution. According
to him, "the role of the artist is to denounce what he sees wrong in
society," but, he argues, "to give solutions escapes the artist."[95] Like
Sembene, a number of black African filmmakers also acknowledge that
a single film cannot create a revolution. In his discussion of Third World
revolutionary films, Gabriel points out that it is in the film's role as a
denouncer that Sembene attaches its revolutionary potential, thus, for
Sembene, "a film can be revolutionary without creating an actual revolution."[96] Here one can easily sense some irony or discrepancy in Sembene's understanding of the distinction between art and revolution and
the interpretation of that distinction if one should contrast it with his
powerful screen images. Toward the end of *Mandabi,* for instance, the
postman (Bah) unleashes the powerful warning "Nous changerons tout
cela" (We shall change all this). Considering this statement within the
situation in which it is delivered (the protagonist having gone through
societal injustice and dehumanization), there is no doubt that a call for
change has just been made. That the audience did not react en masse by
trooping out into the streets to fight for their rights does not necessarily
indicate that passivity or the need for revolutionary change was not
implied.

Like most other African or Third World filmmakers or theorists, most of Sembene's films are open-ended in much the same way that Fanon's ideological construction leaves his views susceptible to various interpretations. Sembene once remarked, "I had no belief that after people saw it [Mandabi] they would go out and make revolution,"[97] yet the director remained committed to the "collective optimism" that he stressed all along in this film and particularly in the film's closing prophetic statement, "We shall change all this." The strength of collective endeavor in Mandabi is comparable to the individual experience Hondo turns into a collective one in Soleil O. Toward the end of the film, the hero is seen fleeing into the bush apparently shocked and disgusted (considering his own depravity) after seeing a French family waste food. He falls upon the roots of a tree, his mind swirling with haunting images of martyred revolutionaries—Patrice Lumumba, Che Guevara, Ben Barka, and Malcolm X—and with machine-gun fire resounding in his ears. Here image and sound coalesce into a revolutionary whole, and on the symbolic level, the hero can only find salvation in his own roots. All of this emphasizes the restructuring of consciousness as a necessary precondition for a genuinely "new" society. Thus, as in Fanon's writings, in the films of Hondo and Sembene it is the structure itself that dramatizes the ideological dimension of the whole project. How then does identification with one's heritage guide and shape the social practices of Hondo's and Sembene's aesthetic and artistic maturity?

It is the contention of this writer that black African cinema, like any other filmmaking practice or national cinema, does not have to reinvent the conventions of cinema in order to remove it from the dominant film practice. Rather, the filmmakers of a particular region, depending on cultural tastes and historical circumstances, might opt to create aesthetic strategies that build upon the already existing traditions of the dominant cinemas. Much black African and Latin American cinema has adopted this counterhegemonic strategy.

The artistic and aesthetic development of Hondo and Sembene is attributable to a number of cumulative influences ranging from all aspects of their culture and education (traditional, colonial, and neocolonial) to their Marxist or pan-Africanist ideological orientations. In their films, no one specific influence can be said to override the others. Among the aesthetic influences we find elements of Italian neorealism, Brechtian epic theater, avant-garde as well as Russian-Marxist aesthetics and cultural practices, all now refurbished to conform to the social tendencies of the African people and forming the basis on which political practice of cinema can be sustained. In reaching this goal, however, Hondo's and Sembene's styles are diametrically opposed to each other.

While Sembene's style is more relaxed, Hondo's is very personal and combative, yet they are both revolutionary in content and treatment. Both approaches have been linked with the kind of mass mobilization or "call for action" sentiments found in Fanon's work and subsequently in Third World theories and Third Cinema practices. Their films provoke thought and instigate action.

In regard to Hondo's film style, Pfaff notes a "syncopated eruptive tone that reminds one of the stylistically disruptive tone of some French speaking black literary writers such as Frantz Fanon, Léon Damas and Aimé Césaire."[98] Indeed, Hondo eschews the type of linear narrative structure that composes most African films. This is why European film critics have likened his style of filmmaking to the militant anticlassicism of Godard and European avant-garde theater. Since it was Sembene's films that opened up African cinema to the outside world, his film style substantiated the notion that African films "tend to engage in building a new style from the ground up."[99] While *Borom Sarret, Black Girl,* and *Mandabi* might be considered annoyingly slow paced, African and European viewers were stunned by the way Hondo's film style confronted and demystified dominant film practices. While Hondo's images gyrate in a camera movement that provides a powerful climactic shock, Sembene's depend on linear structuring and explication of minute details—letting things happen in a natural time continuum.

Sembene frequently argues that the "deliberate" slow pacing of his films works to the advantage of his target audience, that is, the illiterates who may not understand the meaning of the messages conveyed if a rapid succession of images bombards the screen.[100] But Hondo does not see fast camera movement or the rapid succession of images as inhibiting understanding. According to him, "It has often happened that those who understood it [*Soleil O*] best are illiterate," arguing that it has always been the proletariat who must explain his films to the intellectuals because the former can identify with it.[101] Both filmmakers invoke African oral storytelling technique as their primary influence. Directorial style and individual application of oral tradition to film narrative structures compose the major differences in these filmmakers' work. Hondo has stated that "there is no dichotomy between style and content . . . [since] it is the content which imposes a style."[102] He goes on to state that in his country, and throughout Africa, "when people talk about a specific thing, they may digress and come back to their initial topic. . . . We shall not tell a linear story as it happens in Hollywood but we should narrate it as an African and the African way."[103]

The basic differences in the approach of both filmmakers is particularly discernible within the context of African oral narrative patterns.

As already stated in chapter 1, in this context stories, even familiar ones, can be told in different ways. It is the idiosyncrasies of stylization that enhance the power of these artists' audio and visual imagery. This is an important phenomenon and a reason why Hondo's and Sembene's aesthetic differences must be viewed in terms of oral tradition rather than judged exclusively according to avant-garde, Godardian, Brechtian, Hollywood, or European aesthetic norms. As both filmmakers have demonstrated, the modifications they introduce on the level of structure via oral tradition tend to highlight the situations they portray and the kind of struggle their images evoke, as well as demand that their audience identify with the images and participate in the struggles ahead.

Sembene may not argue with Hondo that there is no dichotomy between style and content, but the question is, does their content actually impose a style? Hondo believes firmly that it does, and a look at *Soleil O* and the films following it ratifies this claim. Whereas Hondo's strategy is to montage unrelated sequences (reminiscent of Dziga Vertov of the former Soviet Union),[104] Sembene uses static camerawork and the effects of the long take (reminiscent of André Bazin's notion of psychological identification in the audience-image relationship)[105] to reach the same goal.

Sembene's *Borom Sarret, Black Girl,* and *Mandabi,* as well as Hondo's *Soleil O,* are all revelatory attempts from this period to express African and pan-African imagery. *Borom Sarret* deals with the contradictions of a taxi driver's life in newly independent Senegal, while *Black Girl* and *Mandabi* treat, respectively, the disparity between affluent French colonialists and their oppressed French maid and an allegorical exploration of corruption and exploitation, and *Soleil O* is preoccupied with French racism and mistreatment of African expatriates living in France. These films embody rich themes and cogent inquiry into aspects of African life as well as change film structure by exploring new forms of representation, new perspectives. William Van Wert's observation that Third World artists have proven that "Marxist theory could go beyond static dialectical oppositions, could coexist very well with surrealist metaphors, with African music, with Indian folklore"[106] best applies to Hondo's and Sembene's film practice. In their films, as well as in many other African films, elements of neorealist Marxist, avant-garde, and Brechtian strategies parallel the African oral narrative tradition, becoming incorporated into their films as part of an authentic black African film language. Similarly, the digression that takes place in African oral narrative structure works on two levels in Hondo's and Sembene's films. In conventional cinema, subplots and transitions replace this element of digression found in the African oral narrative pattern. Whereas in *Borom Sarret, Black Girl,* and *Mandabi,* Sembene prefers flashbacks (a derivative of oral tradition) to well-developed sub-plot, Hondo, in *Soleil O,* uses nonsequential episodic patterns as the primary component of this digression. This opposing strategy confirms the point that in most black African film initiative, and authenticity, and not acceptability, is the test. Interestingly, the kind of dichotomy just mentioned actually becomes an aspect of the representation of Africa and its realities by Africans from an African perspective.

As we have shown, methodological differences underlie how this reality should be portrayed. But neither Hondo nor Sembene vilifies the other for this, and in fact, in the next chapters we shall explore further the strategies informing contemporary African aesthetics. These elements frequently combine to form the integral force shaping the construction of the "real" picture of social and domestic life that was lacking in the escapist entertainment cinema of the COMACICO-SECMA years.

3

Developments in
Anglophone Film
Production

Working for the Decolonization
of the Picture

In most English-speaking African countries, people have demanded what was variously called the "national film industry," "indigenous film production," or "national cinema" out of concern for what they regard as the undesirable sociocultural and psychological impact of foreign films.[1] Before independence (and in some cases the situation has not changed), foreigners had total control over film distribution and exhibition. They imported films into English-speaking African countries from the United States, Britain, China, Hong Kong, and India. Needless to say, the films identified ideologically and aesthetically with the sociocultural values of the producer nation—in all ramifications they are different from those of the African continent.

Black Africans realize that U.S. films pervade the market. For example, Tarzan movies, regardless of their negative impact on African culture as a whole, were exhibited with impunity. The most devastating cultural damage these films did to Africa was to instill in the minds of most of the viewers the "dominating image" of the white man over the African. Then came the impact of the westerns. The characters were always tough, fast-shooting horsemen—the U.S. cowboys. Their main objective was to shoot and kill the American Indian by the thousands as the cowboys drove them from their land and slaughtered the buffalo. It is difficult to say if viewers' excitement paralleled the horrifying scenes, but the most disturbing aspect is that African youth acquired new attitudes from the movies. As one critic put it, "Every street had its Django and Palooka, while every 'tough guy' around saw himself as the undisputed double of John Wayne."[2] In Nigeria, Chinese films introduced martial arts, which then became popular among Nigerian youth.

It is important to note that while the Indian and Kung Fu movies play in urban theaters, U.S. films have had a double advantage—exhibiting in theaters as well as in mobile cinemas that penetrate every nook and cranny of the rural areas. The mobile cinema has been an integral arm of capitalistic multinational companies that use the cinema to reach villagers (who have no access to television or radio) to advertise their products. The operation begins with the mobile cinema van arriving in the village during the day, announcing through amplified loudspeakers the arrival of *Silima Ofe* (free cinema), scheduled for that evening. The venue is usually an open field—either a school compound or community ground. When potential customers pack the space, products are advertised (via oral announcements) followed by a film. Halfway through (or at times more than once depending on its length) the film is stopped to enable the merchants to sell their goods to the audience. For most villagers, *Silima Ofe* provides great entertainment and often their first opportunity to watch a moving image on screen.[3] But critics have found drawbacks to this rural foray, as there were no warnings of violence, sex, or obscene language on screen; also, *Silima Ofe* has no age restrictions.

African vulnerability to the ideology of mass media did not end with the negative images promoted in film. In what amounts to political [intelligence tests] on the part of the new African nations, another type of exploitation came in the form of comic magazines or "look-reads" as they are known in the publishing field. Before look-reads became known to Africans, they had been popular in Italy and other parts of Europe, and when they were introduced into South Africa in 1965, the financial prospects were very encouraging. South Africa in turn introduced them to the English-speaking African countries. Published by *Drum Publications*, they were printed in England under different guises—*Drum Publication of Nigeria* and *Drum Publication of East Africa*—the sub-Saharan African issues did not mention South Africa by name for the obvious political repercussion it might have on sales throughout the rest of Africa. These picture magazines remind one of comic books, the only difference being that the action is photographed, not drawn. The contents are action-packed, and, like western films, the hero is tough, smart, witty, and indomitable. Designed to extend the excitement offered by movies, they targeted African youth. In a country like Kenya, for example, the comic magazine registered more sales than any of the country's daily newspapers.[4]

Like John Wayne of the American western, Lance Spearman, the hero of African comic magazines (otherwise known as Spear magazines), is macho and tough. In an attempt to be authentic, though, Lance Spearman is, of course, black. *Drum* came up with other black heroes for their publications: Fearless Fang, a black "Tarzan," is hefty and powerful and wears leopard-skin shorts and a lion-tooth neckless; the Stranger is a black "Lone Ranger" who goes about everywhere on a white horse called Devil-Wind. While the adventures of Fearless Fang are derivative of Edgar Rice Burroughs's fictitious African stories, the Stranger is a bastardization of hybrid, popular culture. The main character is superhuman, he roams about in a cowboy town called "Vultures Roost," and he confronts black gunslingers named Jake, Ringo, Scarface, Trigger-Fingers, and the Dragon brothers. The African who tends the bar in the saloon is named Shorty. As if the lunacy exhibited in this character is not enough to pollute African culture, the substandard language of the look-reads, derived from old movies and pulp magazines, is atrocious. "Wonder who is this hombre?" and "Git behind me girlie, 'cause lead's gonna start flying,"[5] are a couple of the kinds of idioms, with no relevance to African culture, that the magazines use. I do not know of any literate youth in Nigeria, for example, who hated the comic magazines. They enjoyed scrambling for them and reading them, not knowing or caring how escapist they really were.

Spanning the colonial to neocolonial period, it is easy to discern that there is a growing propensity for African youth to hold in high esteem all things European or American over all things African. Indeed, if one gives credence to Fanon's theories on the psychology of the colonized, then Africa's fear of cultural pollution is comprehensible. African people have good grounds to examine the inconsistency of a foreign-African cultural mix and to evaluate it appropriately. For instance, from the shores of West Africa to the Horn, and down to the multilayered ethnicity of Kenya, the unabashed, exhibitionist imitation of Western cultural patterns has caused much concern and commentary. The impact of foreign movies, television programs, and music videos is seen as the conduit for this cultural alienation.

This unhindered embrace of all things Western has even encouraged young men and women to fantasize about the "new" look of Michael Jackson, the enigmatic icon of American pop music who is known to have "surgically altered his appearance" and to have "added an odd cleft to his chin and made his lips thinner . . . blurring his racial heritage."[6] During a three-month run in Kenya of an American music video *Breaking,* it was reported that "youths donned baggy trousers and sleeveless shirts and permed their hair to resemble the movie's hero, Shabadoo. And like their African-American idol, the teenagers shuffled through the city in a break-dance gait, speaking in a ridiculous New York accent."[7] Similarly, television broadcasters, politicians, and other Nigerians interviewed during the twenty-fifth anniversary of Nigerian broadcasting felt that foreign programs, which are allocated more than one-third of air time, "had even helped to erode the country's culture."[8] While others contend that this process amounts to foreign encroachment on the interpretation and dissemination of information concerning Africa's reality, some view it as a cheap and shoddy way of denying Africa's youth the pride of identifying with their roots and the ability to uncover their own values. In other words, prolonged exposure to foreign programs will only alienate African viewers from their own cultural legacy, leaving them better educated and better informed about other countries. This could result in youths becoming what one Nigerian observer has aptly termed "misfits who parrot British ways of life and imitate the American tongue."[9] It is not uncommon, for instance, to hear radio announcers and disc jockeys speak in butchered foreign accents. Dele Jegede, in an article entitled "Popular Culture and Popular Music: The Nigerian Experience," notes that in a 1984 disco competition held in Lagos, the youths who participated wore T-shirts with inscriptions such as "LA 1984, Thriller," but none expressing sentiments about Lagos or Nigeria.[10]

Criticism of the cultural regression implicit in the above observations seems to have gained impetus from the acknowledgment that traditional African societies are collapsing under the weight of rapid change. Such is the situation that has disturbed not only the traditionalists of the African culture but concerned citizens who want to see indigenous cultures preserved. The best way to do so, some envisioned, was to extend the decolonization process of the sixties to cinema and television.

The Battle of the Frames: Film, Television, and Bureaucracy

The story of cinema in Africa offers a lesson in the struggle against bureaucratic and economic forces which began in colonial times and reach into the present. In the anglophone region, the struggle for survival has a long history of expediency and entrepreneurial maneuverability which makes film production activities quite different in purpose—politically or economically—from those of the francophone region.

Even though there exists a tripartite structure for what could have been a flourishing film industry in these anglophone states (as in Nigeria and Ghana, for example), a chasm has grown between independent filmmakers and government and bureaucratically motivated television functionaries eroding cooperation at all levels and preventing the establishment of film industries. Despite the acknowledgment of cinema's positive role in Africa's developing countries, the dream of establishing film industries in each of these countries appears to have remained just that—a dream. But this dream has been kept alive by independent filmmakers, who, through funding efforts of their own, have managed to make feature films. Before chronicling the type of films made in this region, it is pertinent to examine the television industry, particularly the government's involvement and its continual support of didactic documentary films and television programs to the detriment of feature film production. In some countries an example of this would be a television station's abandonment of its film unit in favor of a video format. The purpose here is to show that if properly organized, television in black Africa could provide the base for the structuring of a viable film industry.

Different patterns of film production within francophone and anglophone regions derive from the contrasting ideological pursuits of the colonial French and British governments. For example, while the French pursued the so-called assimilationist policy, British involvement with its colonies was pragmatic business. Similarly, observers point out that while the French "gave" feature film to its colonies, the British "gave" theirs documentary. This notion supports the argument that the cultural policy adopted by France encouraged film production in the francophone region whereas in the anglophone region, where film production did not pass the economic priority test, the former colonies resolved to cling to the tradition of British documentary filmmaking. The anglophone documentary tradition emphasizes selected areas of national concern; for instance, tourism, educational documentaries, and propaganda films, especially those about the political engagement of heads of state and high-ranking government functionaries.

Clearly these kinds of documentaries could not provide the bold challenge needed to combat the impact of foreign films, nor could they satisfy the appetite of citizens who see meaningful results emerging only from a well-coordinated national industry. From this standpoint, television now finds itself unavoidably playing a dual role in the crusade for cultural justice. In a positive role, many television stations do produce culturally relevant programs. But with Africa's economic situation worsening, government funding of television programs and documentary films has been significantly cut, forcing stations to operate on lower budgets, which hampers funding for innovative projects. In its negative aspect, television stations established immediately after independence had not planned for adequate indigenous programming to fill their air time. Consequently, foreign programs filled the vacuum.

Considering that television programming in these countries often serves to promote the narrow interests of the regime in power—civilian or military—television too often becomes the voice and praise-singer of governments, mingled with frugal doses of entertainment and instructional programs. In some cases that transcend this situation, we find programs of real interest motivating national consciousness. In most African states, finding a willing audience has never been a problem for locally produced television programs, especially if they are authentic and devoid of apish Westernisms or indigenous banality.[11]

Ghana's television, considered one of the legacies of the late president Kwame Nkrumah, was inaugurated in 1965, eight years after independence. Transmitting in black and white until 1986, when a grant from the Japanese government enabled a successful transformation to color, Ghana Broadcasting Corporation–Television (GBC-TV), which had stopped issuing television licenses to the public, is reportedly considering their restoration in the face of improved services.[12] The impetus television had early on seems to have been revived under the government of Jerry Rawlings, who expressed concern about combating "cultural colonialism" through cooperation with television writers and producers bent on using television to foster education and entertainment. Regardless of initial drawbacks, GBC-TV is growing and some of its programs have been quite successful. For example, one of its oldest, "Osofo Dadzie," has been running since 1972 and continues to be GBC-TV's most-watched program. This hour-long Sunday evening drama focuses on aspects of life in Ghanaian society. According to *West Africa*'s critic Nanabanyin Dadson, as long as the social vices portrayed in this program "remain relevant," "Osofo Dadzie" will continue to inspire Monday morning discussions "at work places, markets, and schools."[13] Among the vices it describes are bribery, corruption, nepotism, profiteering, and greed. The secret of its success seems to lie in the subtle humor with which it exposes the social ills and contradictions of this evolving society. In addition, its authentic local setting is so real—as one admirer put it—that people just cannot stop laughing at themselves.

With the popularity of "Osofo Dadzie," GBC-TV has made some commercial incursions—dubbing the program and others onto video cassettes for distribution in Ghana and abroad. But this is "the fourth spin-off of the "Osofo Dadzie" success, following live stage performances, publication of a comic strip series, and the making of feature-length video films."[14] Administrators hope this enhanced profitability will relieve the government of its financial burden and commitment to GBC-TV.

In addition to the television network, Ghana has a national film production center, the Ghana Film Industry Corporation (GFIC), established in 1957 after Ghana's independence from Britain. This corporation is the offspring of the old Gold Coast Film Unit (deriving its name from Ghana's colonial one), formed in 1948 by the British as an extension of the Colonial Information Service. The major difference in the two groups' structures was that the Gold Coast Film Unit was not a viable self-sustaining production unit upon which a national film industry could be built during postcolonial restructuring. Ghana's quest to integrate film into its national culture led to its having an enviable modern amenity and a sophisticated production center. According to the production center's first director, Sam Aryetey, Ghana possessed "the best cinematographic infrastructure in tropical Africa."[15]

After independence, when Kwame Nkrumah took the reins of power as Ghana's first president, film distribution and production were nationalized, thus putting the spotlight on a national industry. In the years 1957 to 1966, modern film production facilities sprang up. Facilities readily available included film and sound studios, 35mm and 16mm black and white processing laboratories, and editing rooms. The GFIC's deterioration began with the overthrow of Nkrumah's government. One of the restructuring activities of the new regime was to confiscate the films made by the corporation which, the military charged, helped build the president's "personality cult." A new director, Sam Aryetey, a filmmaker, was appointed to direct the activities of the GFIC. Apart from producing some important newsreels, between 1968 and 1972 the corporation had to its credit a number of culturally significant feature films. They include Ghana's first feature film, *No Tears For Ananse* (1968) by Sam Aryetey, which was based on a traditional Ananse folktale; *I Told You So* (1970) by Egbert Adjesu, which featured Bob Cole, the famous Ghanaian comedian and actor; and *Do Your Own Thing* (1971) by Bernard Odidja, trained at the BBC in London, whose subject concerned the local music scene and a young Ghanaian girl aspiring to become a soul singer.

Such an encouraging development should have indicated a positive future for Ghana's film industry in terms of a large output of feature films. The GFIC had a unique status as the first venture of its kind in Africa with facilities to make films from conception to finish, or as Senegalese filmmaker Paulin Soumanou Vieyra put it, the GFIC "had equipment capable of completing a dozen feature films a year."[16] But as it turned out, the initial impetus of the GFIC seems to have fallen by the wayside. Its foremost problems were administrative, culminating in the pursuit of an incorrect policy that was not only going to slow down the progress of aspiring Ghanaian filmmakers but was also detrimental to the economic role envisaged for the corporation as a self-sustaining industry. Aryetey embarked upon a policy of coproduction with European countries at the expense of local filmmakers who needed financial assistance to function. The result of his involvement with the Italian director Giorgio Bontempi in the making of *Contact* (1976) and with Mike Fleetwood in the making of *The Visitor* (1983) was financially catastrophic. Because of these dismal box-office failures, the GFIC was less inclined to push for further government financial assistance. For over a decade the corporation was incapacitated, producing no feature films either on its own or in partnership with foreign producers.

However, the GFIC has not neglected its social responsibility in making documentary films, having produced a steady output of documentaries partly because it is easier to get government funding for films about political development programs, public enlightenment, and education. *Solidarity in Struggle* (1984) has brought recognition to and solidified the achievements of the corporation's documentary production. Shown at the 1985 Pan-African Film Festival in Ougadougou, it won the Golden Camera Award. But since the decade of the 1980s, in which Ghana experienced its slowest economic growth since independence, one would assume that the GFIC has settled comfortably and solely into documentary film production.

Kenyan television is virtually under the control of the government. Since 1985 that control has further tightened to promote political propaganda. According to Joseph Odindo, television critic for the *Nation* (newspaper of Nairobi), complaints from viewers range from the impact of non-African programs to the numerous hours devoted to "routine speeches by government officials and songs and slogans of the sole party [the Kenyan African National Union], and mediocre drama productions."[17] Like Ghana, however, some encouraging developments have lately been instigated as the government is now increasing indigenous programming and exchanging productions with other African countries. Odindo cites growing audience interest in entertainment programs and documentaries relating to African culture. According to him, "musical shows from Cameroon and Congo distributed through the Union of National Radio and Television organizations of Africa (URTNA)" are well received in Kenya. It is also widely believed that the informal educational programs imported from Côte d'Ivoire helped to increase "preventive health care and agricultural techniques." Another boost in audience expectation came from what Odindo describes as the smashing of "third-rate studio comedies [of Kenyan television] with a crisply produced romantic drama on teenage pregnancies."[18]

The fourteen-part series, "Usiniharakishe" (Don't rush me), was banned, however, after only two episodes following protests registered by parents who found the episodes' treatment of premarital sex too lascivious.

In 1987 a new and effective method was developed. The soap opera "Tushauriane" (Let's discuss it) was a bold move by the Kenyan government in its effort to disseminate information about birth control to this East African nation, which has about a 4 percent population growth rate—the world's highest. Produced by the Voice of Kenya, the series is reportedly based on what has been described as a "scientifically researched communication technique" similar to the one developed and broadcast in Mexico in 1977–78. "Tushauriane" was produced with great care, avoiding the type of problems that marred the acceptance of its predecessor.

To achieve the intended goal, the producers developed situations for the characters designed to parallel those of the audience's experience. This Kenyan experiment indicates how black African film and television aesthetics seek to establish their identity by exploring the social conditions of the entire populace. Nonetheless, a strict production code emphasizes a realistic choice of images. This strategy creates a "people's media"; in time, projects like this can help reverse the failed attempts by foreign film and television producers to deal with Africa's social issues.

In anglophone states, commitment to film and television production assumes various forms of implementation. As elsewhere, funding of productions through state-sponsored agencies is the most common procedure. The Voice of Kenya Film Production Unit has produced a number of documentary films for the Voice of Kenya and other government agencies. The Kenyan Institute of Mass Communication (KIMC), established with the help of the then Federal Republic of Germany, offers both training and facilities for production. The KIMC has facilities for 16mm production, sound transfer, editing, and dubbing, as well as a laboratory. Its activities have so far been limited to the production of tourist-attraction films, educational, and informational documentary films. Sao Gamba, who made several short films here (*Waters of Mombasa, Passport to Adventure, Immashoi of Massai*), tried his hand at fiction filmmaking—a bold attempt considering fiction films have never been a priority in Kenya. The result was *Kolormask* (1985), a film about the collision of African and European cultures. Its story concerns the personal dichotomies of a Kenyan student returning home with his European wife to find their marriage threatened by Kenyan-British cultural differences. Shown at the 1987 Pan-African Film Festival in Ouagadougou, *Kolormask* was "criticized for being too exotic in its emphasis on documenting African cultures."[19]

The Kenyan Film Corporation (KFC), established in 1968, is a government agency charged with the promotion and growth of the film industry and is also responsible for the distribution of films, but to date it has only been active in distribution. U.S. movies make up the bulk of the films it imports, followed by Indian romantic melodramas and Chinese Kung Fu films which are primarily exhibited in cities. The KFC also has exhibited a few African films, with more anticipated in the near future. In addition, Kenya has a well-organized mobile cinema industry that takes films "on wheels" to a rural audience. The Ministry of Information and Broadcasting, Federal Films Limited, and the Film Corporation of Kenya are three major organizations that operate mobile cinemas. The Ministry of Information and Broadcasting distributes "educational" and "nation-building" films, is government funded, and does not accept advertising. The other mobile cinema companies are basically advertising agencies offering services to multinational companies, with entertainment films used as a "crowd gatherer."

Nigerian television in its present form has become mired in a malady of political public relations. The country's first television station (which was the first in Africa) began transmitting in 1959 from Ibadan, the capital of Western Nigeria (now Oyo State). This was one year before Nigeria's independence. The oil boom of the 1970s heralded the creation of new states within Nigeria and the establishment of television stations that came to be known as the Nigerian Television Authority (NTA), now numbering well over thirty-seven. Within each state, by right entitled to one federally owned television station, the number increased during the second republic. At that time, state governments, hoping to disseminate information from the perspective of party ideology, established television stations named after their states. It was here that the states' uncompromising attitude reached an unprecedented height when they began to use their stations to confront federal television stations, which as a rule were loyal to the ruling party controlling the federal government. When the power in the state was of the same party as the federal government, the state television stations painted negative pictures of the opposition. Each of these stations sang the praises and bolstered the egos of political leaders. Although the return to military rule did bring restraint of a kind, Nigerian broadcasters have not refrained from making television the tom-tom that drums the praises of top federal government functionaries and luminaries in the state capitals.

In the early years of Nigerian television, the studios functioned along with the film divisions, whose films, notably documentaries, made a major impact on programming. By the mid-1970s, however, the significance of celluloid power had waned, and in the 1980s film was largely displaced by the video format. With all the television stations abandoning their filmmaking units, their equipment has been tragically left to rust away. Even while relying on video, owing to its low operational cost, the major problem still facing the NTA is maintenance of equipment. The Authority has more unusable equipment discarded as junk than it has equipment functioning in the field. As a phenomenon symptomatic of the general condition tolerated by all government establishments in Nigeria, it would require a separate study to explain the reasons why a lack of cooperation cripples productivity in this part of the world.

Vincent Maduka, the former director general of the NTA, acknowledged the Authority's problems as twofold: (1) human, neglecting to hire people with the "right aptitude and potential" for both the job and further training for the job; and (2) material, in that lack of money and technology form inhibiting factors.[20] The director did not blame the NTA's misfortune on the problem of funding alone, which every other government director has blamed for the agency's incompetency and poor performance. The NTA would have been able to, in his own words, "perform twice as well . . . with the same amount of money if . . . the staff [had been] better motivated . . . more excited and persistent about what they [could] do and what television [could] do."[21] His words echo the views of some disenchanted observers and, specifically, my own contention that mediocrity has become an institution the NTA may not be able to demolish.[22]

To combat such a situation, adequate hiring procedures should take the place of the somewhat random selection of cameramen, directors, or producers by executives (sometimes political appointees). Currently, administrators see the opportunity to practice tribalism, favoritism, and nepotism by giving creative jobs to their brothers, sisters, nephews and nieces, girlfriends, and others without qualifications for the job they are employed to do. Although the NTA is an autonomous institution, its budget is provided by the federal government and, as indicated, television's first and foremost role is to capture every aspect of the government's propaganda about its accomplishments and what it proposes to do; also, it must build up policymakers' egos. It makes some coordinated efforts to put on a few entertainment programs (though marred by shoestring budgets), sports, and some educational programs (which the government is more willing to finance) and to share other transmission time. Clearly, the news and current affairs units are better equipped. This is understandable since it is this branch that contributes to the personality cult of leaders. It offers formulaic praises of leaders'

"The New Village Headmaster"; *Nigeria*. Courtesy of Nigeria Television Authority.

lives accompanied by still photographs that remain endlessly fixed on the screen; such a combination of image and sound sums up the aura of the images transmitted daily.

From their initial stages, comedy and drama have been the staple of programming provided by the NTA's entertainment wing, and most of these are very popular with the audience. For example, the oldest and most highly rated television program to date is "The Village Headmaster" series, which has been running for more than two decades and, as its renaming to "The New Village Headmaster" indicates, seems to have come to stay permanently. The cast and crew have changed and so has its format, which moved from studio to location shooting. The NTA long ago devised a system of broadcasting which it calls "network programming," whereby some selected programs are transmitted to the entire nation from its headquarters in Lagos. Network programming also selects items like documentary films produced in other states on a quota basis and shows them nationally. Although Nigeria's "quota policy"[23] is considered retrogressive by critics, network programming still elicits cultural education and knowledge through varied entertainment choices and viewpoints, widening the path of knowledge about events in other states.

Besides "The Village Headmaster," produced in Lagos, Enugu produces "New Masquerade" and Kaduna, "Samanja." Many more entertainment programs do not make it to the national network for one reason or another. In its quest for expansion with acceptable quality programs (its limited resources notwithstanding) the NTA vigorously seeks sponsorship by multinational corporations, and response from this commercial sector has helped the NTA generate funds and become (partially) competitive. Out of this endeavor, the 1980s has witnessed joint or partial partnership with independent producers, and "Cock Crow at Dawn," "Moment of Truth," and "Mirror in the Sun" have all achieved international recognition and all have won the Union of National Radio and Television Broadcasting Organizations of Africa (URTNA) awards at various times. Corporate sponsorship is encouraging, but given the worsening economic outlook and the hardening austerity measures the government has imposed, corporate sponsorship of programs has dwindled. Hardest hit are young independent producers. As an example, the producers of "Mirror in the Sun," a popular television series based on family life, hoped that the program would be sponsored by the manufacturers and importers of child-care products in Nigeria, but foreign exchange restrictions then crippled manufacturing industries and import and retail businesses, leaving shelves for baby products empty.[24]

Television's role in national development no doubt should seek to communicate indigenous issues of social concern. But for television to become "the conscience of the nation," it must pursue a philosophy of decolonizing the mind. Raising consciousness has been an arduous task for African television establishments and for the NTA in particular. A recent NTA program, "Basi and Company," raises yet again questions regarding the appropriateness of using European languages for African film, television, and literature.

For "The Village Headmaster" and most other popular comedy shows on Nigerian television, (the language that delivers the laughs is pidgin English.) This does not mean that other programs produced in standard English do not captivate the audience. In fact, "Basi and Company" uses pidgin English to satirize Nigerians and the audience loves it. Reminiscent of Sembene's *Xala*, which articulates questions of language, culture, and power, television in Nigeria and Ghana, for instance, commonly uses as a structure the oppositions resulting from Africa's dual existence (Western cultural influences upon traditional culture). In its programs we find symbols of this two-sidedness in characters who represent the colonized imitators of European fashion, who speak the Queen's English, wear ties and suits, and love Western music, fast cars, and money; other characters represent a progressive

"The New Village Headmaster"; *Nigeria*. Courtesy of Nigeria Television Authority.

synthesis of Africa and Europe. They speak good English but prefer to communicate in pidgin English (now a written language that combines English words with African grammar and syntax) and are more attuned to traditional cultures. Here, societal conflicts, contingent upon the languages used to express them, bring to the audience a strong charge of political, social, and cultural tension.

"Basi and Company," produced by Saros International, an independent production company, airs every Wednesday and attracts an estimated ⸱udience of over thirty million people—drawing about the same crowd as "The Village Headmaster." And like Ghana's "Osofo Dadzie," its subject is real and the structure similar—hammering on Nigeria's social vices, especially the self-destructive, get-rich-quick mentality regarded as the cankerworm ravaging the socioeconomic fabric of this once-rich African nation. The episodes have plots that revolve around the star of the show, Basi, whose character is the topic of conversation everywhere in the country. He reveals the contemporary societal atmosphere. He is at once a dreamer and a con artist. The social atmosphere that "Basi and Company" lampoons stems from the country's mood in the 1970s. At that time, in the glory years of Nigeria's oil wealth, national income rose dramatically. (Economic and political power were so closely intertwined that Nigeria even flexed its muscles with Britain by nationalizing British Petroleum in Nigeria as a signal of what was to come if the British-sponsored Lancaster talk[25] did not tilt in favor of Zimbabwean independence.) A social and cultural dilemma emerged from this sudden influx of wealth. Unfortunate consequences occurred in the nation's psychology when unscrupulous individuals acquired millions of naira without working for it. As a social critic, "Basi's" evangelism is didactic. It stresses the need for citizens to eschew materialism and return to hard work as the best way for Nigeria to stand up again after its wealth has been looted by its own unscrupulous people.

While "Basi's" theme wins universal approval, and while the series constitutes an effective way to use film and television to focus on important issues, its method is still controversial. It uses standard English at a time when African filmmakers and literary essayists are urging Africans to make films and write novels in the African languages. In fact, Nigeria's then minister of information, Tony Momoh, praised the show for its good English. This statement ratifies the official government's thinking that substandard English (pidgin) used on television is partly to blame for low scores in the General Certificate of Education English-language examination for Nigerian students.[26] A similar view was expressed by the producer, Saro-Wiwa, who stated that the nation "should go for proper English so we can relate to the rest of the world."[27] Such an opportunistic statement defies the interest of the uneducated masses who form the majority of the population and who probably suffer most from the wrath of social decay that "Basi and Company" attacks. In the old Bendel State (now Edo and Delta states), for example, there is an ongoing interaction between the literate and illiterate communities, based on the fact that pidgin English is widely used and understood by the uneducated. Television here uses pidgin English programs (including six o'clock nightly world news) to provide an antidote for the lack of linguistic unity. Sadly, this nation's lawmakers did not have the foresight at independence years ago to institute, if necessary by mandate, a national language in order to create unity within the country. The fact is that language barriers institute tribalism and tribalism is the greatest saboteur of Nigerian unity.

"Basi and Company" has other qualities in its role as the promoter of national culture. Its authenticity is exemplified in the characters played by the two female stars, Ikpo-Douglas and Mildred Iweka. These women are for Nigerian women what Vanna White, the hostess of "Wheel of Fortune," represents for some American women—someone distinct, though for materialistic reasons. For example, "Basi's" women appear in the episodes looking gorgeous—always clad in traditional attire. Because Nigerian women love to keep up with fashion and because these two women represent tradition, the program is especially captivating. Women viewers often want to copy current head-tie fashions to make them stand out beautifully and ostentatiously, or to know how to match a head-tie with a wrapper (just as some American women who tune in to "Wheel of Fortune" want to see "what Vanna is wearing tonight"). "Basi" thus represents pride in what is African, thereby deconstructing the myth perpetuated by colonial ideology that African culture is not good enough. Now we can see that television used imaginatively in a proper way becomes a potent catalyst for changing practices and attitudes, and it can also articulate a challenge for accelerated development.

Despite this partial but inevitable opening to independent television production, the NTA (from the effect of financial and bureaucratic red tape) still cannot sustain its air time with indigenous productions. The NTA has no agreement with the Federal Film Unit to show its documentaries on a regular basis. Instead, it uses monotonous reruns and fills program schedules with foreign music videos, American and British films, and sitcoms. Up to now it has not been deemed necessary to integrate NTA facilities with those at the Federal Ministry of Information to initiate feature film production. The story of the Federal Film Unit is a depressing one; it has failed to utilize its facilities and expertise to build a viable film industry in Nigeria. As stated in its agenda, the Federal Film Unit is assigned the task of documentary production and exhibition and that was integrated with the Federal Ministry of Information shortly after independence. The Film Unit has large departments for film direction, script-writing, still and live-action camerawork, and facilities for animation, sound track work, film editing, laboratory processing, and equipment maintenance. Because its activity was supposed to sustain the requirement of federal agencies throughout the country, the Film Unit has a large staff estimated at more than five hundred people on its payroll. But as Françoise Balogun aptly states in her book *The Cinema in Nigeria,* this establishment, to be effective, requires "extensive reorganization and reorientation, since the informative and educative role it is supposed to play is considered impeded by the inertia of an obsolete and inefficient administration."[28]

Among the well-known documentary films recently made by the Federal Film Unit are *Transition* (1980), about the swearing into office of Alhaji Shehu Shagari, the first executive president of Nigeria, a ceremony also marking the change to civilian rule after twenty-three years of military rule; *Framework for Survival* (1981), focusing on agricultural development; followed by *22d Independence Celebration at Abuja* (1982) and a series of documentaries about that capital city. These films have not been well distributed as there are no properly developed channels for them. They are only seen at Nigerian embassies abroad and occasionally on school premises within Nigeria. One of the most important films made by the Federal Film Unit is the epic documentary *Shaihu Umar* (1976) by Adamu Halilu. Because of its religious theme and because it is the first feature film shot in the Hausa language, it is historically important. Adapted from a novel by the late prime minister, Alhaji Sir Abubakar Tafawa Balewa, the film examines the role of the Muslim religion in African society, a theme similar to those pursued in Senegal in such films as Mahama Johnson Traoré's *Njangaan* (1975) and Ousmane Sembene's *Xala* (1974) and *Ceddo* (1976). All three directors are of Muslim upbringing but differ ideologically on the subject's treatment.

Shaihu Umar tells the story of a Hausa boy in the last century who was enslaved and taken to the Arab world, where he was adopted by Abulkarim. Brought up as a Muslim, he rose within the ranks, becoming a chief Imam. His nostalgic feelings overshadow his success, prompting him to return to his homeland. In a series of adventures and challenged by many obstacles, he arrives at Nafata, a village in northern Nigeria, where he settles comfortably, spreading the word of the Koran. In terms of historical significance this film may be important in some circles, but its focus is too limited to serve as historical documentation. It breaks no new ground in terms of African enlightenment or the promotion of national consciousness aimed at decolonization. Rather, the filmmaker chooses to glorify Islam by emphasizing its goodwill mission in Africa in the same manner that the Europeans found justification to accord "civilizing" status to colonialism and Christianity. Like other documentary films made by the Federal Film Unit, it too was not well distributed.

The majority of documentary films made by the Federal Film Unit and television programs made by the NTA lack focus and are deliberately slanted to appease the ruling oligarchs. Jibrin Ibrahim, the indefatigable critic of Nigerian media, has forcefully explained why this major NTA flaw is at the expense of the Nigerian public. Even in programs that are popular with the audience and in documentaries on serious national themes, Ibrahim notes, the public is not adequately informed about their government and social reality. It will be beneficial to quote Jibrin Ibrahim at length on this point. Of "The Village Headmaster" series he has written that

> the Kabiyesi (the traditional ruler or Chief) is presented as an embodiment of justice and fatherly wisdom in spite of the fact that the so-called

["natural rulers" have been shown to be nothing but comprador agents of colonial and neocolonial masters in the forefront of land grabbing, tax extraction, and other forms of ruling class intimidation) The problems of Oja Village [where the drama is set] are always caused either by outsiders or by ignorance and simplicity of village folk. The system, as it were, is assumed to be good and the role of government that of modernizer.

[The Federal Government has produced] a number of documentaries on Abuja [the new federal capital]. What is stressed in these documentaries are the problems of Lagos and the necessity [to move the capital here, where land is plentiful for expansion]; the smooth, fast and efficient way in which physical development is proceeding in the new capital, etc. The reality that nothing much has been actually built is negated. The truth that Abuja is one of the world's biggest scandals in terms of corruption, public looting, etc., is never raised. The Nigerian people are deceived that their money is being wisely spent.[29]

Likewise, *Shaihu Umar,* as a defense of Islamic theology and practices, is simplistic in its methodology, refusing to allow any negative portrayal of Muslim imperialism and its encounter with Africa. Regarding the ideological bankruptcy of this work (in terms of the use of film to express Africa's sociocultural reality), Kyalo Mativo's observation is very pertinent:

Like Alhaji Adamu Halilu, Mahama Traoré, the director of *Njangaan,* is, by his own confession, "a believer and practitioner" of the Islamic religion. But that is the full extent of their similarity. Where one glorifies, the other condemns the way the religion has been socially used. When the one defends, the other attacks the heirarchal despotism of the religion; if the one solicits admiration for, the other denounces the brutality of its leaders, and so on and so forth.[30]

The NTA rarely receives favorable critical appraisals for its prosaic productions. Often the plots are ill-developed, the dialogue heavy-handed, and the performance level is equivalent to the actions of provoked market women or male traders who sell produce or retail merchandise in any Nigerian open air market. Furthermore, the much-talked-about mediocrity of the NTA is epitomized in the bumpy and unsteady camera work of some NTA productions. But since some of these comedies and dramas are made in the studio, and since even on location a tripod and braces can remedy such difficulties, one cannot help but conclude that NTA cameramen (no matter how many years of service) have not graduated to full-fledged professionalism.[31] This rank amateurism has not only diminished the aesthetic quality of television programs but is also rampant in mainstream Nigerian independent filmmaking practices outside of television and constitutes a serious impediment to public enlightenment and education.

Tanzania has an Audio Visual Institute that has been functioning since 1974, with facilities for filmmaking, a processing laboratory, and sound-mixing and sound-effects equipment. Like the Kenyan Institute of Mass Communication, the institute provides training for film technicians and has also produced educational and national-interest documentaries. A breakthrough in fiction film production came in 1985 when a Tanzanian-U.S. team coproduced *Arusi ya Mariamu* (The marriage of Mariamu), a thirty-six-minute film directed by Nanga Yoma Ngoge and Ron Mulvihill (U.S.). Here is a narrative that displays the triumph of traditional over modern medicine, all conveyed through professional cinematography. Not surprisingly this film won several awards, including the Journalists and Critics Award at the 1985 Pan-African Film Festival in Ouagadougou, Burkina Faso. Set in a contemporary Tanzania, the film depicts its heroine Mariamu's childhood fears of traditional doctors, carrying over into adulthood. Seriously ill, she refuses traditional healing methods, preferring to be treated in a hospital with modern medicine. However, after treatment by a traditional doctor, the cause of her sickness is detected and she overcomes her fear in the process of recovery; the synopsis distributed by the American Museum of Natural History explains that we "follow her physical, psychological, and spiritual transformation."

As the audience follows Mariamu toward recovery, through a series of vignettes of contemporary indoor and outdoor scenes, the film assumes the qualities of educational docudrama. Constructed in solid sequences of strong narrative episodes free of incongruities, it highlights the same kind of directness *in puris naturalibus* in emotional potency reminiscent of synecdochic rhetoric—the method that Sergei Eisenstein, the Soviet director and theorist, codified as montage. In other words, in *The Marriage of Mariamu* separate elements in the film's sequences are held together by montage or combined to make a meaning greater than the total sum of its parts. Thus, in scenes of alienation, inclusion, self-disgust, and despair-shifting-to-triumph, the film's message becomes unequivocal: victory for the indigenous healing processes over Western medicine. By giving recognition to indigenous medical practices as an alternative to Western medical practice, the film makes a strong political and ideological statement, reversing the tendentious portrayal of native doctors in dominant cinemas as devilish "witch doctors." In its most powerful scenes, as when the men and women gather to discuss and share opposing views on traditional and modern medicine, the tensions between "tradition" and "modernity," between necessity and choice, are ubiquitous and reflect real African conditions. So, too, when the modern African medical doctor talks about sending tests done in Africa overseas for analysis (in fact, he recommends that patients be transferred to the native or traditional doctor for a quick and effective cure), the African viewer understands. This sounds like political satire in a sense, but one not intended to make the African leader blink; rather, it serves as a revelation of a state of bewilderment afflicting Tanzania or any other African community, and African leaders do not like to wash their dirty linen in public. But it is a matter of raising the right issues, and as the Reverend Jesse Jackson has rightly pointed out, "We know that what is right will eventually become political, while what is political may never be right."[32]

In addition to the aspects of the film already praised, there are other cinematic assets worth mentioning. On the technical side, the film is a pleasure to watch, mostly because of the excellent integration of the ritual scenes into the structure without diminishing the impact of the story line. In this regard *The Marriage of Mariamu* succeeds where most African films fail. African films are replete with ritual scenes, but one must admit that most of them are poorly conceived. Not only do the gory scenes impede those films' impact, they are also distracting. A case in point would be protracted camera observation of sharpening a knife, the actual severing of the goat's or cock's head, and its death throes in a pool of blood.[33] What is the viewer supposed to be thinking about—the psychology or the anthropology of ritual sacrifices? When I first saw the scene, I thought I was viewing just another badly rendered ritual. But my second viewing of this film, about fifteen months later, convinced me that the ritual was more integrated into the structure than in most African films I have seen.

There is such a large breakthrough in the film industry in Zimbabwe that people are calling it the African Hollywood, although the country is mainly a location spot for foreign filmmakers. Filmmaking is an old tradition in Zimbabwe thanks in part to a good climate that is conducive toward year-round filming, the beauty of the country, and its proximity to Kenya, where filmmaking opportunities abound. Rory Kilalea, a Zimbabwean production manager who has extensive knowledge of film activities in eastern and southern Africa, notes that both countries "offer a variety of shooting locations so that filmmakers such as Sir Richard Attenborough are able to shoot beach scenes in Kenya and town and country scenes in Zimbabwe."[34]

Zimbabwe now has a Central Film Laboratory (CFL) that offers facilities for film production and training and also acts "as a financing vehicle" to foreign producers. In a recent survey of the Zimbabwean film industry, *Images* reported CFL's role in securing an eight million dollar loan from Barclays Bank with which it partly financed the making of Attenborough's *Cry Freedom* (1987)—18 percent of the thirty-nine-million-dollar production cost of the film.[35] In addition, two other banks in Zimbabwe, the Merchant Bank of Central Africa and Standard Chartered Merchant Bank Zimbabwe Limited, have set up film finance units that are proving to be immensely attractive to foreign filmmakers. Zimbabwe has no formal film training schools, but filmmakers in dire need of technical support can save a lot of money by training and utilizing the services of local citizens. It was in this light that Sarah Radclyffe, the producer of *A World Apart* (1987), based on the "childhood of Ruth First and Joe Slovo's daughter," trained some Zimbabwean personnel. Satisfied with the competence of the trainees, she even asked one of them, "Godwin Mauro, to do the final shot."[36]

At this initial stage the CFL seems to be functioning to the exclusion and detriment of local filmmakers, though it is seeking ways to expand their roles. The government plans to open a film institute for the training of filmmakers in all aspects of film production. In 1987, the Zimbabwean Film, Television, and Allied Workers' Association (ZIFTAWA) was inaugurated. Among its duties are "to provide crew employment and information to visiting local production companies; arrange pension, insurance, and medical coverage for paid-up members; and encourage the training of local people in the film business."[37]

The Zimbabwean government's promising look toward feature film production and its interest in developing a sound infrastructure for film financing, training skilled personnel, and establishing modern processing facilities no doubt raises excitement and encouragement within the African continent. Indeed, it would be very advantageous if Zimbabwean and African filmmakers were encouraged to use the facilities and were provided with the same kind of support and involvement that is given to Richard Attenborough and other Western filmmakers. For example, during the making of *Cry Freedom* and *Soweto, Images* reported that the Ministry of Home Affairs handled traffic and controlled the crowds in suburban locations, the Ministry of Defense provided army vehicles, the Ministry of Natural Resources and Tourism was in charge of supervising locations, and the Ministry of Justice, Legal, and Parliamentary Affairs gave Attenborough the courtroom used for staging the trial scene. Probably nowhere in anglophone or francophone Africa has such a royal reception been given to African filmmakers, who endlessly complain about the lack of cooperation from their governments or government departments. Eddie Ugbomah of Nigeria had to design the soldier's uniforms and guns used in his film *The Death of a Black President*, which was made in Nigeria and is home to the largest army in Africa, and Kwaw Ansah of Ghana has been so frustrated as an independent filmmaker that he threatened to quit film-making.

So far, Zimbabwean government production has been limited to tele-vision programs, tourist films, and educational documentaries. A co-production in 1988 resulted in a film called *Consequence*. Directed by John Riber (U.S.) of the Development Through Self-Reliance and inde-pendent Zimbabwean filmmaker Olley Maruma, this film, which deals with the problem of teenage pregnancy, is hardly a Zimbabwean film. It is totally financed by American agencies concerned with population control. As other African countries are targets for its distribution, it was wise for Mr. Riber to exploit and utilize the services of African consultants, African actors, and an African codirector. However, with such exposure one hopes to see Mr. Maruma's own future engagement emerge out of this exploitation, which will be viewed in terms of Zim-babwean and African indigenous production, and more importantly reach the level of self-sufficiency that would create alternatives to the ''white frame.''

Soweto and *Cry Freedom* touch African hearts if not by content, then by their titles. They both deal with sensitive African themes, but the focus is on white characters rather than black ones. One would expect to see some day the real Steven Biko film, hopefully by an African from an African perspective—one that does not simplify his-tory in order to please a certain audience. There are too many exploita-tive films and books about Biko, the Mandelas, and South Africa with no deep focus on the real evil—apartheid. It is in this direction that one hopes the Zimbabwean government's CFL will be advantageous to the African cause, if only it uses its facilities to advance the black pride and self-sufficiency that Biko advocated and died for, and for which Mandela was jailed for more than twenty-seven years and still struggles for to this day.

Our survey has shown that given the right incentive the anglophone cinema industry could prosper. While there is interest in a few countries in going beyond documentary filmmaking, some simply are deadlocked, and efforts by independent filmmakers to break through the financial and bureaucratic morass hindering the industry's takeoff remain stiffled. Ghana and Nigeria have managed to end this stalemate, and a few individuals have begun to create an independent cinema.

The Formation of Independent Cinema in Ghana and Nigeria

It is most plausible to discuss the formation of independent cinema in Ghana and Nigeria in terms of the divisions created by the sociopolitical tumult of the postindependence era. As is the case of most African countries, they have not been able to follow their political freedom decades after independence with economic and cultural autonomy despite the promises of early independent years. Given the threat of political and economic instability, the fear of cultural stagnation in the midst of political turmoil is a growing concern.

Ghana and Nigeria are like identical twins. In times of prosperity both countries have competed against each other or rallied together for a common cause in the pan-African spirit. In times of adversity both have expelled each other's nationals, but even in hard times they still celebrate an annual soccer competition. Both have experienced successive military coups and coups d'état, inept government, and unprecedented looting of government treasuries by officials, whether clothed in civilian garb or military uniforms. In recent years, their economies have been severely battered, forcing them to mortgage themselves to the World Bank and the International Monetary Fund (IMF). Their currencies depreciated and became almost worthless following the implementation of IMF recommendations to the benefit of Western manufacturers and exporters, business people who pay very little for their African raw materials.[38]

Ghana was rich in agricultural products and mineral resources, at one time the world's largest producer of cocoa and exporter of manganese. Nigeria, also once the largest producer and exporter of cocoa and palm oil and still an exporter of oil and member of OPEC, earned the title "African giant" because of its agricultural and mineral richness. Yet neither country has advanced economically—in fact, the masses languish in poverty. In both cases, if the preindependence years were about formulating the idea of freedom and economic emancipation, the early years following that independence no doubt brought prosperity. But in later years that prosperity evaporated and the ensuing years have proven the lessons of the obstacles to that prosperity. The forces behind the obstacles are manifold. This is how two journalists have described the postindependence dilemmas of Ghana and Nigeria. David Lamb, on Ghana, has written that

> black Africa's dreams were born in that West African country; they are also buried there, temporarily at least, in the folly and greed of soldier chiefs whose misrule spanned [decades]. The Ghanaians, a proud, extroverted, and educated people, shake their heads in wonderment today over what their country has become. Can this destitute, demoralized place, they ask, be the once thriving "Black Star of Africa," which in 1957 became the first black African nation to win its independence?[39]

And about Nigeria's senseless emphasis on materialism, Stanley Meisler has observed that

the most depressing aspect of life in Nigeria is the atmosphere created
by military rule. The soldiers are arrogant and bullying, for the army's
enormous growth has come at the cost of discipline and training. Gone
is the image of the honest soldier who seizes power to save the country
from the corruption of politicians. The black Mercedes of the politicians
have been replaced by the khaki Mercedes of the soldiers, and officers
have made fortunes in bribery, looting, and profiteering.[40]

After thirteen years in power, the ruling military in Nigeria did hand
over authority to the civilian democracy. This government lasted four
years until another military coup. But regarding the economic corruption of the civilian government headed by Alhaji Shehu Shagari, Ali
Mazrui notes the mass condemnation of this government as "pirates
and robbers," stating that "never was a country's economic promise
so quickly reduced to economic rampage."[41] Similarly, Ghana had a
civilian government from 1979 to 1981, headed by Hilla Limann. Like
Nigeria, it tolerated "political openness on one side and economic corruption, drift, and decay on the other."[42] Nigeria and Ghana have since
reverted to military "corrective" regimes and both are trying to hand
over power again to democratically elected civilian governments.

If this civil-military pendulum has failed to induce transformation of
the society, what is going to do it—an invitation to the colonialists to
return, as onetime governor of Imo State, Sam Mbakwe, once suggested? The 1980s was marred by economic decay and people fleeing
hardship while the 1990s has witnessed a mass exodus to foreign lands.
Even those who cannot leave, but who have relatives abroad, send
their pregnant wives overseas to deliver their children, hoping that
future solace can be found for their children with American, British,
and French passports. As a result, many Ghanaians and Nigerians now
have dual citizenship (at least on paper) and are prepared to switch to
whichever economic climate is beneficial.

Apart from the crumbling infrastructure, the system of production
in Africa is bound by acute constraints. One of these is certainly the
scarcity of foreign exchange. In order to explain how this has forced
government allocations in order of priority, we shall turn again to the
effects of the IMF and examine how its policies have continued to
stifle small-scale industries, import and export businesses, and general
consumption patterns. We have already stated that Ghana and Nigeria
are implementing IMF recommendations, even though the latter has
not accepted its loan. Using Nigeria as an example, in 1984 the official
exchange value of the naira was one dollar for one and one-half naira.
But under the IMF's "Structural Adjustment Program" (SAP) the Federal Bank of Nigeria has been forced to buy dollars (as well as pounds,

francs, and so forth) at international exchange rates and to sell them in Nigeria at from one dollar equaling four naira—when the program was first initiated—up to one dollar for twenty-five naira. Because nearly all commodities are imported, prices now have to increase to reflect the new dollar value plus a percentage allowance for profit—but all of this without raising salaries to meet the new dollar value. This is why the smallest car in Nigeria, the Volkswagen Beetle, which carried a price tag of six thousand naira in 1984, cost fifty-six thousand naira in 1990. The annual salary of a holder of a bachelor's degree at "level 08" is still under four thousand naira. Such a graduate would have to be an armed robber to qualify for a Volkswagen. Food prices have also risen, as have building materials, transportation, education, and any and all necessities of life. And filmmakers who had already experienced difficulties raising money to make films must now be prepared to pay ten to twenty-five times more than before to make one film, unless, of course, they find foreign partners.

Before we examine the work of the individual contributors to the development of independent cinema in Ghana and Nigeria, it is necessary to state that success in feature film production in these countries has always pretty much been a matter of the survival of the fittest—even before the 1980s and 1990s economic predicament. Film production activities are defined more by the funding source than observance of nationalistic tendencies. As will be shown, films here display a marked tendency toward social realism and sometimes political (albeit generally innocuous) questioning of contemporary events apparently meant to fulfill entertainment functions. But these films are aesthetically limited and hardly constitute a radical alternative to the dominant cinemas. Nor do they evidence any deep connection with the concepts of art in the definition of "national culture" formulated by Amilcar Cabral or Frantz Fanon. They do not even profess to be fulfilling the promises of an African cinema of decolonization or to encompass the criteria of the Third World–Third Cinema aesthetic formulations discussed in chapter 2.

President Kwame Nkrumah of Ghana was a founding father of pan-Africanism, as was President Nnamdi Azikiwe of Nigeria. In the case of the former, his vision of black and African consciousness helped shape independent movements throughout Africa and influenced civil rights movements as far away as the United States. Hence one might expect filmmaking in Ghana and Nigeria to be influenced by this pan-African vision in the same way that the philosophies of Cabral and Fanon continue to influence African and Third World filmmakers. Under the aegis of this guidance, the vital aspect of putting the cinema in the service of national development would be to contribute to the relaying of messages about the history, needs, and aspirations of the people, to touch the consciousness, and to inspire change or question the status quo. But the refusal to pursue these goals culminates in the imitation of Western models of representation, which for African critics (in particular those concerned with defining and promoting a "national" cinema) represents a Western capitalist inclination toward profit at the expense of "genuine" art. However, rather than examine independent filmmaking in Ghana and Nigeria solely in these terms, it is also valid to see film practices in terms of odds breaking and dream making.

Ghana: Contrasts in Ideology and Practice

The Ghana Film Corporation's initial impetus of the 1960s produced some feature films (although few, it was an impressive start), including *No Tears For Anase*, *I Told You So*, and *Genesis Chapter X* (1977). But this remarkable start was doomed by the corporation's futile incursion into coproductions that proved to be box-office disasters. Feature film production was only to pick up once again in the 1980s through the coordinated fund-raising efforts of independent producers. Out of this effort, six feature films have already been produced in this decade by Ghanaian directors: Kwaw Painstil Ansah's *Love Brewed in the African Pot* (1981) and *Heritage . . . Africa* (1988); Alto Yanney's *His Majesty's Sergeant* (1984); and King Ampaw's *Kukurantumi* (1984) and *Juju* (1986). John Akomfrah, a young, talented Ghanaian filmmaker based in London, deserves special recognition—in passing—for the remarkable creativity and daring political stance of his films *Handsworth Songs* (1986) and *Testament* (1988), which are best discussed along with the black British film movement. In Africa and abroad, *Love Brewed, Heritage . . . Africa,* and *Juju* are the best known Ghanaian films, and it is in these works that the contrasts in ideology and film practice in Ghanaian independent film production is most apparent. Both Ansah and Ampaw produce their films through their own production companies by raising money from different sources; similarly, they both adopted narrative patterns popular with the audience. But they differ ideologically in terms of fund-raising methods. For independence of thought and creative autonomy, Ansah does not accept foreign money or partnership, while Ampaw thrives financially by coproducing with foreign companies and utilizing foreign funds—a measure that he sees as not affecting his creative antonomy.

The independence of thought and maneuverability with which independent filmmakers need to approach their craft requires being free from bureaucratic or corporate intervention in aesthetic decisions. But in striving for such independence, as we shall show, filmmakers often shift their focus to strategies of appealing to popular audience tastes which guarantee the recouping of capital investment and profit for new investment. It is in this respect that Sembene's and Hondo's idealistic desire to galvanize the African masses differs radically from Ansah's and Ampaw's mere commercial propensities. While Sembene and Hondo favor didactic, political, or propagandistic films, Ansah and Ampaw take pains not to alienate their audience. This does not mean that Ansah's or Ampaw's films are entirely devoid of the didactic or political, or the well-meaning imagination favored by the Organization of African Filmmakers. Some critics, however, argue that these qualities are integrated into the film structure from a commercial perspective rather than as part of a conscious strategy to decolonize the mind or to foster individual or national transformation. (My analysis of *Heritage . . . Africa* in chapter 5 argues just the opposite, that the dynamic structure is charged with sociopolitical tension and cultural reflections.) The films of Ansah and Ampaw reveal a union between art and freedom of expression, box-office enticement, and audience satisfaction, a strategy that worked well in GBC-TV programs that were well received by the audience. This basic focus sustains their strategy. They have managed to hold onto it successfully through the fusion of comedy and melodrama in their articulation of contemporary conflicts—specifically, the clash of the new and the traditional in Africa.

The search for private funding to make films has never been an easy process for independent filmmakers anywhere in the world. One of the Ghanaian filmmakers who has endured the traumas of this arduous process is Ansah, whose recent successes have established him as one of the leading independent African filmmakers. Because of a lack of sufficient funding, he took ten years to complete *Love Brewed in the African Pot*. He kept submitting the script for many years, seeking loans from financial establishments. When he finally received a loan (two million ceddis, about fifty thousand dollars) from the Social Security Bank, he used his father-in-law's house as collateral. Like some other African filmmakers, Ansah avoids entering into coproductions with foreign producers and the humiliations associated with this union. As in the circumstances we have already mentioned regarding the francophone patterns of development, Ansah favors the retention of artistic dignity and sovereignty in such a personally expressive art form as the cinema; that is, he avoids the temptation to portray Africa according to the dictates of foreign financiers.

Filmed in English, *Love Brewed* revolves around a typical Ghanaian neocolonial elite family and provides an accurate portrayal of class prejudices and distinctions that have emerged in African societies fol-

Kwaw P. Ansah: Love Brewed in the African Pot; *Ghana, 1981.* Courtesy of Kwaw P. Ansah.

lowing their inundation with Western values. It is accurate in the sense that this story could just as well have taken place in any part of black Africa that has experienced imperial domination and independence from that domination. But this film is not a critique of that domination, nor of the discrepancies in the status of the postindependence elite who have taken over the remnants of colonial powers. Rather, Ansah has cleverly utilized a popular theme that is true to African life, and the experiences of the film's characters are similar to many individuals' experiences in contemporary Africa.

Basically, *Love Brewed* is the story of the love affair between Aba Appiah and Joe Quansah and the inevitable social pressures in operation under the circumstances transpiring in 1951. Aba is high-school educated and a trained dressmaker who falls in love with Joe Quansah, a semi-illiterate automobile mechanic and the son of a fisherman. Aba's father, Kofi Appiah, a retired civil servant, who at first looks like a tyrant owing to his domineering attitude, wants his daughter to marry into the upper middle class. He favors a lawyer, Mr. Bensah, son of another counselor. But Aba shuns materialism, choosing instead to marry Joe, whom she loves and whose lower-class status is not important to her. To the surprise of everyone, including Aba's mother, her disciplinarian father, though initially aghast at Aba's decision, ultimately acquiesces to his daughter's wishes. What follows Aba's unprecedented marriage to Joe is, in Vincent Canby's words, "one love match in which everything goes wrong."[43] This film employs a comic structure in which a number of themes are strung together with sagacious humor and satire in order to illustrate the dual and conflicting life-style of the Ghanaian elite class (though not rendered with the political pungency of Ousmane Sembene's *Xala* and *Ceddo* or Idrissa Ouedraogo's *Poko*).

Dealing with such issues as acculturation, alienation, elitism, the generation gap, inequality, traditional healing versus modern medicine, religion, lust, love, jealousy, and, above all, personal belief and conviction never before so well combined in any one black African film, Ansah unfolds the interlocking elements of an ongoing historical and cultural process. In *Love Brewed,* old and new values collide. This fine piece of work can be most admired for its directorial competence in dealing with these issues visually (surprisingly, this is Ansah's first feature).

Different elements combine to enhance the film's narrative structure. Ansah uses a succession of subplots to create situations in which traditional values are pitted against Western ones, but does not condemn or detail the polarities of this cultural duopoly. He in fact tries to balance the equilibrium; his treatment of each consequence, however, does suggest that Africa's culture is a culture in transition and that the opposing elements are just as raucous as the film demonstrates. The plot establishes Kofi Appiah as a hybrid character who wears Western suits with a colonial hat, and who prefers European schnapps to the locally brewed gin, *akpeteshie*. But the irony appears when Aba has a mental breakdown over her misbegotten love affair with Joe. Kofi's frame of mind parallels the local adage that states that "a beggar has no choice." Determined to see his daughter's recovery, he momentarily recites the "Hail Mary"—to no avail—but without an iota of doubt he resorts first to the traditional healing process before turning to Western medicine. In fact, he does not stand aloof watching the native medicine men perform their healing rituals. He actually participates in the interpretation of the incantations as well as in the killing of the sacrificial fowl, pretending though that he has not. The very shot suggesting this, which also makes him a hypocrite, is the severing of the fowl's neck from its body; we see him turn his eyes from this gory scene in apparent disgust. Here, Ansah plays to his audience's emotions. It reminds the Africans watching this film of the baptismal rites of growing up, when parents warn their children that all those teachers wearing chaplets on their necks, all those civil servants in suits, have got "juju" (charms) in their pockets. It is a spellbinding message that emphasizes that Western education or adopting Western behavioral patterns does not necessarily shield one from traditional handicaps or from becoming the one who inflicts such handicaps on others.

Western acculturation is a serious problem in African societies and has become a recurring theme in black African cinema. Its encroachment on traditional values is epitomized in *Love Brewed* by Kofi's perplexity over Aba's choice for *akua*, the traditional wedding ceremony, as against the Christian (Western) church wedding. In one scene, Ansah dramatizes Kofi's notion of an "ideal" wedding in what appears to be a lesson on the best cinematic uses of the flash-forward. During a well-done dream sequence, while the traditional wedding is going on, Kofi, who stayed away, is seen reminiscing about the type of wedding he had envisioned:

> Kwaw Ansah intercuts between Kofi's dream of the ideal wedding (Aba, Mr. Bensah, relatives and guests in snow-white flowing robes and immaculate tuxedos, church bells, and organ serenading Aba's march down the aisle on the arm of her father, a Christian priest and choir, a motorcade, a majestic cake with white icing, champagne . . .) with the actual wedding (Joe, Aba, and guests in modest traditional outfits, Ghanaian musical instruments, songs and dances, a traditional priest, *akpeteshie*).[44]

Love Brewed sustains its powerful grip with scenes of emotional appeal, nurtured by remarkable performances. George Wilson plays Kofi Appiah, the bullying, disappointed, and condescending father, and the experienced Nigerian actress, Jumoke Debayo, plays Araba Mansah, the good and subservient housewife. Together the roles of Aba and Joe, whose traits reveal class and generational inequality, represent a progressive synthesis of assimilated and traditional Africa (as opposed to Appiah's myopic view of progress and success). Above all, the story is as convincing as it is simple; Ansah being explicit about the multiple implications of colonially inspired acculturation as an omnipresent cultural process. Cementing Ansah's mark of achievement is his brilliant photography (good daylight and night-lighting contrasts) and the integration of varying elements of conventional and traditional dramaturgy in his narrative structure. In an exemplary fashion, Ansah juggles satire, comedy, and melodrama in what at first seems to be a Western-derived narrative style, and then finally shifts to embrace the African oral narrative pattern. By utilizing this unique combination, he demonstrates that as a trained filmmaker he understands the rudiments of conventional photography and the need to apply traditional patterns of narrative, and in this sense he recalls the other African filmmakers discussed in chapter 2—if not in ideology, at least in terms of theme, purpose, and zeal. This probably explains the cogent reason cited for the film's two international awards: the jury's special Peacock Award at the Eighth International Film Festival of India in New Delhi in 1981 for its "genuine and talented attempt to find a national and cultural identity," and the Oumarou Ganda Prize (named for the late talented filmmaker from Niger) at the seventh Pan-African Film Festival in Ouagadougou, Burkina Faso, in 1981 "for a most remarkable direction and production in line with African realities."[45] *Love Brewed* was highly successful and enjoyed wide distribution in Ghana, Kenya, Liberia, and Sierra Leone, where it ran uninterrupted in theaters for three months, breaking all box-office records.[46] It is also one of the English-speaking African films that has enjoyed wide distribution outside Africa, having been shown in Asia, Europe, and the United States.

Technically *Love Brewed* is not without some faults, among which are editing problems. This film should have been twenty to twenty-five minutes shorter, which brings us to the question of relevance in regard to the ritualistic sequence when Aba is taken to the traditional healers. One can understand why, on the symbolic level, Ansah decided to bring Kofi, portrayed throughout the film as denying his heritage, back to tradition. In the case of professionals who carry "juju" in their pockets, this powerful episode explains the solid tendency on the part of the Westernized elite to hold onto traditional beliefs. But the way in which this ritualistic sequence was executed distracts from the film's narrative structure. A mere diversion, this latter part is more effective in focusing the viewer's attention on the anthropology of African native medicine and rituals than in authenticating the process of returning to one's tradition, which is in part supportive of the lesson of the love story. Similarly, one might question the necessity of the second flashback, particularly when the non-African mask and the red paint (which did not exactly resemble blood) prove to be ineffective and unconvincing. This part should have been eliminated entirely. Apart from these obvious flaws, this director has, however, proven his potential and could become a formidable black African filmmaker.

On another level, *Love Brewed*'s significance in the development of Ghanaian and African cinema is worth mentioning. Ansah's use of a Nigerian actress has also proven that if such bilateral cooperation is mutually reciprocated in the areas of human and material resources, black African film production would be far from languishing. But the sort of cooperation that seems to be multiplying the number of Ghanaian feature films is not derived from inter-African initiative. As it has turned out, the Ghanaian film industry's success in the 1980s was increasingly dependent on coproduction between that country and Europe as exemplified in the work of King Ampaw, launched in 1984.

But before Ampaw came into the limelight, Ansah's cousin, Ato Yanney, made his debut in feature film production with *His Majesty's Sergeant* (1984), a story about race relations. Set in the jungles of Burma during World War II, the film focuses on three soldiers who get separated from their units and find refuge in a cave. One of the men, a white private, does not want to take orders from the ranking African sergeant. Like many other English-speaking African films, this film has not been widely distributed.

Since raising money to make films is a grueling exercise, particularly for black African filmmakers, they either stick to this arduous process no matter how long it takes (four to ten years in the experiences of Hondo, Sembene, Traoré, and a host of others) or seek partnership with foreign producers or financiers, ultimately facing the consequences of having to acquiesce in paternalism and the creative restrictions entailed in such deals. While Sembene, Hondo, and Cissé, and to some extent Balogun, are wary of the effects of coproduction, although all have benefited from foreign financial assistance, Ghana's Ampaw (who understands the merits of such a venture) sees no threat from it if the African director can ensure that the story does not falsify African reality. In some respects, however, this is ambiguous. When dealing with *Visages de femmes* in the next chapter, we shall show that falsifying reality does not necessarily affect the story level alone, but can also initiate a polemical discussion of how a film is structured. Misrepresentation could also be found in character performances in terms of their relationship to cultural codes of dramaturgy or to elements of the mise-en-scène.

The primary reason that some African filmmakers opt for coproduction extends far beyond the raising of capital. The recuperation of that capital and the generation of profit for reinvestment into another film project is essential (especially if the film generates enough money in dollars, pounds, or francs, since foreign exchange is too rare these days to be spared by African governments). In this respect cinema would be of service to economic development, but unfortunately it does not work this way in Africa. The regrettable fact is that African governments failed in the 1980s to revitalize and make concrete the hopes raised in the 1960s for a viable African economy. Since there is no singularly buoyant economy among the nations to serve as a role model, the pernicious retardation of progressive growth is aggravated by the lack of any political quest for effective cooperation among black African nations, particularly in the economic sphere. We have heard of the Economic Community of West African States (ECOWAS), East Afri-

can Community (EAC), and so on, but their actual influence is minis-
cule, since they have no sound agenda for economic transformation or
ability to implement the long-awaited economic miracle.

In the film industry there is also a question of the nonviability of
African cinema. Lack of government interest or ineffective government
participation has contributed immensely to the crippling of the industry,
reducing it to an individualistic endeavor. Black Africans in general
have not been able to organize national productions or regional coproductions with one another that effectively utilize existing facilities in
Ghana, Burkina Faso, or Zimbabwe. Coordinated national and inter-
African distribution cartels have also failed to emerge. If they existed
and were effective, it would provide a progressively expanded market
in terms of financial recuperation and investment. Generating adequate
finances to make a film is one insurance of its completion, but faced
with Africa's dry and austere economic climate, waiting for funds from
government sources is like waiting for the rains to moisten the taproots
of a drought-stricken scrub plant already starved by the hostile Saharan
climate. For films to be made, some filmmakers have to swallow their
pride and accept foreign financing.

Ampaw is one such filmmaker who, through coproduction, has produced two features in two years as opposed to Ansah's two in seventeen
years—operationally and economically a remarkable breakthrough by
African standards. Although his coproduction strategy appears to be
the right strategy for the times, it remains to be seen if it is a precedent
that can be emulated by other cash-stricken, aspiring black African
filmmakers.

A coproduction between Ampaw's production company, Afromov-
ies, and Reinery Film Produktion of West Germany, *Kukurantumi,* a
film that uses humor and pathos to tell a contemporary African story,
is this director's first feature-length film. Focusing on the usual themes
treated by most African films—that is, rural-urban migration, corruption, polygamy, prostitution, and the general clash between tradition
and Western values—the film is strung together as vignettes of Africa's
evolving modern societies which reflect typical contemporary urban
cultures.

The story begins in the small village of Kukurantumi where Addey,
a hardworking lorry driver, lives with his family. While he shuttles his
bus between the village and the city (Accra), his wife and daughters
do the farm work. He is plagued by a series of mishaps that plunge
him into debt. He must pay his creditors, so he decides that one of
his daughters, Abena, should get married. Contrary to what would be
regarded as the "usual," traditional pattern of loyalty and respect,
Abena turns down the offer to marry her father's choice, Mensah, a

prosperous businessman from Accra (old enough to be her father), whom she does not love. To avoid an open confrontation with her father, Abena leaves home, heading for the big city. The city Ampaw's film depicts is a typical African urban melting pot characterized by perennial overcrowding, unemployment, and assorted social hardships. When night arrives, it eclipses the daylight horrors; drinking, music, and dancing, along with prostitution, provide merriment. For villagers, passion for the city is immeasurable. The city, the locus of cultural hybridization, represents civilization, money, and the status to which everyone aspires. But without skills it is very hard to find a job. Even with a good education or skill a person still has to have the right connections, a go-between, to find a job. Men of position and power expect young girls to use their bodies as bargaining tools, sometimes for nonexistent jobs. In *Kukurantumi* Abena has no college education or skill. The only avenue to survival is to emulate her friend Mary, who initiates her into prostitution—the quickest and sometimes the only way for a young woman to enter into urban life. Ampaw's narrative strategy here unfolds the shifting status of Addey and his daughter's existence, revealing not only the social inequalities existing in contemporary Ghanaian society but the corruption, deceit, and the selfishness associated with the need to earn money for one's livelihood. It also vividly illustrates elements of the moral turpitude that continue to torpedo traditional values once considered indestructible.

The contrast between traditional Africa and modern Africa is forcefully illustrated in the scene in which Addey's lorry pulls to the side of the road. One by one, the passengers alight. One by one, they wait for their turn to dip into their pockets to pay the conductor—the face of the conductor and faces of the passengers simultaneously radiate with smiles and intense palpable joy and pride during this payment procedure. For anyone who grew up in the 1950s and 1960s and has witnessed how life in Africa has deteriorated in the 1970s and 1980s in the aftermath of various political and societal upheavals, we are reminded that in the "good old days" you didn't have to pay the travel fare at a specially designated zone called "motor garage" where passengers are subjected to the menacing threats of hooligans and vagabonds who use the garage for crime. This scene reminds one of Africa in harmony—tranquil Africa, Africa before the civil wars that proliferated illegal ownership of rifles, shotguns, and machine guns; Africa before the emergence of oppressive neocolonial dictatorships, when straightforward business was conducted more freely.

The film reflects indigenous concerns. Its plot was carefully worked out, though the director delves overly long into melodrama. Technically, some scenes are poorly lit and the print grainy, probably because

King Ampaw: Kukurantumi: The Road to Accra; *Ghana, 1983.* Courtesy of the British Film Institute.

of the use of the wrong raw stock or of low light that did not conform with the film's exposure specifications. Ampaw seems to have attached special importance to framing. Characteristically, his long-shot compositions make good use of mise-en-scène; some events in the background balance what might have become empty, dull spaces.

The problem of sound (sometimes improperly synchronized with the image) is less disturbing than the use of English, which poses a paramount dilemma for the film's narrative. *Kukurantumi* exhibits the same type of problem often seen in English-language television dramas or theater productions by university students; stiffness in oral delivery mars otherwise well-written plays. In this film, we see a serious theme of important sociohistorical significance acted out by inexperienced, nonprofessional actors who appear to be trying to remember their English lines. Absent is the natural flow of words, gestures, and movements—all of which are inextricable components of Africa's oral communication pattern.

The spoken word has a psychological as well as a cultural identification that affects the interpretation of meaning in any given circumstance. African languages are diverse, and most of them are naturally very guttural and gesticular; as body language and communication devices their application to situations may render the mood depicted or meaning intelligible or even perplexing. This means that the professional actor speaking in a foreign language may not be as convincing, on the level of the image signification and cultural dramaturgical patterns, as the amateur whose oratory and mannerism of expression are identified with the local flavor. This film, despite its genuine concern with African conflicts, still falls short of visually holding the audience. It would most likely strike the indigenous audience as contrived; its artificiality might be more convincing to a Western audience. However, this is Ampaw's first feature-length film, and it does clearly display competence and enormous potential.

Following this initial success, the GFIC, according to a *West Africa* review of December 1986, was encouraged to team up with the German company that coproduced *Kukurantumi* to make *Juju,* which Ampaw codirected with Ingrid Metner, a West German.[47] This film was shot in Accra, Koforidua, Oyoko, and Tema in Ghana with a West German and Ghanaian film crew and an all-Ghanaian cast. The story is about a village chief who sends his nephew to college only to discover on his return that his ward has been inspired with a new idea, a plan for a community development project that would provide a bore hole and good drinking water for the village as opposed to his own plan to build a new palace. In this unadulterated political satire against Africa's numerous misplaced priorities, the filmmaker seems to be reminding his viewers that no culture is static and that some old values must be discarded to accommodate urgent needs. The theme depicted here is quite new to the anglophone cinema, but it echoes the concerns expressed in francophonic films such as *Mol* (1957–1966) by Senegal's Paulin Soumanou Vieyra and *Le retour de Tiéman* (1962) by Mali's Djibril Kouyaté, which stress the need for technological development alongside cultural development.

Ansah's new film *Heritage . . . Africa* was completed in 1988. The script was ready in 1982 but the loan from three Ghanaian banks (Social Security, Ghana Commercial, and National Investment) did not mature until March 1987, when he was then able to commence shooting. Made on a budget of over two hundred million cedis (about half a million dollars) this film's historical theme, dealing with, among other issues, colonialism, alienation, acculturation, and misguided priorities, establishes another cinematic landmark in the history of Ghanaian cinema. Shot in English with some sequences in Fanti dialect with English subtitles, *Heritage* is one of the most powerful and innovative African films to have come out of anglophone Africa.

While Ansah has made yet another fascinating contribution to the development of Ghanaian cinema, his experience with filmmaking in Ghana has been one of frustration and bitterness. He once declared that *Heritage* could be his last feature film. Although he is not abandoning filmmaking entirely, he plans "to move into broadcast quality U-matic video format because of the relatively low costs involved."[48] With approximately one film in ten years, he does not feel it is worth "the mental and physical toll" that caused him to collapse twice and be hospitalized as a result of trauma suffered at the hands of uncooperative Ghanaian bank officials and government functionaries. He considers the situation simply a "bad climate for creativity." But as *Heritage* continues to win more awards (the first was the 1989 FESPACO grand prize, the Étalon de Yennega; another was a 1991 FESPACO Institute of Black People's Award worth five million CFA francs), the director admits he is under increasing pressure to make more films.[49] A man of principle who has devoted his art to combating the misrepresentation of Africa, Ansah could have utilized foreign funding to make this film in record time. Based on personal convictions, he turned down a coproduction offer. This offer, like economic aid given to Africa (usually with strings attached), came with the stipulation that he tone down his script for a more "balanced" and sympathetic treatment of the colonizers.[50]

Nigeria: Paradox of Mediocrity?

Writing on "The Image of Nigeria's Culture," Lindsay Barrett notes that at the time of Nigeria's independence in 1960, two aspects of the nation's cultural profile were discernible—"innovation" and "conservatism."[51] According to Barrett, writers, painters, and sculptors represented a "visionary" tendency that sought to reenvision the nature of Nigerian society, while the bureaucratic sphere (or "traditionalist" class) fell prey to self-serving opportunism. This created an inevitable ideological clash; the first group depended on the second to stand firmly in the pursuit of nationalistic tendencies, but because the second was ideologically bankrupt, the aspirations of the first were impeded. This is the strong focus of Lindsay's argument—his observation that policymakers in successive Nigerian governments have failed to recognize the nation's creative artistic endeavor and "expressions of artistic independence" by young Nigerian artists as positive contributions in line with national cultural development. Instead, postcolonial governments have viewed these works as not ideologically supportive of the tradi-

Kwaw P. Ansah: Heritage . . . Africa; *Ghana, 1988.* Courtesy of Kwaw P. Ansah.

tionalist vision of art and culture. Such thinking has only eroded the establishment of the cultural policy needed to expand and strengthen creative potential and make concrete the nation's cultural identity.

That this aspiration is still illusory explains the nonchalant attitude toward art and culture on the part of Nigeria's successive policymakers. As the nation moved deeper into a postcolonial era, arrogation of power, self-centeredness, and corruption took precedence over everything else, including art and culture. This inspired the political confusion that was to follow: successive military regimes, and one short-lived, democratically elected, civilian "gang-of-looters" that was Shehu Shagari's government. The sociopolitical commotion nurtured here demolished in toto the engendering of innovative consciousness through art and culture and the nurturing of original creative power. As Barrett puts it, "Nigeria's creative profile became disinterestingly unadventurous," since national cultural policies continued to enshrine

the conservation of traditional ritual forms in a decorative cocoon of syncophancy and to present the result as nationalist art. As a result, Nigerian art festivals rarely reveal new values or new forms of creative

expression as a matter of routine, because bureaucratic introspection
militates against creative experimentation.[52]

Although one may not subscribe wholly to this view in regards to
other arts, perhaps symbolizing the epitome of Nigeria's legislative
hindsight and military rashness is the establishment of the Nigerian
Film Corporation (NFC). Established by Military Decree Number 61
in 1979, it was not until May 1982 that it was inaugurated by civilian
legislative consent. The NFC, consisting of a Board of Directors, a
Chairman, and a General Manager (the Chief Executive), had grandiose
plans for a gigantic film complex. It is the corporation's job to function
in the area of film production for domestic use and for export, to encourage local film production and help develop those already in existence
through a financial assistance program, to acquire and distribute films,
to provide equipment for film production, to establish national film
archives, and to train technicians and professionals to man the film
industry. So far almost none of this has been accomplished, and although the corporation can now boast of a color laboratory which it
claims is the first of its kind in black Africa, it has nothing to show in
practical terms for its activities. It has made no films of significant
value for public consumption to justify the huge sum of money it has
squandered. Why, one might ask, does the government even bother to
maintain high-ranking NFC executives whom it continues to send on
reckless and expensive overseas trips that result in no actual film production? But having witnessed Nigeria's organization and sponsorship
of the World Trade Fair to promote the technological prowess of the
industrialized nations when it had only carved calabashes to show,
one cannot be too surprised about the NFC and this nation's inept
bureaucracy.

Similarly, Nigeria staged the first World Black and African Festival
of Arts and Culture (FESTAC) only to dominate its entries with mediocre shows while rejecting artistically creative ones in favor of pandering
to specific interest groups. Retrospectively, Nigeria's public utilities
have a history of mind-boggling waste and incompetence, overstaffing,
and corruption (or what Chinua Achebe has aptly termed the "mediocrity cult"). Achebe's observation culminates in the indisputable fact of
Nigeria's moral and ethical laxity, noting that this "is a country where
it would be difficult to point to one important job held by the most
competent person."[53] This also illustrates why, in spite of this nation's
enormous wealth, abject poverty and economic disintegration are so
severe that the World Bank reclassified Nigeria from a "middle income" country to a "low income country."[54] In view of the fact that
thirty-two years have passed since independence, and the country still

cannot boast of a regular pipe-borne water supply, a reliable power grid, or a working telephone system, one would be skeptical if the NFC functioned productively even if the government had chosen to pour enough money into it as originally envisaged in the glory years.

The inconsistencies outlined above illustrate briefly Nigeria's cultural policy since independence. Because there has been no real incentive to foster the growth of a national creative media, private individuals have taken upon themselves the challenge to create and develop indigenous productions in the cinema and theater (which in most cases have been integrated), in spite of colossal financial and material limitations. It is here that two traditions of filmmaking emerge in Nigeria: folkloric and mythological films in the tradition of the Yoruba traveling theater, rendered in a filmic style that has no parallel to any of the dominant cinemas; and films whose themes are developed and executed in a style that is typical of mainstream Hollywood.

What one would call the beginning of indigenous film production in Nigeria began in 1970 with the making of the controversial *Son of Africa*. Produced by Fedfilm Limited, a Lebanese-Nigerian production company, and released as the first Nigerian full-length feature film, *Son of Africa* stirred up enormous disputes as some people thought that the Nigerian contribution was too minimal to accord the film serious status. Although a joint venture, the bulk of financial backing is said to have come from the Lebanese. Also, the leading performers were Lebanese, with the exception of one Nigerian, Funsho Adeolu. The technicians who worked on the film were also mainly Lebanese, and critics even wondered if *Son of Africa* would not be more appropriately renamed "Daughters of Lebanon," since the film is replete with Lebanese belly dancers.[55] Another criticism was the treatment of the theme—the fight against currency counterfeiters—as lacking a Nigerian perspective.[56] Therefore, the person credited with pioneering indigenous film production in Nigeria is Francis Oladele, whose company, Calpenny Nigeria Films Limited, together with Herald production, an American company, and Omega Film, a Swedish company, coproduced *Kongi's Harvest* (1970). Like *Son of Africa,* it also claimed to be the first full-length Nigerian feature film,[57] an adaption of a play by Wole Soyinka, the Nigerian playwright and 1985 Nobel Laureate.

Directed by Ossie Davis, a prominent African-American actor and playwright turned director, *Kongi's Harvest* was shot entirely on location in Ibadan, Oyo, and Abeokuta. It focuses on contemporary Nigerian social reality, satirizing the power politics reminiscent of the first republic. According to the director, this film "concerns itself with the struggle for power between a dictator who represents the distortion of all that is new, and an old decrepit king, who represents the corruption of all that is old. Caught in between are average people, old people, students and farmers, who try to find their way out between two violent struggles."[58] The thematic audacity of *Kongi's Harvest* does not surprise anyone since it was taken from the work of a versatile social critic, but in technical features and stylistics this film exhibits poor craftsmanship and a serious problem of adaptation. Since the film deviates enormously from the screenplay, the author of the script, Wole Soyinka (who also starred in it), disclaimed it when it was released.[59]

The imperfections in *Kongi's Harvest* sound a high note of warning to aspiring Nigerian filmmakers. As we shall see in the course of this study, this problem is not only visible in literary adaptations but also in theatrical adaptations on which the majority of Nigerian films are based. From a technical point of view, Oladele's and Davis's efforts illustrate how exacting it is to galvanize the manpower required in such a highly technical trade as filmmaking in a country where a deficiency of trained technicians in such areas as sound recording, camera operation, and lighting is acute. Complicating the film's success further was the problem of exhibition. The major theaters failed or refused to handle the film, and although it had only limited showings in improvised theaters, this was not enough to give it the required publicity to boost the size of Nigerian and African audiences.

In Oladele's next film, *Bullfrog in the Sun* (1971), one notices an attempt to come to terms with problems of adaptation. Like *Kongi's Harvest,* this film is an adaptation of two novels, *Things Fall Apart* and *No Longer At Ease,* both by Nigeria's well-known novelist, Chinua Achebe. The title of the film has since been changed to reflect the original title of one of the novels, *Things Fall Apart* (which we shall use). Shot in Nigeria, this film is a joint Calpenny (Nigeria), Cine 3 (West Germany), and Niagram (U.S.) production. It was directed by West Germany's Hans-Juergen Pohland, coproduced by Francis Oladele, and its international cast included Johnny Sekka and Elizabeth Toro. Like Soyinka with *Kongi's Harvest,* Achebe was not pleased with the film version of his two novels, but given the fact that the makers chose to shuttle between one novel and the other, it is easy to see why it would be impossible to be completely faithful to either one of the original works.

Things Fall Apart tells "the story of Obi Okonkwo, an idealistic, adventurous [Igbo man], desperately trying to prevent the holocaust towards which his country is drifting and at the same time fighting to overcome traditional African values in order to marry his pregnant girlfriend who comes from an 'untouchable' group within his society. Obi seizes a radio station in an effort to expose the corruption of the politicians in his community and is charged with treason. A military coup frees him in time to flee to the east and participate in the civil war. His survival and reunion with his woman and child are told against a brilliantly iridescent picture of the Nigeria of Obi's grandfather, whose resistance to British colonialism ended in personal tragedy.''[60] Following a sociohistorical path, indicative of Nigeria's emancipation, this film constitutes a tapestry of caustic vignettes of contemporary life amongst pervasive scenes of squalor and corruption.

Things Fall Apart is more cinematically inventive and has fewer technical flaws than *Kongi's Harvest*. The intercutting between scenes of the two novels is imaginative and well done. It displays no disturbing editing problems, although the occasional juxtaposition of scenes is sometimes confusing. In spite of stunning performances by Johnny Sekka (as Obi) and Elizabeth Toro (as Clara), these qualities do not give the film a sufficient boost for commercial success. *Things Fall Apart* managed to play commercially in Africa but received a mixed reception. The attempt to raise funds to launch a full-scale commercial release in the United States failed; the opportunity for American viewers came only when some eastern public broadcasting stations aired it on television. Since 1971 Oladele has not produced a commercially distributed film.

Around the same time, Ola Balogun, a young and enterprising scholar, arrived on the Nigerian moviemaking scene. He was initiated into the rudiments of cinematography at the Institut des Hautes Etudes Cinématographiques (IDHEC) in Paris. Some years later, after graduation, he wrote a doctoral dissertation on documentary films. He has held various posts in the Nigerian Civil Service: Press Attaché at the Nigerian Embassy in Paris; editor for the Federal Film Unit, Lagos; Research Fellow at the University of Ife, Ile-Ife; and audiovisual specialist at the National Museum in Lagos. He is the director of such short documentary films as *One Nigeria* (1969), *Les ponts de Paris* (The bridges of Paris, 1971), *Fire in the Afternoon* (1971), *Thundergod* (1971), *Nupe Masquerade* (1972), *In the Beginning* (1972), and *Owuama, a New Yam Festival* (1973). With his tenure at the University of Ife and at the National Museum, he was able to muster the material and financial resources required for the making of his first film, *Alpha* (1972). A pseudoautobiographical work lacking definite focus, this film, produced on a small budget, is low-key and very experimental.

By 1973 Balogun was already saturated with a working atmosphere inhibitive of creativity at the University of Ife and the National Museum. Eager to establish what he called ''a forum for the promotion of our culture,''[61] he formed his own production company, Afrocult Foundation Limited, in 1973, and since then he has used it as the platform for subsequent film productions. But before any feature-length film rolled out of this company, two medium-length films—*Vivre* (To live, 1974), a film about a paralyzed friend, and *Nigersteel* (1975), a government-commissioned film illustrating Nigeria's industrialization—set the stage. *Amadi* (1975) was Afrocult Foundation's first full-length feature. This film, which employs documentary techniques and fictional narrative structure, breaks new ground on the Nigerian cinematographic scene, not in technical or aesthetic terms but by being the first Nigerian film shot in a local language, Igbo (with English subtitles), one of Nigeria's main languages in this nation of over two hundred dialects.

Ola Balogun is a Yoruba, born in Aba, who speaks fluent Igbo. He has been given much credit for this language breakthrough, but the fact that *Amadi* was made with the support of the then East Central State government, located in the heart of Igboland and completely controlled by the Igbos, probably explains the language preference. Moreover, the film would not have been credible had the director used any Nigerian language other than Igbo to make a film about Igbo people.

The issues dealt with in *Amadi* resemble the themes mentioned earlier in chapter 2 regarding francophone African cinema. These include the young man returning home to his village after an unsuccessful adventure to the city; the depiction of modern agricultural techniques; the foregrounding of religion—in what looks like an appeal for the resuscitation of traditional cults and methods of worship; and also the depiction of the contradictions between modern Africa and the rural world of Africa. While acknowledging the film's technical infirmities and lack of cinematic innovation, the director's wife, Françoise Balogun, has written that *Amadi* nevertheless "gives a feeling of newness and . . . raised a keen interest among Nigerian viewers."[62] Although *Amadi* was successful with the Nigerian audience, this enthusiasm, which increased awareness of the need for a viable film industry, was not reinforced by the federal government or any other state government. As the potential of the film medium's utilization for national development further eroded, so did "the potential validity of cooperative links between policy formulation in the arts and the growth of new expressions,"[63] that is, creativity and the raising of consciousness through film.

Amadi generated an unprecedented awareness, demonstrating also the potential for the use of local languages to galvanize audiences. Balogun was quick to utilize this strategy to the advantage of his fledgling production company. His next film, *Ajani-Ogun* (1975), the second feature to be produced by Afrocult, is black Africa's first musical. Shot entirely in the Yoruba language, it tells the story of a young hunter, Ajani-Ogun, who is determined to recover his late father's land, which was misappropriated by a corrupt politician, Chief Abayomi, with the complicity of some mischievous public officials. Between Ajani-Ogun and the Chief is a young and beautiful village girl—the perennial love triangle. Meandering through miscellaneous issues, together with the development of a confrontation between Ajani-Ogun and Abayomi, *Ajani-Ogun* becomes a social essay that indicts the corrupt elements of Nigerian society. It also goes further, tracing the roots of this corruption to the colonial-neocolonial transition, casting blame on the elite as exemplified by Samoye, a greedy and unscrupulous character inclined to enter into shady deals with anybody. He connives with Abayomi, the dishonest and arrogant feudal politician, to cheat and strip the society of its material wealth. In this film, Balogun encompasses the imagery of contemporary Africa, blending it with traditional African narrative patterns. In doing this, he uses African music and dance not only as a colorful background highly indicative of African culture (specifically of Yoruba culture) but also in a fashion that seems to be arguing for the values, significance, and meaning of the African identity. The cinematographic realization of the tradition and structure of the Yoruba traveling theater poses the problem of adapting theatrical plays to film. Technically, this film is replete with continuity problems and overacting by nonprofessionals. The dances and songs are overemphasized, thus becoming monotonous. But these problems did not seem to bother the audiences, who were enthralled by the local setting of the film.

Ajani-Ogun is a product of exemplary collaboration between a veteran stage actor and "King of the Theater," Duro Ladipo, and an industrious and enterprising young filmmaker, Ola Balogun. At the time of the film's release, the Yoruba traveling theater was at the pinnacle of its popularity, and Duro Ladipo's theater group comprising the cast expedited the film's tremendous success, especially among the Yoruba audience for which it was intended. To this audience, who stampeded to the theaters, the appearance of Duro Ladipo and his theater group was much more appealing than the conventions of cinematography. *Ajani-Ogun* also marked a turning point in Balogun's career, for from that time on he was to turn his lens perpetually onto the Yoruba theatrical culture whenever his attempt at conventional cinematography failed. This film's box-office popularity spurred the get-rich-quick mentality underlying Nigeria's business practices. It also had a profound influence on the pattern and future of filmmaking in Yorubaland. It was *Ajani*'s success and the promise of financial reward that led to the proliferation of filming Yoruba theater by its practitioners, who had already realized many years of lucrative practice on the dramatic stage.

Among the dramatists who made an early plunge into filmmaking were Hubert Ogunde, one of the most celebrated dramatists of the

Nigerian theater with an unparalleled ability to gather a large audience; Moses Olaiya (alias Baba Sala), a famous and renowned stage comedian; Ade Falayan (alias Ade Love), the former "Lover Boy" and tour de force of the Nigerian theater who broke with Moses Olaiya to start his own group. Previously unknown theater groups also jumped into filmmaking, all of them governed by the same ambition—to use film as an extension of their theater practice and to enhance remuneration. "Theater on screen" became very popular. Its audience appeal (mainly in Yoruba geographical areas) and box-office returns were high, making people believe, at this initial stage, that the golden years of Nigerian (read: Yoruba) cinema had finally arrived.

Contrary to this assumption, the so-called prosperous years of filmed theater had nothing to do with the creation of a long-lasting cinema industry for Nigeria or the development of a genre based on the Yoruba's popular traveling theater. It was an enterprise born out of greed and lack of concern for cinematic creativity and is truly second-rate entertainment since the artistic excellence of the Yoruba traveling theater's stage performance is an enduring tradition. The so-called thriving years of the Yoruba tradition of filmed theater are unfortunately characterized by a purveyance of mediocrity as genial art; worse still, what is today known as "Nigerian cinema" revolves around this type of filmmaking. Such a practice negates the original code of traditional Yoruba traveling theater, which Joel Adedeji, the historian of this tradition, termed "intensive professionalism."[64] While noting that "professionalism in the theater" resulted in the proliferation of troupes, he categorically stated that "it encouraged competition which, in turn, improved the theatrical art."[65] But in the case of the integration of theater with cinema, the reverse has been the case. This tradition lacks the substance that is emblematic of the "golden age" of Senegalese cinema, which, in the work of Ousmane Sembene, Paulin Soumanou Vieyra, Ababacar Samb, Momar Thiam, and others, champions the political and cultural use of cinema for consciousness-raising and giving a sense of direction to national enlightenment and development.

Ajani-Ogun's success moved the Indo-Nigerian Film Distribution Company to finance the making of *Musik-Man* (1976), coproduced with Afrocult Foundation and directed by Balogun. Shot in English and pidgin English, this film is a quasi-musical whose language preference was aimed at broadening national audience appeal. This rather ambitious and well-conceived project (albeit marred by some technical incompetence) regrettably failed to produce a magnetic grip on the audience like that of its predecessor. The abundance of humor in *Musik-Man,* if properly integrated, would have made the film more entertaining. As it is, *Musik-Man* remains a failed experiment rather than an African Chaplinesque comedy.

Musik-Man's failure forced Balogun to redirect his strategy. The choices were clear; either continue to make films utilizing conventional cinematographic methods and appeal to a national audience, as in *Musik-Man,* risking both dismal box-office returns and jeopardizing a blossoming career, or continue in the tradition of filming Yoruba theater whose theater actors' popularity guaranteed profit. Opting for the latter course, Françoise Balogun admits that there was a Yoruba audience waiting for another *Ajani-Ogun.*[66]

At the time of the failure of *Musik-Man,* and stemming from the euphoria created by *Ajani*'s success, the theater practitioners, who had formed their own film production companies by printing letterheads (even though they had no cameras and filmmaking equipment and no prior film training), were anxiously awaiting a film director to transfer their plays to the screen. So, Ade Folayan, a popular theater actor who played the leading role in *Ajani,* and now the proprietor and head of Ade Love Theater Company and Friendship Motion Pictures Limited, a film production and distribution company respectively, established a partnership with Balogun which led to the making of *Ija Ominira* (Fight for freedom, 1977). This film is an adaptation of a novel by Adebayo Faleti and is also taken from the stage adaptation as performed by Folayan and his theater group and other participating Yoruba traditional theater groups. The story concerns a king, a hated tyrant who is banished by his own subjects. The completion of this film came amid a tumultuous clash of interests between Balogun and Folayan. *Ija Ominira*'s success, in spite of this, was immeasurable—recouping its production costs in less than one year.

The following year, a deal with Brazilian financiers made Balogun temporarily abandon the Yoruba tradition of theater reproduction on film, in order to direct *A deusa negra* (Black goddess, 1978). Produced by Embrafilme of Brazil and the Afrocult Foundation, it was shot in Brazil in Portuguese and dubbed into English with some prints containing French subtitles. Unlike Balogun's other films to date, whose distribution is mainly restricted to Nigeria and some international festivals, *Black Goddess* has been distributed outside of Africa. It won a prize from the International Catholic Office of the Cinema as well as a prize for best film music at the 1980 Carthage Film Festival. Although critically acclaimed, the film poses a dilemma regarding the question of cinematographic representation of the supernatural. This problem becomes more apparent in his later films whose structures are embellished with excursions into mythology and folklore. In Africa's oral narrative structure, references to the supernatural are legion and audiences have no problem understanding their incorporation into stories. But in cinema, as Balogun's later films show, representation of the supernatural is not as effective. We shall deal with this issue in more detail later as it manifests in the films discussed.

Returning to Nigeria, Balogun teamed up once again with another veteran of the Yoruba traveling theater, Chief Hubert Ogunde, who wanted to adapt one of his most popular plays, "Aiye," for the screen. Ogunde had no formal training in filmmaking, but like Ade Folayan, he too had a film production-distribution company, Ogunde Films. Coproduced by Ogunde Films and Afrocult Foundation, and directed by Balogun, *Aiye* (1979) portrays "the struggle between the forces of good in the person of 'babalawo' (traditional healer and priest) and evil forces incarnated by witches in a Yoruba village."[67] This film utilized the services of an estimated two hundred persons, actors from Ogunde's theater group as well as those from other theater groups.[68] The technical crew comprised both French and Nigerian experts. The netherworld of witches was given prominence by a barrage of special effects suggesting an exploration of the deeper mystical world of the supernatural, designed to entertain the audience with a taste of intrigue. The presence of Ogunde, the star of this film, was an added factor in the film's appeal and success. It grossed over three hundred thousand naira (approximately four hundred fifty thousand dollars) in one week in Lagos alone.

Balogun's collaboration with theater czars has never been cordial.[69] After each coproduction he would attempt an individual production on his own, but each attempt was rebuffed by the audience. The problem is threefold: he has established himself as the reputable director of the "Yoruba" cinema so that each time he comes up with something different, his audience (who expects to be amused and entertained with gags, slapstick, and singing and dancing, as in the theater-film tradition) is easily disappointed; the audiences he tries to reach have, for a long time, been indoctrinated with foreign films, so that anything short of a thriller, with physical action, fistfighting, or combat reminiscent of foreign films, is unable to attract Nigeria's adamant crowd; and since there is no effective distribution outlet, one is not sure how well the films will be received by the audience outside the Yoruba-language area.

By 1980, Nigerian film production was still oscillating between idealism and actuality. The enthusiasm raised by filmmakers in the 1970s had not yet resulted in a recognizable masterpiece. A major attempt to break this impasse came from Balogun, whose undertakings, once again outside the confines of the theater tradition, resulted in the realization of *Cry Freedom* (1981). This film (probably this indefatigable director's boldest endeavor at seeking his own creative autonomy) was inspired by *Carcase for Hounds* by Meja Mwangi of Kenya, a novel about the Mau Mau struggle. The story deals with colonialism and the liberation movement in Africa and tells of a group of guerrillas fighting a war of independence against the colonial administration. The rationales motivating the opposing forces are set in ideological conflict and structural situations are made to illustrate the struggle for liberation.

Thematically and stylistically *Cry Freedom* is different in many ways from Balogun's earlier films. It is an ambitious leap toward the production of cinema that elicits knowledge and understanding of African history. Shot in Ghana with an international cast, here is a story of continental relevance, one that deals with African social and historical problems—an area that has been awaiting serious cinematographic exploitation from an indigenous perspective; and yet *Cry Freedom* did not draw a good-sized audience. Why would such a film dealing with Africa's political problems, touching the continent's sensibility regarding freedom, independence, and the search for political, social, and cultural identity, fail to attract a large audience? Could it be that audiences (Nigerian audiences specifically) are apolitical? Lamenting the dilemma of the low audiences turnout, Françoise Balogun noted:

> The film which was born of good intentions and of the will to give a message in a didactic way, is interesting in that it tries to express the African point of view. . . . Intellectuals who enjoy abstractions in films praised it, but the popular audience who, above all, wants a good story, rebuked it because spectators want a war film with battle scenes and blood and are indifferent to moral and political lessons.[70]

Although the film style of *Cry Freedom* embraces the dominant features of the Hollywood mode of representation, it seems that the director's technique has failed to make enough concessions to a popular audience spoiled by lengthy exposure to American "B" movies, Italian spaghetti westerns, Hong Kong karate and Chinese kung fu films, and Indian romance melodramas. By contrast, the director's "focus of interest," observes Mario Relich, "in fact, seems to be not action as such, but in depicting what characterizes a guerrilla's struggle for freedom from colonial tutelage with the utmost clarity."[71] But why would *Aiye* and *Ija Ominira* be box-office hits even though in technical terms *Cry Freedom* is cinematographically more ingenious? Here, thematically and stylistically, authenticity and originality may be a crucial factor. To explore this further, we will refer to the African novel as an example. Many African novels derive authenticity from theme and method of exposition (in which the infusion of oral tradition is very important) and are popular with African readers who identify with their objectives, styles, and African story lines. As already illustrated, this

Ola Balogun: Cry Freedom; *Nigeria, 1981.* Courtesy of the Françoise Pfaff Collection.

audience appeal also applies to the films of the theater tradition, not from the point of how well the filmic conventions were applied but in terms of identification with the social and cultural ramification of theatricalities. While Nigerian novels may be well conceived and comparable in quality to their African counterparts, Nigerian films are of low quality in comparison to cinema in the rest of Africa.

With regard to the audience, it seems the implication of their unresponsive attitude is clear; a filmmaker who chooses to utilize a dominant film style to address contemporary issues and wants to entice Nigeria's complex audience, must do it in a way that is convincing and competitive. But more important, most people (both critics and spectators) insist that Nigerian cinema be based on the African model of representation. If such a model incorporates foreign models its integration must not obliterate the Africanness and creativity that make such works worthwhile contributions to culture and dialogue.

On the basis of this premise, we would attempt further explication with reference to the autonomy and authenticity, the originality and creative essence that have sustained mass appeal of African visual and performing arts. The basic contention here is that artistic conception and execution must still possess a virtuosity that is contingent upon sheer know-how. Therefore, if this philosophy were to govern film production in Nigeria the result would reflect pure artistic integrity. In the interest of African identity artistic creativity should and can transcend the commercialism of that art and also rise above sectionalism and profit. If traditional African art of the kind that influenced Picasso, the kind that adorns numerous books on art and is acclaimed worldwide in many cosmopolitan museums, is rarely created these days or no longer exists, it is because art is now art for money's sake. Still, in the face of this commercial onslaught, there are areas of the performing arts that continue to display unparalleled creativity. These are artists who, despite a lack of cultural policies in their countries to promote their work, are motivated by self-assurance and self-discipline, eschewing, in Barrett's terms, the "conservative and neorealistic tradition of colonial illustration" to place their work in pursuit of development.

In Nigeria for instance, as in many other African countries, such talented visual artists as Demas Nwoko, Erhabor Emokpae, Clara Ugbodagba-Ngu, Yusuf A. Grillo, Bruce Onobrakpeya, and many others including, of course, "Afro-beat" musician Fela Anikulapo-Kuti, have instituted a genealogy of artistic legacy. It is true that some of them have made money out of their sweat, but that has not tampered with their creative instincts. Their work provides a composite representation of highly codified images that make the African elements in which they are embodied become more spectacular.[72] They represent a high level of cultural assertiveness.

This assertiveness is perhaps best exemplified by the work of Fela Anikulapo-Kuti. In music, Fela Anikulapo-Kuti has demonstrated that he epitomizes a lifetime commitment toward uplifting black people—a commitment that makes him one of the dominant voices speaking fearlessly for African freedom. His music is based on the complex authentic interactive rhythms of African persuasion—an amalgamation of jazz, highlife, juju, traditional rhythms, and chanted declamations—which he dubbed "Afro beat." But the style with which Fela combines all this music, observes Randall F. Grass, is "in the far more sophisticated context of African rhythms."[73] Fela is a Yoruba, and in Yorubaland music and life are inseparable. In this land there are numerous musicians playing traditional "juju" and "apala" music. Famous among them are I. K. Dairo, Sunny Ade, and Ebenezer Obey. But Fela's music is much more imaginative, stylized, self-confident, and politicized in probing inner and external Africa.[74] While Fela refrains from praise singing, Ebenezer Obe and Sunny Ade, the exponents of juju music, indulge in cheap commercialization. They use their music to sing the praises of rich people—chief, doctor, lawyer, military officer, business tycoon, respected members of the Yoruba community, and even those who may have found their wealth through questionable means. Here, the praised patron would go wild and shower the musicians (yes, spray him, in Nigerian terminology) with new currency notes.

Fela's music is widely accepted and cuts across Nigeria's ethnic boundaries, with lyrics composed in both Yoruba and pidgin English. His nightclub, the "Shrine," is the "OAU" (Organization of African Unity) of Nigeria's ethnic mix where the haves and have-nots are united for mutual celebration and worship, "a rallying point for pan-African progressivism."[75] The "new society" that his music calls to the "Shrine" is, as Grass notes, "pan-ethnic and pan-generational,"[76] which the government, filmmakers, and artists alike could emulate. Where the narrowly focused juju music or, in the case of cinema, the Yoruba tradition of film and theater failed, Fela's music succeeds.

Returning to our discussion of Nigerian cinematic trends, the box-office disaster of *Cry Freedom* once again reasserts what Françoise Balogun has described as her husband's "pendular movement." Balogun accepted the offer from Moses Olaiya Adejumo (alias Baba Sala) to direct the filmic adaptation of one of his popular plays. A coproduction agreement between them led to the making of *Orun Moorun* (Heaven is hot, 1982). As in the case of other films in this tradition mentioned earlier, actors from Adejumo's theater group, as well as other groups from the Yoruba theater, comprised the cast. Like the other films, it was shot in Yoruba with English subtitles. Like *Aiye,* a conglomeration of special effects—animation and video—were lavishly combined with Baba Sala's "comic ingenuity" to electrify the audience. As expected, *Orun Moorun* was very successful. *Orun Moorun* is an alluring drama of "social messages subtly telegraphed across the screen: the perils of sudden, unearned wealth (owo ojiji, in Yoruba) rampant in contemporary Nigeria, the menace of pot-bellied, damasked (or laced) millionaires who "spray" wads of naira like used tickets."[77] This film is very funny even though the subject depicted touches on a shameful Nigerian habit.

Like the previously mentioned films in this category, the audience who viewed the film left with their shirts soaked in tears of laughter. Such an audience is transported into a world of magic with wonderful animation and video effects that highlight the ghost scenes. But this type of effect requires enormous research to devise a way in which to unite scenes and sequences with suitable conventional devices. This filmmaker's directorial problems began with the inability to handle

those posed by the representation of theatrical performances in cinematographically accepted terms and the unconvincing way the Yoruba
folktales have been sloppily handled in film after film.

The ability of the director to use the film medium, not only to repro-
duce "reality" but to rearrange that "reality" according to his desire,
demonstrates his creative potential. This calls for proper innovative
practices: mobility of the camera, variation of distances, change of
angles, perspectives, or if you will, utilization of transitions and montage (editing) for various applications. Many of the aforementioned
filmic characteristics, if incorporated into the films made in Nigeria,
would undoubtedly improve their quality. For example, *Orun Moorun*
exhibited too many directional problems—ineffective use or poorly applied transitional devices—and thus resulted in continuity problems.
Skillful employment of conventional elements of cinematography, for
example, close-ups, cut-aways, cut-ins, and careful editing, would have
bridged the disharmony between the long-takes and the overacted
scenes of *Ajani-Ogun*. Balogun's frequent incursion into metaphysics
similarly once again fails to achieve relevance in cinematographic representational terms. Some aspects of traditional mythology clearly are
best described orally (as in oral storytelling) or through literature (as
in African novels and plays in which the reader is left to imagine the
wonders described) rather than in cinematographic translation where
clashing juxtaposition of images and special effects obfuscate the story
line and the unraveling of the mystical content. But this does not mean
that cinematic representation of particular aspects of folktales that deal
with metaphysics is not practicable (as, for example, in Cissé's film
Yeelen, 1987). The opportunistic tendencies hidden in the shadow of
special effects can be avoided by enlisting the services of a creative
team and scriptwriters who are capable of developing the themes into
a good treatment without destroying the Africanness or originality of
such stories.

Some critics have called this tradition of filmmaking opportunistic,
dull-witted, self-indulgent, what Niyi Osundare calls "glorification of
cheap folklorism" involving the common themes of superstition, witchcraft, and magic. While acknowledging that *Aiye* is not technically deficient, Osundare left the theater wondering what he gained from the
movie—"just laugh[ter] or marvel at the power of witches?"[78] Falusi
Fola sees most Nigerian films made since 1975 as portraying the country
in its ancient, primitive state while neglecting present-day advance-
ments. According to him, these films are no different from Tarzan movies, since what is usually presented to the audience "are scenes shot
in deserted villages and farmsteads."[79]

After *Orun Moorun,* Balogun made no other films with the theater

practitioners, since every one of their coproductions had ended in bitterness. After this film, in the same year, Balogun completed *Money
Power* (1982). Produced by Afrocult Foundation, it was shot in Yoruba
with English and French subtitles. The film, according to the Afrocult
Foundation press release, is "a penetrating look at the overpowering
role of the naira currency in contemporary Nigerian society." Although
it is not set solely within the framework of the Yoruba filmed theater
tradition, it has some typical comic elements in its structure. The enlist-
ment of popular actors—all prodigious artists and entertainers—parallels the commercial tendency of the theater tradition. Even its title and
language indicate that the film was designed to

> please the normal Nigerian (and especially Yoruba) audience for the sim-
> ple reason that the characters are recognizable, the content is equally
> recognizable and there are several moments of situation comedy [reminis-
> cent of the characters playing them] that are very familiar to anybody
> who has walked into a Lagos office, worked in one, been near a rich
> man in a big "Agbada," has chased a woman or been chased by one. Such
> familiar elements such as political thuggery, bribery, and lovesickness are
> all present.[80]

This poignant attack on Nigeria's social decadence no doubt has won
Balogun credit for having, if only momentarily, avoided the practice
of romanticizing (through his collaboration with theater practitioners)
the art of filmmaking. However, as with his other works, there is much
still to be analyzed concerning Balogun's view of this theme. *Money
Power* exhibits what Bentsi-Enchill terms "a kind of comic-book episodic treatment"—resulting from deficient and unconvincing characterization. Thus,

> Chief B. C. Ade could only be called the main character because his
> nickname was the film's title; otherwise young and honest journalist Jide
> deserved to be the principal, but neither of them was allowed to achieve
> that prominence.[81]

And in structural terms, there were too many episodes that should have
been treated as a clear-cut, simple story, but

> which relied more on stringing together those appealing touches of recog-
> nizable reality than condensing those touches as the base for a more
> powerful plot. This type of deficiency could be seen in the passages where
> the lovesick Jide sings Yemi's name for what feels like five minutes, or
> the card game scene ending in a messy fight, or worst of all, when Ade's
> chief gorilla warns Akinwale not to campaign against "Money Power":
> for a thug who pleads with his boss to let him "finish" Akinwale, his

actual performance of dissuasion is unconvincing. Thus, the moments of dramatic potential where both the story line and the camera focus closely on emotions, tend to be overdone or underdone.[82]

This raises the question of the rationale for the extraordinary length of the movie. Given the moderate cost of only three hundred fifty thousand naira (approximately five hundred fifty thousand dollars),[83] one wonders if a sequel at a tightly controlled and appealing length would not have been more appropriate than its present double feature length of three hours and thirty minutes.

With the temporary exit of Balogun (this illustrious director is still too young and too ambitious to be counted out) the theater moguls are now in full control of film production in Nigeria. By 1979 the popularity of this tradition of "theater on the screen" was so potent that the dramatists whom Balogun had worked for started to direct their own films and other less popular dramatists also jumped on the bandwagon. While some enlisted the help of professionals, others felt that the experience of working with Balogun had qualified them to become full-fledged film directors. This was born out of the belief that as long as they had theater groups to sing and dance, all that filmmaking required was for someone to point the camera and trigger away.

Ade Folayan became the first to roll out a feature length film in this direction, *Kadara* (1979), followed by *Ija Orogun* (1982), *Taxi Driver* (1983), *Iyaniwura* (1985), *Ojun Ajaye* (1986), *Mose Bolatan* (1986) and *Taxi Driver II* (1987). All were made in the Yoruba language and did very well at the box office. *Kadara* was also dubbed into Hausa (a major Nigerian language), a commendable entrepreneurial decision aimed at broadening Folayan's commercial base outside of Yorubaland. Herbert Ogunde, who enlisted Freddie Goode as codirector along with some other British technicians, made two successful films: *Jaiyesinmi* (1981), and *Aropin N'Tenia* (1982) in Yoruba (the latter with English subtitles), and featured the Ogunde theater group and other Yoruba theater troupes. Moses Olaiya Adejumo codirected *Aare Agbaye* (1983) with Olowomoruoje. Produced by Adejumo's Alawada Film Company, the cast also came from his theater company and other participating Yoruba theater groups. In an attempt to internationalize his production and distribution enterprise (though this film was shot in Yoruba), he had English and French subtitles. However, because this film displayed too many technical flaws, it was not as successful as his first film, *Orun Moorun*.

Other films made under the Yoruba theater tradition include *Efunsetan Oniwura* (1982), which was produced by Ishola Ogunsola and directed by Bankole Bello, who was the camera assistant for *Ajani-*

Ogun, sound engineer for *Ija Ominira,* and a former cinematographer at the University of Ife. *Ireke Onibudo* (1982), which was adapted from a novel by Fagunwa, was produced by Bayo Aderounmu and codirected by Tunde Kelani and Bayo Aderounmu. *Anikura* (1983), produced by Ayo Rasak, directed by Tunde Kelani, and *Lisabi Agbongbo Akala* (1986), codirected by Olowomoruoje and Akin Oguagbe, are among the other numerous films made under this tradition.

Having traced the formation of the Yoruba tradition of filmed theater, I shall return to the other type of Nigerian cinema, that is, the one modeled after the dominant tradition. One of the pioneers of Nigerian cinema is Sanya Dosunmu, who believes in the use of film in establishing the cultural dynamics of the Nigerian condition. He found his creative vocation in television as the cocreator of the popular series "The Village Headmaster." In the same year that Balogun made *Amadi* and *Ajani-Ogun,* Dosunmu's first, and sadly his only, feature film, *Dinner with the Devil* (1975), was released. It deals with the problematic aspects of Nigeria's sociocultural problems and impugns all forms of corruption—moral delinquencies as well as infidelity. In theme and creativity this film is exemplary, first for being one of its kind in Nigeria's cinematographic aspiration by veritably depicting patterns of life. Second, in contradistinction to "Village Headmaster's" emphasis on talking heads, the emphasis is on narrative patterns delineated through characterization. In addition, the indigenous juju music of Sunny Ade is interspersed throughout the film. These creative features are phenomenal if only for the exaltation of the quest for authenticity, thus revitalizing the discourse on using indigenous Nigerian images in films and television. In spite of the film's success, the director has chosen to settle down at his home base, in Abeokuta, where he has a film distribution and exhibition business.

In pursuit of an indigenous film industry, filmmakers concerned with the paucity of film production in Nigeria continued to spread their dragnet, trying to garner from home and abroad financial and material resources for its implementation. It is along these lines that producer Ladi Ladebo sought and utilized the acting talent of Jab Adu, a seasoned and popular Nigerian television actor of "The Village Headmaster" fame. He had also served as coproducer and actor in the production of *Countdown at Kusini* (1976), a joint Nigerian-U.S. production, directed by America's Ossie Davis (who had directed *Kongi's Harvest* in Nigeria six years prior to this). However, owing to complications following the shooting process and the recusance following postproduction in the U.S., the distribution of this film suffered immensely.

As a long-standing African adage would have it, disappointment sometimes prompts renewed efforts. So when another attempt to involve some black Americans to collaborate in a film project failed, Ladebo, Jab Adu, and the newcomer, Kola Ogunnaike, teamed up to counter what they regarded as black American intransigence by launching the production of *Bisi, Daughter of the River* (1976). Funded by Chief M. K. O. Abiola, a Lagos-based business tycoon, this film was directed by Jab Adu. It is the story of Bisi, a young woman born in the coastal town of Badagry, a few kilometers from Lagos, the then federal capital of Nigeria. Her father, who is entrenched in the belief that Bisi is a gift to him, originating from Yemoja the river goddess, insists his daughter must be a priestess so that she can serve the goddess. Rather than accept this mythical proposition, Bisi chooses to disobey her father and moves to Lagos where she works as a secretary for Paul Banji, a businessman. There she falls in love with Banji's business partner and friend, Dexter Raymond. This connection with Raymond momentarily cuts off any hope of her return to Badagry. Babalola, an archenemy of Paul Banji, is intent on usurping the progress of the Banji-Raymond business by killing Dexter and Bisi. Aware that Babalola's bandits are coming to murder her, the frightened Bisi escapes to Badagry. Paul and Dexter go to Badagry in search of her, their arrival coinciding with the celebration of the Festival of Yemoja. Dexter and Bisi are out walking when Babalola's thugs, dressed as masqueraders, ambush them. The couple attempts a dramatic escape in a boat but Bisi accidently falls into the river and drowns in full view of the Yemoja worshippers. The river goddess has claimed her servant.

Bisi, Daughter of the River was shot in English (not surprising since the production reflected Nigeria's "national character"—with producers, technicians, and cast comprised of people of various ethnic origins) and completed and released in the same year as Balogun and Folayan's *Ija Ominira*. Both films were popular with the audience. *Ija Ominira* relied heavily on the famed theater actor Folayan and on other popular acting groups of the Yoruba traveling theater and the Yoruba dialect to capture the audience, while *Bisi* relied on famous names in show business, Jab Adu and Patricia Ebigwei, along with heavy publicity, to create an impact. The slogan that advertised *Bisi,* "Made in Nigeria by Nigerians and acted by Nigerians for Nigerians," still remains fresh in the minds of local film buffs whenever *Bisi* is mentioned. With these remarkable achievements, elated Nigerian audiences hoped that this double dose of interesting and entertaining features signified more local thrills in the future.

As with Sanya Dosunmu, who has made only one feature film (*Dinner with the Devil*), Jab Adu, who aside from the thirty-nine-part television series "The Adio Family," which he directed (televised by NTA), has made no other feature films since 1977. The filmmaker's withdrawal into obscurity is, however, connected with the difficulties of making films in Nigeria; or to be more accurate, the problem of getting anything organized in Nigeria. Yet independent producers continue to fight the challenges imposed by financial and bureaucratic constraints.

One of the most prominent independent filmmakers outside the Yoruba theater and film tradition is Eddie Ugbomah, who launched his career in 1977 (and is now the foremost Nigerian filmmaker in terms of the number of feature films made) with the release of *The Rise and Fall of Dr. Onyenusi*. He has since made more feature films: *The Mask* (1979), *Oil Doom* (1981), *Bulos 80* (1982), *The Boy Is Good* (1982), *Vengeance of the Cult* shot in 1982, released in 1984, and *The Death of a Black President* (1983)—all shot in 16mm with the exception of *The Mask*, which is in 35mm. Trained in London, Eddie Ugbomah graduated in journalism and drama and later in film and television production. He worked for some time at the BBC, and he played minor roles in such films as *Doctor No, Guns of Batasi,* and *Sharpeville Massacre,* before forming his own black theater group. Returning to Nigeria, he started film production in 1976, producing all his films through his company Edifosa Film Enterprise or through Third World Production as in the case of *The Death of a Black President*. Unlike any other model of film production in this country, Ugbomah's creative zeal is inspired by contemporary social, political, and cultural events, tackled in English or in pidgin English. Given the preponderance of dialects or languages in Nigeria, for him, this language choice has special significance. Ugbomah is from the Igbo ethnic group of Delta State of Nigeria, but his operative base is Lagos, the capital and the point of convergence of the country's diverse ethnic groups. Lagos is the heart of Yorubaland, and although in terms of ethnic loyalty the Yorubas are very cohesive and are less likely to communicate in English or pidgin English, numerous other groups do so. In other words, while Ugbomah targets the general populace, which is harder to please, the filmmaker who shoots in Yoruba can easily recoup his investment in the Yoruba area because there is always a ready audience.

In Ugbomah's films, we find the treatment of violence and corruption, lost dignity, and other societal issues constituting a critique of neocolonial and externally motivated Nigerian problems. This concern echoes the disdain of the moral and bureaucratic ineptitude that permeated the mood of the 1970s. By the mid-1970s, when Ugbomah began his career, Nigeria's oil production had reached its pinnacle and the devastating civil war had ended. But that did not mean equitable distribution of Nigeria's wealth, nor did it turn the country into an egalitarian society. In this period, Nigerians became, in the words of one social commentator, "morbidly acquisitive," and money became the domi-

nating criterion of value. Greed, the lust for material wealth and
"money power," created indiscipline within the rank and file of the
military-cum-civilian oligarchy; abominable inflation of government
contract awards (with kickbacks of 10 to 15 percent and over, depending on the level of the financial excesses of the signed contract), bribery
and corruption, and the menace of armed robbery and lawlessness were
all rampant.

Ugbomah's first feature film, *The Rise and Fall of Dr. Oyenusi,* takes
its theme from the times—armed robberies and the ruthless killing of
innocent citizens typical of the callous criminality of Ishola Oyenusi
(alias "Dr." Oyenusi), whose gang terrorized the city of Lagos in the
early 1970s. Although Dr. Oyenusi was captured and executed, his
death did not erase the fear instilled in the Lagosians. Nor did it erase
the fear that his legacy could be resuscitated by his underworld cohorts.
Ugbomah could not find anyone to play the part of Dr. Onyenusi, for
everyone feared retribution from the "Dr.'s" gang, so the director
played the role himself. Since then Ugbomah has played the leading
role in all his feature films. On another level, there were people who
felt that Oyenusi's story was best left buried along with him; an enraged
medical doctor whose name is also Oyenusi, but who is not related to
the King of the Underworld, sought litigation to stop the shooting of the
film. Ugbomah's provision store was burglarized, the thieves sending a
letter to him pledging to return the stolen goods when he dropped the
idea of making the film. The defiant director, however, could not be
stopped.

The Rise and Fall of Dr. Oyenusi is Ugbomah's first film and no
doubt exhibits some traces of amateurism. While the film could not be
commended for cinematic innovativeness, the maker must be remembered for having the courage to depict the undepictable. As a fearless
social historian who through the celluloid medium drives breath into
people's social consciousness, he has opened up new areas of inquiry
for Nigerian filmmakers. Given the theme, complexity, and sensitivity
of its social relevance, one must admit that in the absence of collaborating, experienced professionals—technicians and performers—shortcomings are bound to exist. In any case, the film provides a useful
experience that will hopefully strengthen future enterprises.

Ugbomah's next film, *The Mask* (1979), introduced a cultural and
historical subject of national importance. It portrays and exposes the
shameless looting by Africa's colonizers and the subsequent incarcera-
tion of Africa's art objects in British museums, following the kind of
similar protests registered in *You Hide Me* (1972) by Ghana's Kwate
Nee-Owoo and in *Les statues meurent aussi* (Statues also die, 1953)
by Alain Resnais and Chris Marker. The retrieval of one of Africa's

most cherished cultural symbols, a famous highly stylized and intricately carved face of Queen Adesua of Benin, which was stolen by the British around 1897 when their forces invaded Benin City, provides the central theme of the film. This mask was chosen as the symbol of FESTAC '77 and was the cause of a political wrangle between the British government and the Nigerian government when all efforts made by the latter to reclaim the mask failed to win the approbation of a defiant British government.

In this film, Ugbomah dramatizes a rescue operation that would have returned the mask to Nigeria. The film is a true story that uses a fictional narrative structure. Major Obi (played by Ugbomah), the hero of this film, embarks on a secret mission to London to organize a break-in of the British Museum to retrieve the mask and return it to Nigeria. He receives training in military tactics, and on reaching London (where most of the action is staged) he confronts a series of obstacles. The complex situation set in truncated subplots is an example of discontinuity of cinematic structure. Poor acting coupled with appearances of unidentifiable characters who, in the words of a *West Africa* correspondent, "fortuitously appear at times of crises,"[84] make it even more confusing. This film displays the symptoms of directorial bankruptcy, low-level craftsmanship, inability to apply transitional devices for effective structural continuity, poor synchronization of the sound track in one of the early scenes, and incompetent editing. Here, the enlisting of experts in the areas of scriptwriting and directing and of cameramen and other technicians to render essential services undoubtedly would have remedied these aesthetic problems. The story is authentic and deeply African, yet its execution replicates the poor taste of Hollywood's style of representation. Describing this film as "following in 007's footsteps," Nigerian critic Niyi Osundare noted *The Mask*'s avowed similarity to the American James Bond series.[85] This observation echoes that of the anonymous *West African* correspondent above: the main character, Obi, typifies the macho James Bond image; his bravery, sexuality, and indomitability parallel that of the typical, always victorious Hollywood star. Rather than provide an African model of cinematic representation, this sensational vehicle combines an African version of James Bond with Shaft.[86] Within its historical and cultural context, Ugbomah's work is viewed as vulgar, overcommercialized, and exploitative—labels which the film director rejects totally. In Ugbomah's view, *The Mask* is an important work that is culturally and politically enlightening. According to him, it was "made first and foremost as a kind of getting even with Britain. The British stole our treasures, they felt the impact of the film's message, and hence the BBC was forced to make *Whose Treasure, Ours or Theirs?* as a counter response. I was flown to London to discuss the topic when it aired on the British Broadcasting Corporation.''[87]

Ugbomah's career flourished into the 1980s with *Oil Doom* (1981), which (as the name implies) lampoons the nation's predicament caused by the oil boom of the 1970s, *Bulos '80* (1982), *The Boy Is Good, The Death of a Black President, Vengeance of the Cult, Esan* (1985), *Apalara* (1986), plus other titles not mentioned here. He makes at least one film per year. Reacting to the commercial tendencies of filmmaking of this sort, Charles R. Larson indicated that ''in an attempt to make a movie marketable both in Africa and in the West, the producers chose the middle ground and apparently please no one.''[88] Ugbomah pursues this commercial tendency through the infusion of Hollywood clichés, such as the display of affluence and the occasional mixing of ''kinky'' sex with gun-toting, which in many ways undercuts the film's intended message. Even his most acclaimed film, *The Death of a Black President* (1983), shows the problems that existed in his other films, including unconvincing characterizations, here made worse by the actors' difficulty in delivering their English language lines with fluency. However, this film, which deals with the assassination of Nigeria's former leader, General Murtala Muhammed, is a remarkable improvement over the director's previous efforts. Enthusiastic, if pedestrian, the standard of acting here is higher and indeed brilliant in the case of some of the performers. This film, which, amid the problems encountered from uncooperative Nigerian government functionaries,[89] cost over three million dollars to produce, is undoubtedly Ugbomah's best.

Like other Nigerian filmmakers, Ugbomah faces distribution and exhibition problems. Nigerian films made in the 1980s have either received limited showings or are unknown. The documentary feature *Shaihu Umar* (1976) by Adamu Halilu, who has since made such feature films as *Kanta of Kebbi* (1984) in the Hausa language and *Moment of Truth* (1981) in English; *Blues for a Prodigal* (1984) by author Wole Soyinka (and banned for some time by the government); *The Song Bird* (1986) by Mayo Ogundipe; *Parcel Post* (1982) by Segun Oyekunle; and *Turning Point* (1980) and *Him Don Die* (1982) by N. Frank Ukadike have all received only lecture room showings.

This chapter has established that film practice in the anglophone region is not ideologically patterned on the francophone model discussed in chapter 2. While filmmakers here meet with enormous financial constraints (even more severe than their francophone counterparts), they are also responsible for compounding some of the other problems affecting the quality of their films. In Nigeria, for instance, filmmaking is a family business. Quality work is not likely to emerge from a situation in which the filmmaker is the director, the professional scriptwriter, the professional actor, and the exhibitor. In most cases he is not trained in any of the above; and in the case of some theater practitioners, the proprietors are the sole beneficiaries since their wives, children, and relatives comprise the cast.

Ola Balogun, Eddie Ugbomah, Adamu Halilu, and others outside the theater companies have made significant steps toward the search for a Nigerian film industry. Their contributions have shown commitment to the building of a national film culture. However, all these are only adjuncts to a fine-tuned cinematic procedure. And if this contribution is to be improved, the elimination of most of the problems exhibited in these films should be considered forthwith. They could be tackled through a division of labor whereby professionals would work together, plan together, and share ideas for the sake of quality. In this regard one would hope that a coordinated dialogue for common ground, aiming for regional and continental cooperation in all aspects of filmmaking, would provide a forum for the reorganization of production strategies.

If, as is widely believed, the pursuit of profit is the main cause of this loss of artistic integrity, the desire to please the audience is another. If, on the one hand, Nigerian films become commercially viable and are able to generate lucrative investment returns for further production, that is progress. On the other hand, if poor quality invites the condemnation of all films made in the anglophone states as "mediocre," by Mbye Cham's observation,[90] "money power" would only worsen the insipid cinematic representation of a society in dire need of better treatment.

4

The Cultural Context of
Black African Cinema

Post-1970 and the Introspective
Phase

In terms of the problems of film financing, production, distribution, and
exhibition, the first decade of black African cinema clearly indicates
the attachment of its growth to the economic, political, and social contexts of the African situation. This dialectic of text and context engendered experiments in theme, style, and approach to filmmaking. In the
1970s and 1980s, cinema became more introspective, directed toward
addressing contemporary African issues—colonialism and neocolonialism, social and cultural conflicts. Often styles were deeply rooted in
African concepts of storytelling and specifically in the oral tradition.
The fusion of oral tradition with filmic narrative structure became an
important characteristic of African filmmaking, toward which almost
all filmmakers now lean and to which the level of its maturity is attributed. Even in the lusophone African countries, where a sophisticated
revolutionary approach to film production reflects the struggle for self-
determination, the liberationist documentaries also invoke this pan-
African structure (the oral tradition). However, as we have already
pointed out, government subsidy for film production still remains elu-
sive, and only an enormous increase in coproduction with foreign countries has enabled the production of feature-length films in black Africa.
This chapter explores the perspectives of black African cinema in the
1970s and 1980s (bearing in mind the issues touched on in chapter 3),
focusing on the expanding themes and the questioning aspects of films

of this period, on joint productions with African and foreign countries, on patterns of oral tradition in the structures of recent films, and on the liberationist tendencies of lusophone and South African documentaries.

This inquiry into aspects of traditional culture and history as they relate to the film medium is here linked to a discussion of black African film practice in terms of its technological means of image production and traditional forms of communication. This combination of these devices parallels the dichotomy of existence permeating modern African history, a history generally evaluated through the understanding of internal squabbles and of conflicts associated with influences from eastern or western European countries. This contradiction also becomes apparent in the representation of this reality, the problem being the challenge posed by the integration of modern and traditional media, that is, the problem of finding ways to continue the bond between traditional and modern modes of representation and communication without distracting from the traditional ways or detouring the advancement toward modernity. Despite the general hegemony of Hollywood and European dominant conventions, black African film practice is strenuously attempting to modify these conventions—narratively, aesthetically, and ideologically—to suit the culture and situation under which black Africans have to function.[1]

In 1971, two films from Senegal notably advanced this challenge—Ousmane Sembene's *Emitai* (God of thunder) and Ababacar Samb-Makharam's *Kodou*. Based on actual events, *Emitai*, set during the Second World War, relates the history of resistance in the village of Effok in Casamance (southern Senegal) to the French colonial army, which forcibly drafted able-bodied African males and coerced the villagers into giving thirty-seven kilos (sixty-seven pounds) of rice per person to support France's war efforts. Stunning visual moments serve to enhance the film's message. For example, French soldiers are shown tying up village elders and the heads-of-family, holding them against their will to force their children out of hiding so that they can be drafted. And when they are shown defenseless and in direct and bloody confrontation, being wiped out by guns of the heavily armed French soldiers, the filmmaker not only invokes emotions but lays bare the ugliness of colonialism, revealing the oppressive lives of a dominated people. Roy Armes notes that Sembene's handling of this subject avoids both false heroics (no single hero, only mass heroes) and the psychologizing so typical of a Western approach.[2] But as a film that vehemently denounces colonialism, it is also a revolutionary conscience awakener to tenets of traditional values which the filmmaker sees as needing reexamination.

An illustration of the French colonial mission in Africa reveals its operational and opportunistic tendencies. France's conquest of African countries was fulfilled by using Christian missionaries, civilian administrators, and the military. Apart from its own white soldiers (commissioned and noncommissioned officers), black Africans comprised the forcibly recruited mercenaries (albeit meagerly paid and inadequately trained) who were marched to the front lines of European wars. Some of them were positioned to suppress any insurrection that might occur in the territories. Sembene himself was one of the draftees, and his analysis of this debilitating aspect of French subjugation in *Emitai* is no less than a testimony to France's usurpation and hybridization of African traditions. In this regard, the film uses three languages—Diola, French, and pidgin French to emphasize the confusion evinced in the French policy of assimilation. This indictment becomes vivid in the scene in which African soldiers are shown speaking broken French. One notices that in this process of "Frenchifying" and "de-Africanizing," African soldiers are no longer identified by any specific origin or ethnic trait.

Regarding the aspect of traditional values implied as needing reexamination, one such illustration in *Emitai* is the scene in which Sembene questions the wisdom of adhering to the myths of traditional African religions. The black characters in this film are Diola and are inherently cohesive and resistant to foreign influence, exemplifying what we might call relentless traditionalists who represent authentic African values. The dynamics of their religious conviction are tied to cosmological facts; for them, the human being is part of the universe controlled by cosmic forces visible and invisible. While their belief in a supreme deity is unquestioned, they aspire for intimate contact with the spirits that control the universe.[3] This source of contact takes the form of offerings and sacrifices by the community's high priests, who appease the gods who may be responsible for life, death, famine, disease, and disaster.

By Diola tradition, according to Pfaff, rice has special significance and, accordingly, women oppose the selling of this staple. It is a sacred entity whose production ensures a communal bond as well as subsistence, hence the women who produce the rice ignore the military might of the colonialists and wage stiff resistance against its confiscation. In the film, women spearhead the attack on the invading forces by hiding their rice and refusing to give it up. The army responds by putting the women out in the scorching sun and threatening to incarcerate them and burn down the village. The men, still in hiding and behaving according to Diola custom, ruminate about the inability of the gods to prevent such a problem from taking place in their community. Through a parallel montage, Sembene alternates between the scene of the men appeasing the gods and the women waging stiff resistance against the French

Ousmane Sembene: Emitai (*God of Thunder*); *Senegal, 1971.* Courtesy of the British Film Institute.

army. Reminiscent of Amilcar Cabral's notion of "national culture," Sembene's position regarding religion and traditional custom implies that the gods induce a passivity that acts as a conduit for submission and resignation in the face of aggression. However, this aspect of culture is not treated with contempt; rather, it is implied that since traditions are no longer static in these modern times, some of the old ways must be reexamined and either encouraged or rejected. This position, as we shall see, is reflected in the work of other black African filmmakers, Souleymane Cissé's in particular.

In *Kodou,* filmmaker Samb-Makharam, popularly known as Samb, offers a different perspective on national culture and, like Sembene, in a cinematic language all his own, deals with the conflict of the individual and the community. Set in a traditional environment, the story concerns the central character, Kodou, who one day decides (without obtaining the prior approval of her parents) to have her upper lip tattooed in the traditional way. But this ritual female tradition involves pain, and in her society, ability to endure such pain is a mark of gallantry signifying maturity. However, Kodou undergoes the process, finds the pain unbearable, and runs away. Her inability to cope with the tattooing automatically degrades her before her peer group while also debasing the pride and confidence her family has in her. Rejected by everyone, the young girl is traumatized and driven insane. She is taken to a European doctor who is unable to help her. Finally she is cured by a native doctor (a traditional medicine man).

Rendered in a cinematic language that gives priority to furthering an awareness of traditional culture, *Kodou* opens the way for a vivid examination and understanding of the situation being scrutinized. Replete with the contradictions of contemporary Africa—traditional values caught up with infiltrating Western ways—this film suggests that certain customs should not be allowed to vanish in the face of encroaching Western values. The film's noticeable cinematographic deficiencies are here compensated for by a meticulous examination of the theme depicted. By contrasting sequences of the Western psychotherapy available to patients at the Fann Psychiatric Hospital in Dakar with scenes of the "Ndepp," a traditional ritual that cures Kodou of her madness, *Kodou* transcends a mere recording of vignettes of contradictory African life. Pierre Hafner contends that the quality of the film must also be judged by the director's ability "to avoid giving a simplistic and schematic solution to the crucial problem of cultural traumatism."[4] Furthermore, *Kodou,* like *Emitai,* compels its viewer to reflect upon Senegal's ambiguities in relation to its accumulating political, economic, social, and cultural problems.

An attempt to link commercial tendencies with recognizable social issues is prominent in Henri Duparc's film *Abusuan* (The family; Côte d'Ivoire, 1972). The issues addressed are parasitism, whereby dependents exert a heavy financial burden on a successful family member, juvenile delinquency, and urban-rural migration. Unfortunately, unlike *Kodou*, *Abusuan* fails to probe the causes and effects of the situations under examination, nor is it capable, like *Emitai*, of sharpening the film's political perspectives in order to invoke the audience's participation. In Côte d'Ivoire, this film was financially successful, but like the Nigerian commercial films discussed in chapter 3, African critics concerned with its lack of detail and authenticity greeted its commercial exuberance with mixed reviews.

By contrast, Gnoan Roger M'Bala's *Amanié* (What news, 1972) and Étienne N'dabian Vodio's *Le cri du muezzin* (The muezzin's call, 1972), both from Côte d'Ivoire, offer a more radical, critical, and penetrating awareness of social issues. While both films humorously satirize urban life, the ferocious critique of societal inadequacies here helps to focus attention on these dilemmas. The films explore the theme of the delusive aspects of neocolonialism, the lure of material success, and the struggle for well-being amidst deceit, prostitution, and thievery—most of which are diseases afflicting the alienated middle-class elite. These themes are taken up again in the satiric study of the neocolonial African bourgeoisie's taste for women, villas, cars, and money in *F.V.V.A.—Femmes, villa, voiture, argent* (1972) by Niger's Mustapha Allassane and coproduced by Niger and Burkina Faso.

F.V.V.A. deals with the trials of Ali, a young clerk who slowly drifts away from modesty and honesty into a life of corruption and, finally, imprisonment. The perils it impugns are perennial in "new" African societies: unscrupulous accumulation of wealth, forced or arranged marriages, the ambiguous role of marabouts, parasitism and its consequences within the family, and the cupidity of modern African women. The unusual quality of this film lies not so much in mise-en-scène as in the originality of the work and the relaxed expressiveness of thought and technique of its director, a remarkable development in this nascent African cinema. The wit and eloquence displayed here and in other films by Allassane obviously earns him recognition as the foremost filmmaker of Niger and one of black Africa's most prolific. The political imperatives of his criticisms are clear, and even in *Toula ou le génie des eaux* (The water spirit, 1973), which relates a traditional fable, this defiant director explicitly asserts his politics: "I did not make *Toula* for the mere pleasure of adapting one of Boubou Hama's legends to the screen, but rather to draw attention to the agonizing problem of drought which could very well be solved if adequate measures were really taken."[5] In the film, one gets the message that this accusation focuses not only on the local governments whose areas are affected by the drought but also on all international bodies or relief agencies that could come to the aid of the suffering masses.

The evolution of African cinematic practice resonates with social trauma as well as hope—in this case, the optimism and uncertainty, the intense emotions, strength, and vitality, and the afflictions of a disorganized continent in perennial struggle and at the crossroads of change. In cinematic introspective studies of Africa's reality, it is no longer a question of filmic practicability, but rather a matter of how best to depict actual realities using an aesthetic responsive to the continent's rhythms and cadences. While Oumarou Ganda's *Saitane* (Satan; Niger, 1973) uses humor and comic acerbity (à la *F.V.V.A.*) to attack the excesses of local marabouts, haunting visionary images are posited within the politics of culture and tradition with a style resonant with powerful and ancient oral traditions. In like manner, Congo's first feature-length film, *La rancon d'une alliance* (The disadvantages of an alliance, 1973) by Sebastien Kamba, an adaptation of Jean Malonga's novel *The Legend of Mofoumou Ma Mazono* made with the assistance of the French Ministry of Coopération and shot in French, offers insight into the precolonial strife of two African societies. This film explores a variety of issues such as kinship structures and the position of women in a traditional setting. A bold cinematic evaluation of traditional mores, it nevertheless lacks the kind of spirit of filmic innovation that might influence or induce other black African filmmakers to reassess their film styles.

In *Touki-Bouki* (The hyenas' journey; Senegal, 1973), Djibril Diop Mambety breaks this aesthetic gridlock, typifying a trend dedicated to total decolonization of both the content and style of movies (which is not to suggest that Mambety is endowed with the type of ideological motivation that regulates the work of Sembene, Hondo, and as we shall see, Cissé). Made with financial support from the government of Senegal, *Touki-Bouki* deplores the mentality of African youths who want to leave their mother countries to take refuge in European cities. Mouri, a former shepherd, meets Anta, a university student, and talks her into sharing his dream of living in France. Lacking the money to undertake such an expensive journey, they devise a series of bizarre misadventures consisting of stealing the money collected from a wrestling match (after breaking the coffer, they discover that it contains a contestant's fetish—a skull and amulet), and visiting Charlie (a homosexual who had earlier made a pass at Mouri), whose expensive wardrobe Mouri steals while Anta takes a wallet from one of his guests. At the last minute, with boat ticket in hand, Mouri cannot bring himself to leave Senegal.

Touki-Bouki exemplifies a rich reservoir of creative leitmotifs around which Mambety's ingenious oeuvre revolves. He undertakes to explore themes of youth and their dreams (love, alienation, fear, justice, and urban stress), processing them as symptoms of the problematics of development, in which "the normal course of events is continuously interrupted, attacked, and finally regenerated through dream sequences, hallucinations, lyrical interruptions, ultimately surrealism."[6] The unconventional manner in which space, time, and events are juxtaposed compels one to appreciate the film as a non-narrative whose collage of cultural, political, and sexual imagery offers a wide array of connotative assumptions. For example, while non-African critics have read the film as an avant-gardist manipulation of reality, an Africanist analysis would attempt a reconfigurative reading that synthesizes the narrative components and reads the images as representing an indictment of contemporary African life-styles and sociopolitical situations in disarray. Mouri and his girlfriend, Anta, feel the urge to leave Senegal. But the film ironizes the dreamworld, France, where they hope to go. Within their present world, however, is overpowering colonial subjugation—even in independent Senegal. The French sit on a luxury yacht and mock Africans by comparing them to "barren intellectuals" and "big children." This scene is intercut with haunting frenetic montage images of livestock being slaughtered. This powerful sequence, reminiscent of *Hour of the Furnaces,* in which this kind of comparison has been made before, vividly lays bare the problematic social, political, and economic relationship between the colonizer and the colonized. At this point the film's structure calls attention not only to device, reflexivity, and deconstruction but also to the unique system of semiotics that is clearly being affirmed.

Touki-Bouki eschews didacticism while maintaining a commitment to liberated African film practice. In both content and style, the film makes intellectual demands that challenge the viewer. It does so by hybridization, appropriating and then subverting conventional film techniques and the thematic-narrative elements of traditional African tales. The film's stylistic sophistication surpasses previous experimentations within African cinema and is replete with well-integrated symbolism of typical African sociocultural codes, effective visual metaphors, and intelligible juxtaposition of images of reality and fiction which force frequent action and reaction between opposite poles. The film lacks the slow pacing and linear structuring that so characterizes and stigmatizes most African cinema. The editing strategy subverts spatial, temporal, and graphic continuity: disjunctive editing, jump cuts, and calculated disparities between sound and image violate domi-

Djibril Diop Mambety: Touki-Bouki (*The Hyenas' Journey*); *Senegal, 1974.*
Courtesy of Djibril Diop Mambety/Waka Films AG.

nant patterns of representation within both Western and African cinema, thus contributing to the fascination of the film.

The eruptive style of *Touki-Bouki* is sustained by a restless mise-en-
scène that culminates in a series of shifts and transgressions originating
from unconventional viewpoints no longer bound by conservative dramaturgy or the principles of oral tradition (even though the title itself,
"Bouki," is a popular character in oral tradition). Earlier, this tactic
was explored in Med Hondo's *Soleil O* (1969), but not with the kind
of violation of continuity created in *Touki-Bouki* by what Metz calls
the "nondiegetic insert."[7] While *Soleil O* has no real narrative structure, *Touki-Bouki*'s is disrupted by the insertion of "cut-aways," metaphoric or symbolic shots that do not belong to the space and time of
the main narrative. In conventional narrative structure this cut-away
would be replaced by a "cut-in," a shot, usually close up, to emphasize
visual specificity. We find a typical illustration in the lovemaking sequence of *Touki-Bouki*. Anta is seen on the beach as she undresses,
but what would have been her process of lying down readying for the

act of lovemaking is abruptly interrupted. The director then cuts to animal images of sheep being slaughtered, followed by a close-up shot of foaming waves. When he cuts back to the scene of lovemaking, what the viewer sees is not the contact motion of two bodies but Anta's fingers clutching a cross hanging on the rear of Mouri's motorbike. The movement of her fingers and the off-screen sound we hear juxtaposed with the foamy waves suggest the orgasmic burst of the encounter. This well-orchestrated sequence is presented without violating the moral codes pertaining to sex within the African tradition, where indecent exposure and overt promiscuity are taboo.

Elements of the image juxtapositions cited above have been used previously as a prominent strategy to counter dominant narrative tradition. David Bordwell and Kristin Thompson in *Film Art* point to examples in films like Fritz Lang's *Fury* (1936), in which gossiping housewives are intercut with clucking hens, and *Deep Throat* (1973), in which a shot of orgasm is juxtaposed with the launching of a missile. More complex examples abound in the work of Eisenstein. In *Strike* (1925) images of workers being massacred are juxtaposed with a bull being slaughtered. And in Godard's films it is not uncommon to see shots of posters, newspaper or magazine advertisements, and photographs being used to disrupt the time and space continuum of film scenes. Willing to go against the grain of narrative convention, Mambety intersperses comedy and drama, Western narrative style, and oral tradition in a manner that recalls Shklovsky's injunction to "bare the device."[8] This stylistic hybridization draws the viewer's attention to distinguishing between the real and imagined events, prompting participation in the search for the "implicit" or "connotative" meanings of the images represented. In this way the audience's film-viewing experience is pushed to a higher level of understanding. The question here is not necessarily the importance of realistic portrayal of actual events but rather how a filmmaker can utilize different elements of storytelling technique in order to create phantasms reflective of a society's shortcomings, which Mambety wants understood in dialectical terms. But for a fuller, more exact understanding of Mambety's creative fecundity and of its implications for the differences and tensions between African filmmakers and critics, we must look to his position on the aesthetics of African cinema.

According to Ferid Boughedir, *Touki-Bouki* belongs to an "intellectualistic trend of avant-gardist stylistic research."[9] Guided by the notion that cinema in black Africa must be an art which should be pushed toward international significance, Mambety understands that within this effort the development of a personal style with a high level of artistic and technical sophistication is a sine qua non. He deplores the exasperating simplicity of African cinema. His complaint is not directed toward its ideological focus but to "the level of form."[10] He also does not hide his contempt toward dogmatically inhibitive views on creative methods and derides African filmmakers who deceitfully proclaim the structural flaws of their films as "a stylistic component related to the filmmakers' African personality."[11] It is in this vein that he avoids films with didactic or political overtones. For him, cinema must be free of the seductive ambiguities and servitudes of dominant production. He believes in freedom of expression and diversity of style as the vivifying determinants of a counterpractice to the established codes of cinematic representation. Although he professes to be apolitical in a politically charged African world, the views he expresses in *Touki-Bouki* are not at all severed from politics, in the same manner that the moral overtones highlighting former shepherd Mouri's quest for the future are indicative of didactic reasoning.

This film also demonstrates how creative use of oral tradition in the construction of cinematic narrative structure can authenticate and enhance the aesthetics of black African cinema. *Touki-Bouki*, translated from Wolof (one of Senegal's languages), means "the hyenas' journey." In West African oral tradition, this animal (symbolic of "trickery and social marginality"), notoriously known for its greed and mischievousness, and for its repulsive, nasty smell, is cleverly associated with the film's main character as well as with other participants. "It is accordingly," Pfaff notes, "that the animal is used by Mambety in his story, which again opposes nonconventional individuals to the established mores and laws of society."[12] On the one hand, the restructuring of African oral storytelling technique renders his work cinematic. On the other, its experimental character personalizes the work, asserting creativity and authorial voice.

The rhythm of daily life as Mambety's camera portrays it at the beginning of the film is either slow or fast. The camera develops a masterful choreography as it dictates the pace of events; it chases and pans with electrifying speed every object within its vicinity. In African films, until 1973 when *Touki-Bouki* was made (with the exception of Med Hondo's films), the camera has been either static or languid with little movement. Mambety's paramount concern has been to develop what might be termed an "African eclecticism." If this creative stance constitutes audacious "rebellion" against the established tradition of African cinema—that is, the slow-paced, linear narrative style typical of *Emitai, Kodou,* and many other African films—in *Touki-Bouki* this pattern is destroyed. What we see is a harbinger of the creative autonomy now favored by the younger generation of black African filmmakers. It is important here to state that while Mambety clarifies without simplification, Sembene, in contrast, attaches importance to simplicity of detail. Yet, as with many other African filmmakers, their differing tactics produce insightful images of the continent's complex formation and patterns of refurbishment of the cultural patrimony.

Black African cinema received a unique boost in 1974, this time from a woman, Safi Faye[13] of Senegal, whose feature-length film *Kaddu Beykat* (Peasant letter, 1974) made an impression in international film festivals as an authentic African ethnographic film. Like *Xala, Kaddu Beykat,* a black-and-white fictionalized introspective documentary, is also very political, delivering pungent attacks on the Senegalese government for its failure to deal with the agricultural predicaments imposed by the hazards of monoculture. (This failure resulted in what Kwame Nkrumah calls the disintegration of the "communalist socio-economic patterns" of Africa.[14] Nkrumah traces this disaster to the beginning of imperialism and colonialism, noting that it was the introduction of export crops such as cocoa and coffee that gradually tied the economy of the colonies to the world capitalist markets that inundated Africa with capitalism, individualism, and private ownership. Although these crops are produced in Africa, in reality the prices are regulated in foreign markets. So, in the Senegalese village of Beykat, peanuts are the essential cash crop and fluctuation of prices leaves the farmers in peril. It is the adverse impact of such measures upon producers (the plight of the peasants) that inspired the theme of *Kaddu Beykat.*

Structured in the form of a letter to a friend about village life, this film interlaces themes of village life, temporality, and work, from dawn to dusk. Here, Faye's camera follows the village from its awakening, showing peasants in their daily routine, doing domestic chores, working in the dusty fields, singing work songs, enjoying family meals, with glimpses of traditional medicine practices and the customs of courtship and marriage. We see the village elders in their traditional evening meetings remembering the old days when everything was abundant, now expressing fear and concern about an unpredictable future. The style of this film does not conform to what Michelson calls the "meta-cinematic paradigm"[15] or to the manipulation of the process of production, for example, as in René Clair's *Paris qui dort,* or to the "camera pyrotechnics," as Leyda calls them,[16] of Dziga Vertov's *The Man with a Movie Camera.* Rather, its rhythm and rhyme is enunciated by an analytical ethnographic and socioanthropological approach to filmmaking (from an African perspective). This filmic approach reveals not only Faye's training in ethnography but also her observational skill, seen in her foregrounding of genuine cultural details typical of the daily routine. Her style would influence foreign filmmakers (whose ethnographic African films hitherto bear the trademark of exoticism) toward a more meaningful approach to studying Africa through film.

Although there are technical problems in this film, the "serene authoritative touch" seen here is so wide in scope and so satisfying that one cannot but concur with Clyde Taylor that "something new was being brought to African visual art."[17] Faye's participatory involvement is one of intense observation. Because she belongs to the society being filmed, Faye successfully persuaded the participants (who are not professional actors) to remain themselves before the camera, as she stays behind as far as possible, "watching" without trying to disturb the flow of events. *Kaddu Beykat* is a powerful and haunting sociopolitical statement that was unfortunately banned in Senegal, preventing the dissemination of its rich message.

If by reproaching bureaucratic ineptitude *Kaddu Beykat* carries complex social, economic, political, and historical thematic freight, *Xala* (1974), by Ousmane Sembene, is an allegorical tale of corruption told with simplicity and bathed in biting satire exposing the emerging neocolonial bourgeoisie. This ringing critique of an excessively corrupt national leadership underscores the disappointment and affliction in neocolonial Senegal, and in Africa in general. *Xala* succinctly recapitulates many of the important motifs in African cinema—concern about the role of syncretic religions, the relationship between colonizer and colonized, and the neocolonialist quagmire generally.

The film narrates the rise and fall of its chief protagonist, El Hadj Abdou Kader Beye, a prototype of the new breed of Senegalese businessman in the import-export sector of the newly independent country's new economy. (El Hadj means "pilgrim." In the Islamic faith it refers to a man who has been on a pilgrimage to Mecca and has returned to his home in a "holy state." The spelling varies depending on the country of usage, namely, El Hadj, Alhaj, or Alhaji, and a woman pilgrim is referred to as Adja or Alhaja.) His ascension to power culminates in his membership in the Chamber of Commerce. As a sign of status, El Hadj decides to take a third wife. On the night of the ceremony he suffers from "xala," a temporary impotency caused by a spell cast on him by a beggar, a former landowner whom he had once cheated. As a result, El Hadj is confronted with the problem of regaining his potency to consummate his marriage. The problem becomes so all-consuming that he neglects his business affairs and his responsibilities as a member of the Chamber of Commerce. He finds himself in deep financial trouble as he devotes all his time consulting with the marabouts to have the curse removed so that his potency can be restored.

Basically, *Xala*'s story is straightforward and direct. On the one hand, *Xala* is a comedy told in the typical African storytelling tradition

Ousmane Sembene: Xala; *Senegal, 1974.* Courtesy of the British Film Institute.

to illustrate a simple moral tale. On the other hand, the film poignantly brings to the surface the gullibility of Africa's elite, or what may be termed the nouveaux riches.[18] Sembene sees this elite class of Africans, the heirs to the colonial power structure, as just as perfidious and exploitative as the colonialists they replaced. Sembene denounces their misplaced priorities, their selfishness, and their appetite for imported luxuries—cars, wigs, attaché cases, three-piece suits, air-conditioning, sunglasses, green lawns with twirling sprinklers, American soda pop, French bottled water, and champagne.

Xala derives its effectiveness from the reality it derides, and from the treatment of these issues in Sembene's narrative style, using, for example, the ironic juxtaposition of opposites. From the very beginning of the film, Sembene draws a sharp distinction between the two main classes in Africa, the ruling class and the subject class. While the Chamber of Commerce represents the state, its members represent the exploiting class that shares money looted from the government treasury, while the oppressed sing and dance for independence. So too does El

Hadj's sexual impotence denounce metaphorically Africa's socioeconomic impotence as seen through the miserable conditions of its peasants, beggars, and unemployed. The acerbity with which Sembene's social criticism is lodged in this film is so harsh that the Senegalese censors insisted on cutting out ten scenes from the prints shown in Africa. The director had to distribute "fliers which indicated the scenes which got cut so people [could] get a sense for what is missing."[19]

Sembene, who has been criticized in the past for the lugubrious pace of his films, exhibits a different expertise in *Xala*. An example of his swift cutting is when, at the request of El Hadj, the president of the Chamber of Commerce arrives to hear El Hadj's story of his impotence:

Shot 215	President:	*Walks into El Hadj's office.*
Shot 216	President:	*Laughing, sits.*
Shot 217	President:	The potion was excellent. I see you haven't changed your clothes.
Shot 218	El Hadj:	That's not it. I didn't get it up. Nothing . . .
Shot 219	President:	What?
Shot 220	El Hadj:	No erection last night. The matron says that I have the xala.
Shot 221	President:	Oh shit.
Shot 222	El Hadj:	That's why I need you.
Shot 223	President:	Who did that to you?
Shot 224	El Hadj:	*Stands up.*
Shot 225	President:	*Astonished.*

If we compare *Xala* with *Black Girl* or *Borom Sarret*, we find that Sembene has proven that with practice, perfection of skill is possible, and that denunciation of African film practice need not entail oversimplification of plot and naïveté of style. Although there is a problem with the film's alternation between real time and screen time, many critics agree that this remained a calculation designed to work well with the linear progression of the film's narrative structure. This film makes use of long sequences, long takes, and continuity in relation to real time. Close-ups are not a priority, medium shots dominate, and static shots are preferred to camera movement. But unlike his earlier films, the treatment here enhances the intended didacticism.

Also, Sembene adds to his style the classical Hollywood technique of alternating close-ups with medium shots and medium shots with long shots, though not without some Eisensteinian effects. One particular instance deserves mention. After the remarkable sequence in which El Hadj tells the president about his "xala," El Hadj hears the beggars' music outside his office. In long shot (226) we see fingers playing the strings, followed by a medium shot (227) of El Hadj in the next room looking out. In close-up (228), we see fingers playing the strings, in medium shot (229) we see El Hadj still looking outside, a long shot (230) reveals a group of beggars, some of them standing on crutches, and in medium long shot (231) El Hadj goes to meet the president. Shots 232 to 238 are a series of close-ups similar to the Western newsreel interview style where El Hadj and the president conclude that it is better for hygiene's sake to get rid of the "human rubbish" (the beggars) because their presence in the city is bad for tourism. In some sequences, alternating shots set in motion the film's narrative pace as in the beggars' return to the city to reclaim the environment from which they came. Elsewhere, Sembene contrasts El Hadj's marriage feast with the sharing of the beggars' meager supply of food in order to accentuate the dramatic significance of these two unequal and diverse social spaces.

In both cases, Sembene finds expediency in the use of montage and contrast cuts. Music functions as a good transition device, particularly from shot 226, when the viewer begins to hear the sound of string instruments; but it is not until he cuts to a close-up of the beggar's hands playing the instrument (228) that we learn the source of the music. And Sembene was indeed clever with many staged scenes to direct his audience's attention toward the issues he thinks they should not miss. A typical example is the effective and pronounced use of the shot-reverse shot strategy, not a Sembene priority up to this time, to dramatize the abuse of power by African government functionaries. In *Xala*, Sembene dramatizes the typical character of Africa's neocolonial leaders. As guests start arriving for El Hadj's wedding, Kebe, one of the cabinet ministers, finds time to negotiate a business deal. In medium close-up (106) a businessman is seated and a voice-over is heard as one of the cabinet ministers, walking into the shot, says, "Old boy, what's wrong?" The minister, dressed in a white jacket, sits with the businessman:

Businessman:	Business, business.
Minister:	But it is lively and there are a lot of girls.
Businessman:	Of course, but business . . .
Minister:	And what is your business?
Businessman:	I have a deal going on tourism. I am looking for someone to handle it.
Minister:	If I do, how much?
Businessman:	10 percent.
Minister:	No!
Businessman:	How much?
Minister:	15 percent.
Businessman:	OK, 15 percent.

This is followed by a handshake, but Kebe, who wants to make sure everything has worked out to his advantage, asks how the deal is going to be finalized. The businessman suggests payment by check, but the minister insists that it must be "cash on the line," because he leaves no traces in his deals. In this scene, the check is not accepted because it could implicate the minister in corrupt practices. But elsewhere, when El Hadj, in a legitimate deal, pays the marabout with a check for services provided to cure his "xala," the check becomes legal tender (although it bounces).

A film with many humorous scenes, *Xala* is imbued with psychological depth evoking both pathos and laughter. The contradictory roles of the check are just one of the multiple confusions in the film, emblematic of neocolonial African administration. Sembene's microscopic view of Africa will continue to awaken people's consciousness (Africans and non-Africans) to the "xalarous" afflictions of Africa for a long time to come. The issues he portrayed in 1974 are still burningly relevant nineteen years after the film was released.

Although religion is not the central issue in *Xala,* Sembene alludes to it through El Hadj, a devout Muslim, thereby putting Islam at the focal point of Africa's corruption. Presented merely as a prelude to Islam's role in the tension between imported structure and the old resilient culture, this issue is elaborated on in Sembene's next film *Ceddo* (1976). The story of *Ceddo* is set in what appears to be the late eighteenth or early nineteenth century when North African Arabs scrambled for Islamic expansion into Africa. This expedition was pursued aggressively, forcing Africans to convert to Islam and submit to its ideology. For those who resisted this mandatory indoctrination, death was the penalty. While some Africans submitted to the invading forces, others fled and migrated, and many opted to defend their cultural identity, waging stiff resistance. In Senegal, such were the Ceddos, from whom Sembene's film derives its theme.

Ceddo begins in an African village heavily infiltrated by Islamic intrusion. The king of the village and some of his subjects succumb to the ideological orbit of the Islamic faith. The Muslim Imam, having accomplished this goal, now wants to extend his dragnet by converting still more villagers. The king, heeding the Imam's advice, imposes undue punishment on resisters who choose to cling to their native gods and belief in African culture. A distressed villager, a *ceddo,* gallantly protests the king's weakness by kidnapping the king's daughter and pledging to free her only when the king restores the identity usurped by Islam. However, the king dies and the Imam takes charge of the throne, launching the conversion drive forcefully and brutally and in the end

Ousmane Sembene: Ceddo; *Senegal, 1976.* Courtesy of the British Film Institute.

rescuing the princess, whom he intends to marry. The Imam is eventually slain by the princess.

[The liberated role Sembene accords this female drastically violates
Islamic doctrine of relegating a woman to second-class citizenry] By
doing this Sembene proposes a new vision for Africa. In line with his
masterful tradition of heightening awareness of the obstacles to
progress eroding Africa, here Sembene takes his audience across the
continent, penetrating deeply into its history as it pertains to Islamic
and Catholic expeditions into sub-Saharan Africa, European slave
trade, and Africa's response to foreign invasion. Though the film revolves around these issues, *Ceddo* is an iconoclastic film, devastatingly
antireligious, focusing mainly on the Islamic impact and particularly
questioning the subjugation entrenched in its ideology and the acceptance of this ideology by Africans to the extent of rendering traditional
cultures impotent. Sembene deals with "cruel sweet truth," with an
aspect of African history that has often been distorted, in the sense
that Muslims are seldom depicted as disruptive of African culture as
the Christians have been.

Sembene is so committed to African affairs that he could, in the
interest of preservation of national culture, point out the contradictions

in Africa as he sees them, even in his own sect. *Ceddo* is indeed prophetic! Sembene's vision of the vestiges of confusion deriving from imported ideologies makes one reflect upon the disastrous consequences lodged in the gulf between opposing imported religions. In Nigeria for instance, since 1980, periodic eruptions of political violence by the militant Islamic Maitatsine[20] movement have left hundreds of people dead. Similarly, Muslim students of northern Nigerian universities, invoking Islamic fundamentalism, have gone on rampages, decimating Christians and animists and wantonly destroying their property. With the revival of indigenous cultures (vis-à-vis traditional religion) off the agenda in these regions, Islam is indeed waxing in strength. In fact, in modern African countries there is increased agitation toward the creation of Islamic republics. Islamic penal law, known as *Sharia*, is in effect in some countries and is the driving force in the rivalry between Sudan's Muslim-dominated north and its Christian-populated animist south. (In the same manner, and contrary to what is maintained in Muslim countries like Saudi Arabia, Iran, and Pakistan, the title Alhaji or Alhaja is gaining precedence over hard-earned internationally acclaimed qualifications. Hence it is common practice in Nigeria or Ghana, for instance, that a former pilgrim who is a professor with a doctorate degree would be addressed as Alhaji Dr. X; a medical doctor would prefer Alhaji first before Dr. X; and an army general would prefer Alhaji before general.)

Hence, *Ceddo* is about cultural colonialism; Sembene's recognition of Africa's surrender to this type of foreign ideology led him to ask whether Africa will ever again hold onto its own traditions and values. Since this bitter question was too hard-hitting for the Christian president, Leopold Sédar Senghor, of Muslim-dominated Senegal to swallow, the film was banned for eight years. The official reason the government gave for this prohibition was that *Ceddo* was spelled with two "d's" instead of one.

Mahama Johnson Traoré's *Njangaan* (also spelled *Ndiongane*; Senegal, 1975) and Alhaji Adamu Halilu's *Shaihu Umar* (Nigeria, 1976) are two other films that express views about the Muslim religion in African societies—but from different perspectives.[21] While *Njangaan* strongly impugns the misuse of Islam in the exploitation of children, for instance, *Shaihu Umar* masks the blemishes in the Islamic African expedition (such as slavery, tyranny, and murder), giving it a "civilizing" status and glorifying its mission. Traoré, who earlier in his career had made *Reouh-Takh* (Big city, 1972), a film Senegalese authorities banned for being too critical of that country's sociopolitical laxities, was not deterred and made *Njangaan,* a ferocious and unrelenting attack on what the director calls "spiritual colonization."[22] Like Sembene, Traoré advocates political use of cinema. Although he does not condemn entertainment films, he believes that African filmmakers must not "try to impose a vision of life that is alien to Africa."[23] This philosophy of reasoning binds Sembene and Traoré together and separates them from Halilu in their quest for African identity.

All three filmmakers are Muslims; Sembene and Traoré perhaps not as ardent and alienated as Halilu (as his title Alhaji appears to indicate). In fact, Halilu's film is an adaptation of a novel whose author, the former prime minister of Nigeria, a Muslim devotee with two alien titles, Alhaji Sir Abubakar Tafawa Balewa. Sembene's and Traoré's "rebellion" can be understood from their commitment to focus their lens on what is wrong in African society, even in their own cultural "backyard." While they understand Islam to be a form of alienation that derives from Arab countries in the same way that political and economic colonization of Africa came from France, Britain, and others, they do not condemn the Islamic institution as a whole, but rather the oppression and deception they see in its practice.

Njangaan, Traoré's best-known work to date, jointly produced by the now defunct Société Nationale de Cinéma (SNC) of Senegal and Sunu Films, is a true story that exposes the exploitation of children by Islamic Imams under the guise of the Muslim religion. In this film, Njangaan is a young boy in a Koranic school headed by a marabout who sends the schoolchildren out to hustle in the streets and beg for money, which ends up in his pocket as payment for their education. The boy's parents, who believe that Koranic education is unparalleled, do not raise any objections. It is during one of these outings that Njangaan is hit and killed by a Mercedes Benz and his father accepts this cruel fate as the will of Allah.

Ceddo and *Njangaan* celebrate lessons in history with authenticity, hard work, dedication, talent, and ingenuity. *Njangaan's* ending calls the viewer's attention to the same themes vigorously emphasized in *Ceddo*—[an examination of Africa's bankrupt social institutions and the submission of indigenous traditions to alien forces.] Both films simultaneously reveal and denounce the mechanisms of alienation responsible for the disintegration of indigenous cultural identities.

In this same period, films emerging from different countries expressed broad-based issues of general concern rather than those of the individual filmmaker. Thus, in Cameroon, for example, forced marriages, excessive dowries, and emancipation of women find treatment in Jean Pierre Dikongue-Pipa's *Muna Moto* (The other child, 1975), Daniel Kamwa's *Pousse-pousse* (Pedicab, 1975), and *Le prix de la liberté* (The price of freedom, 1978). In Senegal, Moussa Bathily's *Tiyabu Biru* (Circumcision, 1977) focuses on that topic. In Mali, Alkaly Kaba's

Wamba (Between water and fire, 1976) examines the caste system and social inequality, while Souleymane Cissé's *Baara* (Work, 1976) looks at class struggle. In Benin, Richard de Meideros's *Le nouveau venu* (The newcomer, 1977) explores bureaucracy and corruption; in Ethiopia, Haile Gerima's *Harvest: 3,000 Years* (1976) takes on feudal repression; and in Mauritania, Med Hondo's *West Indies* (1979) presents the mechanisms of colonization and slavery.

Of utmost significance to the period's development are the stated objectives of the Federation Pan-Africain de Cinéastes (FEPACI) meeting held in Algiers in 1975.[24] Its charter invokes the need for African films to play an educational role in bringing to consciousness African reality and African problems. Their recommendations can be seen as an important shift toward relating all aspects of production to the culture of the receiver—the African audience. Here, too, lies the importance of film signification, which is not to be randomly chosen but to be put at the center of the process of negotiating interactive ideas of meaning, closely related to Roland Barthes's idea of "two orders of signification"—the denotative and connotative.[25] On the denotative (*what* is photographed) and connotative (*how* it is photographed) levels, the meaning of this new construction of African reality is to be produced through a union of negotiation among the author, the text, and the audience. It seems to this writer that the FEPACI resolution envisages the possibility that by activating various signifiying elements, they can function as determinants of the level of emotion a film can generate in the process of public enlightenment. Hence, while such films as Tidiane Aw's *Le bracelet de bronze* (1974) and Kamwa's *Pousse-pousse* were box-office hits, they were being attacked by critics "for being overwhelmingly spectacular and less committed to demystifying neocolonialism," while directors like Sembene, Hondo, and Traoré were being commended for "de-emphasizing the sensational and commercial aspects and emphasizing instructional values,"[26] thus raising consciousness and awareness of African situations.

In this regard, although certain aspects of Dikongue-Pipa's *Muna Moto,* Cameroon's first feature and an award-winning parable on the dowry system and woman's place in society, could be said to be sensational in its approach, it manages to qualify such an opinion through its stylistic amalgam within a poetic structure. This amalgam includes flashbacks, dream and fantasy sequences, the fusion of oral tradition and dominant narrative principles, and an editing strategy that incorporates abnormal juxtapositions independent of the time and space continuum. As a director who admires Ingmar Bergman, Luis Buñuel, Sembene, and Cissé,[27] Dikongue-Pipa's distinctive vision, often lyrical, is neither entirely Western nor entirely African. The film synthesizes indigenous African concerns with a peculiarly personal response to a societal inequity—the spiraling dowry as fixed by the elders. Though the film attacks the abuses of traditional culture, it does not hesitate to attribute this profligacy to colonialism's introduction of money. In precolonial Africa the dowry was only a symbolic gesture whereby a single kola nut had a treasured cultural significance as opposed to the huge sum of money now involved in getting married.[28] *Muna Moto* deals with a continental fact. While its theme is imbued with moral and political overtones, in the observation of an anonymous commentator in *Sequence* magazine, it is neither "moralistic" nor "politicized."[29] It is simply a beautiful film endorsed as one of the best in black African cinema history.

Muna Moto, Harvest: 3,000 Years, Baara, and *West Indies* are examples of allegorical dramas firmly rooted in oral traditions. They deal with controversial issues rendered in inventive styles emanating from the search for African film language. Visually and narratively, they do not conform to the dominant mode of representation. The filmmakers' technical virtuosity, fused with strong political convictions, enables them to eschew the caricatures fabricated by European and American filmmakers and to promote a genuine understanding of Africa's socio-economic complexity. The inquiry, imagination, and ideological positioning posited in these films are illuminating. Cissé, Gerima, and Hondo represent an intellectual class of African filmmakers trained in American and European universities and film schools. The analytical prowess they bring to their work is a direct result of this training, experience, and the understanding of the need to build upon what the pioneers have already established. The primary concern here is the exploitation of film's full aesthetic possibilities and political potential. Like the pioneering films of the sixties, these African films continue to focus on the diverse problems that envelop various segments of African communities, including the black diaspora—as in the case of *West Indies.* This motivation prompted the expansion and proliferation of new ideas, new creativity, and a new trend that is now giving independent African cinema fresh focus.

"The films of Soulemane [*sic*] Cissé of Mali, trained in Moscow (like Sembene and Sara [*sic*] Maldoror)," notes Clyde Taylor, "have found a form that lies somewhere between the extended parables of Sembene and the disrupting strategies of Med Hondo and Haile Gerima."[30] In recognition of the creative might of this humble filmmaker, Roy Armes also observes that Sembene's work "is matched for critical rigor and creative excitement by Cissé in three masterly features of increasing stylistic complexity: *Den Muso* (The young girl, 1974), *Baara* (Work, 1979), and *Finye* (The wind, 1982)"[31]—to which one should now add

Yeelen (Brightness, 1987). In fact, *Baara* enjoyed immense popular success, becoming the first African film shown in 1982 in prime-time on a French television station (FR3), and *Yeelen* has played at the Samuel Goldwyn Theaters in Los Angeles, California, and at the Public Theater in New York City.

In their authentic depiction of Africa, Cissé's films, as social dramas, cannot avoid being political and didactic. For him, film must "address issues of the utmost concern and implication to his society, with the hope of positive change."[32] The first film made after his Moscow education, *Cinq jours d'une vie* (Five days in a life, 1972) criticized the poor practical education offered by Africa's Koranic schools (an issue dealt with by Traoré in *Njangaan*) and also delved into aspects of urban hardships suffered by the young, unskilled people who rush to the cities in search of jobs (a topic treated in Ampaw's *Kukurantumi*). Following this is *Den Muso,* about a young, mute, unwed pregnant woman whose story Cissé uses to denounce parental attitudes toward daughters who are ostracized for going against tradition. *Baara* introduces a critical view of trade unionism never before explored in African cinema in the same way that *Finye* offers insight into Africa's military regimes.

Made with the help of France's Institut National de l'Audio Visual, *Baara* conducts a filmic foray into Bamako, the capital city of Mali, cinematically examining daily life, with exquisite attention to detail. The film opens with an extreme close-up of Balla Diarra, a porter, sweating profusely. As the camera pulls back, we notice that this young man is not moving fast, but rather in slow motion, walking in an environment engulfed in flames. This figure embodies the image of itinerant workers, as in Sembene's *Borom Sarret,* who flock to the cities in search of jobs; the flame metaphorically symbolizes the frightening urban life seen here as the center of corruption, greed, retrogression, and injustice where everything moves at a snail's pace (as the slow motion seemingly suggests). On one of his rounds, Balla Diarra meets a young engineer, Balla Traoré, who befriends him. Traoré offers him a job in the factory where he works. The engineer's humane attitude toward the factory workers initiates Diarra into the laborers' struggle against the oppression by a factory boss who personifies the new class of African elite. The unfeeling factory boss murders his wife, whom he accuses of infidelity, and has the popular engineer killed for his involvement with the trade union. This provokes, ironically, exactly what the factory boss was trying to suppress—a general revolt.

Among the social and political messages raised here, one instance is especially touching. It concerns the character of the young engineer, portrayed as self-effacing and who identifies with the working class. This is made clear when he stresses his objection to being addressed

Souleymane Cissé: Baara (*Work*); *Senegal, 1978.* Courtesy of the British Film Institute.

as the "Boss." "My name is Traoré," he retorts. It is here that Cissé pinpoints a very important virulent affliction of African society. This film is also about etiquette, dedication, and patriotism and seems to be saying, "Do whatever you do well and without discrimination or class consciousness." For those factory workers who have witnessed indigenous engineers wearing ties and spotless shirts in production lines, standing aloof, giving orders, and pointing out to the fitter mechanic (lower technician) which part of the machine to loosen and fix, *Baara* would impress them as a film that could also pass for an industrial training program and that could undoubtedly help eliminate pride and prejudice in every facet of contemporary life—if the content is absorbed as intended.

This film is a conglomeration of thematic elements cleverly woven together to bring the viewer to an empathetic perception of the underlying social problems. While showing the humane aspects of the engineer, the director also devotes time to revealing his bad character (as in the maltreatment of his wife). The depiction of the engineer is sociologically acute and biographically nuanced; he is portrayed as a fallible member of the upper class who nevertheless identifies with the struggles of the workers. The various elements operating in the episodes are unified by the narrative strategy employed—specifically related to the Marxist notion of history as essentially collective. For example, while *Baara* does not discard the sense of individual identity, it expresses the congeniality of a collective force. The latter is the larger perspective the film aspires to, and even when motivations and responses are examined through individual characters, this collective endeavor is never sacrificed. Cissé conveys this sense of the whole through expert direction, good acting by nonprofessional actors, and fine camera work, along with his skillful use of music, which strengthens the film's impact on the audience. However, some of his scenes still tend to drag, and some lack coherent editing. For example, a woman's hands in close-up rubbing cream on her palm and fingers is a rather tedious shot, lasting more than forty seconds before the camera zooms out to reveal her identity. One would have assumed that Africans already know what body lotion is and how to apply it to the body.

Haile Gerima's *Harvest: 3,000 Years* is one of the most highly acclaimed films made in black Africa. A professor of film at Howard University, this director openly acknowledges the influences of Sembene and Hondo for their insistence on communicating through African culture but maintains that he identifies more with Hondo "in terms of anger," sharing "his obsession with history and self-reliance."[33] Indeed, in *Harvest* one sees the same type of strong historical portrayal, dialectical structuring, and the disruptive film language typical of Hondo and reflective of the angry response to centuries of oppression.

Harvest, a painful testimony about Ethiopia's societal conflict, was shot in Amharic, the major language of that country. The cost, raised by the filmmaker with the assistance of some friends, was twenty thousand dollars. Using the services of the peasant community, including Gerima's own family members, this film utilizes documentary and ethnographic techniques to capture the perils of a millennia of agonizing poverty and oppression endured by Ethiopia's peasants. In its revelation of a contemporary family's struggle for survival under a feudalistic landowner, the entire system of class inequality and subjugation is chronicled (reminiscent of the entire African situation), where, according to the fliers accompanying the film's showing, "the harvest of centuries of oppression limits the masses' feelings of freedom to overturn class tyranny." The yearning for justice is loudly proclaimed through the character of a veteran, a madman whom Gerima makes a symbol of political wisdom and who finally kills the repressive landlord who expropriated his land while he was at war.

Gerima's film is subversive in both content and style. A film that dramatizes the process of societal transformation, it illustrates its inevitability with a revolutionary cinematic technique in which elaborate compositions create hypnotic images rendered through good camera work, strong editing strategy, as well as an innovative use of music and silence. To call attention to the mechanics of oppression in the village (a situation the film presents as atrocious and deplorable), Gerima's strategy is to invoke sympathy for the peasants as well as to justify the need for violence as the only avenue left for the repossession of one's dignity. Here again, as in most African films, Fanon's concept of what is deemed the necessarily violent restructuring of African political systems manifests itself in the structure and in the severity of the denunciation of the neocolonial systems. For example, the portrayal of the landlord and his unpatriotic practices, his ruthlessness, and his usurpation of power conveyed in all their vivid and tragic dimensions allude to Fanon's thesis on "the pitfalls of national consciousness." In *The Wretched of the Earth,* Fanon argues that

> the national bourgeoisie of underdeveloped countries is not engaged in production, nor in invention, nor building, nor labor; it is completely canalized into activities of the intermediary type. Its innermost vocation seems to be to keep in the running and to be part of the racket. . . . Seen through its eyes, its mission has nothing to do with transforming the nation.[34]

The politics of the film can be seen emerging from the juxtaposition of opposites; thus, the feudal landlord is presented as lazy, repressive, exploitative, and comfortable, while the vassals who work for him are the hardworking, even subservient victims of poverty. Here is a Marxist activist dialectical arrangement situated within the politics of pan-Africanism comparable to the film structuring of Sembene, Hondo, and Cissé. Within the film's pattern of binary oppositions we find a blend of oral narrative art where symbols, metaphors, and connotations interact with other elements of the filmic mode for a unity of purpose and unparalleled emotional impact. Similarly, as in the oral tradition, in which the storyteller's repetitious verbosity highlights certain aspects of reality, the repetitious sequences[35] in *Harvest* encourage audience contemplation of the meaning of the images and also provide a way for the filmmaker to exert his authorial voice, strengthening the emotional tone of the film. This method clarifies the position of the peasants under feudal repression even though various Eurocentric criticisms have denounced the technique. Clyde Taylor's brilliant summation is indeed very apt:

Gerima's slow-paced, black and white staging transports his spectacle beyond neorealism into a timeless collective memory. The grace and elegance of the peasants' movements, the unalienated, unsentimental firmness of their love for each other, the eloquent testimony of their faces in this nearly silent film, the spirituality of the daily culture, impart to their story an antiquity of Biblical resonance. In one scene the peasant father makes a long trek up the hill to bow to the rebukes of the landlord who is seated atop with a view of his domain. In a dream sequence, a young woman and her parents are driven through the fields, yoked like oxen to a plough, a whip cracking overhead. These images are unforgettable. Such moments make *Harvest* more convincing than fact or fiction.[36]

There is no question that *Harvest* is a landmark in the search for a model African film aesthetic. The camera work is very sophisticated, but the pacing is extremely slow. A second viewing of the film, however, convinced me that the slow pace contributed to setting the emotional tone of the entire film as it unearthed the highly repressive situation and the revolt and violence that ensued. This slow pacing also increases the audience's awareness, enabling them to grasp some minute details that might lead to questions and answers after the projector lamp dims and the theater lights go on again. *Harvest* was shot in 16mm and blown up to 35mm to conform to the projection facilities in Ethiopia, but as of this writing, not surprisingly, it has not been officially shown in that country, although pirated video copies of the film are hawked on the streets of Addis Ababa.[37] It is also the only film Gerima has made in his native Ethiopia. Although he has made several other features in the United States, their themes concern black American experiences, and those films are consequently seen as belonging to the African American independent film movement.

If Gerima's *Harvest* is an inexorably authentic depiction of Africa's reality, the search for the heart of things is made concrete by Hondo's *West Indies*. This film, an exuberant, phenomenal musical pageant, utilizes song, dance, and exotic costumes to create an exhilarating, spellbinding filmic opera with colorful cinematography. The film traces with candor black people's history, the perennial past and present oppression in the black diaspora from French colonialism, slavery, and the postindependence era to the effort to combat this bondage. Shot on an enormous slave-ship set that was constructed in a vast abandoned Citroën factory in Paris, this film is exceptional for its huge budget of $1.35 million—surpassing the cost of any other African film. Hondo's theater experience and many years of cultivating a personal artistic expression can be seen in full gear. Culminating in extraordinary choreography, linked with music and camera movement, an interesting and dramatic force of geographical and historical analysis of an entire culture is displayed.

The film critic Teshome Gabriel, noticing the "experimental forms" in effect here, opined that Hondo's "camera moves where it pleases; {he almost paints with it trying even to penetrate man's inner consciousness."[38] Similarly, the film's unique structure takes place against an epic backdrop—all the action on the ship is either sung or danced, as Armes notes, "acted in symbolic fashion—there is no mistaking the clarity of its analysis of the mechanisms of colonization, slavery"[39] and African accomplices in this dehumanization. The basic philosophy inspiring Hondo's unrestrained creativity, which this author has dwelled upon in chapter 2, can further be traced to the illuminating rhetoric of this ebullient director. In his own analysis, Hondo states that

> our languages, the richness of our history must bring something unique to our cinema. This is why I often say that African filmmakers should be wary of imitating. When one has a particular history, a people with its own way of walking, shaking hands, looking at other people, eating rice, one should film this in a different way, impose a language and make the image serve this language.[40]

Having aroused critical excitement with his first feature, *Soleil O*, a film about an immigrant Arab and black community in France, Hondo's films continued to focus a critical lens on the relationship between Africa and its colonial masters. Thus, his long documentary *Les bicots-nègres, vos voisins* (Arabs and niggers, your neighbors, 1973) encompasses a study of many forms of oppression of Africans, calling attention to the ill-treatment of the North African Arab and black African immigrant labor forces in France. *Nous aurons toute la mort pour dormir* (We will have the whole of death to sleep in, 1977) and *Polisario, un peuple en armes* (Polisario, a people in arms, 1979) elaborate on the Polisario armed resistance against the Mauritanian and Moroccan forces begun in 1975. In the last two films Hondo relates the effects of bloody war on the abysmal living standards in refugee camps. This was followed by *West Indies* and his 1987 epic *Sarraounia*.

Sarraounia further elevates this indefatigable and versatile director to a position of well-earned recognition. This epic film, like Hondo's other ambitious projects, has generated a good deal of excitement in African and international film festivals (attacked in France, though, for being too Manichean). The film also demonstrates a marked shift in strategy from his earlier work. *Sarraounia* is political, less didactic, and features a credible story line. Although the pace of the film lacks the rapid movement of *Soleil O*, this and other shifts in strategy are typical Hondo characteristics. Since the pacing and style of his films are dictated by their themes, the tactics used in *Sarraounia* distance the viewer, giving him or her "respect for the soul of tradition," Hondo notes, "to impose a vision would not be honest."[41]

By 1980, black African cinema had reached a point where it was possible to talk not only about its thematic richness and diversity but also about its aesthetic sophistication. Although much remains to be accomplished regarding the latter, given the frugality of budgets under which films are produced on the continent, an imposing aesthetic excellence is visibly established. While films of the 1970s had already dealt extensively with the search for an African film language and theme, in the 1980s a furtherance of this procedure led to the production of mature films built on past experience. Building on the tradition of the recent past, these films continue to demystify colonial misconceptions. Although some persist in paying homage to the cinematic models of the "pioneers" of African cinema, others have attempted to forge an African aesthetic that combines both the oral tradition and avant-gardist modes. Herein follow some names and titles, some of which have been discussed previously, bearing in mind that while some of the films considered are thematically and aesthetically noteworthy, others may be significant for different reasons.

Sey Seyeti (One man, several wives; Senegal, 1980) by Ben Diogoye Beye dramatizes the impact of polygamy in modern Senegal, exploring the complexities of a new law that requires couples to sign a declaration before the wedding stating whether the bridegroom will remain monogamous. An ambitious project, dealing with an important and controversial topic, this film unfortunately gathers too many diverse themes rendering the treatment slipshod. *Djeli* (1980) by Côte d'Ivoire's Kramo-Lanciné Fadika, and financed by the director with the help of friends, is highly indebted to oral narrative technique. It deals with the contradictions and ambiguities of African tradition (implying the need to change) with cinematographic competence. In this film, social inequalities are emblematic of the caste system in Côte d'Ivoire, whereby griots, who are considered lower class, cannot marry outside their caste. The same masterful procedure is seen dictating the authenticity of *La chapelle* (The chapel; Congo, 1980) by Jean-Michel Tchissoukou. The winner of the Prix de l'Originalité Africaine at the 1981 FESPACO, it was made for the Office National du Cinéma (ONACI) in Congo. Set in the 1930s, it explores the issue of imported religions in Africa (in this case Christianity), and the many forms of deculturalizations it espoused. Others include Ola Balogun's *Cry Freedom* (Nigeria, 1981) and Kwaw Ansah's *Love Brewed in the African Pot* (Ghana, 1981), both self-financed.

The problem of the inability to unite various themes in a coherent structure as posed in *Sey Seyeti* is solved in *Jom* (The story of a people; Senegal, 1981) by Ababacar Samb-Makharam. This politically didactic film is a typical example of how the oral art of storytelling can be integrated with dominant cinematic narrative form to forge a personal film style, or, in a broader sense, African film language, and shall be discussed in this context later. Another politically inspired film of this year is the hard-hitting *Poko* (Burkina Faso) by Idrissa Ouedraogo, which received FESPACO's 1981 Grand Prize for best short. Made on a shoestring budget, this twenty-minute short highlights the problem of villagers who pay taxes and yet have neither medical facilities nor means of transportation in times of emergencies. It portrays the experiences of a young pregnant woman who develops complications and needs urgent medical attention. Because there is no transportation to take her to the city, she is taken by cart, which proves to be too slow, and she dies on the way. The pacing of the film is as slow as that of the journey portrayed, both combining to generate intense emotions in this depiction of catatonic government indifference to the plight of Burkina Faso's peasant communities. Such pungent candor also highlights the political tendency of *En résidence surveillée* (Under house arrest; Senegal, 1981) by Soumanou Vieyra. This film lampoons self-destructive currents in contemporary black African society, the frequency of military coups, and the mechanisms of coups d'état. Military topics had previously been a "restricted" area forbidden to independent black African filmmakers. Although the film is technically flawed and lacks the coherent flow of Souleymane Cissé's portrayal of a similar theme in *Finye* the political impact of *En résidence surveillée* is as vivid as it is inspirational.

Thematically, *Finye* highlights the opposite polarities of tradition as exemplified in the situation of women in West Africa, social conflicts faced by urban youth, polygamy, and corruption within politics, business, and the military. Noting that *Finye* is the first African film to probe in serious depth the "workings of power in an African society under military rule," Roy Armes pinpointed Cissé's effective strategy in the director's choice of

> complex figures who can represent the ambiguities of the times, and he is careful to place the young in a context of traditional African beliefs and values. Though the bulk of the film is shot with a close and precisely focused realism, Cissé does not remain at a simple observational level. His social analysis is sufficiently rich to contain purely symbolic acts and his style subtle enough to shift effortlessly into moments of literal unreality.[42]

The title of the film itself illustrates Cissé's obsession with social realism. It is "composed of ideograms in the Bambara language that represent the evident traces of a heritage to be preserved . . . or perhaps to be discovered."[43] The powerful wind that blows through the film is indicative of the opening epigraph that reads, "The wind awakens the thought of man." An ideological statement reflecting Cissé's concern for the inevitable changes within the African system, it accentuates the overall connotation of *Finye*'s x-ray images of contemporary African societies in a manner reminiscent of *Xala*. Apart from his directorial skill, the audacity with which this astute, diminutive director portrays military and other societal decadence is immeasurable. Ironically, *Finye* was partly financed by the military government of Mali. Tolerance and maturity prevailing, the government demonstrated that it is capable of listening to constructive criticism.[44]

Les coopérants (The cooperative effort; Cameroon, 1982), directed by Arthur Si Bita, finds inspiration in social drama pitting enlightened urban students against village-life conditions. Like *Finye,* which was partly funded by the government but was relentless in criticizing government lapses, Bita's film, funded by Fonds de Developpement de l'Industrie Cinématographique (FODC), is also very critical of the corruption among government functionaries. An interesting exposé of certain aspects of traditional culture and Cameroonian life-styles, *Les coopérants* is technically well polished and focused. It moves at a faster pace than many African films; and unlike *Jom,* for instance, it is not didactic. The musical score by Pierre Akendengue, who also scored the music used in *Sarraounia,* adds impact. However, the startlingly authentic juxtaposition of the sound track is flawed by a rather disconcerting syncretic structure of the image track; to many critics, the disturbing aspect of Bita's strategy is his resorting to an international thriller tradition, a choice that has not only devalued the moralistic tone of the film but also tends to blemish his creative accomplishment, especially if this work is to be examined in relation to our discourse concerning the search for authentic film language resonating from African cultural traditions. It is in this sense that, although we find elements of Western genre in *Touki-Bouki,* this film cannot be put into the same category (thriller) with *Les coopérants.*

By contrast, *Wend Kuuni* (Burkina Faso, 1982) and *Naitou* (Guinea, 1982) by Moussa Kemoko Diakite, within the cultural context of artistic authenticity, can be classified as distinctly African. They both explore, with conviction, the role of African oral tradition as a creative foundation in cinematic narrative, which is why, in all their manifestions, the techniques owe no allegiance to the stylistic trends of other cultures. But the same cannot be said of the highly successful *Visages de femmes*

(Faces of women; Côte d'Ivoire, 1985) by Désiré Ecaré, which was shown on Bravo cable television in the U.S. Although highly indebted to the technique of oral storytelling, the film indulges in a Hollywood kind of sexual exploitation which, like the thriller elements found in *Les coopérants*, it may be argued, does not accurately fit into the concept of genuine African aesthetics.

Naitou should be given adequate attention in future discussions of oral tradition in structural narrative. It is a special film, a major breakthrough in originality and film language, and one-of-a-kind in the history of black African cinema. It is an African tale of Naitou, a young orphan girl in a polygamous home, badly mistreated by the jealous stepmother who killed her real mother. The film has no dialogue, only music and dance performed by the Ballet Africain de Guinée, which provides many of the multifarious African art forms employed in the film. This "film-ballet" is self-explanatory and can be understood without the aid of subtitles, voice-over, or dubbing. For lack of space, this author has chosen to examine the impact of music and dance, both essential elements of oral tradition, within the structure of black African cinema and in *Visages de femmes*.

Another film worth mentioning in this list of significant African films of the 1980s is Ferid Boughedir's *Camera d' Afrique: 20 Years of African Cinema* (Tunisia, 1983), a valuable documentary and visual history of African films and filmmakers. This film provides extensive film clips of "the best African films" and includes interviews with Ola Balogun, Souleymane Cissé, Oumarou Ganda, Med Hondo, Jean Pierre Dikongue-Pipa, Safi Faye, Gaston Kaboré, and Ousmane Sembene. And no list would be complete without Idrissa Ouedraogo's *Issa le tisserand* (Isa the weaver; Burkina Faso, 1985) and *Yaaba* (1989); Ngangura Mweze and Benoit Lamy's raucous musical comedy *La vie est belle* (Life is rosy; Zaire, 1985); Cissé's *Yeelen* (Mali, 1987); Sembene's *Camp de Thiaroye* (Senegal, 1987); Hondo's *Sarraounia* (Mauritania, 1987); and *Mortu Nega* (Guinea-Bissau, 1988) by Flora Gomes. Others include Gaston Kaboré's *Zan Boko* (Burkina Faso, 1988) and Kwaw Ansah's *Heritage . . . Africa* (Ghana, 1988), most of which are presented in chapter 5.

This list of impressive films of this period is by no means exhaustive, nor does the significance of these films reside solely· in the hurdles crossed leading to their production, artistic maturity, and integrity. It shows that these enterprising filmmakers, given the right incentive, are capable of catapulting black African cinema into a productive industry. Sembene once noted, "Our low-budget films are the beginning of a greater future of better African films."[45] The aesthetic success attained so far advocates the introduction of new elements of production and creativity which in turn justify its survival. Therefore, adequate funding is needed to buy equipment and to build exhibition houses where films would be promoted. Since it is almost impossible to generate funds from local sources, nearly all of the films are coproduced and cofinanced by foreign sponsors. Even in Senegal, once considered the most dynamic film center of sub-Saharan Africa, production had abated by the mid-1970s. Sources of state and independent financing were dwindling daily, complicated by the temporary withdrawal of the French Coopération funds. Financing was restored, however, in 1980 when President Fran-çois Mitterrand came to power, once again boosting francophone film production. For other African nations facing economic hardship, it was a matter of seeking money to provide *garri* (toasted cassava [manioc] flour) to feed the teeming population rather than support luxuries (as the cinema is considered).

With the exception of *La chapelle, Wend Kuuni,* and *Les coop-érants,* which were financed by state sponsorship, and *Cry Freedom* and *Love Brewed,* whose productions were independently financed, most of the other films made in the 1980s were not entirely funded by African sources. (And even the first three films had to be *promoted* with French money.) The plight of young aspiring filmmakers is even more pathetic. *N'tturudu* (Guinea-Bissau, 1987), Umban u'Kset's first feature; the shorts *Yellow Fever Taximan* (1985) and *Hommage* (1985), award-winning films by Cameroon's Jean-Marie Teno; and *Poète de l'amour* (Poet of love; Senegal, 1986) by David Ika Diop, featured in the Second Washington, D.C. Film Fest of 1988 all exemplify the work of brilliant directors who might generate significant future surprises. Although paltry financial assistance from the French Coopération helped in part to complete these works, the unresolved problem of distribution and exhibition poses an eternal dilemma for these young filmmakers. It was pitifully disappointing to watch Africa's young filmmakers at this festival and in New York during the United States Information Agency's (USIA) sponsored meetings with film directors and heads of film institutes and studios; they scurried for attention in pursuit of American distributors, even though these filmmakers are still lamenting their past dealings with them, which they acknowledge have not yet yielded encouraging financial results.

Since African films are known to the outside world via international film festivals, it is logical that films coproduced by France are given preference, leaving many good films relatively unknown. To date, Paris still exercises dominant control over international exhibition and recog-nition of African films. Owing to distribution and exhibition problems, more and more African talent remains undiscovered. Manthia Diawara and Elizabeth Robinson, citing *Nyamanton* (The garbage boys; Mali,

1986) by Cheick Oumar Sissoko, advance this notion of France's
"techno-paternalism." This film, described as "a significant turning
point in African cinema" (and which was able to defeat this system
since it was not made with French Coopération funds), did not enjoy
the same promotional and exhibitional advantages accorded African
films produced by France. Diawara and Robinson note that "usually,
when France coproduces African films," not only does it make sure
that French technicians are employed but "it also places [the films] in
festivals, invites the press to see them, and sometimes distributes them
in Paris theaters and on French television."[46] For African films produced outside of France's circuit, trying to break into the system is
excruciating.

In an interview in *New Africa* (April 1988), Hondo lamented the
absence of a coordinated African distribution cartel. Commenting on
how African films that do not sing the chorus of French ideology are
"assassinated" in France he deplored African bureaucratic ineptitude,
cultural inertia, and indifference to cinema. He pointed out that African
biennial film festivals—in Ouagadougou (Burkina Faso) for pan-African
cinema and in Carthage (Tunisia) for Arab and African films—have not
fostered foreign and local interest in the exhibition and distribution
of African cinema. Hondo also blames this stagnation on the political
instability ravaging African countries, noting that as soon as an "intellectual minister" who happens to understand the importance of cinema
is appointed and is willing to contribute positively, all too often he is
replaced or killed (as in the case of President Thomas Sankara).

Captain Sankara, the young and charismatic leader of the West African nation of Burkina Faso, which translates as "the land of democratic
and honest people" (formerly Upper Volta), who was assassinated,
allegedly by close associates, must be remembered for being the only
African leader who was wholeheartedly committed to the development
of African cinema. To the dismay of Africans and lovers of cinema
elsewhere, it is incredible that this country of only eight million people
(and which the World Bank ranked as the poorest in the world after
Ethiopia and Bangladesh) continues to champion the transformation
of the African film industry. Not only has this country demonstrated
continuous willingness to finance local and interstate African productions (one of them being Hondo's *Sarraounia*), it has persistently hosted
the continent's longest ongoing film festival, which started in 1969.
Sankara was exemplary in strengthening this commitment in the 1980s.
This genuine revolutionary gained a reputation as "the angry young
voice of Africa." He had a strong vision for Africa and its culture and
for black African films "as a bridge between nations and peoples."[47]
A realist in a world of fatalists, President Sankara brought energizing

Ouagadougou: Place des Cinéastes Africains. Sculpture celebrating Ouagadougou as the place of African
cinema. Courtesy of FESPACO Permanent Secre-
tariat.

candor to the Tenth FESPACO held a few months before he was killed
at the age of thirty-seven.

Sankara was detested by corrupt older African leaders for his unorthodox ideas and his outspokenness, decency, and good leadership.
To African youth, whom the postindependence era has provided with
nothing other than misery and deprivation, he is still regarded even
after his death as mentor, idol, and symbol of resurrected progressivism. With regard to how his death affects black African cinema, we
cannot say with any certainty whether his successors possess Sankara's
dynamism but African cinema clearly has received one more setback.

The 1980s showed a coordinated struggle against almost three decades of a dearth of facilities and have revealed that the most viable way

of maintaining the continuous flow of African film production would be an increase in coproduction. Emmanuel Sanon-Doba of Burkina Faso coproduced with Cuba a film called *Desebagato* (The last salary, 1985). It was a disappointing film, castigated by African critics for its stereotypical portrayal of African women. Expansion of coproduction with Latin America is progressing, involving Fernando Birri of Argentina, the director of the Havana International Film School.[48] Britain's Channel 4 television is also involved in backing African productions, such as *Cinéma Arabe,* a documentary by Ferid Boughedir used to introduce a season of screenings of Arab films on Channel 4. They have also partially financed Sembene's six-part TV miniseries "Samory Toure," which is about a legendary African known for his stand against French colonialism, and *Ouaga: African Cinema Now* (1988) and *Ama* (1990/91), both coproduced by Efiri Tete Films and codirected by Kwate Nee-Owoo and Kwesi Owusu of Ghana. *Ouaga,* a documentary on the tenth anniversary of FESPACO, explores the question of form, content, and structure of African cinema through interviews with African directors.

Oral Tradition and the Aesthetics of Black African Cinema

Black African cinema and African artisan crafts, both influential vectors of oral tradition, share a sociocultural structure—a system of ideas and images—as collective synthesis of a society that never tires of defining itself to itself and to the rest of the world. Here lies the core of a tradition that gathers elements of reflection and introspection, provoking real-life discussion of the African condition. Using allegorical means, black African cinema achieves this, thus placing new emphasis on the well-known African tradition of making a point with stories—an important aspect of African life not widely disseminated to the outside world, except in literary circles.

The structure of African storytelling is composed of a variety of cultural and symbolic configurations. Much of this variety has been discussed in chapter 1, where I noted that its significance is enunciated in the cohesive web surrounding the relationship among the text, the spectator (audience), and the performing artist (orator-narrator). This symbiotic relationship among the artist, text, and spectator, which African writers have so eloquently stressed,[49] has also posed problems for African novelists and filmmakers, problems concerning language and the means of technical reproduction—the Africanization of the medium. For example, writing in Africa's languages is inhibiting since numerous languages abound. Chinua Achebe, Nigeria's veteran novelist, felt that the English language was capable of transporting his African views, noting that the language must "be a new English still in full communion with its ancestral home but altered to suit its new African surroundings."[50] This view is antithetical to Ngugi wa Thiong'o's radical advocacy of writing in African languages in order to restructure African literature.[51] Like other controversial passages in the article from which Achebe's statement was extracted, and seen in conjunction with early African writers who held similar views and who are often criticized by African writers,[52] Ngugi's dictum would also be limited and fails to provide an antidote to the problems of Ousmane Sembene, a novelist turned filmmaker. Anxious to spread his messages beyond conventional boundaries, specifically to the illiterate community (the peasants), Sembene resorted to making films. Oral dissemination of information is slow. The printed word is faster, but illiteracy reduces its efficacy. With film, the visual images can spread the message more effectively. Even if the language used poses some problems, the message of the film image is still discernible to the viewer. Written literature and film depend on technology, but film transcends oral tradition and literature because it allows for wider coverage by producing audio and visual images simultaneously.[53]

The choice of film production means acceptance of European technology and codes of representation. But as to their application in the African context, it was only a short time before African filmmakers discovered the means of integrating traditional aesthetics into the stylistic repertory of world cinema. These modes of representation would resonate with indigenous codes and African sensibility. Like the African novels which developed precisely out of this instrument of cultural symbiosis, one of the expedient ways to inject African cinema with a dose of authenticity is to exploit the interlocking elements of the continent's cultural heritage. This tremendous fund of African imagery, ritual-spiritual language, music, dance, metaphor and proverbs, the mythic components and poetic resonances of the oral traditions, when adopted to filmic codes, would produce film aesthetics that are African.

Black African cinema, in this regard, has already dedicated itself to a genuine refurbishment of the continent's culture. The significance of its services to the African people is that it is persistent in highlighting images of historical experience, cultural identity, and national consciousness in past and present struggles. Whether some of the views expressed remain optimistic or pessimistic, whether they provide solutions to the impending crisis or not, the point is that these films are presenting debatable issues to the public by utilizing African cultural associations in a unique fashion no foreigner is capable of providing. How has African cinema imbued the dominant film structure with oral tradition to penetrate the African condition and bring to the surface

African facts to inform the public? Is this tradition holding, and how has it been utilized in filmic narrative patterns?

Oral tradition and the aesthetics of African cinema are becoming the subject of exploration by African film historians and critics whose studies are pertinent to the understanding of African film practice. While Mbye Cham[54] links Sembene's storytelling capability to that of the *gewel* (griot or storyteller) and the *lekbat* (also storyteller), François Pfaff[55] sees this trait encompassing Sembene's narrative techniques in such films as *Borom Sarret, Xala,* and *Ceddo,* where the griot's role is elaborated. In another perspective, while Manthia Diawara[56] analyzes the role of the griot in Sembene's films, this analysis is extended to the work of other directors—providing a detailed examination of oral tradition as an aesthetic device in cinematic narrative in the same way that Teshome Gabriel[57] explores oral narrative and film form in *Harvest: 3,000 Years.*

Clearly, the topic of oral tradition and the aesthetics of African cinema is wide-ranging enough that it demands exploration from diverse perspectives to broaden the dialogue and to study its application to specific films. My task here is to engage some salient principles of narrative functioning and explore the full effect of oral narrative as a force for "Africanizing" film language. Among the variable patterns of oral literature serving as influences, I shall be considering such elements as interventions and digressions that help to shift points of view in time and space; dramatic illustrations carved out of multiple narrative voices, for example, the story-within-a-story; transgressions by means of flashback and flash-forward; and music as narrative structure.

Let me start by declaring that the process of narration in black African films is an outgrowth of the oral tales and the epic poem narrative tradition.[58] The African cinema, like its counterpart the African novel, has antecedents in African oral literature. The most important element in oral literature (as in the novel and the cinema) is the story, which builds the structure, the climax, and the resolution. In order to establish how oral tradition operates in the aesthetic mode, it is essential to posit the structure of oral art (the interconnected system of signifiers and cultural codes) that enables the construction and creation of alternative cinematic forms.

Ababacar Samb-Makharam's *Jom,* coproduced with Germany's Zweites Deutschen Fernsehen (ZDF television), is a good example of black African cinematic strategy completely reliant on oral tradition. In this film, a griot relates to his listeners the story of Dieri Dior (Oumar Seck), who murders a French colonial administrator. In the rage that follows the revenge, Dieri, rather than surrender, decides to die a dignified death by killing himself. The ramifications of this dignified act are recalled through the story of Khaly during a present-day labor strike. A strike breaks out in 1980 in a large industrial complex. As a result, two opposing groups emerge. While one fights for better salaries and for the reinstatement of retrenched workers, the other sabotages this effort by accepting management's new proposals. This precipitates Khaly, the griot, to step up his role as trustee of traditional values, to serve as the catalyst for unification of the opposing sides. Khaly plays the guitar and sings words of wisdom. Recollecting the past, he tells the story of Prince Dieri, the ruler who had died honorably rather than lose his "jom" (dignity, courage, or respect).

Narrated by a griot, the film reveals the multidisciplinary talent of the storyteller. Samb-Makharam acknowledges in his production notes that the griot "is also an endless source where painters, writers, historians, filmmakers, archivists, storytellers, and musicians can come to feed their imaginations."[59] In the oral tradition, the griot is endowed with multiple functions, as musician, dancer, and storyteller; he is the storehouse of oral tradition. The peripatetic nature of his performance enables him to recount to listeners the history of the entire community. His audience can in turn pass such knowledge on to others who are not present, in an endless transmission—passing from mother to sons and daughters, generation to generation. It is this type of knowledge that would precipitate, if need be, mass mobilization.

In *Jom*, Samb-Makharam uses oral storytelling techniques to create a visual definition of sociopolitical African history as seen through the virtues of "jom." According to the director, Jom is a Wolof concept that has no direct equivalent in English but loosely translated means the origin of all virtues, "dignity, courage, respect." Jom is concerned with traditional values, equality for all, respect, and efficiency. The director adds in his production note that

> it guides the lives and behaviors of thousands of people in West Africa. For them, it is Jom which makes a man and not his family origins or his wealth. Jom protects us against the absurdities of life. It keeps us away from lies and cowardice. . . . Jom is beyond God and beyond evil.[60]

This film's absorbing narrative is imbued with simple oral art, and a parallel between film and the folktale is skillfully drawn. It juxtaposes the past with the present, the colonial with the contemporary. In the tradition of oral patterns, *Jom* proclaims loyalty to indigenous values, exhibiting cultural symbols and political knowledge in a somewhat didactic manner. Samb-Makharam's gradual sense of discovery is evoked by cultural codes and symbols that reveal a series of paradoxes. Colonial domination engenders indigenous resistance, which in turn pro-

Ababacar Samb-Makharam: Jom, ou l'histoire d'un peuple (*Jom, or The Story of a People*); *Senegal, 1981.* Courtesy of the Françoise Pfaff Collection.

duces the bourgeois elites of neocolonialism. The film proceeds to suggest ways in which to alleviate the inequities of the neocolonial order and restore "rights and dignity." At the heart of the film the director places the protagonist, the griot, not a star in the Hollywood system, in a position relating his own response to African events. In this film, the griot defines the thematic specificity that shapes the entire narrative structure. Samb-Makharam sees the filmmaker as an educator or an artist who must "be viewed as a conscious member of a society, as sculptors used to be in traditional African societies."[61] Here, the filmmaker's service to this society parallels the typical role of the griot in the oral tradition who must function as a "living archive of his people's tradition."[62] In this film, as in oral art, the griot, song, dance, metaphors, and the story-within-a-story mark the film's exemplary articulation of cultural forms. All of these are successfully used to embellish the thematic, stylistic, and structural elements of the film's episodic treatment.

The moral chord *Jom* strikes lies in the sociopolitical message revealed through vital oppositions. The schism is between striking workers who hold tenaciously to their demands and those who express equally fervent opposition to the strike. The film, like the storyteller's art, contains an ethical component that is deeply embedded in the quotidian recounting of events, a dimension, for example, typified by the oppression it depicts.[63] Here is a calculated accent on historicity authenticated by the performance of Khaly (the griot), which allows the spirit of "jom" to penetrate the minds of the people, if not to enable them to participate in the envisaged transition to an improved society, at the least to hope to remain collective associates of that desire. *Jom* is an ideological expression, a visual anthem, and to paraphrase J. Hoberman, a "political-aesthetic manifesto."[64] Samb-Makharam makes clear in this film that although his character Khaly catalyzes action through his transmission of ancient wisdom and knowledge, it is actually the masses who instigate the act. The film is therefore not primarily about individual heroism but rather about commitment and collective endeavor, which can achieve success only if the collective will is achieved.

The expansion of knowledge seen through the energetic and extraordinary dance toward the end of the film signifies this communal aspiration embodied in the griot's tale and its didacticism. This celebrated and "jom"-inspired dance contributed to the liberation of the community's oppressed maids. That the dancer is a woman, a *griottes,* means that a griot can be anybody in the society who transmits messages to the people.[65] Although this scene is too long, the photography, camera work, and editing are very impressive. The dancer illustrates one of the principal functions of oral tradition, which is the passing from the esoteric to the exoteric, that is, the extension of the information provided by the griot and transmitted by a spectator or ordinary member of the public to the masses as typified by the "griottes" (the female dancer). This dance attracted a large and admiring crowd, which is to say that in this didactic emphasis, "jom" pushes for a commitment to patriotism and communal response to the society's problems. *Jom*'s populism underlies a revisionist approach to modernity from the traditional. Although the film emphasizes class struggle, through a skillful interplay of tradition and modernity it also delves into aspects of resistance against colonization (Dieri murders a colonial officer) and neocolonization (opposition to the blandishment of Mr. Diop, director general of the industrial complex). It is still from the griot's perspective that the messages become haunting. The images are clearly slanted to highlight the dramatic and emotional emphasis on moral issues intrinsic to oral culture.

Operating on the basis of teaching the philosophy of "jom," the film shifts in subject. For example, in the opening scene a wife complains that her husband is unproductive by spending a lot of time painting pictures, and another wife is infuriated by her husband's idleness. She drags him into their matrimonial home and beat him. Following this sequence, however, we are introduced to the 1980 strike scene and from there to the colonial period where Prince Dieri fights and kills a French colonialist, and such other incidents as the dance sequence, which also occurs in modern times, presumably 1980. The events in the film, in other words, take place in truncated periods of time. *Jom* uses this strategy to expedite the technique of flashbacks, multiple narrative voices, the story-within-a-story, and movement in time and space. This strategy serves as a necessary process of adding emphasis and reinforcement to segment details, functioning in the manner of Marxist dialectic by which knowledge of full meaning in the end emanates from combining such pieces to make a whole. These pieces in no way disrupt the narrative verisimilitude of *Jom*; they are essential thematic and formal concerns of oral tradition that African filmmakers and writers adopt for elaboration of stylistic ranges. This technique allows the director to experiment with form and content, to move freely through these times and spaces—backward from 1980 to 1900, forward through the 1930s and 1940s, and returning to the 1980s—going through important Senegalese historical times spanning colonialism to the age of nationalism and independence. By emphasizing neocolonial repressions, *Jom* alludes to future problems that might necessitate interconnected journeys to the past in order to express the present by drawing on historical documentation. From this point of view, the griot will not outlive his usefulness as the embodiment of "jom," since he might be needed again to narrate history and to mobilize the masses. In this film, the griot serves as the code to which all references are made, culturally, ideologically, and filmically. Prior to *Jom,* in such African films as *Borom Sarret, Xala,* and *Ceddo,* griots played prominent roles, but none of these films assigned griots structural dominance as *Jom* does.

If in *Jom* Samb-Makharam's structure illustrates the use of a historical narrative form of storytelling, Kaboré's *Wend Kuuni* is a prototype of creative candor for its definitive advancement in the effort to utilize specifically African cultural elements to create indigenous cinematic aesthetics. Basically, *Wend Kuuni* is a revival of the family-oriented film fashioned after the African oral tale tradition; it depicts a young boy's traumatic experience of losing one family and finding another.

The film's story derives from tranquil Africa, in the peaceful precolonial days of the Mossi Empire before the arrival of the white man. The film opens with a close-up of a woman crying, sitting in her hut, as she holds her son in her arms. A man tells her that her husband, a hunter who has been missing for the past thirteen months, must have died or else he would have returned home by now. There is no reason, he says, for her to be crying as she might as well make up her mind to remarry so that her little son can have an adoptive father. She does not see this as a solace and instead decides to escape with her son. The hermeneutic teaser ends here as the credits of the film appear. The story continues when a man on his trading route, riding a donkey, discovers a boy lying unconscious in the bush. He helps the boy by giving him water to drink and takes him on the back of his donkey to the nearest village. When he questions the boy about his circumstances and condition, the boy does not respond—he is mute. Nobody in the village is able to identify the boy, so the trader leaves him with a family until his parents can come and claim him. When no one comes after many months, the village chief confers with his people and his temporary family is allowed to adopt him. The boy is given a name, Wend Kuuni (meaning "the gift of God"), by his new adoptive parents, Tinga and Lale, who have a female child of their own called Pongneré. Being the same age, the children have no problem in relating as brother and sister despite Wend Kuuni's muteness. Both assist in family activities; she helps her mother with domestic chores, while he tends the herd of cattle with their father.

One day Wend Kuuni's peace is abruptly shattered when, in the bush, he discovers the body of a neighbor hanging from a tree limb. Traumatized by this gruesome event, the boy regains his speech, thus fulfilling Pongneré's dream prophecy in which she saw Wend Kuuni speaking. Wend Kuuni tells his own story, stating that his muteness was caused by the emotional trauma suffered as a result of seeing his mother die in the bush after being ostracized and chased out of their village by denizens who accused her of being a witch and for refusing to remarry according to custom.

Wend Kuuni is beautifully photographed, with the pacing of the film matching the rhythm of the pastoral village scenes in which it is set. Kaboré's film has a Sembenean quality that pays respect to the master. This filmmaker, who, after watching Sembene's *Xala*, "realized that the cinema could be used as a tool to express African culture,"[66] was to abandon his earlier profession (he holds a doctorate in history) to become a filmmaker after graduating from the French film school l'Ecole Supérieure d'Etudes Cinématographiques (ESEC). Made with the crew supplied by Centre National du Cinéma of Burkina Faso and financed by that country's national film funding agency, Fonds de Promotion et d'Extension de l'Activité Cinématographique, *Wend Kuuni*, Kaboré's first feature and the first feature film to be "entirely produced by the state of Burkina Faso,"[67] is the first black African film to be awarded a César (Le César de la Francophonie) and has many other awards to its credit as well.

Wend Kuuni, like *Jom*, shows how stories functioning on the level of plot and subplot can coalesce into a synthetic artistic entity. Although in both films, thematic-cum-cinematic specificities distinguish their structures as cinematic equivalents of a griot's tale, the griot's roles are markedly different. While in *Jom* the story is told by the griot, in *Wend Kuuni* the physicality of the storyteller is effaced. Here the director uses documentary technique and offscreen laconic narration (voiceover) to render the images comprehensible, as opposed to *Jom,* in which the griot articulates directly to the camera and audience. (We should note that voice-over narration is also a common oral narrative feature, not belonging entirely to cinematic documentary technique). The offscreen narration in this film is closer to its function in oral tradition. Markedly distinct from mainstream talking heads, it is harmonious with the simplicity of the story line. Even though the film's structure encompasses different stories, there is a natural flow of events. In this film, the storyteller emerges out of the structure of a cleverly integrated dominant (Western) and generic (cultural) mode of representation and not out of the physicality and invincibility of the griot whose oration we intermittently hear when some point needs clarification. It is clear here that Kaboré sought to construct a rhythm that creates an atmosphere of accountability, dwelling on the audience-text-artist (griot) relationship so characteristic of Africa's oral literature.

This lyrical film, which shows the boy being abandoned in the bush and becoming mute, employs multiple narrative voices. Using the story-within-a-story strategy to further this design, *Wend Kuuni* not only shows the tragedy that renders the boy mute but also uses another tragedy to restore his speech and open him up to society, to whom he then relates his experience. In simple oral narrative, this could take the form of linear structuring, but in its cinematic rendering, episodic sequential units introduce three stories that merge into one. In his detailed examination of *Wend Kuuni's* structure, Diawara notes that this synthesis, starting from the first sequence at the opening of the film, in which a husband is declared missing, "calls for a set of other [functions] which constitute the deep structure of [the] autonomous story"—the emerging new story.[68] This strategy not only saturates the structure with an air of confident exploration of oral storytelling techniques mixed with cinematic conventions, it makes this film a dignified work of experimentation, and, like *Jom,* proves that subscription to this culturally inspired aesthetic control asserts limitless thematic and stylistic diversity. For example, from the beginning of the film, we are introduced to what seems to be a simple linear tale of one family's problems. Within a short time, the story digresses to incorporate other stories (making it a community story that is, in effect, still part of the family story but which in turn establishes or alludes to "new functions," "new order").[69] Thus, we learn that a husband is missing—we witness the pain and anguish of a grieving wife wondering about what to do next. We see a boy found in the bush lying unconscious. He regains consciousness in the village and is adopted by a couple who have only one daughter (a situation that Diawara, citing Djibril T. Niane's *Sundiata: An Epic of Old Mali,* finds alluding to the "wanted son" myth of the oral tradition, and which could function as another autonomous story).[70] This smooth transition is then interrupted by the sudden death of a neighbor. This last part leads to the climax and resolution of the whole. The interruption forms a highly orchestrated sequence in which a woman publicly accuses her aging husband of being impotent. Unable to endure this embarrassment, the old man takes his life by hanging himself. The next day Wend Kuuni discovers his hanging body and the emotional trauma he experiences results in the regaining of his speech.

Reinforcing this story-within-a-story strategy is Wend Kuuni's recapitulation of his family's past experiences, which are deliberately left untold in the beginning of the film. For instance, when the boy starts to tell Pongneré his story, Kaboré uses a flashback to show the search for the missing husband whom we know to be a hunter. In a normal linear oral narrative structure, we would have been informed earlier that Wend Kuuni and his mother were driven out of their burning hut by irate villagers who accused her of being a witch and that they were lost in the forest, sick and dejected, until the woman gave up and died. Subsequently, Wend Kuuni's mother is already in the process of dying before a shot shows her husband hunting, thereby establishing his livelihood, a good use of flashback reminiscent of *Jom*'s pungency. Typical of the oral narrative pattern, the story should have started with "one day there was a woman who lived in such-and-such village with her son, so-and-so," but the film departs from such a linear structure. Even though Wend Kuuni was about nine years old, we are not told his real name even after he regains his speech. In the film's attempt to clarify, it imposes a critical set of assumptions and even represses the social, cultural, and historical rendering of oral tradition. The point here is that in cinema it is possible to rearrange pieces of information and still tell a sensible story. While it is also possible to rearrange parts of a story in a verbal language, in the oral tradition *some* stories are simply followed or retold according to how they were transmitted by one's forefathers many years ago. But the artists' freedom is limitless if they are allowed to experiment with form, utilizing their ingenuity to assert authorial control. Hence Kaboré appropriates and then subverts the linear structure of oral narrative for maximum effect.

If one of the principal constituents of oral tradition is the organization, examination, and interpretation of society's past and present, *Wend Kuuni* shows that the fragmentation of linear images and their

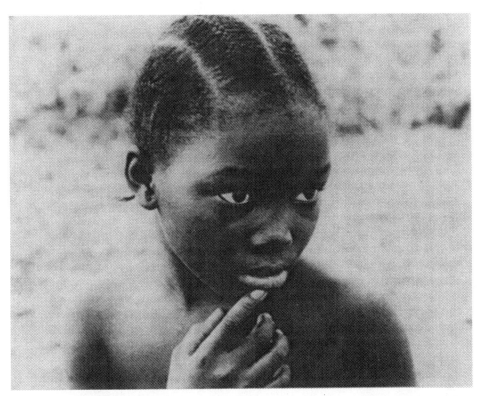

Gaston Kaboré: Wend Kuuni (*God's Gift*); *Burkina Faso, 1982.* Courtesy of the British Film Institute.

remolding in "new configurations and contexts," to use E. H. Gombrich's phrase,[71] can be achieved by blending oral art with cinematic art. In this film, the whole process of juxtaposition is conveyed by *découpage,*[72] specifically through parallel montage, extensive use of continuity editing, and with admirable characterization and performances by the nonprofessional cast. These elements, also comprising shifts and transgressions (of oral tradition and dominant cinematic conventions), assist in capturing the graphic images of the boy's transformation and the centralization of the film's rugged humanist qualities. As the narrative shows, Kaboré eschews chronological order by inverting the linearity of the tale as it would be told in oral narrative by employing the above filmic devices. But this is not the only quality that gives this film its captivating power; the melodrama built on Wend Kuuni's tragedy catches our attention as we follow the plot through the invocation to new depths of despair, mounting suspense, climax, and resolution.

Another interesting feature of oral literature found in *Wend Kuuni* is the use of indigenous language and repetitions. The language used in this film is Mooré, an indigenous language. In using it, Kaboré attempts to recapture the poetic resonances, the common symbols, simplicity, and the structure of traditional African storytelling art. Even though dialogue is used sparingly, it is in accordance with the new philosophy of reasoning—Africanization of the film language whereby the narrative style transcends the spoken word. Segun Oyekunle has already touched on this issue when he observed that *Wend Kuuni* "could be understood without understanding the African language used," because the "scripting, the film narrative, and the use of dramatic and common symbols"[73] are all directed toward the breaking of language barriers.

The use of repetitive images in this film occurs as flashbacks from Wend Kuuni's point of view in relating his mother's plight, which is minimally hinted at in the beginning of the film. Repetition of shots or sequences have been used in such African films as *Emitai, Xala,* and *Ceddo* by Ousmane Sembene, and more combatively, as a structural device in Haile Gerima's *Harvest: 3,000 Years.* In this latter case it not only establishes rhythm and pace but is used as a principle of opposition (structure of opposites) to emphasize the etiology of neocolonial decadence.

There is no doubt that *Wend Kuuni* illustrates how oral narrative techniques affect cinematic structure and how cinematic convention affects oral art. A clear example would be to see their functions in terms of the associations between cultural and dominant cinematic models, which in this film do not impair the authenticity of the cultural symbols and thematic alignments of the visually narrated African tale. Examining Kaboré's aesthetics within this perspective, it is interesting to see how the unity of *Wend Kuuni*'s narrative structure emerges from fragments and juxtapositions, from a bold individual style carved out of dual stylistic possibilities. Although most of the fundamental codes work by inversions and subversions, they are still advantageous to the fostering of indigenous aesthetics. For instance, it is possible on the one hand to see the element of subversion and inversion in the film in terms of Diawara's observation that archetypal stories are not narrated "successively and in their entirety" and that where "the events of certain functions appear simultaneously in more than one archetypal story," they have a tendency to introduce "additional meanings."[74] On the other hand, here is an expanded thematic and stylistic alignment positioned to subvert the classical documentary codes, a careful arrangement of profilmic and extrafilmic material condensed for impact. Otherwise, such a well-guided search for the depth of creative autonomy would not transcend the limitations imposed by what is accepted as a "standard" feature-length film. On the level of the signified, this filmic process is not immersed in nostalgia but is directed at awakening consciousness, and in doing so is indebted to the oral art.

If oral tradition, as is argued by the notable traditionalist of African culture and specialist in oral tradition A. Hampaté Bâ of Mali, is "a great school of life" that serves "to create a particular man to sculpt the African soul,"[75] then this philosophy has prevailed in black African film practice where the impulse to combine particular visions is an intracontinental strategy that suggests dialogic links between various African cultural practices. In this vein, *Visages de femmes* by Désiré Ecaré, makes a different contribution to black African film aesthetics through oral tradition. Ecaré's innovative use of song and dance, here functioning as a vital narrative element, holds the film's structure together while other significant cultural oral traditions come into focus. Constructed in two autonomous parts, this award-winning film, which took twelve years to complete, was shot in French and in such Ivorian dialects as Baoulé, Jula, and Bété[76] (with English subtitles in the American prints). *Visages de femmes* is notorious for having Africa's steamiest erotica. It was the first film to be prohibited in Côte d'Ivoire for its explicit love scenes and nudity.

Visages de femmes begins with ten minutes of song and dance. Beautifully composed and shot mostly in close-up with a few medium shots, it begins with two drummers dexterously providing the exhilarating music that draws a large village crowd in colorful traditional attire together, happily dancing the two-step. This wonderful scene, masterfully choreographed, catches the gay exuberance of the denizens of Loupou, in a sequence so compelling that J. Hoberman noted that "one would be proud to show [it to] a Martian as evidence of life on earth."[77] There is no dialogue omnisciently telling the viewer what is happening. The visuals are self-explanatory, providing an introduction to the African culture. This leads us to the first of two stories, filmed ten years apart (the first shot in 1973 and the last in 1983) and differing in tone.

The first story is set in a small village. Brou (Kouadio Brou) and his wife N'Guéssan (Albertine N'Guéssan) are working on the communal farm together with Affoue (Mahile Véronique) and other villagers. Brou's brother, Kouassi (Sidiki Bakaba), wearing a leisure suit with zippered pockets, has recently arrived from the capital to visit. He prefers smoking cigarettes and standing around flirting with his sister-in-law N'Guéssan and her lascivious friend Affoue. Brou chastises

Kouassi for this, calling him a "smart ass intellectual." Brou suspects his wife of being attracted to Kouassi, and the situation is aggravated by town gossip when Brou is told that his wife was seen holding hands with Kouassi. However, at this point it is not N'Guéssan that Kouassi compromises. One day, Kouassi follows Affoue into the woods where she has gone to fetch water. They end up frolicking naked among the trees and making love in the quiet, cool, easy-flowing waters of the shallow river.

We then shift to the second story, which concerns an enterprising woman named Bernadette (Eugénie Cissé Roland) who lives and works in Abidjan, the capital of Côte d'Ivoire. She owns a fish-smoking business and is by nature a very industrious person. Making a good living, she nonetheless spends most of her earnings on the parasites around her—her husband and uncle, who claim "women and money do not go together," her daughters, who are in college, and her nephew. Bernadette wants a bank loan so she can expand her business to include a restaurant but encounters an obstacle when an uncooperative bank manager tells her that, even though she makes a lot of money, her house is only worth three million French francs—not enough collateral to secure her the requested loan.

Employing satire and comedy, Ecaré puts Bernadette in the role of a superwoman, a domineering character who wants either to see the power of men curtailed or women doing everything possible to be powerful and aggressive like the men. In the beginning sequence of this second story, Bernadette is shown preaching this message to one of her daughters, saying that after her exams she should go to military school and get tough like a man. (Her daughters are sophisticated in their ways and have their own ideas about how to get along in a male-dominated society.) With this type of attitude, and with the widespread public and official corruption, Bernadette is aware that no meaningful economic project can prosper in a sociopolitical climate such as that of Côte d'Ivoire and, therefore, Africa. She has no choice but to be a hard worker and disciplinarian; undeterred by her sex, she is equal to the implied male-dominant African environment.

Like other filmmakers mentioned, who base their creative approach on oral tradition, Désiré Ecaré, actor, dramatist, and filmmaker who studied at the Institut des Hautes Etudes Cinématographiques (IDHEC) in Paris, also believes oral tradition to be a mainstay of African film language. In his work, oral tradition functions as a way of conceiving cinematic structure, a way of seeing, a view of the cosmic universe, and a way of articulating political and cultural possibilities. This means that, while the structural underpinnings in his films revolve around this cultural precept, his work is also based on an ideology that seeks to debunk rigid methodologies. Like Kaboré, Ecaré favors multiple narrative structure, as opposed to, for instance, Sembene's linear narrative style. But where Kaboré and Sembene clarify through simplicity and meticulous attention to detail, Ecaré uses an elliptical film style reminiscent of Hondo, where character delineation and situations are provided without full detail. In *Visages de femmes,* evidence of this can be found in the song and dance sequence in which various characters intermingle and disappear at will without ever signifying structural deficiency or impeding understanding. In Hondo's *Soleil O,* for instance, there is no real story line—only juxtaposed images of oppression and resistance. Continuity is no real factor; rather, it is the imaginative use of sound and music which provides the sense of unity in a manner similar to that in *Visages de femmes,* in which dancing and singing constitute the narrative thread that holds the apparent disparate themes together.

Maintaining and then expanding upon the type of structural rhythm and the aesthetic and thematic concerns found in Ecaré's previous films *Concerto pour un exil* (Concerto for an exile, 1968) and *À nous deux, France* (Beware of France, 1970), *Visages de femmes* is crafted around excellently choreographed dancing and singing. As in grammatical construction, where a punctuation mark breaks a sentence, the dancing and singing sequences play a similar role in the story line. Both are elements of form and content reinforcing the structure without breaking the flow of the diegesis; both also function as well-intended transition devices. In traditional African cultures the reason why oral tradition has had such an enormous impact on communication is its reliance on one of the most powerful elements of culture, the indigenous language, for its exposition. Since the employment of the oral tradition reflects patterns of everyday life, the narrative trajectory is easily understood. This sensitivity to a particular cultural heritage promotes a greater level of self-awareness and suggests avenues of social change. In *Visages de femmes,* one of the principal elements influencing the construction of its structure is song and dance. Before we explore how song and dance have been used in the structure of this film, it is necessary to delineate their cultural significance within African oral tradition.

From the marvelously well-orchestrated opening sequence of this film, one is immediately struck with the conviction that African music, as the adage goes, can emerge from African dance steps, lyrics can take their cue from oral poetry, and live performances can be a reassemblage of African rituals and folk opera. In the oral tradition, music and dance serve as bridges to the animating forces of nature, which is why in traditional cultures they are inextricably linked with aspects of everyday life. In this function, every rhythm generated is associated with

Désiré Ecaré: Visages de femmes (*Faces of Women*); Côte d'Ivoire, 1985.
Courtesy of New Yorker Films.

particular activities, where rhythmic complexities serve to differentiate
one particular African song and dance from another and one function
from another. The rhythm of African music and dance is inspiring in
its sophisticated and intended form. It evokes and manifests the cadences of creation, life and death struggles, and generally accompanies
ordinary ceremonies usually requiring a group of musicians and dancers
who perform communally with no strings attached. Contrary to the
negative anthropological misinterpretations of African song and dance
in Western films and television, which usually emphasize the exotic,
for Africans, song and dance are not just accessories to life, they are
transmitters of culture, indispensable to African existence.

I noted earlier that *Visages de femmes* intersperses ritual performance along with song and dance in the film's narrative to form a web
that binds the stories together. This narrative pattern is an invocation
of cultural imperatives symptomatic of the African way of life. In this
tradition, for instance, it is common practice for peasants working collectively or individually to interrupt their speeches with song in the
same way that in the African storytelling tradition main narratives are
interrupted to allow interconnecting stories to be sung or danced. In
the style of cinematic flashback and flash-forward, the song emerges

out of what has happened, what has been said or done before, drawing attention to what follows and what may later develop. In this respect, the songs and dances highlight the continuity and the progression of the action. Let me illustrate by examining the instances in which such musical sequences are used in *Visages de femme*.

After Brou succeeds in convincing Kouassi that he should leave in two days' time to visit their grandmother who lives in the village of Broukro (in an apparent attempt to send him away from his wife, N'Guéssan), we learn within a short time that N'Guéssan also plans a trip during the same period of time to visit her mother in a town less than one mile away from Broukro. Before this, the visuals have already established N'Guéssan's and Kouassi's intimacy and intentions. At one point during one of their clandestine meetings, N'Guéssan asks Kouassi, "What will I do if you leave?" Both of them run to the bush in a jubilant mood; the scene is interrupted by village women singing:

> So they left.
> Kouassi for his village
> N'Guéssan for her mother's.
> But the two villages were very close.
> Less than a mile apart, they say.
> So, it's in Kouassi's arms that she spent most of her time.
> And her husband heard about it.

It is clear from the song what has already happened, and more important, that Brou is aware of all. The question now is, what is he going to do about it? (Notice that gossip here assumes an important role as in the well-dramatized earlier scene in which men playing the *isha* game gossip about N'Guéssan's and Kouassi's relationship.)[78] In subsequent scenes Brou engages N'Guéssan in incessant squabbles and accusations, followed by N'Guéssan's perennial denials of an affair with his brother. Ecaré has broadly emphasized contemporary women's contempt toward male domination in this film and shown their liberationist inclinations. This attitude is obviously slanted to correspond with the mood typified by the next sequence of song and dance, filled with premonitory lyrics with which the village women fire their rhetorical salvo:

> Men never trust us.
> And there are so many honest women.
> Oh, yes, so many honest women.
> Men can't appreciate honesty.
> They see the worst in everything.
> Especially when there's nothing to hide.
> Oh yes, when there's nothing.

What does a man deserve who cannot trust?
He deserves one thing only.
And what is that?
To be deceived.
Yes, to be deceived.
Let me tell you what I do to my man,
my husband who is always spying on me,
suspicious of me.
Follow me! And you'll see the life.

(Notice the repetition of lines, an essential feature of oral storytelling; in film it becomes repetition of scene, used for emphatic purposes.) In this sequence, in verse, chants, and gestures, the women warn about future consequences, and the touting expression of the first song graduates from moralist gossip and innuendo to a call for action and finally rebellion.[79] As the next scene shows, the film's images of sexual exploitation and vehement denial negate the moralist tendencies. In a protracted ten-minute sexual encounter, it is Affoue (not N'Guéssan, whose flirtatious overtures had earlier received extensive coverage) who makes love in the river with Kouassi. Functioning more as a flashforward of what the possessive and distrustful husband should expect from a liberated African woman, the all-woman chorus in the next scene explains this motive:

You'll see if the husband suspects anything.
He'll believe everything he is told.
Everything. Everything . . .
But do you think that will teach him a lesson?

In the next shot, Affoue is returning home, Kouassi following behind. When her husband asks where she has been for such a long time, she refers to the basin of water she has fetched from the river. Affoue's husband does not seem to distrust her. He is not suspicious, like Brou, who continues with the surveillance of N'Guéssan's relationship with his brother and finally triumphs in the end when he catches N'Guéssan one night waiting for Kouassi at their regular meeting place under the branches of a big tree.

Let us consider some other cultural and symbolic configurations of African storytelling employed in the structure of *Visages de femmes*, notably body language emanating from music and clothing, and humor, an important additive. In African culture, body language and clothing communicate in the same way as art—sculpture, song, dance, and storytelling. As stated earlier, African music is one of the art forms that reveals the expression of the black soul. In this film, drumbeat and hand clapping are the cultural components of oral tradition that illuminate the musical sequences. In the opening scene, for instance, the inner feeling of an entire community is expressed by the rhythm of drumbeats, which not only transmit messages but also move the feet to pound the ground as, in Francis Bebey's words, "the rhythm of the music whose notes are in turn transformed into dance steps."[80] Thus, just as drumbeats in the traditional pastoral village signify dissemination of news or the sending of messages to adjoining villages, when the drums in *Visages de femmes* begin to throb and the circle of dancers in colorful traditional garb begin to two-step into action, cultural context is tested and affirmed. There is no doubt that the drumbeat epitomizes the strength and influences of African music—"a music that speaks in rhythms that dance," to borrow Bebey's felicitous description.[81] Although the function of the drum, which produces the music, is the same in terms of information dissemination and entertainment, we know that the drums themselves differ from region to region, culture to culture. But everywhere competence in handling them is required. The ability to drum different messages that people will understand demands a special technique. (While *Visages de femmes* demonstrates this type of dexterity, the Nigerian film *Parcel Post* [1982] by Segun Oyekunle illustrates a different kind of drum where the griot, using a two-headed Yoruba "talking drum," reproduces nuances of the spoken language.)[82]

In the second, third, and fourth song-and-dance numbers, in which the drum does not produce the music, Ecaré's emphasis shifts to the women's gesticular movements and gait; here body language takes the cue from the reflections of absorbed drumbeats. This omnipresent characteristic of the drum in the African musical world is highly esteemed—as these sequences show. Even when the drum itself is not directing the rhythm or the dance steps, "its presence is reflected by hand clapping, stomping, or the repetition of certain rhythmic onomatopoeias that are all artifices that imitate the drum beat."[83]

In West Africa, for example, art and life are interwoven in the same fashion in which Ecaré's characters illustrate the inseparability of clothing and body language—attire as creative language. The men and women in the dance sequences are gaily dressed in African print fabrics, the *ankara*. The vibrant colors and patterns of the stylistic African designs match the unique way wrappers are artistically tied to the shoulders of the men and to the waists of women with matching blouses and head-ties. The clothes worn here reveal information about the people and their culture. We see a cultural response to the interpretation of traditional life, and the information given also illustrates an understanding of nature's lines of demarcation such as age and marital and economic status, all attesting to the dignity of African men and women.

The importance of humor in oral art is immeasurable, too. Since it is the duty of the oral artist to demonstrate his artistic ingenuity, it is common practice that he add certain flavorful details to entice the audience. While some artists employ this strategy to cover up structural flaws, it may also be used to address politically sensitive issues that African leaders may otherwise find objectionable. Utilizing the latter strategy, Ecaré believes that "one can remain pleasant while being subversive . . . and say terrible things with a disarming style."[84] One such application concerns the second story of *Visages de femmes*. When Bernadette relates how badly she was treated at the bank manager's office where she went to seek a loan to expand her business, her older daughter, T'Cheley, a sophisticated woman with an appetite for Western fashion, offers her own view of life in contemporary Africa:

> Our bank is in our thighs, our breasts and our ass; with these we have got all the power; with my backside, Mother, I can get the government toppled tomorrow if I want. I can get a new Ambassador appointed to Paris, to Peking and even to the Vatican. The Pope won't twig, God and women always see eye to eye. For that you've got to be twenty and good looking.

Bernadette shrugs to herself in disbelief. But this sequence touches on the corruption and economic impotence that is indicative of the administration. Sembene has effectively used this kind of caustic humor and satire to deal with such societal inefficiencies and decadence. In Ecaré's case, however, this political message loses its grip owing to hyperbole.

Finally, oral tradition also influences the theme of the extended family system in Africa which is in part a contributor to the sub-Saharan economic quagmire. Under this system, as shown in the second story of the film (and also touched upon in Henry Duparc's *Abusuan* and Oumarou Ganda's *F.V.V.A.*), any member of the family who commands an average income or by rank is head of the family, is expected to shoulder the responsibility of relatives—brothers, sisters, cousins, nieces, nephews, and in-laws. In the form of oral narrative, *Visages de femmes* creates this kind of atmosphere and makes one look at it as a preternatural African affair. *Visages de femmes* ends as it began, with a chorus of singing and dancing villagers. We hear the director's voice-over narrate, "You've too many plans, too many for a woman, your brothers say, 'Money is for eating.' So let's eat what's left, let's join the others, let's do as they do, let's dance with them."

I have shown how filmmakers in search of personal style invert or subvert aesthetic codes. Returning to this topic it is necessary to relate it to Ecaré's virtuosity. It is obvious that Ecaré's protracted sex segment is rather lurid, which, to some critics, makes it an extreme act of iconoclasm far removed from African respectability. It is one thing, in search of independent film style, to subvert or invert the chronological parameters of oral storytelling technique, as in *Wend Kuuni,* but it is quite another to subvert traditional moral codes, especially if there is a suspicion of an ulterior motive for doing so. *Visages de femmes* exhibits an unrestrained indulgence in eroticism. It is not nudity per se that most violates the traditional African moral approach to the private areas of the human body, but the dramatization of the various techniques of sexual intercourse, a sequence that shows Kouassi and Affoue in the river, "squishing and splashing," as J. Hoberman puts it, "in the original waterbed if not the amniotic fluid itself."[85] The traditional African moral code does not permit such public exposure or even reference to certain parts of the body by their real names. This sequence, if judged by this standard, takes on a grotesque, almost parodistic garishness, so completely at odds as it is with established tradition. Tight editing and two or three shots as opposed to its present ten minutes would have sufficed to curtail the emphasis on sexual exploitation. Similarly, medium and long shots as opposed to tight close-ups would have made the visual less plastic especially with regard to body contact and suggestive ecstasies. Ecaré could have chosen to use suggestive shots as in the beautifully orchestrated love scene of *Touki-Bouki,* where a woman takes off the top part of her clothing (her complete nudity is not shown), a clenched fist grasping a Dogon cross (a symbol of fertility from Mali) hanging on a motorbike indicates sexual encounter, while a cut to a powerful wave suggests an orgasmic burst.

How much external influence contributed to this overt exposure is hard to discern. Although the director received financial help from France, it is too minimal to influence ideological and aesthetic decision. But considering the hard times the director had gone through trying to raise money for this film, it is possible that in the interest of future productions Ecaré thought he should explore new possibilities. With such defiance, *Visages de femmes* may not have been intended for extensive public viewing in the hard-to-find African exhibition houses that may have found a "genuine" excuse to shut their doors against it, except of course, in clandestine screening. It may well have been intended primarily for the foreign film market.

Ecaré may argue (but perhaps not publicly) that this love scene is only a ten-minute nude sequence tagged for export and thrown in for the titillation of his Western audiences. The fact is, if you take this sequence out, the film is completely African. The differences between African and Western concepts of love and lovemaking and their abuses in dramatic forms have been elaborated in an article by Joseph Okpaku entitled "African Critical Standards for African Literature and the Arts."[86] The author notes that the African believes in "implicit or understood love" while he sees the Westerners' notion of love "explicit and dramatized." For the African, "kisses, hand holding in public amounts to a show-off aimed at a third party," which, in aesthetic terms, he considers "superficial and melodramatic."[87] This explains why kissing, explicitly suggestive scenes, and public display of erotic matter are not common features of "genuine" black African cinema.

In a sense, Ecaré can be seen irreducibly moving with the times by willingly applying antitraditional posture to the analysis of modern Africa, but the method used, it may be argued, does not provide a careful examination of social mores. Films before *Visages de femmes,* such as Sembene's *Xala* and *Ceddo* and Cissé's *Den Muso* and *Finye* have all inverted aspects of social mores to create a dialectical process of looking at African traditions. By implication, they suggest a reexamination of such structures and possible changes relevant to our modern times, but with clear intentions. How do these assumptions manifest themselves in *Visage des femmes*'s structure, particularly in the characters of Kouassi and Affoue? It is possible to interpret the nude sequence as a feminist squeal or a phallocentric construction in which the woman's body no longer "holds the look" or "plays to and signifies male desire"[88]—to reverse Laura Mulvey's and other feminist film theory assumptions—with the implications bouncing against the two characters. Both bodies can be considered sexual objects coded for erotic spectacle and the gaze of both male and female spectators—she for her body and he for his penis. This flaw notwithstanding, *Visages de femmes* is a good film. What it lacks in social mores, it gains in mise-en-scène, thematic and stylistic reliance on oral tradition in its quest to give definition to indigenous artistic possibilities.

Similarly, we have shown that black African film practice is endowed with the dynamic of endogenous oral art. This has facilitated the maturity of black African cinema, which has been able to incorporate oral tradition's communication and reception codes to give us a basis on which to appreciate what is truly Africa's and will lead us to examine how this African art has been expanded to effect the dynamics of liberation and reconstruction.

Film and the Politics of Liberation

In Africa's desperate struggle for freedom, cinema has proven to be as valuable an asset as other communication media, and in countries with high illiteracy rates, as we shall see, it is even more valuable as a powerful instrument of ideological education. In general, however, these messages originate from the necessity to mount penetrating campaigns and are not only aimed at providing an explanation for the struggle and mobilization effort needed to sustain the revolution. Andres R. Hernandez observes:

> To understand the role of cinema in a revolutionary society, it is necessary to emphasize that the transformation of social reality attempted by a true revolution includes not only the fight against underdevelopment, the organization and growth of productive forces under a new system of social relations, but also and simultaneously, at least in the cases of China and Cuba, the concerted attempt to develop a new man, in dialectical relationship to the new society being created.[89]

In the lusophone African countries of Angola, Guinea-Bissau, and Mozambique, where the liberation movement has undertaken massive programs of political education, the Cuban format seems to have provided a role model in helping map out the future, specifically, in the building of a new man (new society), the central concern of any movement fighting to break away from colonial bondage. While this strategy has succeeded in the lusophone countries (former Portuguese African colonies), the grinding tragedy of apartheid has limited its spread to the liberation struggles of the African National Congress (ANC). There is space here to state only some general lines of development or underdevelopment; South African film history and media activities have been exhaustively covered elsewhere.[90] South Africa, site of the most repressive society in the world, is unfortunately not the base for the most militant liberationist film indicative of oppressed societies.

For too long the oppression in southern Africa has been inadequately explained to America, Europe, and the rest of the world from the black African perspective. Just as the apartheid regime is immersed in an overabundance of military hardware, so has it developed a formidable public relations expertise to confuse the world. With this propaganda machine, and with the collaboration of its overseas cohorts, South Africa has managed to suppress adequate coverage of the truth about apartheid. Not too long ago the South African film *The Gods Must Be Crazy* (1984) by Jamie Uys gave large audiences from around the world unprecedented enjoyment by ridiculing Africans. This film portrays them as incompetents who are unable to take their destiny in their own hands. But it is the Broederbond (white Afrikaner mafia, and authors of apartheid doctrine) that is denying the world the truth about the displaced Khoisan people (''Bushmen''), whose tragedy Uys turned into comedy. *The Gods Must Be Crazy*, despite this obvious slant, remained the longest-running foreign film in New York theater history.[91]

In its effort to suppress the truth, the Afrikaner government of South Africa, like the colonial governments of other parts of Africa discussed in chapter 1 and other repressive governments of the world, is apprehensive about images conveyed by film and television. According to Keyan Tomaselli, the white South African author and critic, "The State uses the media strategically," and he warns that "action against film-makers" may be becoming like the situation in "Argentina—where people have lost their lives or been tortured for making films."[92] This probably explains why protest filmmaking is invisible in South Africa. Why can't the ANC, the group championing the fight for independence, make ideologically explicit films channeled to address the horrors of apartheid? Films of that kind could have been made in neighboring independent African states.[93] Recently the ANC missed a golden opportunity to exploit the power of the motion picture when it failed to capitalize on the ideological ramifications proffered in the powerful South African Broadway play *Sarafina*. Before the tension that underlies these statements are explored, it is necessary to give a brief historical account of black South African cinema since 1967.

Understandably, there is a plethora of feature, documentary, and television films on South Africa (e.g., *Cry Freedom, Mapantsula, A World Apart, Sarafina,* and *Witness to Apartheid*) as well as a flurry of books focusing on Biko, the Mandelas, Tambo, and Tutu, but these are not by any means deeply African. It is in this light that we remember the zeal of two pioneer films, *End of Dialogue* (1967) and *Last Grave at Dimbaza* (1974), both produced by Morena Films, a film group of exiled black and white South Africans living in Britain, headed by Nana Mahomo, who now lives in Washington, D.C. The first film, *End of Dialogue,* shot clandestinely in South Africa by Africans, is a powerful indictment of the apartheid system, portraying the social and political injustices permeating the lives of black Africans. The impact of this film in international communities was so intense that the government of South Africa was forced to make a film called *Black Man Alive* (1975) to counter its effect.

The second film by the same group, *Last Grave at Dimbaza,* was also secretly filmed in South Africa, and to this day it remains the most important film by an African to painstakingly examine the African condition under apartheid. This film depicts Dimbaza, a black township and one of the homelands where blacks are crowded together in ramshackle apartments, and contrasts its poverty, misery, and squalor with the affluence of urban and rural whites. In addition, migratory labor laws oblige blacks to carry passbooks (in white areas), dispossession of which means automatic imprisonment. The most ignominious

Oliver Schmitz/Thomas Mogotlane: Mapantsula; *South Africa, 1988.* Courtesy of California Newsreel.

Nana Mahoma: Last Grave at Dimbaza; *South Africa, 1974.* Courtesy of the British Film Institute.

aspect of this policy is the law that compels black males working in white industrial cities to live in camps separated from their wives and children (who are many miles away in the homelands), allowing only one visit home annually. Numerous other apartheid issues abound in this film.[94] In sum, the Afrikaner notion of blacks is made explicit when the former Minister of Bantu Affairs, speaking in the film, states that "African males from the homelands have no rights whatsoever in South Africa, they are only in South Africa to sell their labor." This film is such an educational lightning rod that it leaves one gasping at the evils of apartheid. The film is so powerful that, in the words of Susan J. Hall, "it will shake the apathy of the most quiescent."[95] Although *Last Grave at Dimbaza* is most noteworthy, Lionel Ngankane's film on Mandela and the more recent work of Nana Mahomo must also be acknowledged. But as independent films they are rarely seen, due in part to exhibition problems, and hence do not represent a challenge to the mainstream.

Centuries of Afrikaner domination of this country have left black South Africans alienated. There is the need now more than ever in light of the euphoria following Mandela's release from prison and anticipated majority rule for the ANC to pursue a policy of cultural resuscitation which will serve to retain the social dynamics of African tradition. This will not only shape the development of black South African art and culture now but will also encourage the production of more art and artists of caliber and integrity: more Miriam Makebas, Hugh Masekelas, Molefe Phetos, Nana Mahomos and more *Sarafinas*.

Sarafina, a black South African play presented on Broadway, has been very successful as a powerful tool of political enlightenment concerning oppression in that country. A lackluster documentary version of *Sarafina*, directed by Nigel Nobel, was hurriedly assembled in New York at the height of the play's popularity when it dominated Broadway. It is, however, unfortunate that Nobel's film is barely a movie version of the hard hitting Broadway play, critically acclaimed for its political acerbity. It is not surprising that his documentary, which became a character study of the performers rather than an indictment of apartheid, was a box-office flop. It is devoid of the sociopolitical engagement and moves too far away from the use of film as a tool of liberation or a medium of enlightenment—the Hondonian or Sembenean style—given its "hot" theme.

A new version of *Sarafina* (1992), a full-blown musical, has been released. My viewing of this film has confirmed my earlier criticism of Nobel's *Sarafina* and the commercial propensity of the play's creator, Mbogeni Ngema. The new *Sarafina*, directed by Darrell James Roodts, stars Whoopi Goldberg as Mary Masembuko, the rebellious schoolteacher. As I watched Goldberg, struggling with her shaky African accent, I marveled at the absence of the actress who played the schoolteacher in the original play. Her performance was electrifying and very convincing. Goldberg, who disappears midway through the film after she is taken away by apartheid security agents, remains only a celebrity whose presence is to guarantee box-office returns. She is not an authentic icon of liberation. Her presence signifies a sell-your-soul kind of pandering to foreign interest, the type of control African filmmakers long resisted. The film's structure alternates between the main story line and sudden bursts of exuberant song and dance sequences. The dance sequences are disturbing for their transformation of the stage play's original "music of liberation" to that of reductionist stylization or what one might as well term bastardized "Zuluism" symptomatic of Hollywood-MTV music video allure. Michael Peters, who choreographed *Sarafina* with Mbogeni Ngema, is well known in Hollywood. He also choreographed Michael Jackson's "Thriller" and "Beat It," which is not surprising since the profit motive in *Sarafina* takes precedence over education. What is relevant to our discourse here is the fact that the dance sequences lack the emotional and psychological

Oliver Schmitz/Thomas Mogotlane: Mapantsula; *South Africa, 1988.* Courtesy of California Newsreel.

persuasion of the protest songs and dances we see on television news, albeit briefly, by youths, for example, who carry corpses of their fellow comrades, victims of apartheid police brutality.

The point I make here about *Sarafina* and the function of art and culture in liberation struggles is clear. If there are elements of disingenuousness in the articulation of both political and cultural patterns, it lies in the distancing effects Whoopi Goldberg and the stylized music and dance steps have on the viewer. Mama Africa, Miriam Makeba, is magnificent in her role. So also is Leleti Khumalo and the other South African actors and actresses who play their parts well and convincingly irrespective of the visible clichés of Hollywood. Having seen the play twice, I am also convinced that the teacher in the original cast is more authentic. This is indeed sad because the producers of *Sarafina* (the play) have made a retrograde decision that is reminiscent of the 1970s, when in the United States there was a spate of black films made by white producers which, needless to say, were exploitative. But economic exploitation is not the question here. Rather, there are competent black

Oliver Schmitz/Thomas Mogotlane: Mapantsula; *South Africa, 1988.* Courtesy of the British Film Institute.

African directors, like Med Hondo, who made the musical, *West Indies,* who could effectively transfer *Sarafina* to the screen and more important, do it from an African perspective without simplifying history to entertain certain audiences. Darrell James Roodt, however, is a known critic of apartheid. His film *A Place of Weeping* (1986), which focused on the killing of a black farmhand by an Afrikaner employer, attests to this fact. But on the level of political and emotional impact, both his *Sarafina* and Nobel's documentary version of *Sarafina* lack the grip and intensity of *West Indies,* which was made with historical accuracy in mind. In my judgment, since the theater version is completely African and successful, would it not have made more sense to have the movie version made in the same pattern? In this vein, having Whoopi Goldberg play the lead role and not using a black African director or even assistant director is a tactical blunder motivated by "big bucks" at the expense of the real revolution—freedom for the people.

Cinema in Angola and Mozambique has some resonance with Brechtian aesthetics, especially those elements of Brecht that emphasize art as a practice that produces knowledge. But unlike Brecht, the mode of representation here stresses ideological factors reminiscent of revolutionary Cuba where cinema has been used to advance a massive program of political indoctrination and education. As Cuba's central focus was on the building of a "new man," so Angola, Guinea-Bissau, and Mozambique aspired to create a new society, and the cinema was believed to be the most powerful medium of information by which ideological messages could be imparted to their people, the majority of whom cannot read or write. The purpose and ideology of the lusophone African film practice can be found in important articles and interviews by the filmmakers.[96]

Alan Rosenthal maintains that the dilemma of "how to present history on film" continues to challenge filmmakers and claims that "in essence the problem has two different aspects—how to access and evaluate the past, and how to help understand the present and possibly change the future."[97] This process of evaluation is especially applicable to Latin America, particularly Cuba, where the cinema has been an instrument for the pursuit of revolutionary goals and national identity. Rosenthal's observations refer to *When the Mountains Tremble* (1985) by Pamela Yates, Thomas Sigel, and Peter Kinoy, an impressive documentary film that chronicles political repression in Guatemala. The film fuses traditional narrative technique with experimental interludes in which a Guatemalan woman recalls her own tragic personal history. This film is very revolutionary in its imagistic content and approach and in its use of a highly effective traditional narrative trajectory. Similar thematic and formal concerns have recently emerged in African documentaries. African contemporary history is beginning to be filmed with just such documentary audacity.

In anglophone states, priority has been given to documentary filmmaking, but even there the boldest efforts still lack the revolutionary zeal of Cuban and Latin American approaches. They have not been able to challenge or confront serious social, cultural, historical, and political issues with the kind of innovative approach characteristic of such films as *When the Mountains Tremble* or *Playa Girón* (Cuba, 1973) by Manuel Herrera. But with the budding lusophone documentaries a new and important chapter of African cinematic strategy has emerged. In Angola, Guinea-Bissau, and Mozambique, revolutionary film practices have developed out of struggles for freedom. The structure and goals of such documentaries and the pronouncements of their practitioners bear connotations of aspirations engendered in the works and polemics of Third World-Third Cinema film practice and film theory. In the cases of the lusophone African former colonies, cinema adopts the form of conscious didactic structure embedded in revolutionary ideology. Hence, producing documentaries that are deliberately slanted toward decolonization and that contribute to the process of developing a new consciousness enlightens the masses and instills in them a new revolutionary awareness that will enable them to understand contemporary realities and to participate in the struggle for total freedom—just as documentaries have been used in Cuba, for instance, where cinema became a fundamental tool indispensable in the revolutionary transformation of a distressed society.

Unlike anglophone and francophone African states, which had vestiges of film production facilities prior to independence, the lusophone countries had none, nor did they possess any technical training in this area until after independence in 1975. According to Ron Hallis, the Portuguese filmmakers who worked in Mozambique had no

> interest in developing African cinema or allowing the young African workers they employed, and exploited, a chance to learn the whole process of filmmaking. The few Mozambicans to work as assistants to the Portuguese were sequestered in tedious jobs, refused access to higher knowledge, and even forbidden to enter each other's work space.[98]

Yet even before independence, film played an important role in the lives of the lusophone African people. This came about because Portugal had refused to grant independence to its colonies, and for the nationalist movements that responded with armed struggle, media coverage was necessary to explain their perspective. Even though they did not possess the technical know-how to make films, they realized that film was a vital tool of liberation. They embarked upon film production, mainly documentaries, by inviting foreign filmmakers to follow the activities of the guerrillas and thus bring the war to the attention of both the local population and the world.

The first films made about the liberation movements and the war in Portuguese African territories include *Angola: Journey to a War* (1961), produced by NBC news with photographers and correspondents assigned to examine both the rebel and the Portuguese sides of the struggle; *Medina Boe* (1969), a Cuban newsreel that deals with the liberationist struggles in Portuguese Guinea-Bissau, depicting the atrocities committed by the Portuguese forces; *Venceremos* (We shall win, 1967), made inside Mozambique by a Yugoslavian film crew, dealing with guerrilla activities; *Viva FRELIMO* (1969), made by a Dutch television documentary crew; and *A luta continua* (The struggle continues, 1972) and *O povo organizado* (The people organized, 1975) by Robert Van Lierop, an African-American. All these films are anticolonialist films that not only helped to explain the conflict but also advanced consciousness, a vital requisite for revolution.

Consciousness-raising was accentuated in many ways in these films, although there were many discrepancies. For example, comparing the anticolonialist films of this period, John Stone finds that while NBC's *Journey to a War* maintains avowed neutrality by refusing to apportion any blame to Portuguese imperialism, Yugoslavia's vapid *Venceremos* weakens the intensity of revolutionary vibrancy and tranquilizes the audience.[99] In contrast, *Viva FRELIMO, A luta continua,* and *O povo organizado* forcefully probe the reasons for the armed struggle. Credence is justifiably given to the guerrilla struggle, in counterdistinction to the negativity of the Western media which, as a rule, branded the guerrillas "terrorists." Thus *A luta continua, Viva FRELIMO,* and *O povo organizado* give prominence to the political imperatives of the freedom fighters. The guerrillas are portrayed positively, depicted not simply as victims but as courageous individuals actively struggling against a superior colonial army. The films emphasize a didactic structure; when the freedom fighters are seen in training and in action, for instance, the camera also follows the local inhabitants in their contribution to the struggle and their collective commitment to the war effort. This situation is well documented in *A luta continua,* in which guerrilla training and activities are juxtaposed with the images of women and children in makeshift classrooms in the bush, reading, writing, and at times singing cultural and revolutionary songs that are indeed emotionally and psychologically penetrating.

The overall strategy of the film addresses the guerrillas' appeal for the need to create a society not partitioned by hierarchical variations, where there would be common dialogue between the sexes, the elders, and the masses. As Stone has pointed out, the lasting effect of this strategy derives from the priority of "service" to the community rather than of leaders exercising domineering powers over members of the community.[100] Echoing Fanon's theory of the African revolution, which calls for the rejection of bourgeois materialism in favor of indigenous revolutionary philosophy, this call could not have been better heeded than in the lusophone world, home of the revolutionary leader Amilcar Cabral, a leading theorist of African revolution. As with Fanon, the need to establish indigenous mobilization and organization of the masses for struggle against colonial power is one of Cabral's primary concerns. Although his theory focused on preindependence liberation strategies, he was also concerned about neocolonial effects, especially the question of leadership. For Cabral, this entails "identity and dignity,"[101] stressing the role of the organizer and the organized:

> The leaders . . . drawn generally from the petite bourgeoisie . . . having
> to live day by day with the various peasant groups in the heart of the

rural populations come to know the people better. . . . On their side the working masses and, in particular, the peasants who are usually illiterate and never have moved beyond the boundaries of their village or region . . . realize their crucial role in the struggle; they break the bonds of the village universe to integrate progressively into the country and the world. . . . They strengthen their political awareness by struggle.[102]

In the lusophone world, the struggle for self-determination led the freedom fighters to discover the use of the cinema as one of several weapons of revolution. Consequently, when it was time to establish their respective film industries after independence, it was quite clear (following the stylistic options offered by the earlier films made about the revolution) which cinematic pattern to adopt. According to Pedro Pimente, the assistant director of the Mozambique Film Institute (Instituto Nacional de Cinema or INC), it would be too reductive not to change the dominant image to "produce a new thing, the product of a new ideology."[103]

As the situations in Cuba and China have proven, the press and the cinema can indeed become powerful instruments for ideological education. But, at the time of independence in Mozambique and Angola, adult illiteracy was 95 percent and 70 percent respectively[104] and dissemination of information via print was simply not plausible. Television did not appear until after independence and although radio had existed in these countries since 1936, privately owned radio sets were rare. The movie theaters in the Portuguese territories existed for the colonialists. Ironically, black deprivation was advantageous in the sense that after independence it was easier for the masses to be receptive to the new educational films rather than, say, in Cuba, where American, Latin American, as well as eastern and western European films flourished before the revolutionary films emerged. The same is true of other African countries. The product of this new discovery became, for Angola, Guinea-Bissau, and Mozambique, the adoption of a documentary film practice rooted in the philosophy of socialist ideology and distinct to a remarkable degree from the informative and educative documentary filmmaking in anglophone Africa.

The struggle for independence by the Popular Movement for the Liberation of Angola (MPLA) was covered by the news media of foreign countries and was the subject of television documentaries and dramatic narrative films. Best known among these films is Sarah Maldoror's celebrated *Sambizanga* (1972). Although this filmmaker from Guadeloupe is of African decent, she might well be regarded as a foreigner. Her long service to the black and African causes and her marriage to a prominent Angolan nationalist, however, have well earned her the status of a native African. Before *Sambizanga,* she had made *Monangambee* (1970), a short film in Algeria about an African political activist languishing in a Portuguese jail. Both films were adapted from stories by the Angolan novelist Luandino Vieira.

Sambizanga, Maldoror's best-known work, was shot in the People's Republic of the Congo under the auspices of French technicians and a cast of nonprofessional actors with strong affiliation to the MPLA and the African Party for the Independence of Guinea and Cape Verde Islands (PAIGC). Based on the MPLA's liberation struggle, this film depicts the Portuguese atrocities and repression inflicted on Africans fighting for their freedom and self-determination. Set in the 1960s, the film opens with the main protagonist, the militant Angolan revolutionary Domingo, being arrested and jailed by colonial armed renegades, and in danger of being tortured to death for refusing to implicate other members of the clandestine liberation movement to which he belongs.

The film's celebration of defiant courage is exemplified by a sequence in which Domingo's wife decides to find her husband. Her search ultimately culminates in the news of her husband's death. The film ends with African revolutionaries seen plotting an attack on the loathsome Luanda prison, notorious for its torture of dissidents. The film is structured with a deliberate feminist slant aimed at giving credibility to women's active participation and involvement in this dangerous liberation struggle. This emphasis, lengthily dealt with, dilutes the impact of the film's concern with armed guerrilla struggle. Thus, regarding its effectiveness, some critics thought that this deficiency amounted to romanticizing what could have constituted a forceful delineation of a liberationist uprising.[105] However, *Sambizanga* ultimately ratifies, with an indelible stamp, African revolutionary agitation. It raises consciousness and awareness of how mass mobilization and collective endeavor can help accomplish the arduous task of revolution.

The combined efforts of French, Brazilian, and Angolan filmmakers who learned filmmaking by working with foreign television and film crews during the years of struggle propelled the production of several short films during Angola's first year of independence. Ruy Duarte de Carvalho, a Portuguese who became a naturalized citizen in 1975, Abrantes Menas, Antonio Ole, and novelist Luandino Vieira (who later became the director of the Angolan Film Institute [IAC], in 1977) were among the notable directors. The films made in 1975 were *Angola, guerre du peuple,* a short film directed by Bruno Muel about the MPLA and its revolutionary struggles; *Generação,* directed by Carvalho, a documentary on three leading Angolan poets, Agostinho Neto (onetime head of MPLA), Antonio Jacinto, and Viriato da Cruz; *Sou Angolano, trabalho come força* (I am Angolan, I work with strength), an overall

Sarah Maldoror: Sambizanga; *Angola, 1972.* Courtesy of the British Film Institute.

title given to a series of eleven documentaries on Angola and considered the most ambitious of this collective endeavor by the filmmakers mentioned above.

Duarte Carvalho and Antonio Ole have established themselves as the most formidable of Angolan filmmakers. Among numerous other films, *Presente Angolano, tempo Mumuila,* made between 1979 and 1981 by Carvalho, comprises a series of ten socially and culturally oriented films; *Aprender para melhor servir* (Learn in order to serve better, 1976), *Un orchestre Angolais, les (N'Gole Ritmos)* (The rhythm of N'Gola Ritmos, 1977), and *No caminho das estrelas* (Pathway to the stars, 1980) are impressive tributes by Ole to the first president of Angola. Significantly, the Angolan authorities have committed themselves to an output of short and medium-length documentary films and television production (acquired in 1975), which is steadily progressing well into the present. Amidst its meager resources, the first feature-length films to roll out of IAC's production facilities are Carvalho's *Faz la coragem, camarada!* (Courage, comrade! 1977), Orlando Fortunato's *Memória de um dia* (Memory of a day, 1984), and the institute's first fictional film, Ruy Duarte's *Nelisita,* not produced until 1983. The structure of *Nelisita* is heavily indebted to oral tradition and a mixture of documentary technique that not only reflects many years of association with documentary films but also a major strategy focusing on audience reception and absorption of the sociocultural and political content of the film.

In Guinea-Bissau, film was a didactic tool for fostering revolutionary objectives. It was used to explain the armed struggle, to educate the masses, and to emphasize the battle victories achieved at the front. At the invitation of PAIGC's freedom fighters, during the struggle foreign filmmakers from Cuba, England, France, Holland, Italy, Sweden, and other countries covered the uprising. It was this involvement that yielded such films as *Terrorist Attack* (1968) by the British journalist Basil Davidson, about the invasion of PAIGC's headquarters by the Portuguese forces, and *No pincha* (1970) by a French television crew, depicting the enormous solidarity of the relationship between the liberation movement of PAIGC and the citizens of Guinea. In 1971 Sarah Maldoror began a film project called *Des fusils pour Banta* (Guns for Banta) with a team of Algerian technicians. Dealing with the liberation forces of Cabral in Guinea-Bissau, this film was started but never completed because of a dispute between Maldoror and some Algerian financiers.

After independence, Guinean film prospects faltered with only a paltry amount of documentary productions coming out of an uncoordinated film industry. In 1978 a thirty-minute documentary on the return

Ruy Duarte: Nelisita; *Angola, 1983.* Nwachukwu
Ukadike Collection.

of Cabral's body was made, followed by a UNICEF-sponsored twenty-
minute film, *Les jours d'Anonco* (In Anonco's time), about children.
The first Guinea-Bissau feature-length film, *N'tturudu* (1987), by musi-
cian-actor-director Umban u'Kset, was shown at the Film Fest D.C.
in May 1988. This promising young director is a man to watch. This
film is a gentle comedy, furtive in its own unique way, exploring many
themes common to black African cinema—the status quo versus
change, country versus city, and the generation gap. *Mortu Nega,*
Guinea-Bissau's second feature, produced by the Instituto Nacional de
Cinema, dramatizes the war of independence against the Portuguese
army and the problem of adapting to the new reality of living in pain
among ruins of war as well as amidst the joy of newly acquired freedom.

In colonial territories, cultural expressions of protest and resistance

Umban U'Kset: N'tturudu; *Guinea-Bissau, 1987.* Nwachukwu Ukadike Collection.

are inextricably bound up with the solidarity of the members of cultures who are victims of colonial repression. The Mozambican example demonstrates that artistic expression can indeed help to stimulate national consciousness, as when the National Front for the Liberation of Mozambique (FRELIMO) allowed cinema to systematically integrate and develop with their emerging tradition of popular resistance. Cinema eventually became a recognizable factor of such consciousness formation from the early stages of the liberation struggle to the postindependence era. Furthermore, reaction and responses to colonial domination may depend on the magnitude of such repression and mass resentment of that repression, as well as on the political leadership and ideology directing that reaction. For example, while countries like Ghana, Nigeria, and Tanzania did not engage the British in a long and protracted guerrilla war for independence, Angola, Mozambique, and Guinea-Bissau have had to fight for more than a decade for their independence. When this happens, Fanon's thesis on violence as the only "language" that the colonizer understands gains credence. This strategy, which was directed by socialist ideologies and collective militancy, was instrumental in the freedom of the colonies after five hundred years of Portuguese domination.

Beginning with the inspiration emerging from *A luta continua* and *O povo organizado,* made during the struggle and after independence respectively, the role that the film medium was to play in the new nation was beginning to become clear. The significance of both films (and of some other films made about the struggle such as *Viva FRELIMO*) is measured not only in their exemplary documentation of the transformation occurring during this period but also in their illustration of film's potential for bringing about such a transformation. The leaders of Mozambique, themselves architects of that change and witnesses of the role earlier played by the film medium, were ready to exploit it in pursuit of their revolutionary agenda. The Mozambique film industry was launched with precision—with the establishment of Instituto Nacional de Cinema—only five months after independence. Mozambique had no trained filmmakers of its own during this period, so the film institute began to operate by recruiting foreign directors. This arrangement saw the realization of films like *Um ano de independência* by Luis Patraquim and Fernando Silva (Brazil), a historical documentary depicting the long struggle for independence from the beginning of the insurrection until the first year of independence, and *Mapai,* also by Silva, on the attack of Mozambican villages such as Mapai by Ian Smith's Rhodesian army, both made in 1976. The year 1977 was especially productive, as documentary output from the young Mozambican movie industry increased. The film *25,* directed by Celso Lucas and José Celso-Correa (both Brazilians), was the most ambitious of the projects and takes its theme from history: Mozambique under Portuguese domination and the revolution that toppled it. A classic documentary, this film is a photographic legend that combines "fiction and documentary, color and black and white, tragedy and humor, epic poem and travesty," and was considered the most successful movie until then.[106]

In pursuit of its revolutionary ideology, and to make this new film industry indigenous, "coopérantes" from Britain, Brazil, and Canada were recruited to teach film production at the National Film Institute. These include Brazilian director of photography Murrillo Salles (of *Dona Flor* fame) and director Ruy Guerra (*Os fuzis,* The guns), and the Canadians Glen Hodgins, a sound man, Ophera Hallis, an editor, and Ron Hallis, a documentary filmmaker.[107] This initiative produced Mozambican filmmakers like Camillo de Sousa, Luis Simoa, and João Costa, and the infrastructure provided by the institute enabled people like Pedro Pimente and others who trained in Cuba and Paris, as well as exiled filmmakers like Ruy Guerra, to function. Guerra became the director of the institute in 1978, and in fact his years of filmmaking experience were an added advantage here. He was trained at the Institute des Hautes Etudes Cinématographiques in Paris and on graduation went to Brazil, where he established himself as one of the best directors of the Cinema Novo. His films in Brazil include *Os cafajestes* (The beach of desire, 1962) and *Os fuzis* (The guns, 1964). Following this development, the institute was well equipped with experienced professionals when it launched the production of a monthly documentary film series called *Kuxa Kanema* (The birth of cinema), coined from two Mozambican dialects, "Kuxa" in Runga, spoken in the north, meaning "birth," and "Kanema" in Makua, spoken in the south, meaning "image."[108] The new endeavor simply reflects ideological affirmation entrenched in the socialist cinematic objective of a new nation aspiring to transform its society. As a questioning cinema that scrutinizes every aspect of life, it is to be informative, producing images of Mozambican reality and realities elsewhere. In accordance with this, there is no "neutral" image in Mozambique, since film is exquisitely political and imparts and reflects the revolutionary process.

Between 1978 and 1979 the institute produced ten documentaries in the *Kuxa Kanema* series as well as two feature-length films: *Estas são as armas* (These are the weapons, 1978), directed by Murrillo Salles, a compilation documentary dealing with the struggle against Portuguese colonialism and Rhodesian aggression that became the first Mozambican film to win first prize, the Silver Dove, at the Leipzig International Film Festival in 1978;[109] and *Mueda: Memória e massacre* (Mueda: Memory and massacre, 1979) by Ruy Guerra, a film on the annual reenactment of the 1960 massacre of six hundred Mozambicans by Portuguese troops in the town of Mueda. By all indications a unique film, this fictional account of an actual event depicts the merciless liquidation of people agitating for self-determination on 16 June 1960, just before the beginning of the revolution. A social, political, and educational film expressing a liberationist socialist ideology, *Mueda* powerfully expresses the people's history in an unconventional cinematographic language. This revolutionary zeal lies within the style of execution maintained throughout the structure of the whole film. Shot in black and white, Guerra's film mixes fiction with documentary, capturing the actual dramatization of the massacre and interspersing the sequence with interviews of participants and eyewitnesses to the original massacre. It is through this disruption of continuity that the film achieves its emotional intensity. But this strategy is made even more effective by the use of hand-held camera shots producing jerky images that give the audience a feeling of authenticity of news reporting—a feeling of the massacre just having occurred. The most moving moments of this film are the eyewitness accounts of killings as seen through the eyes and experience of the elderly survivors that interrupt the fictional dramatization to tell and authenticate the story.

The style of *Mueda* is reminiscent of *Playa Girón,* a film about the Bay of Pigs disaster, which critics believe revolutionized approaches to documentary films, and of *When the Mountains Tremble,* a film about political repression in Guatemala. In *Playa Girón,* eyewitnesses and participants in the Bay of Pigs incident re-create their roles in the battle. This method introduces the viewer to the developments as they actually happened, by people who were really there. A witness is moved to the scene where the actual event occurred and is reenacted. With this approach, Teshome Gabriel points out, the film "acquires a self-reflective dimension as it reveals the process of its construction while foregrounding the problematic relation between history (the events) and fiction (the re-creation). At the same time, a participation in the fiction of the same people who were involved in the incident vests the reenactment with a credibility that would have been unattainable otherwise."[110]

Similarly, *When the Mountains Tremble*'s captivating power and emotional intensity is provided through the experiences of a survivor who witnessed the atrocities committed by government security agents. As in Guerra's film, the witness in this film also interrupts the flow of sequences to give an account of government killings. Although the insertion of this personal account through editing was an afterthought, the effectiveness of its strategy is stunning. The unusual rich background displayed here "is provided by the experiences of Nobel Peace Prize winner Rigoberta Menchu, a Christian Indian" who, through the threads of her story, exposes as never before "the courage of her people, the tragedy of greed, corruption and repression"[111] in contemporary Guatemalan history. Although Yates's, Sigel's, and Kinoy's method is controversial, it adds to the credibility of the film's condemnation of the pogrom credited to the government forces; here we see bodies lying everywhere and a woman telling how her family was massacred. This makes the criticism of such an approach somewhat irrelevant. This radical departure in style is capable of producing the political implications illustrated above.

Guerra, who was born in Mozambique, lives in Brazil and worked as a film director at a time when Brazilian cinema was being radically restructured. The creative zeal he brought to *Mueda* had already been demonstrated in *Os fuzis,* a film he directed in Brazil. This film was made at the time Cinema Novo was at its aesthetic zenith and was considered one of the best in this tradition. As in the case of *Mueda,* where "real events" interrupt the fictional story line, in *Os fuzis,* the documentary sequences are interrupted by fictional events. *Mueda* and *When the Mountains Tremble* both apply revolutionary strategies to invoke our attention to the plight of a people; we see the tragedy that befalls them and identify with their culture and the magnitude of brutality they suffer from repressive regimes. In both cases, as the story unfolds detailing the murder of defenseless citizens, the witnesses' stories become a national story—a chance to evaluate the past, assess the present, and possibly instigate changes for the future. *Mueda* does not attempt to hide the political obligations of its structure or attempt to obliterate the distortions created by distinctions between fiction, documentary, and real events. In fact, such distinctions become apparent as we watch the film, hence such alignment (division, if you will) helps to explain what has happened and what is happening, thereby bringing the audience nearer to the actual event.

Offensiva (The offensive, 1980), by Camillo de Sousa, shows the late president of Mozambique, Samora Machel, doing impressive investigative reporting. In this film the president proved that incompetence, bureaucratization, mismanagement, carelessness, indiscipline, wrong working methods, theft, sabotage, and destruction of merchandise and equipment are the handiwork of enemies of the revolution who, for political reasons, destroy the nation's development projects so that socialism will be blamed. In this moving documentary, the president visited factories, warehouses, and the country's housing corporation—unannounced. The camera in cinéma vérité style catches people unaware, revealing an unprecedented man-made maladministration. President Machel's oratory is combined with photographic innovativeness, as when the camera frame-by-frame zooms in, à la *Wavelength,* to the still photograph of apartheid South African President P. W. Botha (allowing the audience to identify this symbol of destabilization). *Abaixo o apartheid* (They dare cross our border, 1981), by José Cardoso, shows clips of the dead and officers of the Mozambican armed forces who admit, as they are successively identified, collaborating with South Africa.

The Film Institute of Mozambique also released three made-for-television shorts that premiered in New York City in September 1988 and used the same strategy to generate public awareness and condemnation of Renamo's incessant guerrilla attacks on lives and property. All made in 1988, *Escola em armas* (School in arms) shows a school destroyed when guerrillas attack. Dramatizing the actual attack, an eyewitness—a member of the government troops who helped repel the attack—tells how it happened, displaying the bandit's weapons. *Os deslocados* (The refugees) depicts a multitude of refugees, also victims of the war. An example of human misery that presents people with little or no clothing, women and children who have lost all of their belongings to the bandits, and those whose legs have either been blown off or severed by Renamo mines or machetes, this film tells how the refugees, on a long trek to safety, eat anything to keep alive. *A criança e a sua difícil reintegração* (The child and his difficult reintegration) is about government efforts, some of them futile, to reintegrate the children of the streets into society. Concern for the future is one of the themes depicted in Carlos Henriques's (Angola) and João Costa's (Mozambique) *Pamberi ne Zimbabwe* (Let's fight for Zimbabwe, 1981), a landmark film coproduced by the film institutes of Mozambique and Angola on the independence of Zimbabwe, and in *Os comprometidos* (The treatment of traitors, 1983), a group production also made at the film institutes.

The pace of Angolan and Mozambican film production has seemed to slow down. Political instability prevails in both countries. Although a cease-fire is holding in Angola, transition to a "unity" government and economic difficulties may force the government to redirect its financial commitment from the film industries to other more urgent and pressing needs. The war, which has been raging in Angola since 1975, pits the government of José Eduardo dos Santos against the National Union for the Total Independence of Angola (UNITA), the rebel group led by Jonas Savimbi. It has shattered the economy of this former Portuguese colony, creating a large number of refugees and rendering the countryside uninhabitable. Complicating an already chaotic political situation is superpower meddling. East and West hegemonic ideologies, until the collapse of communism in eastern Europe, vied for Angola as a critical pawn in their competition for imperialistic expansion. While the Soviet Union provided Angola with MIG-23 jet fighters, M1-24 helicopters, Ilyshin cargo jets, T-62 tanks, antiaircraft missiles and armored personnel carriers, the U.S. provided Stinger antiaircraft missiles and other covert logistical support (the amount involved kept secret by the Reagan and Bush administrations) to Savimbi forces who are also armed and financed by apartheid South Africa. In addition, other nations have also become accessories to the deaths of millions of Africans by participating in armament sales: Belgium sold bullets and artillery shells; Brazil sold jeeps and trucks; Britain sold jeeps and military radios; France sold military helicopters; Japan, uniforms; Spain and Switzerland, training aircraft; and West Germany, trucks and communications equipment,[112] draining more than half of Angola's export earnings from oil.

Similarly, Mozambique is locked in a sixteen-year-old war, and like Angola's, it too is exacerbated by foreign meddling. Fighting the government forces is a rebel group called Renamo, a Portuguese acronym for the Mozambique National Resistance (MNR). Like UNITA, Renamo's armed renegades use callous sabotage and terrorism to direct its operations. This includes indiscriminate killings and raping of villagers, destruction of property, and the cutting off of villagers' ears, noses, and fingers. These "bandidos armados" (armed bandits) are thought of by the local Mozambican population in the same way that the Ovimbundu[113] people of Angola regard Savimbi and his clones, as "butchers of Cuito."[114] Like UNITA, Renamo wantonly destroys rail lines, sabotages bridges, roads, water and electricity supplies, and terrorizes farmers. Even though these gangs of killers are unpopular with their own people, whom they aspire to lead, they are allowed to maintain offices in Washington, D.C. (at the Heritage Foundation Headquarters), and, as the *New York Times* revealed, a group of U.S. businessmen and conservative and evangelical circles still finance these Mozambican murderers.[115] Stemming from narrow political conviction, their obsession with communism makes them haters of any government that some ideologues label "Marxist." They blindly support any group of Africans or any Third World country whose leaders describe themselves as "freedom fighters." In fact, neither Angola nor Mozambique pose a threat to the U.S. or its interests in any way. Despite the large number of Cubans and Soviets who were present in Angola (without the former, the rebels probably would have crushed a legitimate government), it is the Gulf Oil Company and the United States that have been benefiting from the huge oil deposits in Angola's Cabinda region. Apart from Nigeria, Angola is the second largest African supplier of oil to the United States. Significantly, in what amounts to pro-Western liberalization, Angola and Mozambique have taken steps to diversify their economies, and both governments can no longer be considered as ardently Communist. According to *The Economist,* both countries now opt for "better economic policies," encouraging free-market enterprise.[116] But as an Angolan national recently indicated, the social and economic situation would be better if it were not for the war.

Both Angola and Mozambique have proven that film, especially the documentary, has an immense capability of reaching a wide audience and can thus invoke a higher degree of emotional involvement than any other medium of communication. While the documentary role in this respect may be disputed, revolutionary filmmakers tend to hold tenaciously to this claim, agreeing that documentary is easier to manipulate and distort to reflect the ideological position directing its execution and reception.

The films discussed above have shown the heroic liberationist effort with which the lusophone African cinema was created, emphasizing a nationalistic tendency rooted in historical, social, and political themes. Almost all were produced in a documentary format, with very few short fiction and feature-length films. This imbalance is connected with what one might call economic, technical, and political reasons. Emanating from oppression and deprivation, these young nations ravaged by war lacked the financial stability to invest in expensive equipment. Since they had no experienced film directors and technicians, money that could have been used to develop the industry went to the maintenance of expatriate filmmakers imported to help establish new industries. Under this limitation it was not feasible to embark upon mass production of feature films. There is no doubt that the new society under construction is best explained through documentaries, which are cheaper for them to produce and which have effectively, aesthetically, and ideologically proven to be a model for African solidarity. It is hoped that the level of maturity displayed in many of their impressive films will continue to grow.

5

New Developments in
Black African Cinema

*Today, we can summon to memory the
languages of our ancestors. What is
important, though, is the rediscovery of the
power of words of our people. Metropolitan
French, English, Spanish—all languages of
colonization to be colonized in turn.*
—Maryse Conde

*I shall speak about Africa, with confidence
both that some of what I have to say will work
elsewhere in the so-called Third World and
that it will not work at all in some places.*
—Kwame Anthony Appiah

Contours of an Emerging Trend:
Toward a New Cinema?

The ab0ve statements vividly address problems of cultural production
within the African diaspora and Third World societies. With production
processes becoming increasingly validated in terms of new modes of
film practice, this endeavor, utilizing indigenous systems of thought,
is creating aesthetic practices that illuminate developmental struggles.
Even though positive results have emerged from this collective cultural
experience, the urge to give more specific character to cultural products
means widening the indigenous boundaries for the investigation of

modes of representation to provoke discussion. We can see this in the reading of "nativist texts," when interrogation of production processes stimulates the selection, arrangement, and reception of cultural products. African cinema, as already established in previous chapters, is shaped by the producer's avowed determination to move ahead, unencumbered by the legacy of the dominant paradigms.

In recent years innovative works of historical, cultural, political, and aesthetic significance have emerged from "new breed" African filmmakers as well as from the pioneers, enabling us to speak about "interrogation of origins" (that is, transformation of negative conventions into a positive source of signification), "analytical complexities" (exploration of African alterity via sociocultural dynamics), and "aesthetic diversion" (nationalistic practices versus aesthetic internationalism). It is now possible to say that African cinema is at last penetrating the world market with major works of indigenous cultures that explore and adapt their own oral and literary traditions in the articulation of a new film language. Yet, the relationship between the perception of African cinema and the realities it tries to depict is a paradox marked by the filmmakers' indefatigable struggle.

On the one hand, experimental trends inherent in recent developments in African cinema exemplify a characteristic emphasis on film as cultural and political practice. As the concern for economic viability deepens, African cinema can also be understood from the perspective of thematic and aesthetic pluralism. On the other hand, the aesthetic orientation seen at first as hybrid was gainfully used to critique the aesthetics and ideology of alien film practices, later developing as a renovated film language. Also, the employment of oral tradition and other cultural codes that served as the base for indigenous aesthetics also helped to repostulate canonized Western paradigms (modes of production and spectatorship). However, while oral narrative illuminates the paradigmatic exigency of black African film practice, the engendering configurations for the new aesthetic are in danger of being misread as an alienating convention. It is my contention that this alienating posturing is inescapable—involving both the combative didactive practices of nationalistic concerns (Sembene, Hondo, Gerima, Kaboré, Cissé, and Ansah exemplify this category) and the politically compromised aesthetic internationalism of economic concerns (exemplified by the works of Ouedraogo, Sissoko, and Duparc).

In the first instance we have categories of films put in the service of political consciousness, and in the second, films that are thematically audacious and innovative but whose sociopolitical allegory is diffused by pandering to the imitation of alien conventions and commercialization. If it is true within the confines of political consciousness and cultural affirmation that the latter works would be deemed as abandoning the collective consciousness engendered in the pioneering works, it is the recourse to aesthetic internationalism—the fusion of traditional codes with canonized Western forms—with which the films aspire to break through national and international alienation.

Politically conscious films constituted the mainstream, at least through the early eighties, especially in the francophone and lusophone regions. In the late eighties, the new African films created by the new-comers launched the opposition to the dominant didactic formulas. Seeing themselves as no longer in the periphery, the new filmmakers discarded heavy-handed didacticism for narrative conventions that stressed entertainment over instruction. Although the films are still modeled after oral tradition, the majority, as we shall see, cannot be said to be revitalizing film language. There seems to be a movement away from the political use of the film medium, which addresses and relates to authentic cultures and histories, toward a concern with film as an object of anthropological interest. It has been argued that most films employ the same Western ethnographic conventions that have historically worked to limit the understanding of Africa's sociocultural formations.[1] Is African cinema in general lacking the dynamism and experimentalism of the sixties and seventies? How has its film practice developed operational tactics that promote (inter)nationalization of film form and ideological precepts? Has the diversity of textual expressions created new attitudes toward black African film culture? This chapter will provide a matrix of convergent and divergent perspectives by ex-amining recent films, illuminating their historical, sociopolitical, and cultural affirmations, while at the same time foregrounding the ap-proaches and structuring complexities of the emerging trends.

African cinematic practice of the 1980s, if nothing else, has done an enormous job in terms of restating the authentic values of African soci-ety and, given the popularity of some of the films, enhancing the posi-tion of this cinema within the stylistic repertoire of world cinema. With the protean notion of Africa as "cinematographic desert" obsolete, the question is no longer whether Africans can make films. The excitement and expectation offered by recent films compel one to accept that there can be a prosperous African film practice given the right incentives. The unprecedented success of some recent African films, both in criti-cal acclaim as well as in box-office receipts (in Africa, Europe, and the United States), promulgates speculation regarding the emerging trend of new African cinema. Does the current trend constitute what might be considered the quintessence of African cinematographic art and in-dustry? It is with this question in mind that I shall examine *Yeelen* (Brightness, 1987) by Souleymane Cissé, *Yaaba* (1989) and *Tilai* (1990), both by Idrissa Ouedraogo, and the following social-realist films (also

Idrissa Ouedraogo: Yaaba; *Burkina Faso, 1989.* Courtesy of the British Film Institute.

of cultural ramifications): *Finzan* (1989) by Cheick Oumar Sissoko, *Bal poussière* (Dancing in the dust, 1988) by Henri Duparc, and *Zan Boko* (1988) by Gaston Kaboré. I shall also address this study to the historical affirmations in Med Hondo's *Sarraounia* (1987), Kwaw Ansah's *Heritage . . . Africa* (1988), and Ousmane Sembene and Thierno Faty Sow's *Camp de Thiaroye* (The camp at Thiaroye, 1987) and shall examine their historical propensities and methods of construction.

The new African films have not strayed too far from the issues depicted in earlier films, yet the impact of the popular films by the "new breeds" are more strongly felt than that of their predecessors. I will argue that the impact of the popular African films of the eighties is a result of filmic subterfuge: passion for ethnographic information (thematic construction); profilmic and extrafilmic organization (immutable landscape); and aesthetic reconciliation (the incorporation of oral art).

In black African film practice, Ntongela Masilela identifies the historical and cultural meaning of African cinema as relating to the "dialogism" between Frantz Fanon's philosophy of culture and Amilcar Cabral's philosophy of history, noting that the former is a deliberate attempt to restructure Africa's political systems while the latter strives to redraw the map of the "social geography of African history."[2] Applied to the new African cinema of the late eighties, it is possible for one film to embrace both philosophies, as in the cases of *Camp de Thiaroye, Zan Boko, Heritage . . . Africa*, and *Sarraounia*, whose structures exhibit affinities with the social and historical philosophies of Cabral as well as the cultural and political philosophies of Fanon. Although films such as *Yeelen, Tilai, Bal poussière*, and *Finzan* openly exhibit an exquisite affinity with culture, they lack the political candor of Fanon's ideas. Exception, however, can be made for *Yeelen*, whose analytical complexity and (arguably) biased political undercurrents are hidden beneath the umbrella of traditional culture.[3]

The films as indigenous cultural expressions are situated within the social context of multicultural Africa. Hence, the symptomatic trend characterizes a wide range of representation and interpretation from works inspired by African and Third World resentment of Western processes of conversion (*Camp de Thiaroye, Heritage*, and *Sarraounia*) to culture-based representational structure (*Yaaba, Yeelen, Finzan*, and *Zan Boko*). It is this resistance to assimilation that unites black African cinema with Africanists' theories on African culture. Although the films display their "unity on a continental plane . . . they equally differentiate themselves from each other by simultaneously articulating national cultural patterns, national ideological conflicts and national class confrontations,"[4] and, we might also add, national economic patterns. For example, *Bal poussière* could be read as a political film, although its few political jabs get lost in the comedic structure. Yet, like the film's environment, some narrative codes (its theme and music) are typically African. Although the focus of each film is on geographically divergent zones, the contents and significations indicate similarity of purpose and goals. Ideologically, there is the persistent struggle to develop genuine film practice; politically, there is an attempt to use the film medium as a speaking voice of the people; and aesthetically, there is relentless experimentation with film form aimed at achieving indigenous film culture, although it has not been possible to reach this goal. Similarly, there is a profound urge to satisfy the tastes of both African and foreign audiences. Reflecting the economic realities in Africa today, the targeting of foreign audiences connects philosophically with the notion of economic viability, in which effective export of goods enhances the gross national product.

Narration, Transgression, and the Centrality of Culture

Black African film practice rejects all vestiges of colonialism and acculturation. Because cultural assimilation has involved the protracted co-

Idrissa Ouedraogo: Tilai; *Burkina Faso, 1990.* Courtesy of
Waka Films AG.

lonial process of stripping Africans of their individuality, the various
steps taken to counter this process argue for the linkage of self-affirmation with universal consciousness, for example, attachment of the individual to society, and society's place in the centrality and the collectiv-
ity of world culture. This process of inclusion and retrievability,
apropos to what John A. A. Ayoade terms "reculturation and re-Afri-
canization,"[5] echoes the need for the restitution of social institutions
and relations and beliefs and practices congenial to indigenous traditions expressed in nationalist agendas. In his essay "Cultural Restitution and Independent Black Cinema," Tony Gittens identifies some

essential characteristics of indigenous beliefs and practices. He states that "they are usually ritualized and celebrated in a process which helps to engender a sense of national, secular, regional, or ethnic pride, dependent on the type of cohesive force and social priorities binding a particular group together."[6] This explains why cultural productions are viewed critically and, regarding African films considered by Africanists as the epitome of decolonization, there is continuous demand for African dignity to be forcefully depicted on screen. "Dignity," in the words of the late Captain Thomas Sankara, the ex-president of Burkina Faso,

> has not been presented enough [in African films]. The cry from the heart, justice, too, the nobility and the necessity for struggle in Africa, that has not been shown enough. Sometimes one has the impression that Africans are striving in vain in a world of evil men. What we have experienced, what we have suffered, what we are now experiencing, what we are still suffering—this has not been publicized enough and we also know that the media elsewhere in the world are efficacious in preventing people in other countries from understanding the struggle which we are waging here.[7]

African films such as *Yaaba, Tilai, Zan Boko, Yeelen,* and *Finzan* offer meticulous anthropological renditions of African cultures. The films are true to life and do not attempt to rearrange natural settings or modernize them to look foreign. In their cultural manifestations, certain rituals, music, dance, and song, once considered primitive, are frequently adopted motifs in these films. It has not been easy to achieve a way of reconfiguring the images created, of transforming them into counterhegemonic images capable of confronting dominant paradigms in order to engender a sense of African pride and the sort of identity envisaged by Sankara. Sensibility and sensitivity as the mainstay of African film practice, and the need for indigenous characteristics, simply require a formula that presents the environment and characters without running into the Hollywood situation in which non-Western images connote the exotic "Other."

While sympathizing with the pioneering impulse that created African cinema, the "new breed" African filmmaker seeks to advance cinematic strategy beyond the ideologies that have defined the contours of didactic sociopolitical films. In the first place, there has been no inclination toward cultivating the services of professional actors. Second, in the absence of a sound infrastructure to pursue glamorous projects, the filmmakers feel there is an overabundance of local themes and an inexhaustible number of sociocultural motifs with which to sustain production. Thus, as long as village scenery and pastoral landscapes continue to provide the desired spectacle and backgrounds that urban land-scapes lack (for example, skyscrapers that are similar to the ones in Paris, London, and New York), filmmakers capitalize on this simple arithmetic of economics.

The cultural dynamics of African cinema must also be examined within the larger significations of African cultural discourse. Africanist thinking has long recognized the dialectical link between one factor of development and another, in this case, the coalition of cultural and economic enterprises. For example, on the dynamics of culture, Sékou Touré of Guinea notes that "every people must struggle to exist by creating the material means of its existence."[8] For him, culture is "a social process, an infrastructure" whose characteristics are determined by "the level of development of productive forces and the nature of the means of production as determined by the historical and social context."[9] Bringing this point closer within the environs of the dominated people's struggle in Africa in particular, Touré goes on to emphasize that "the cultural level of a people . . . its means of conquering knowledge, its manner of explaining phenomena, will depend on the . . . degree of objectivity and abstraction attained in the heat of action to gain mastery over ever more perfect techniques."[10]

In the African film industry, the tripartite relationship amongst the cultural, economic, and historical forces responsible for the development of African cinema reflects the shifting conditions of African culture and its economy. If the responsibility of the African film industry is to cultivate audiences for African film, then the accomplishments gained in production—the instinct for self-preservation (cultural restitution) and fulfillment (aesthetic development)—must embrace societal and infrastructural requirements (audience reception). As it is now, African cinema has presented African culture both realistically and impressively on screen. But African cinema has not been able to exploit the continent's economic potential. An attempt to pull African film practice out of its current form of marginality can only be achieved if genuine development of the audience and reception patterns are refocused. And, if there is to be a common ground in this film practice, it will undoubtedly be found in the aspect of production to be nurtured rather than patronized in Africa, not perceived as a metaphor for otherness, isolation, and difference but as a continent central to world power institutions, no longer bound to the periphery.

Generally, while African film practice has succeeded in renovating its film language, it can also be argued that it has failed to produce a new African audience capable of exploring different patterns of signification while pondering this "new" African film language. Toward this goal, the most important endeavor would be the making of films that challenge the reception patterns of the African audience. While some African films succeed in attaining this goal, some films actually alienate their audiences, precluding the building of a strong African audience for African films.

Yeleen, Yaaba, Tilai, Zan Boko, and *Finzan* are African films made in the 1980s that have emphasized African culture specifically and, in the case of *Zan Boko,* have contrasted precolonial tranquility with the turbulence of contemporary life. This is not the first time that African culture has been meticulously studied in African cinema. If compared with earlier black African films, these new films show shifting aesthetic and formal concerns. Here we find that the sociocultural dynamics that influence the cinematic language of explication can be both an asset and anathema. In this sense, structural configuration poses methodological questions not only about what the artists are saying with the images they create but also about how they say it. This surging interest in these recent African films stems from the curious anthropological images they proffer, some critics reading them as innovative, others as repugnant. Agreeably, there is vivid concern to stretch inquiries about Africa beyond cultural and anthropological limitations. The crux of the matter is that, while the majority of the films are packed with realistic images of everyday village life, overemphasis on "lowlife" details reinforces the fascination with the exotic African images in Western ethnographic films. Rather than destroying and deconstructing canonized codes of spectatorial fascination through rejuvenated film form and modes of production, some of the films perpetuate marginality and also invite reductionist reading of the films mainly within the confines of ethnographic film discourse.

From another perspective, some critics have argued that the images and verisimilitude present in African films indicate structures that manifest African notions of ethnography, and that by depicting the African peoples the way they are, their cultures and histories, these images explore value systems contrary to Western ethnocentric understanding (in which non-Western images are evaluated by Western norms). In this sense the films are also read as reversing the institutionalized condescension and master-race narcissism offered in Western ethnographic films.[11] It is in this light that we focus on the varying trends of the African films of the eighties by examining their thematic, aesthetic, and textual configurations.

Souleymane Cissé's *Yeelen* (prize winner at the 1987 Cannes Film Festival) epitomizes the daring stance shared by African cinema pioneers. In every respect the filmmaker's quest for an indigenous film structure parallels the film's exploratory tactics and is realized in a complex cinematic style. The film narrates an initiation journey that puts father (Somo Diarra) and son (Nianankoro) on a collision course as they struggle for supremacy in the possession of a special knowledge—the secrets of nature—that is exclusive to the Bambara people of Mali. The father, seeking to prevent his son from acquiring this special knowledge, plans to kill him. But Nianankoro's mother intervenes by sending her son away (into an initiation journey that introduces him to the oral cultures and traditions common to the Sahel). This pilgrimage takes him across the semiarid regions spanning the Bambara to Dogon and Fulani lands, enabling him to acquire the ultimate knowledge that establishes his own supernatural powers.

Cissé documents that this film was accomplished through mutual understanding and respect, by placing the significations of form and content within social, cultural, and historical contexts and in a transgressive mode of address far apart from dogmatic codes and conventions. For example, *Yeelen* could either be seen as promulgating a strict reflectionist or deterministic notion of cultural and social connotations or, more daringly, it could be read as an antitraditionalist allegory that introduces "the correlate" and "the resilient" as dichotomous canons for the critique of tradition and change.[12] The very depiction of the "Komo" secret society, in which the camera lens witnesses the actual initiation, rituals, and ceremonies, would ordinarily have been regarded as sacrilegious and intrusive. In fact, traditional Malians have long been suspicious of what they term "diabolic images" of the magic machine of the devils' creation named *Tiyatra*.[13] But Cissé holds the middle ground between the Western ethnographic conception of the moving image, which seeks out the misery of the Third World, and the falsehood of repressing it on the grounds of cultural intrusion. Thus *Yeelen* is significant for a number of reasons: the film creates a dialectic of old and new; as a critique of culture, it displays new ideas; and as a critique of convention, the filmic strategy suggests a resolute trend in creativity, fresh and focused on African film language. Out of this practice, however, emerge certain questions of perspicacity and contradictions of ideological ramification. I attempt to expedite this study through an examination of Cissé's concern for authenticity and respectful treatment of the subject and the cinematic strategies contiguous to the film's realization.

Structured around mythological patterns, *Yeelen*'s complex narrative allows one to explore the articulation of the precolonial and the traditional. The film's binary structure foregrounds the distinctive dynamic of traditional culture, also revealing its contradictions, such as the antecedent practices indicative of what Kwame Anthony Appiah, in another context, terms "exclusivity of insight."[14] By calling attention to the opposition and rejection that dichotomize traditional systems, Cissé's projection of the inevitability thus centers around apostasy, which works as a revisionist code that, though not on par with traditional systems, enables him to construct the dialectics of culture and morality. By having Diarra refuse to transfer generations of secrets to his son, the viewer is forced to sympathize with Nianankoro when he attempts the retrieval of this knowledge by force. In this respect, the father's action nullifies one of Africa's most cherished traditions—the quest for knowledge—while the son's rebellion is just another case of nonchalance typifying negation of the tradition of morality that is emblematic of respect and loyalty to the elders. The film does not show us, however, that Diarra is not obligated to reveal such secrets to his son since he is too young to be entrusted with the secrets of the Komo, which only members who have attained the rank of "Kore" can possess. According to Kate Ezra, it takes a neophyte "seven-year cycles through six grades of progressively more arcane knowledge" to reach, at old age, the Kore stage.[15] Because the Komo is highly restrictive, and because the powers wielded by the members are all-encompassing, like other secret societies all over the world, it is prone to criticism and rejection. But considering that Cissé's background is in the Soninke, early Islamized marabouts,[16] it is possible that the director is speaking on behalf of his own clan, which may be deprived of admission to this impregnable Bambara knowledge.

The nation of Mali is 90 percent Islamic, and Cissé's view, while its focus is mainly on contemporary Muslim urban and rural society, does not necessarily indicate that traditional systems should be discounted. Rather, he reflects on what has plagued African sensibility for many years. He ponders the potentials of traditional culture—for example, the practice of witchcraft—which is not put at the service of advancement, in what amounts to an Africanist injunction to garner such culture for posterity. Put another way, this implies that beyond its (witchcraft's) present scope, Cissé is advocating a new kind of thinking, a refinement in which such powers are no longer misused but are transformed from destruction to invention, as have been the inspirations that have shaped Western scientific and technological prowess.

It is interesting to note that he has the ability to tell a legendary tale against the backdrop of a cultural motif without resorting to reductionist conventions. His fabulous attention to detail is not simply exploitive, illustrative, or didactic; rather, he develops a way of introducing new cultural perspectives—new ways of looking, discovering, and identifying. He does not select his characters and locations in order to simplify or exoticize them; his composition in depth, camera movement, mise-en-scène, and sound coalesce into what might be termed a discerning vision. Together with the natural movement and mannerisms of his

Souleymane Cissé: Yeelen (*Brightness*); *Mali, 1987.* Courtesy of the British Film Institute.

nonprofessional actors, the distinctions between society and culture and fiction and reality are interrogated as fictional characters are juxtaposed against ritual and the ritualistic to evoke specific sociocultural dynamics. This prerogative, charged with the inclination for authenticity, is attributable to the philosophy emerging from the "mastery of content," as he says, which forces one "to select forms that are appropriate."[17]

In *Yeelen* the characters must go through a series of encounters as part of an initiation process that would enable them to acquire more power and knowledge. In the end, both father and son perish. For Nianankoro to attain the level of maturity necessary to confront his father's prowess means the acquisition of occult powers. He must recover a specter—a long piece of carved wood shaped like a wing which symbolizes knowledge and power—which is the only thing capable of destroying the Komo. Already he has retrieved parts of the missing wing from his mother, and she now reveals to him that the remaining part of the Kore is in the possession of his father's identical twin brother, Djigui, a blind man who fled the Bambara land. Later we learn that Djigui himself lost his sight trying to acquire the Komo secret. A series of encounters which attempts to cast doubt on the relevance of the whole process of this mystical acquisition and the negative connotations of the cult are set in motion: Nianankoro kills Baafing, one of his other uncles who tries to persuade him to give up his revengeful mission. In the land of the Fulanis (Peul), he seduces the king's wife, Attou, proclaiming, "My penis betrayed me." Later he marries her and she bears him a son.

On the other side of the conflict, members of the Komo cult are meeting secretly and deciding what kind of punishment to inflict upon Nianankoro. He must be stopped before he acquires the power to destroy them, and this means destroying him. It is not surprising that his father, armed with the pestle of the Komo, embarks on the dreadful journey of tracking him down. When they finally meet, Cissé unleashes one of cinema's most dramatic moments. Nianankoro, armed with the wing of the Kore, and his father, with the pestle of Komo, stand gazing at each other. In this confrontational stance there is a powerful and unpretentious composition; the extreme close-up of both men's faces compels us to witness a wide range of moving emotions. Few words are exchanged. We see both men perspiring feverishly, and when the tears in Nianankoro's eyes begin to trickle down, both Kore and the pestle emit magical rays. The screen turns translucent, an indication that the competition is over, as both men are destroyed and the earth scorched.

By allowing Attou and her son to survive, Cissé's prophecy is fulfilled. This was first implied when Nianankoro is seen deliberating with Djigui on the parched ground of the Dogon, when we learn that the Komo cult, if unchecked, will continue to use its powers to subjugate the inhabitants. In the last scene, Nianankoro's son is seen walking over a large sand dune through a beautiful desert. He uncovers two "orbs," gives one to his mother, who in turn gives him Nianankoro's *grand boubou* (robe). If an accurate reflection of a particular society is the main point of *Yeelen*'s narrative structure, the film can be read as criticizing redundant aspects of the Komo cult and at the same time presenting it as an authentic culture specifically valorized to project its cultural significance. The film's utilization of the myth of origin with which it embellishes its structure is indicative of the credo of returning to one's roots as a paradigm of reaffirmation, politically as well as aesthetically.

Amie Williams's observation that *Yeelen* and some other African films "dip into the ancient past not to escape the present or lapse into nostalgia but to extract knowledge and history relevant to the present condition of its viewers as dispersed postcolonial subjects"[18] echoes Cissé's contentious stance of transforming spectator intractability (African or Western) into docility, a transformation involving active processes of "looking," "interpreting," and "discovering."

Nianankoro's son's position not only exemplifies hope for Africa but also ratifies, once again, what many Africans have wished for in the postcolonial era: eradication of all forms of dictatorship and the sweeping away of all dictators, tyrants, and corruption, making way for a new generation to emerge. In this sense, the dramatic closure reminiscent of most African films, à la Sembene, withholds judgment. Cissé's *Yeelen* imposes the filmmaker's vision.

Yeelen displays Cissé's powers of directorial invention in its combination of forms. As a poetic celebration of African culture it is dynamic; in the sense of authenticity and cultural iconography and in the sense of indigenous African art form, it is a classical epic reminiscent of the tradition of Sanjata, weaving aspects of repressed cultural motifs—rituals, folklore, and symbols—into a historical tapestry of ritual values. As a cinematic summa encompassing the indigenous and the mainstream, it specifically alludes to styles ranging from Sembene's candid didacticism to Hondo's eruptive style; in it we find the fusion of ethnographic and documentary modes, fiction and reality, cinéma vérité and oral literature.

Although *Yeelen* is not exactly a film that fits well into the tradition of social realism, its pattern of construction reflects a synthesis of ideology and aesthetics that is reminiscent of early Soviet filmmaking. For instance, Vertov's radical documentary practice was distinguished by artistic and innovative editing and camera technique. So too is *Yeelen* in its formalist criteria of mise-en-scène, lighting, photography, and directing, all fused with the cultural components of African oral tradition to produce a distinctive narrative structure and rhythmic patterning that make it brilliantly evocative. It is here that Cissé succeeds where many have failed. However, our concern is not to appraise the film as the "most beautiful film ever to have emerged out of Africa,"[19] as it would be naïve to subscribe to that view, but rather to see it as a dynamic construction whose beautiful photography demystifies the notion of the photogenic. This film compels the viewer to feel as if, in Alice Walker's phrase, "one has been in Africa during several centuries."[20] It is this that is central to our discourse.

Yeelen's inventiveness is also notable in its subversion of linear narrative structure. For example, favoring short vignette over lengthy narrative development, it could be argued, is instrumental to the film's complex structure. Many scenes and sequences are particularly illuminating for various innovative reasons. But this structure emanates from the complex paradigms of the cultures presented in each episode. The purpose is to foreground the use of cultural codes to force the viewer

Souleymane Cissé: Yeelen (*Brightness*); *Mali, 1987.* Courtesy of California Newsreel.

to articulate the complexity of the relationship of precolonial structures to the present. For instance, the film's flashbacks draw attention to the interplay between past and present, and, since the film is replete with so many allusions, it also illuminates the boundaries of fact and fantasy. This means that the language of indigenous modes of inquiry is presented in a dichotomous art that bridges the distinction between the African mode of address (precolonial past) and the technologically inspired mode of representation (neocolonial present). I will expand upon this with specific examples to illustrate that there is a dialectical connection between traditional art forms and the mainstream, based around reconstitution, and I will show how this duality affirms cultural existence and identity in a nonconvoluted fashion.

Nature and scenery have constituted the settings of the majority of African films, although not as a focal point of interest as is the case in Cissé's *Yeelen.* Most of the events take place in the bush, such as the initiations, or on the parched grounds of the Sahel, but these settings are neither romanticized nor reduced to exotic decor in the Hollywood fashion that would deny Africans their culture. Universal significance is accorded nature's gifts; for example, ancestral soil, water, and trees are assigned symbolic values. In the scene in which Nianankoro and Attou are seen bathing, water symbolizes purity and fecundity, and the respect attached to the shooting of this sequence clearly indicates Africa's notion of morality maintaining the human body as a sacred entity. Although seminudity is visible, it is presented in a wholesome, nonsensational way. Similarly, colors are significant, as in the black pigmentation of Attou, Nianankoro, and the close-up shot of Nianankoro's mother as her fingers mix the water in the bowl before she uses it to purify her son. Consider also the shot of the stream water and blue sky, together with the natural shadows cast by the sunlight; these are captured in their purest naturalism. This attention to visual simplicity compels one to think about the close-up shots of the cliff leading to the stream as Cissé's panoramic camera pans slowly around to highlight natural beauty at its best.

In Africa the tree is universally symbolic, and like any other of nature's creations, accorded multiple interpretations. In the West, what is called "woods" may just be as thick as what Hollywood depicts in Africa as "forest" or "jungle." There is what one might call the cosmic tree that Africans believe eternalizes the link between the earth and the cosmic universe, an intermediary between the natural and the supernatural. Trees are also valued for providing basic necessities of life: food, medicine, and knowledge. Residents of the Sahel attach special importance to the baobab tree; it plays an important role in initiations and ceremonies.[21] In *Yeelen* rituals are performed under a baobab tree, which serves as a meeting place for cult members. (Cissé was particularly concerned with appropriate representation of the rituals to instill their significance and meanings in order to transcend the images of Africa offered in ethnographic films.) The tree is also an instrument of power and has mystical dimensions; the wing of Kore and the pestle of Komo (symbols of power and knowledge) are both carved from the tree of wisdom. As cultural "eyes," they are deemed to have seen ancestors come and go. In many African films of the Sahel region there is hardly any one film without the baobab tree.

The level of experimentation, solid as it is here, ratifies Cissé's contention that "knowledge is built and consolidated by one generation [precolonial], it is destroyed by another [colonialism], and recreated by a new generation [indigenous practices]."[22] In his discussion of the production and commodification of African art, Kwame Anthony Appiah distinguishes between the "traditional" and the "neotraditional."[23] "Traditional" African art—likely to be favored by minority African elites, "if they [buy] art"—dons the accoutrements of precolonial established "styles" and "methods," whereas the "neotraditional" is tourist art "produced for the West."[24] Applied to African

Souleymane Cissé: Yeelen (*Brightness*); *Mali, 1987.* Courtesy of the British Film Institute.

cinema, I would argue that there is no precolonial African structure of the cinema, but rather that, as I have stated in chapter 1, oral narrative gave African cinema precolonial traits that were integrated into the postcolonial cinematic paradigm. It is more plausible, therefore, to state that since African cinema originated after independence from two conventions—the mainstream and the indigenous—it exhibits affinities with the "neotraditional" in terms of inception but not in terms of commodification as in the "neotraditional genre" of African art.[25] However, since Africa is deeply immersed in a culture of poverty that worsened in the late eighties, some sections of African film practice transmogrified to what one might call "bitraditional" structures. This in turn, with respect to the popular films of the late 1980s, made them susceptible to exploitation, commercialization, and misinterpretation. Simply put, what is typical about this genre (bitraditional structure) is the choice of a universalist theme distinguished by hybrid conventions, which targets foreign spectators for materialistic ends. Does this mean that the films are incapable of cultivating African film audiences, or confronting and challenging the dominant conventions that Hollywood uses to construct denigrated images of the "other"?

Gaston Kaboré, Idrissa Ouedraogo, and Cheick Oumar Sissoko, Pfaff notes, "seem to have a predilection for the filming of rural life-styles," but their films are "not made with specific ethnographic intentions."[26] But of the monotonous images of women pounding millet or corn, or families cooking or eating, as is the case with almost every film, one cannot help but caution that Africans already know the process of pounding, weaving, and tilling the soil. While these images unquestionably connote vignettes of life as actually lived in the villages, they can only appeal to non-Africans at the expense of alienating African audiences at whom these films are aimed.

We must also acknowledge that in using these images of rural life-styles, some filmmakers have been able to construct culturally, politically, and aesthetically inventive films. One such case is the director Gaston Kaboré. His film *Zan Boko*, like his other feature *Wend Kuuni* (1982), depicts the "confrontation between two humanities," as he puts it, and critically examines the disrupted lives of people forced out of their ancestral village as a result of urban expansion. *Zan Boko*'s main focus is on social justice, corruption, arbitrary misuse of power, acculturation, and freedom of the media to deal with the problems of modernization and urbanization.

Tinga Yerbanga, the film's protagonist, is forced to abandon his ancestral land to urban expansion partly because his wealthy neighbor wants to use the land for a swimming pool. A fearless journalist is thrown into the center of this social injustice when he aspires to reveal Tinga's predicament. His live television current events show mounts a forum on the problem of forced urbanization which Tinga attends. Because it implicates government officials, the show is suddenly cut off the air when the minister of information orders an end to the broadcast.

Zan Boko is a courageous film and ironic in the sense that the very establishment it lampoons, the Ministry of Information, helped to finance the film's production. It thus echoes the audacity and the strategy of denunciation in Cissé's *Finye* and Arthur Si Bita's *Les coopérants*, which also critique the governments that financed them. Kaboré, however, makes it perfectly clear that his film was started before the regime of the late Thomas Sankara was installed.

The film starts at a leisurely pace as ethnographic realism dealing with images of everyday village life. But it uses this meticulous exploration of village culture to inform the audience about the politically charged atmosphere of its second half. Kaboré skillfully transforms what would have been an innocuous and romantic patina of exoticized life into an extremely combative sociopolitical critique. John H. Weakland refers to fiction film as story film that presents "an interpretation of some segment of life by selection, structuring and ordering images of behavior.''[27] Here in *Zan Boko,* this reference is recontextualized as a heuristic device rather than as an ethnographic study, and should not be misunderstood as such. When Kaboré's camera slowly takes its viewers to witness scenes of workers in the field, we are reminded of communal labor activities spanning time immemorial. Women carrying water gourds on their heads do not signify misery; rather, we are informed that it is a way of life. A woman giving birth to a baby outside a modern clinic makes crystal clear the prowess of traditional medicine rather than the backwardness of "witchcraft." When men gather around fires each evening and women chatter, the relevance of oral culture is amplified. These are selections of images that accent sociocultural parameters of this work as reflected by its title, which Kaboré explains in his production notes:

> Amongst many black African cultures the birth of a child is accompanied by rituals that are designed to prepare the introduction and acceptance of a new member of the community. Among the rites practiced by the Mossi in West Africa, is the burial of the mother's placenta. This act consecrates the first bond between the newborn child and the nourishing earth. It is also the home of the ancestors and of the spirits which protect the family and social group. The place where the placenta is buried is called "Zan Boko." These two words are used by the Mossi when speaking of their native land, with a meaning that is at once religious, cultural, historic and emotional but also signifies a real relation with place. "Zan Boko" is an expression of the concepts of "roots" and "identity."

In *Zan Boko* the special relationship of attachment to one's ancestral land is disrupted, turning that energizing cultural icon of existentialism, popularly tagged "son of the soil," into a figure of displacement and disillusion. This obliteration of tradition begins when the modernizing government surveyors arrive and start defacing the "pretty mud brick huts" with "white harsh numerals," in *Variety* reviewer Yung's phrases.[28] In this scene where natural sunlight casts interesting patterns on the wall, Kaboré eloquently dramatizes his concern for relationship and, above all, identity. In an unusual long take, the camera lingers on a nine-year-old boy as he moves gradually toward the numerals of his father's wall, which he laboriously rubs off with a piece of brick. In this sequence Kaboré knows when to alternate psychological time with cinematic time. The first shot establishes the boy's intentions as the spectator is positioned to witness him perform the act. For emotional impact, Kaboré then cuts to a medium close-up of the boy's face, which reveals consternation. Finally, the third shot (a close-up) shows the numbers almost completely erased as the boy's hand goes in and out of the frame—still rubbing. The sadness in his face suggests everlasting memory paralleling the scar of remembrance indelibly etched on the wall. Although the numerals are gone, the wall no longer retains its original look, just as the boy's experience is likely to remain with him as he grows.

Visual collage of village life comprises the tapestry of indigenous cultures which Kaboré exploits for intelligibility. In the second part of the film, when the focus shifts to the interrogation of the role of the media in society, the conflict between the traditional endogenous systems of communication and the technological, imported television culture is dramatized. This dramatization can be seen to represent an imposing dialectic between appropriating Western conventions and deviating from its norms. As an example, *Zan Boko*'s focus is on the problems of urbanization and modernization and their impact on the people and their relationships with the environment. But when the dauntless journalist, Yabre Tounsida, decides to have his current affairs program debate the issue live on television, television's role as a symbol of enlightenment is reversed and it becomes one of disinformation. He introduces his guests, the secretary general of the mayor's office, the general manager of national lands, the general manager of public works, and a sociologist, after which he announces that he was expecting a fifth guest. This guest, Tinga, is deliberately made to appear late in order to disguise the main focus of the show—the misappropriation of his land, nepotism, and governmental corruption.

The whole process of staging a live-action show of this type undercuts the subversive nature of television culture in developing countries such as Burkina Faso. As Tinga walks onto the stage, we can tell that he is in an alien environment. The only forum he knows is the traditional type in which the elders meet under the baobab tree or in the king's court where knowledge is transmitted and disseminated. Like this traditional forum, when Tinga walks into the studio, he offers his hand to the other invited guests only to be told by the host, "It is not necessary to shake hands. Have a seat." He heads toward the floor before Yabre points to an empty seat reserved for him. Momentarily, Tinga is carried away, mesmerized by a beautifully painted backdrop, artificial decor that he finds alienating and far removed from the kind of natural environment replete with fresh air and sunlight where traditional meetings are held as opposed to the air-conditioned room with hot lights pointed at his forehead. The program continues for a short period of time, and when the host acknowledges that Tinga's problem is scheduled to be discussed, the program is ordered off the air. Tinga's presence is symbolic because it is his story that causes rupture, forcing the minister of information to arbitrarily cut off the program.

During this period Kaboré's camera frames the participants in televi-

Gaston Kaboré: Zan Boko; *Burkina Faso, 1988.* Courtesy of California Newsreel.

sion news style, using medium shots and close-ups and eschewing the long takes and long shots that are characteristic of the first part of the film. A female announcer, dressed in a colorful African print with head tie to match, walks in a few seconds after the screen goes blank, to announce, ''We ask every faithful viewer to please excuse us for this technical problem. But our program will continue with the third episode of the magnificent serial 'The Golden Dream,' which will take us to the enchanting Riviera.'' This statement mocks the very identity, the appearance that the announcer represents. In her statements, ''faithful viewer'' and ''enchanting Riviera'' metaphorically connote noncompliance and cultural erasure. Perhaps we would have accepted the naïve excuse for technical problems if the audience were taken to the splendor of Victoria Falls (at the border of Zambia and Zimbabwe) or to Maroko, in Lagos, Nigeria (to witness urban slums, chaos, and helplessness). That a program which aired to debate national problems is replaced by a foreign program suggests a myopic vision that is indicative of national disaster. Kaboré uses this irony to look critically at society, its cultural heritage, and diversity. While questioning, he also subverts and destabilizes anachronistic dichotomies rooted in the traditional and modern.

The pervasive codes of media communication in this circumstance pose a serious challenge to traditional oral communication patterns. The rich man's message is communicated to Tinga via word of mouth as opposed to the newsroom situation in which telephones function as an oppressive device. It is possible for the government dignitaries to connive with one another through the telephone to stop Yabre's broadcast. In both cases, television and telephone, as subversive communication devices, demarcate what we see, how we see it, and how we evaluate the images represented. The interesting thing is that it is through the omnipotence of oral literature, which modern technology here tries to subvert, that *Zan Boko* becomes indefatigable. Therefore, it is right to observe that the film's peculiar hybrid nature is capable of introducing a situation that makes it possible to negotiate between generic codes and cinematic forms both affirmatively and transgressively, creating a nationalist work as Kaboré does.

The film also shows how modern society subverts traditional culture through double standards. A clear example would be the kind of support Tinga's rich neighbor receives from high government functionaries who have sworn to uphold the law of the land and faithfully serve its citizens. It demonstrates how nepotism and personal alliances can easily be used to outmaneuver others in one's own society. The effectiveness of the film derives from the simplicity of Kaboré's style, his editing, camera placement, and mise-en-scène, recalling his concern for "two humanities." In effect, the first part is realized in minimalist editing as every shot, every long take, comes right out of the camera as if unmediated. Characters are observed in normal behavior as they go about their business in the realist traditional sense typical of Satyajit Ray (*Pather Panchali*) and Ousmane Sembene (*Mandabi*), but also incorporated are some elements of the here-is-the-villain-shoot-him structure that is reminiscent of Jorge Sanjine and other Latin American documentary filmmakers[29]—as the pace quickens in the second half. There is manifest interest in community and humanity (the good and bad) in the framing of a disdainful young boy as he aspires to reassert his parents' dignity by erasing the numerals painted on their wall, or an affluent couple's display of insensitivity and double standard as they cannot bear the smell of their neighbor's "soumbala," a condiment that Tinga's wife, Napoko, prepares and sells. In actuality, this condiment is an indispensable cooking staple for both the rich and poor, elite and illiterate.

To show how traditional culture is colliding with contemporary realities, *Zan Boko* reverses the order of traditional mores; confiscation of land goes against the tradition of Mossi culture, and to think of offering money for a piece of land is an act of betrayal. Pfaff notes that "land was collectively owned and assigned to individuals by heads of lineages. . . . Land could, traditionally, be borrowed or inherited but never sold."[30] The griot's words as he sings "The monster has triumphed" in a local outdoor bar endorses the feelings of Tinga, who represents the majority of the underclass who are likely to be trampled on. As he tells his wife, "What bothers me is being treated like outsiders on the land of our ancestors." The problem of illiteracy in the film recalls *Mandabi*'s theme. Because Dieng, the hero of *Mandabi,* cannot read or write (he can only write his name, which works to his detriment), he signs his money order away to an unscrupulous relative. In *Zan Boko,* the lack of education seems to hinder Tinga's comprehension of the television debate regarding his predicament. Like Dieng, he is not stupid. Mirroring that prophetic statement at the end of *Mandabi* when Dieng says, "We shall change all these," in the final shot of *Zan Boko,* Tinga's final statement echoes the voices of the marginalized who make up 90 percent of the population. Looking at Yabre's agonizing face, he says, "I don't understand French but it is easy to see something serious has happened. I urge you to remain true to your convictions and to yourself as human being."

Finzan is the second feature-length film by Sissoko following his successful *Nyamanton* (Garbage boys), winner of a gold medal at the Mannheim Film Festival. *Finzan* is a story about women and their resistance to the social systems and traditions they consider oppressive. The story focuses on the plight of two women: Nanyuma, a mother who is now widowed, and her niece, Fili, a socially sophisticated young woman who has not undergone the traditional clitoridectomy. Nanyuma was married to an older man (possibly as old as her father), who had two other wives. He dies after eight years of their being together. Her predicament is not yet over since tradition demands that she remarry, to her late husband's next of kin, Bala, the village buffoon. This obligation is ratified by the village chief despite Nanyuma's indignation. Nanyuma, however, is in love with a younger bachelor about her own age whom her family rejected as a suitor before her first marriage and who now once again is being denied the opportunity to marry her. She escapes to another village, taking refuge in her brother-in-law's house. This situation sets up a division amongst relatives as her brother-in-law tells her that she is obligated by custom to marry Bala, while Fili supports Nanyuma's position.

In another twist, the film shifts focus to a general emancipation

Cheick Oumar Sissoko: Nyamanton (*Garbage Boys*); *Mali, 1986.* Courtesy of
Vues d'Afrique.

theme designed to reinforce Sissoko's social critique. When a government dignitary arrives and demands that villagers surrender tons of
millet to the government at a fixed price well below market value, the
villagers' protests lead to the king's arrest. He is later freed when the
women mobilize themselves to express their disapproval of his arrest.
The king's freedom in turn empowers the women to protest their own
marginalization—women's role in society and Nanyuma's plight—by
threatening their husbands with a sexual boycott if their requests are
not met.

Meanwhile, Nanyuma is caught and returned to her village, where
she will be forced to marry Bala. Her young sons, who despise this
treatment of their mother, retaliate by planning retribution against Bala.
In subsequent scenes laced with comedy, Bala's water is adulterated
with a poisonous concentration capable of inducing diarrhea and flatu-
lence in order to make him believe that the gods demand that he let
Nanyuma go. Other humiliating measures follow, which really make

him look foolish, including using Koteba "ghost" costumes and voices to send threatening messages to frighten him. However, all these measures do not stop Bala's obsession with Nanyuma, who refuses to consummate her marriage with him. She becomes very friendly with Fili, who is soon to be accused of irreverence toward society for not having endured the required clitoridectomy. This is where the real tragedy lies. The villagers are divided and the women who support the king's position of letting tradition prevail (even though they know that there is a possibility of infection, which might ultimately cause her death) outnumber Fili's supporters. Subdued and helpless, she is forced to undergo the procedure after which she bleeds profusely and is rushed to a hospital by her father.

In the end Nanyuma leaves the village with her youngest son, surprisingly, with no challenge. This occurrence signifies a return to sanity—a progressive synthesis between an antiquated past and demystified present which the director uses to project a remodeled society in which women and men negotiate on an equal basis and solve their problems together.

Like his first feature, *Nyamanton,* which seriously depicts the tragedy of children in Mali's capital city of Bamako, *Finzan* examines traditional systems and culture, vehemently denouncing the contradictions inherent in them. From the beginning of the film one recognizes the handiwork of a professional seeking to give illumined definition to film form and cinematic art. In attempting a compelling narrative style, there is no doubt here that cinematic art reinforces the strategy of rendering explicit the cultural and the political. However, from the perspective of forging indigenous film culture respectful of African sensibility, one is forced to ask if what is presented is not some kind of structural asymmetry that tends to perpetuate the entire paradigm of cinematic representation of African cultures, as Western practices do through seeking the exotic.

The film opens with a graphic reflection on motherhood as a beautifully composed shot of two goats shows them giving birth and straining at their tethers. This shot is followed by a catchy text in French which announces that "a world profile on the condition of women reveals the striking effects of double oppression. Women are 50 percent of the world's population, do about two-thirds of its work, receive barely 10 percent of its income and own less than 1 percent of its property." This statement is not merely descriptive; it also reflects the populist cry for equal justice. For anybody who has been following feminist writings, it could easily be misconstrued as a film made by a woman, or as a United Nations' documentary seeking out Third World "barbaric" cultures for debate. Rather, *Finzan* is a moving account of desperation told with sincerity and boldness, a film that looks at women through an empathetic male's eyes.

Although the film deals with a number of social issues, the main focus revolves around women's emancipation. One focal point centers on the cultural practice of clitoridectomy which, still in effect today in over twenty African countries, by United Nations' estimate, affects from twenty million to seventy million women. This practice has traditional significance in Africa, for excision was thought to be a proper way of guarding virginity as well as discouraging extramarital intercourse and an insatiable sex drive. It is important to restate that the subject of "excision," "female circumcision," or "clitoridectomy," as it is variously called, is a controversial one. From the perspective of a Western cultural norm, the practice is usually denounced as sexual mutilation performed by "ethnic" cultures seen as "barbaric" or "anachronistic." The practice's defenders, on the other hand, see its criticism as nothing short of racist, anti-African diatribe. It is pertinent to emphasize at this point that our reading of *Finzan* is not based on dogmatic principles. Following the same usual pattern of decipherment applicable in all circumstances, ours is not a matter of whether circumcision is still relevant in our present time, or whether one believes in it or not; rather, the main focus is to examine Sissoko's film style and his overall method of analysis.

In *Finzan,* Sissoko presents a critique of indigenous culture in a manner recalling the liberationist injunction to fight for freedom, a call for rebellion. I will argue that while the filmmaker presents this issue with utmost concern, his camera fails to present a detailed examination of the culture from a logical perspective enabling us to understand how the ritual evolved. Rather, what we see is a farcical analysis which treats the subject of excision, in the words of Françoise Lionnet, "peremptorily, in an impassioned, reductionist and/or ethnographic mode which represents the peoples who practice it as backward, misogynistic, and generally lacking in humane and compassionate inclinations."[31]

In a scene preceding the one in which the female traditionalists mobilize to track Fili down, we are shown what appears to be callous attitudes on the part of the children who repeatedly tease Fili for not being circumcised. This parallels the brandishing of a razor by the woman assigned to perform the excision in a macabre manner reminiscent of Bunuel's *Un chien andalou,* where in one of cinema's most bizarre moments, an eyeball is caught in big close-up as it is slit open. The irony here, though, is that Bunuel is a surrealist interested in the bizarre, incongruity, shock, and rejection of causality while Sissoko is a realist who prides himself in representing African reality for the purpose of enlightenment and entertainment. He succeeds in the latter (but not necessarily in *Finzan*), his narrative drawing from the popular Koteba theater combining slapstick comedy and satire with raucous scatological humor. Some of these devices are tried in *Nyamanton* and they work well, but in *Finzan* they function to distance the African spectator from the narrative, particularly in the bush scenes when the little children play tricks on Bala, or when a snake is made to crawl on his body and into his jacket before he smashes its head. Following this, Bala dances, glorifying his prowess for having killed a snake.

Regarding film and entertainment, if *Finzan* is strong in the entertainment sector, it serves to satisfy non-African spectators; it is unilluminating since the film's structure adheres to "the new pressure to seek pleasure and fascination in the exotic"; nor is there sustained cinematic inventiveness to suggest overt insurgency or challenge to the subjugative dominant structures.[32] Throughout the film, Bala's acting cannot go unnoticed. Although he overacts at most times, he instinctually commands professionalism, but his performance alone is not enough to salvage the film from its amateurish style of representation.

Indeed, the question of inventiveness is so often raised by critics and filmmakers who want to emphasize either the equivalence between education and entertainment or cultural productions reflective of genuine indigenous art and aspirations that we must examine its premises. For example, through constructive criticism the relevance of cinematic structure can be tied to its ability to inform the viewer of important sociocultural issues such as excision, which is prone to disdain and misinterpretation. A cautious approach, rather than haphazard assemblage of reality, in my opinion, might best illuminate Africa's "fitful process of shifting from one set of rules to the other" (from colonial and neocolonial influences to cultural critique and changes) when "loyalties are stretched between commandments of the Bible" (missionary influences) and "obligations to the ancestors" (traditionalism).[33]

As Abdou Diouf, the president of Senegal stated,

> Female mutilation is a subject that is taboo. . . . But let us not rush into the error of condemning [genital mutilations] as uncivilized and sanguinary practices. One must beware of describing what is merely an aspect of difference in culture as barbarous. In traditional Africa, sexual mutilations evolved out of a coherent system, with its own values, beliefs, cultural and ritual conduct. They were a necessary ordeal in life because they completed the process incorporating the child in society. These practices, however, raise a problem today because our societies are in a process of major transformation and are coming up against new sociocultural dynamic forces in which such practices have no place or appear to be relics of the past. What is therefore needed are measures to quicken

their demise. The main part of this struggle will be waged by education rather than by anathema and from the inside rather than from the outside. I hope that this struggle will make women free and "disalienated," personifying respect for the eminent dignity of life.[34]

There is ample room from this policy statement for us to agree or agree to disagree. It is interesting how Diouf challenges us with the task of handling the issues and becoming informed as never before about African social systems, beliefs, and thoughts. For Sissoko, *Finzan* "deals with excision as an oppressive practice," but he "does not want it to be known as a film about excision," saying that he "made it generally as a film about women's right and struggle for freedom."[35] Yet it is the "mutilation" sequence, which lasts for less than fifteen minutes, that is the most powerful and talked about because of the way it was shot. In Sissoko's filming of the brutality accompanying the capture and tying together of Nanyuma's hands and feet with a rope that looks to be as fat and strong as that which anchors ships to the docks, the long take, long shot (of hands and feet) and the close-up (of the rope) lingers for an unsympathetic time.

It is true that filmmakers have to contrive an adventure, and Sissoko's automatically finds a center of attraction—the bush and the bizarre. It could be argued that most of the scenes in the bush could have been filmed at a better location or left out entirely and the film would make better sense. To substantiate this claim, let us look at a particular sequence in which Jean Rouch's[36] influence is most profound and retrogressively appropriated. In this sequence, after the king rules in support of Nanyuma's marriage to Bala, she tries to escape from the village by hiding in the bush. This triggers a night search by the villagers, a well-orchestrated sequence comparable to the search sequence in Euzhan Palcy's *Sugar Cane Alley* (1983) (when the whole village, led by José, played by the talented child actor Gary Cadenat, mounts a formidable search for Medouze). Villagers are seen here holding lit torches scrambling to find Nanyuma. No definition of body contour is visible except when certain forms need to be highlighted, as when Nanyuma stops running to oil her body. The only other thing that Sissoko draws our attention to is a close-up chiaroscuro effect of a ferocious lion growling as it charges Nanyuma or the villagers. The lion's menacing presence is shown three times: in the first and third it is visible and in the second we only hear it growling as the villagers run for their lives. This particular sequence is especially disturbing because of the deployment of retrogressive practices reminiscent of African images proffered in Tarzan jungle melodrama films. Fashioning his cinematic structure after this practice, a strange misguided judgment

Cheick Oumar Sissoko: Finzan; *Mali, 1989.* Courtesy of California Newsreel.

that subverts the director's attempt to liberate himself from constrictive norms, canons, and myths the mainstream media has used for a long time to undermine Africa, indicates a failure to deal with the burning question of indigenous mode of African film language—something that has preoccupied the minds of African cineastes since the inception of African cinema. It also highlights the desperation that is in many hearts, African critics and audiences alike: How to completely decolonize the image?

If the goal of African film practice is to formulate strategies for the production of work relevant to pan-Africanism, our concern here is to build a community of support for cultural and creative endeavors and to explore possibilities for collaboration in pan-African spirit. This is emblematic of the position espoused by Kwame Anthony Appiah in my second epigraph to this chapter taken from his essay "Is the Post-in Postmodernism the Post- in Postcolonial?" regarding African art, its commodification, and interpretation. *Finzan* leads one to question what guidelines are necessary to construct a "positive image" of Africa. By "positive image" we mean the representation of what really matters, not that the image has to be favorable and conforming to the values of the norm (hence a critique of Islam and African systems, for instance, in *Ceddo*). That is, "positive" refers to the appropriateness of the method of selecting reality in a particular context. All too often, artists' affinities with specific cultures conjure immediate knowledge; sensitivity to that culture's configurations becomes instinctive. Unfortunately, this is not always the case. *Finzan* is beautifully filmed, as in the opening scenes, where composition-in-depth (deep focus in one case) is used to capture the village environment. The night sequence, while also beautifully shot, defies logic. This sequence, as in so many other scenes in this pockmarked film, is "pretty bad." And if sensible depiction of Africa means working to dismantle demeaning mainstream canons of representation, we might as well ask if *Finzan* has helped to reverse the popular assumptions perpetuated by existing forms of cinema and television. Commodification, as in the "bitraditionalism" discussed above, is not on a par here with African identity and sensitivity, especially the search sequence's "Tarzan" overtones. *Finzan* is a film that no African will watch and feel proud of, nor want to purchase for subsequent viewing. *Finzan* is extremely popular with Western audiences and widely distributed for classroom showings as, according to one critic, "an important new resource for studying rural sociology . . . [that] can bring to Women's Studies curricula a badly needed African perspective."[37]

There are recent African films by aspiring African filmmakers that do not celebrate contemptuous colonial and postcolonial messages which have worked historically to limit knowledge about Africa. Their structures may be steeped in the traditions of ethnographic vérité, but they do not promote the entrenchment of inferiority or the "development of underdevelopment," in Hondo's words, but rather, a development path to artistic maturity. For reaching a truer sense of African reality, they have been able to push art toward a celebratory role of a culture and of a life that is as warmly as it is urgently articulated. In this category are *Saaraba* (1988) by Senegal's Amadou Saalum Seck, which uses utopian motifs to demystify the illusions of independence in postcolonial Africa, and *Angano . . . Angano . . . Tales from Madagascar* (1988), coproduced by Marie-Clemencé and Cesar Paes (Madagascar/France), a highly innovative ethnographic film, brilliantly conceived and evocative, which places oral tradition specifically in its social context. As Donald Cosentino writes in California Newsreel's catalogue, "This film reveals the ever shifting, perhaps illusory, boundary between reality and myth." The others in this selection include Idrissa Ouedraogo's *Yaaba* and *Tilai* (Burkina Faso, 1989 and 1990), to which we will soon return.

Saaraba in Wolof stands for a mythical environment, equivalent to

Marie-Clemencé and Cesar Paes: Angano . . . Angano . . . Tales from Madagascar; *Madagascar/France, 1988.* Courtesy of California Newsreel.

the Western idea of utopia, supposedly free from the troubles of everyday life. Like Kaboré, Seck has a penchant for neorealism, and like
Zan Boko, Saaraba starts as an ethnographic document, changing its
style to a more conventional narrative structure as it progresses. It is
the ethnographic value of the first part, however, that gives the whole
film its African feel. *Saaraba* recapitulates some of the themes that
popularized early African films and their combative posturing. It denounces with unflinching temerity the corruption and lust of materialism and the excesses in the life-style of the older generation of Africans.
In doing this, Seck foregrounds the disillusionment that has crippled
Senegal's younger generation since independence—including the director's age group—who see preindependence promises melting away in
the postcolonial period.

Seck's first feature functions as a political critique and speaks well
of African film projects that scrutinize contemporary developments in
traditional values of the first generation of African filmmakers. As we
notice in *Saaraba* a craving for a personal style, we are also reminded

Amadou Saalum Seck: Saaraba (*Utopia*); *Senegal, 1988.* Courtesy of California Newsreel.

of the future of African cinema, the new direction proposed by the African film practice of the 1980s.

Idrissa Ouedraogo, the dean of the "new wave," citing Burkina Faso as an example, contends that films made in Africa with Africans solely in mind "cannot generate revenue to defray production expenses. If we want them [films] to be truly profitable, we have to internationalize our methods of making films. I personally do not dream of industrializing my films; I try with the little means I have to deal with subjects concerning human beings."[38] It is from this perspective that Ouedraogo has succeeded where many others have not broken the bondage imposed by distribution and exhibition problems. His films have been extremely popular and well received. Africa and its cultures are the mainstay of his thematic convergence, in which the humanistic and the universalist interweave with the ancient and the present—probably deliberately avoiding political confrontations (and confrontations with the status quo).

In terms of universal acceptability and commercial viability, *Yaaba* is exceptional if not unprecedented in the history of black African cin-

Idrissa Ouedraogo: Tilai; *Burkina Faso, 1990.* Courtesy of the British Film Institute.

ema. It is one of the few African films that has made it to international commercial screens, and remarkably so, in box-office terms. Following its critical acclaim at Cannes (it was selected as the opening night event of the Directors Fortnight), the film has played to large, enthusiastic audiences in Africa, Europe, Asia, and the U.S., thus shattering the exclusion of commercial theaters that has long plagued African cinema.

Ouedraogo's next film, *Tilai,* about "incest, revenge, crime and punishment," is the winner of the Special Jury Prize, Cannes, 1990, and also won the Grand Prize of the 12th FESPACO—the coveted Étalon de Yennega. Ouedraogo has since made another film, *A Karim na Sala* (1991), also shown at the latter festival. Bowing to international pressure to produce another miracle following previous successes, this work failed to meet the expectations of people to see a well-polished film like *Yaaba* or *Tilai. A Karim*'s postproduction was reportedly rushed for the 12th FESPACO's opening ceremony. It is a poorly edited film that may never be resurrected from FESPACO.

Yaaba is a deceptively simple parable, filmed in an unadorned, lucid style. It derives its plot from an African tale of the oral tradition. It is the story of two youngsters, Nopoko (the girl) and Bila (the boy), and an elderly woman. The woman is ostracized by the villagers, who accuse her of being a witch and therefore responsible for the village's misfortunes. However, the youngsters recognize that the elderly woman is often blamed for what she has not done and decide to befriend her. They nickname her "Yaaba," meaning grandmother.

Yaaba exemplifies a number of important trends in contemporary African cinema.[39] It is made in a style that could be called "elitist" and "individualistic"—combining various comedic modes with moral nuance in a fashion that reveals the contours of a revivified pan-African strategy. This strategy manifests itself in the shared consensus of African filmmakers' quest for authentic treatment of African issues in a style that not only inscribes African identity in African films but also renders the films competitive in the international market. The "new" African cinema interweaves elements of melodrama, satire, and comedy in a manner that attempts to satisfy the spectator's appetite for entertainment. *Yaaba* typifies this trend and its success and international acclaim exemplify the goals of the new crop of African filmmakers.

The appropriation of neorealist techniques by Third World filmmakers has been well documented, and Ouedraogo fuses the neorealist penchant for eliciting polished performance from nonprofessionals with the African narrative tradition of the griot (oral storyteller). Ordinarily, *Yaaba*'s story, in terms of cinematic storytelling, would be dismissed as too amateurish. But, as in the oral tradition, a story's interest and attraction for an audience depend on how creatively a storyteller embellishes what he has heard or taken from his own experience. Although *Yaaba*'s story line is basically simple, the film itself commands a universal appeal owing to the sophisticated ability of the director to unite all the essential elements operating in the film. Here, bits of humor, comedy, and satire coalesce into an idiosyncratic cinematic style that highlights societal mores and those who attempt to undermine them. In terms of mise-en-scène, every detail is conveyed by the extraordinary framing of a static camera. In a sequence in which the camera lingers on villagers playing a traditional West African game, participants proceed in and out of frame in a fashion that unobtrusively captures the flux of traditional life. Similarly, skillful editing promotes rhythmic progression of disparate episodes. Attention to visual detail is coupled with Francis Bebey's effective score, which makes use of indigenous string and reed instruments to heighten solemn moments (for example, Yaaba's burial) as well as carefree ones.

The film's emotional power is largely due to the choice of Yaaba as the village scapegoat. Her old age leaves her vulnerable to superstition, since elderly people are among those most suspected of being witches. This stigma does not, however, render her any less the quiet woman of wisdom she is. Anyone familiar with African culture knows the tremendous respect accorded elders—which is, of course, withheld from Yaaba. This respect begins in the family and is ordinarily unconditional. The aged, like the sick, for instance, are taken care of within the home, and members of the family, including the extended family, are obligated to contribute their quota. Contrary to what occurs in the West, where, for instance, government welfare programs are substituted for family care, in African society close-knit family relations eliminate the horrors of old age. Old people are indispensable, and above all, they are loved, no matter how rich or destitute they may be. In *Yaaba* the old woman is denied this important benefit of her life, ostracized, and driven to despair by the villagers. Yaaba is apparently childless; although she grew up in the sophisticated caring system of African communalism, she cannot reap the benefits of an extended family, having been dismissed with ignominy. This desertion causes other members of the village community to ridicule her; in one scene we see them throwing stones at her. She survives the resulting wound and it is Nopoko and, even more, Bila, who show sensitivity to her predicament. At one point, when the children call her "Yaaba," she is elated. "This is the first time that someone has called me Grandmother, and that makes me happy," she says, as she and Bila eat the chicken that Bila has stolen from the village to feed her. As a rule, stealing in the village, as in many other societies, contravenes ethical and moral codes. However, there is good reason for Bila to steal the chicken for Yaaba to eat; it is out of sympathy as well as a matter of subsistence, since Yaaba is unable to trap meat for herself.

Nopoko and Bila represent the values of modern Africa and serve as a bridge between the present and the past which is Yaaba's tumultuous environment. Here the film seems to suggest that there is need to abandon superstition and critically examine the causes and effects of all societal circumstances before crucial judgments can be arbitrarily imposed. Yaaba's ordeal reveals that what is associated with the past is not necessarily at odds with the present; her wisdom is reincarnated in the vision of Nopoko and Bila, who in this respect represent both future and hope. This quest for future and hope is strongly entrenched in the solidarity of Bila's prophetic utterance, when, after Yaaba's house is burned down by mean-spirited villagers, we hear him say to her, "I will build another house for you."

In another sequence when Bila is accosted by the village bullies (a group of youngsters about the same age as Bila and Nopoko), a fight ensues and Nopoko rushes to the aid of Bila, and she is cut by a rusty

Idrissa Ouedraogo: Yaaba; *Burkina Faso, 1989.* Courtesy of Waka Films AG.

knife held by one of the assailants. The cut becomes infected and she falls ill, causing her mother to fear she has tetanus. After all medical attention fails to cure Nopoko, it is the medicine of Taryam, a native doctor who is connected with Yaaba, that provides a cure for her ailment. Once again, Yaaba's wisdom prevails. Bila serves as the go-between, the link between Yaaba and the native doctor, although Nopoko's mother must hide Taryam's medicine from her husband, who does not want anything to do with the witch or her native doctor. Nopoko's recovery synthesizes the film's attempt to reconcile past and future. Bila's endeavor to repudiate suspicion, superstition, and ignorance speaks of a desire for understanding between the young and the old, past and present. The temptation to disparage Yaaba's traditionalism and Taryam's values (the healer's medical roots originate from traditional culture) is offset by the fact that recourse to these ancient remedies prolongs Nopoko's and Bila's lives. Ouedraogo's respectful treatment of Taryam is part of the film's dialectic between traditional wisdom and the sometimes dubious "progress" wrought by modernity.

In all African societies, adultery is a sin and divorce is an offense, if not taboo. Within the rural milieu of *Yaaba*, adultery and divorce are condemned, since they threaten communal solidarity and family cohesiveness. In the film, Ouedraogo displays all three, not through commentary but as plot elements meant to entertain spectators, not instruct them. Thus, when he shows us an attractive young woman, Koudi, married to Noaga, an alcoholic, who is having an affair with a local charlatan, it is not surprising that he bypasses the implication of such a serious taboo subject by showing her comically upbraiding her husband for being impotent. Since Noaga is unable to sexually satisfy Koudi, a farcical transference of guilt occurs in which the promiscuous wife absolves herself of any responsibility. Yet, the beautiful woman cannot leave her husband because of the matrimonial bond consecrated in traditional doctrine. This narrative ploy is in sharp contrast to Sembene's *Xala*, a film in which impotence suggests a larger political metaphor, an allegorical strategy that is absent from the more prosaic plot twists of *Yaaba*.

Stealing, bickering, gossiping, eavesdropping, and juvenile mischief are portrayed, no doubt flaunting the strict moral code of a community deemed closely knit. But behavioral strictures are not the primary focus in *Yaaba*, even if the dilemma seems to extend far beyond the mere question of moral decay. Although much of the film's strength lies in its whimsical irony, Ouedraogo nonetheless does not seem to have a clear vision of the African future, and there is cause to wonder whether *Yaaba*'s parabolic structural oppositions truly illuminate societal conflicts. In one sequence, for example, a quarrel breaks out between a couple, but instead of showing them fighting, in the next shot a door opens and both of them end up in a romantic embrace—this is like saying, sarcastically, of course, "If this is how couples fight, no one will ever cry." In another instance, the mother of three delinquent youngsters who are constantly berating other members of the community is shown turning a deaf ear to the misbehavior of her own children.

In *Yaaba*, the director creates expressive rhythm through characterization and meticulous attention to detail. The marvelous performances of the nonprofessional actors increase the stark realism and simplicity of the narrative, which in turn focuses attention on the film's drama. In the end, the spectator is left with the feeling that the compassionate human drama as it unfolds in the village where love, evil, fear, superstition, and intolerance coalesce are revelations that only an insider can convey. For example, by making Yaaba a scapegoat, in this case accused of being a witch and therefore responsible for the evils afflicting the society, the film touches upon a subject that is crucially important for understanding African culture. For instance, in colonialist discourse witchcraft is denigrated as "superstition," "demonic," and "primitive," endemic to the "dark continent." Although the subject of witchcraft is used to enhance the story line, it is not used tendentiously to either valorize African tradition or dismiss it as irrational. In this respect the film exemplifies an African sensibility in its effort to sensitively represent certain aspects of African culture.

The various episodes and segments that compose *Yaaba*'s structure are seamlessly constructed. Along with the utter simplicity of the narrative pattern and his careful attention to detail, Ouedraogo knows when to alternate long takes and fast cutting, silence and sound, light and dark. For example, the scene in which Bila takes food to Yaaba and discovers she has died progresses with rapid cutting—Bila running to inform the villagers and then returning, forward to the burial sequence where the action is slowed down deliberately by the employment of the long take. The scene in which Koudi is seen wanting to have sex with Noaga, her alcoholic husband (which comes to no avail), is showered with chiaroscuro lighting but also features an alternation between silence and sound—reminiscent of Fritz Lang's *M*—that expedites our anticipation. Thus a static camera watches the young beauty as she struggles to arouse her husband, who is snoring loudly. When she fails to awaken him, she resigns to melancholy, twisting and wiggling in silence. This silence is broken momentarily by whistling from outside. When Koudi walks to the window, the camera shows her submerged in light and dark looking out the window into the night until we are made to understand that it is her lover, Razougou, signaling for attention.

The dialogue spoken throughout the film is sparse and delivered in Moore, one of Burkina Faso's mother tongues, with English subtitles, though most people who have seen the film agree it can be understood without them. The emphasis on image over heavy-handed dialogue is increasingly common in African cinema. The multiplicity of African languages demands the breakdown of language barriers, enabling films to cut across boundaries. The desire to internationalize black African cinema in order to gain larger audiences and reap greater financial benefits currently defines the structure of the "new" African film.

However, *Yaaba*'s innovative tendencies seem to obscure some of the flaws in this film: many sequences seem all too predictable owing to the deployment of stock characters and clichéd plot devices. *Yaaba*'s admittedly diverting vignettes do not have the power to suggest the historical resonances achieved by a film such as Hondo's *Sarraounia* or the nuanced depiction of African ritual explored in Cissé's *Yeelen*; but they are clearly antipodal with Sissoko's *Finzan*.

After *Yaaba*, two African films, *La vie est belle* (Life is rosy, 1985) by Ngangura Mweze and Benoit Lamy and *Bal poussière* (Dancing in the dust) by Henri Duparc are distinguished by their engagement with popular culture and Africa's polyphonic rhythms tempered with Holly-

Idrissa Ouedraogo: Yaaba; *Burkina Faso, 1989.* Courtesy of Waka Films AG.

wood enticements. But *La vie est belle* is not at all similar to a Hollywood film. It is an interesting film, an unusual African film, commercial but not trivial.

It was released as a coproduction involving Belgium, France, and Zaire. Ngangura Mweze wrote the script and was assigned a codirector by the authorities in the Belgium Ministry of Culture who provided two-thirds of the financing as a condition for cosponsorship. The outcome of this problematic collaboration is a contemporary comedy, the roots of which are tied to the Zairean popular culture and to commedia dell'arte—television programs of years ago where singing and depiction of the sexes were very popular with the audience.

In *La vie est belle,* Zairean popular theater and music are also used, allowing the audience to experience the Kinshasha boisterous night life. Here, a popular Zairean musician, Papa Wemba, a star and a crowd-pleaser, plays the protagonist, Kourou, a neophyte in the process of exploring the musical road to stardom. Although the film is a musical comedy, it is not strictly structured as an entertainment film using the African prototype of a modern city (Kinshasha) as mere decor. Rather, Kinshasha comes to exemplify many of the film's thematic preoccupations: the city as a fashion capital à la Paris in which we see men and women chicly dressed; the city as a boisterous music capital continually hosting the region's hundreds of musicians, many of them the world's best, in which we find the development of new tunes and dance steps presented as routine;[40] and a city that exhibits the problems of urbanity, the entrenchment of the survival of the fittest. *La vie est belle,* like *Kukurantumi* (also set in a big city, Accra, Ghana), deals with the theme of misplaced priorities, as with the show of affluence in the lust for expensive goods, such as Mercedes Benz cars, polygamy, class division, male-female relations, urban migration, and economic imbalance. Although the structure of the film is comedic, one can still recognize societal discrepancies as they are filtered out of joke-filled scenes that are sometimes humorous and sometimes ironic, as in the scene in which a dwarf who hawks "kamundele"(shish kebab, in Lingala) in front of a nightclub reminds us that "life is rosy" as he watches Kourou and his feisty girlfriend frolic on the doorstep.

Male impotence among the African bourgeoisie, the theme of Sembene's *Xala* (1974), is also explored. However, unlike *Xala,* in which the subject is used as a caustic satire metaphorically signifying the political impotence of Senegal's ruling oligarchs while at the same time valorizing the expediency of traditional medicine, *La vie est belle* uses it to induce laughter. One such moment is when Kourou's rich employer, Nvouandou, comically practices the dance steps prescribed by the traditional medicine man as a cure for his impotence. Ngangura Mweze makes the following observation on the search for a popular film form apropos of a paradigm that argues for a new way of seeing.

> The term "commercial cinema" is quite pejorative, let me call it "popular cinema." I like to make a film that many Africans come and see and feel good with it. If I want to say commercial cinema, it means concocting stories for money, reinforcing it with sex, violence, speeding sports cars . . . that is not what interests me. Rather to make films which are best popular with African culture as well as which will feature African problems and accomplishments at the same time. I don't feel like a teacher or a messenger of a particular idea. I am a filmmaker, as there are carpenters and bricklayers.[41]

Like *La vie est belle,* Henri Duparc's *Bal poussière* makes use of popular forms. The film is replete with entertainment features as in the emerging trends. His, though, is being pushed toward a more bizarre, vulgar tradition, as his new film *Sixième doigt* (Sixth finger, 1991) suggests, which unfortunately is not only nihilistic but also reproduces many of the racial and ethnic stereotypings that African films purport to attack. When these films were shown at the 12th FESPACO, African critics, who still associate "sexual modesty with African dignity and

Ngangura Mweze/Benoit Lamy: La vie est belle (*Life Is Rosy*); *Zaire/Belgium, 1985.* Courtesy of the British Film Institute.

sexual exhibitionism with Western decadence,'' as Rayfield puts it, were very critical of the overblown sexual scenes. On the surface *Bal poussière* is a social comedy focusing specifically on polygamy, making references to corruption, contradictions of tradition and culture, but cannot be taken seriously as the issues are treated with only one thing in mind—amusement.

The focus of *Bal poussière* is a local rich man about fifty years old who is obsessed with power and calls himself Demi Dieu (Demigod). He already has five wives and wants a young school girl, Binta, played by T'Cheley Hanny of *Visages de femmes,* as his sixth wife. She is not happy to have been sent out of the city by her uncle. She meets up by chance with Demi Dieu, who falls in love at first sight and promises to marry her. He is wealthy and Binta's parents agree to Demi Dieu's proposal. As soon as she comes into the household, the rebellious Binta exposes the other more traditional wives to untraditional behavior, such as naked bathing, splitting the family into two factions: those wearing Western-style dresses and those wearing traditional attire. Soon, Demi Dieu, who used to think with his penis, believing, according to the production note, that "a sixth wife will only harmonize

Ngangura Mweze/Benoit Lamy: La vie est belle (*Life Is Rosy*); *Zaire/Belgium,
1985.* Courtesy of the British Film Institute.

the week: a wife for every day of the week and Sunday for the one who behaves best," now knows that that is, after all, not a "supreme reward."

Bal poussière's photography is stunning, the acting exceptional by African film standards. The colors, composition of shots, and rhythm and pacing epitomize polished craftsmanship. It is highly entertaining and is so at the expense of the changing role of African women or women's liberation, although that is exactly what it supposedly argues for. On a few occasions, the film manages a self-conscious attempt at germane criticism. For instance, at one point a prostitute who attempts to seduce a bar client is asked, "And what about AIDS?" Similarly, the film concludes that polygamy is somehow retrogressive, since the overbearing character Demi Dieu mishandles it as he does. Binta is allowed to leave him for the man she loves—in the spirit of a liberated woman—but only when she has proven that she could not be a traditional housewife like Demi Dieu's other wives.

Duparc's structure and his method of construction become questionable in view of his cinematic voyeurism. Consider, for example, his camera's preoccupation with the conspicuous, leering at Binta's features and contours, to expose them in close-up—her bouncing breasts, and in full-screen close-up, her buttocks. For Western viewers, these features may be more gripping and profoundly alluring, but for African critics, including feminists, Duparc's experimental interludes are simply jaundiced, misguided, and stereotypical.

Within the domain of the new African film practice, therefore, nonconformism, more than a flight from established traditions, is rather an inevitable transgressive mode of practice if only to accomplish the Herculean task of getting a good film distributed widely in important theaters. This has led to competition and aesthetic proliferation of inquiry into diverse filmic applications. I argue that some of the conventions used to attain this aspiration have, however, been misappropriated.

Toward the Tradition and the Centrality of the Paradigm

In an interview published in *West Africa,* Haile Gerima, the versatile Ethiopian filmmaker, who at the time was scouting for locations for his film *Sankofa,* was asked to explain why "the past continues to be such fertile soil for African filmmakers."[42] Gerima's new project actually does deal with the past, in a film that explores "the love and conflict between an 18th-century African slave and her mulatto son—the product of rape by white slave traders." The film traces this story through three regions: to the U.S. (Louisiana), Jamaica, and Ghana. "Without the past," Gerima noted, "there is no forward movement, so somehow we have to make peace with, and have an understanding of our past. We cannot physically go back to the past. But we have to look into the past to find out why we have come to where we are now."[43]

The understanding of the past that Gerima is concerned with typifies the "collective" and "universal" ordering of African film structures manifested by the crisis of cultural assimilation imposed by colonialism and recolonization. The recolonization factor arises chiefly from the fact that Western media continues to develop more and more as an enterprise of acculturation, and since many African stories, long forgotten, still need to be told, there is reason to advance knowledge of Africa by exposing the ruptures and discontinuities that constitute the African experience. The priority that continues to drive the initiative still remains to investigate Africa's past in order to interpret history and awaken a great cultural heritage, for example, as a challenge to racist historical myths and assumptions. How can the screen be decolonized? How can film form, content, and style be developed to serve the dissemination of information? How can films contribute to a better knowledge of the African past and present? What are the priorities?

The focus of this section is to examine how the above perspectives have been reorienting African film practice for some years now; that is, the primary concern to constructively engage the African experience in narratives, which, when "presented in the truth of their language and authenticity, become texts of real peoples," in Mudimbe's terms, rather than stereotyped, demeaning, fabricated stories as revelation. It is this kind of disinformation "which does not demand a knowledge of a specific social context, its culture, and language" that some African films are "progressively replacing [with] concrete questions bearing upon contextual authority and the necessity of linking narratives to their cultural and intellectual conditions of possibility."[44]

In recent African films, digging into the African past and recontextualizing it to inform the present has been indefatigably pursued with striking filmic innovations that have initiated a new phase and expanded definitions of the cinematic. In terms of creative autonomy and their themes, *Sarraounia, Camp de Thiaroye,* and *Heritage . . . Africa* can be seen as the precursory voice of new African alterity which, like the alternative Latin American cinemas, is closely aligned with the counterhegemonic tendencies of "Third Cinema." Because the structure of the films is fused with synthesized sociohistorical and cultural information, interrogation of the production processes involves the form and content of what Mudimbe terms the style of "Africanizing" knowledge.

From a general critical perspective, therefore, these films can be seen as recoding conventional film form, bringing to it not only a new range of historical reference but also creating the type of cultural resuscitation referred to by Brazilian modernists as "cultural anthropophagy." The notion of cultural anthropophagy derives from Oswald de Andrade's "utopian desire for a return to a mythical golden age of primitive, matriarchal society, when enemies were eaten not enslaved . . . not the romantic ideal of the noble savage," but rather, as in Montaigne's cannibalism, one "who devours enemies as a supreme act of vengeance."[45] Simply put, cultural anthropophagy seeks to counter the cultural colonialism imposed by Western hegemony by advocating the reversal of the oppressive mechanisms that the colonizer uses to subjugate colonized cultures, recycling them as "raw material" for a new synthesis: in cultural production, this means the creation of an indigenous aesthetic that places art not only in the service of the people but also makes it answerable to their political and cultural specificities. Applied to African cinema, this means of restructuring is the integral arm with which cinematic conventions are linked with speaking in one's own voice. My analysis of *Sarraounia, Camp de Thiaroye,* and *Heritage . . . Africa* will argue that their structures reveal political consciousness indicative of a "supreme act of vengeance," foregrounding situations and colonial atrocities long hidden.

In chapter 2, I noted that in terms of temperament, outlook, and artistic goals, Hondo and Sembene are a study in contrasts, but that their distinctive styles are united by a common ideology. This includes their unflinching interest in African issues and the rendering of cinematic structures with styles emanating from dynamic cultural polyphonic codes. Both filmmakers continue to work from pedagogical perspectives that are nonetheless gripping and emotionally resonant. Most of the time the filmmakers urge the West to acknowledge their ruinous policies toward Africa, or as one student succintly put it in the aftermath of the Gulf War, "their greatest crimes against humanity,"[46] and implore Africans to wake up and work out lasting structures of political and economic stability.

Sarraounia is a landmark of African cinema, the most ambitious for its inventiveness, professionalism, and dedication. It took Hondo seven years to raise the three million dollars required for its production—an uphill task, and by African standards, unprecedented. The screenplay is adapted from the novel of the same title by Abdoulaye Mamani of Niger. The story recounts a true African experience during colonialism, at a time when the French colonial army was plundering its way across the western Sudan from Dakar to Rabat. According to Hondo, he was motivated to show the true "historical value of traditional culture" by bringing to light an important period in Africa's history; Sarraounia, a

Med Hondo: Sarraounia; *Mauritania, 1987.* Courtesy of Med Hondo Films.

Malian queen, led a successful battle against the French colonial forces. Aside from showing "African history in cinema honestly and objectively," the film is also an homage to African women in history, something which has always been downplayed, "ignored or underestimated."[47]

The structure of the film develops along two basic story lines. The first is necessary to provide information about the effects of traditional culture on national resistance and concerns the growing up of a young girl (Sarraounia) as seen from preadolescence to her establishment as queen of the Aznas of Niger. During this first period, when she lives with her adoptive father, she is initiated into mastering traditional secrets, leading her to acquire the power of a respected fierce warrior. On the other side of the story are the French forces, evil and mean-spirited foes, whose psychological warfare includes the raping of women, brutality, and annihilation. As the French forces advance, some of the queen's detractors betray her and her prowess is tested. Determined as ever, with the help of some volunteer forces, she is able to muster defenses capable of restoring her people's dignity. On the eve of the attack by the French forces, a thunderstorm, believed to have come from the spiritual forces at the command of Sarraounia, strikes the French camp, throwing them into confusion as they accuse one another of desertion. This takes place at the same time that the queen is rallying a new defense force to her side. When the invaders attack, Sarraounia's forces inflict demoralizing damage, despite the enemy's powerful guns and cannons—a situation caused by Sarraounia's tactical withdrawal to the bush. The French army finally arrives at the village of Lougou, only to find it a ghost town, confusing them all the more. This disappointment leads them to become very violent and greedy, and their demise comes when disheartened *tirailleurs* (African soldiers of the French colonial army) revolt, killing their white officers.

If Hondo succinctly retrieves in *Sarraounia* an essential chapter of African history, *Camp de Thiaroye,* codirected by Sembene and Thierno Faty Sow, reveals the unfortunate legacy of French colonialism, which the French would have preferred undocumented. The film is based on an actual event, the 1944 massacre by French forces of Senegalese *tirailleurs* stationed at the camp of Thiaroye a few miles outside of Dakar. The *tirailleurs* were billeted there after returning from World War II, having fought for France and now awaiting repatriation to their homes. Sembene's drama unfolds as a revelation of the unsavory relationship between the colonizing army of occupation and the colonized subject. French policy poses a double standard in regarding the *tirailleurs* as French citizens while treating them as colonized subjects, as is clearly illustrated in the film. Sembene shows that the African soldiers' demand for "equal sacrifices," "equal rights," and "equal pay," which the white soldiers enjoy, is legitimate. The French authorities promised to pay the *tirailleurs'* back wages, a demobilization allowance, and five hundred French francs each, plus civilian clothes, only to renege on the promises. A series of other insults and maltreatment by the French authorities (one injustice is the refusal to pay them at the going exchange rate) boil over, forcing the soldiers to mutiny. The *tirailleurs* seize the French commanding officer, who is later released after he promises adequate and prompt compensation. This proves to be a false promise. In the deep of night, after everyone is asleep, the French armored vehicles and artillery roll into the camp, demolishing everything in sight and massacring a large number of the *tirailleurs*. This is how they are rewarded for the sacrifice of untold African lives in the service of France during World War I and II.

The emotional impact of the film derives from a meticulous plotting and selection of details and careful dramatization and characterization. It is a story told from personal experiences, which, in the director's words, "render the film vivid"[48]—Sembene himself having fought for France in World War II—with irrefutable credibility, its authenticity being a hallmark of a truly revisionist history.

The allegorical treatment of both *Sarraounia* and *Camp de Thiaroye* appropriately mirrors the characteristics of a "vindictive" art, only, however, if it forced France to repent and pay adequate compensation. But since these films are intended to contribute knowledge of Africa's repressed history rather than incite violence or retaliation, their revolutionary dynamics echo the nationalistic ideology of using art to scrutinize, disturb to the point of jolting consciences, and, in this case, to haunt, if possible, the propagators of today's imperialistic policies that render ineffective African and Third World struggles. Hondo's words, "You can read my film back under the light of today,"[49] underscore this concern. It is pertinent that we fast-forward at this point to Hondo's and Sembene's strategies of revelation in *Sarraounia* and *Camp de Thiaroye*.

Sarraounia's preoccupation with historical specificities ratifies the contention of cultural theorists that it is the colonizer who "invests the other with its terrors." As Jonathan Rutherford has pointed out, "It is the threat of the dissolution of self that ignites the irrational hatred and hostility as the center struggles to assert and secure its boundaries, that construct self from not-self."[50] As the "barbarously cruel" French forces "slaughter [their] way from Dakar to Rabat"[51] to assert control, it was expedient that African warriors led by Queen Sarraounia mount a formidable defense in the same way that the *tirailleurs* in *Camp de Thiaroye* did when, fed up with French insult, lying, and cheating, they were forced to mutiny. The mutiny staged here as a result of this injustice was simply to draw attention to their cause, seeking a remedy in accordance with the French policy of assimilation since they were supposedly French "citizens." It is not surprising, therefore, that Sembene and Hondo, both at the zenith of their creativity, would illustrate French colonial treatment of Africans with utmost pungency.

Important genre cinematic conventions determine the techniques employed. They include ethnographic methods of observation, appropriation of revolutionary Russian techniques of socialist art, avant-gardist modes of production, all refurbished and fused with oral art. In *Sarraounia,* Hondo frames in long shot the Sahel landscape filled with hazy atmosphere (as if the Supreme Being, frowning at the destruction about to affect her children, decides to dim the cosmic lights in the same way that flags are lowered during national calamities) as the camera witnesses the French colonial army under the command of Captain Voulet advance to decimate the resistance. In the foreground are human bodies planted in single file with only their heads above ground. Mounted soldiers are then seen cutting off the exposed heads with their swords as if they are playing polo. In the following shot four French officers stand talking as if nothing had happened. The remarkable thing about this scene is the way in which it is shot with a static camera positioning the audience to witness the event as if it just happened; it traumatizes as it urges the viewer to meditate on the killings.

In another scene, Hondo's camera deviates from the long shot, static camera positioning as a witness to become a "roaming ambassador" in order to seek and find. In the scene after Sarraounia withdraws to the bush and the disappointed French army retreats, a high-angle camera shot shows the soldiers leaving, and a pan shot reveals some wounded African *tirailleurs* on stretchers. The camera switches angles, following the movement of one of the French officers as he weaves his way through the crowd, shooting and bayoneting the wounded soldiers. One of the latter is shown in close-up as he takes his last breath. The cruelty demonstrated in these sequences ratifies the fact that the French were not interested in the lives of Africans, even those fighting for them; as far as they were concerned, the African soldiers were subhumans.

A scene that substantiates this statement occurs later in the film when the French soldiers on a rampage come across a native shrine. Inside is a big mask ornamented with traditional symbols. Their African counterparts, on spying the mask, are gripped with fear. One French soldier walks fearlessly forward and removes the mask. Putting it on his face he starts to dance around, ridiculing its cultural significance. But his foolishness is only momentary as this flagrant abuse quickly ends when a shrieking cry for help is heard. His face is suddenly covered with angry insects. The next shot shows two other French officers struggling to remove the mask from his face. As they treat him, the camera reveals an African resister in the background mercilessly tied with ropes to a stake and left unattended. This scene is symbolic and makes explicit the French cruelty and contempt toward African cultures. It also illustrates the director's concern to show fetishism as an authentic national culture; the mask as a "cultural product of the people" has traditional values attached to it. (I must point out that the scene's impact would be much more profound if there were traces of insect bites remaining when the camera reveals a close-up on the man's anguished face.)

At FESPACO 1987, where *Sarraounia* won the festival's Grand Prix, the director "was asked whether he had not exaggerated the atrocities committed by the French soldiers, such as playing polo with the decapitated heads of the Africans. He replied that he had drawn his information from respected French histories, including [Jean] Suret-Canale."[52] Hondo's concern for authenticity typifies what he means when he constantly reminds critics and audiences that "every film has its own particular structure."[53] For example, *Sarraounia* eschews the syncopated eruptive tone of *Soleil O* and the swift and painterly camera movement of *West Indies*. In the structure we find a deliberate use of camera that is very relaxed, creating a slow rhythm that leaves no detail unaccounted for. There are a few rapid camera movements, but only when the situation demands it; overall the rhythm is calculated to make the viewers feel as if they are listening to a history lesson, narrated realistically as unmediated events instead of a fact distorted by cinematic pyrotechnics. Similarly, Hondo is careful not to depict the French solely as bad guys. In showing the contradictions inside the colonial camp forced by the resistance, he also uses this resistance to analyze the contradictions among the Africans themselves. Here, as in *Ceddo*, where Sembene posits the impotence of African traditional religions against powerful Islamic encroachment, Hondo shows Africa torn by imported structures. The abandonment of Sarraounia by the Muslim soldiers, who detested her resistance to all foreign structures, including Islam, at a crucial time when Africa's freedom, dignity, and pride were at stake, exemplifies this stance.

Concern for Africa's freedom and dignity is also foremost in Sembene's cinematic analysis of the continent's problematic emancipation and, like Hondo, he is careful about how to put those problems on screen. In *Camp de Thiaroye*, Sembene and Sow's dramatization of the atrocities committed by the French forces shows centuries of exploitation which, as in *Sarraounia*, can be read as mirroring today's realities. Through storytelling ingenuity, character delineation, and mastery of cinematic techniques, the film reveals characteristics already well circumscribed and established. As G. Williams puts it, "Colonies were . . . of value only insofar as they brought material benefits to the mother country."[54] *Camp de Thiaroye* not only shows us the processes the colonizers used to chew away Africa to its bare bones but also the tradition that sometimes reflects the muteness of Africa in the so-called new world order (read: new world disorder) formed under the auspices of Pax Americana. In the film, the most well-defined signifier of this assertion comes in the form of the character of the mute soldier nicknamed "Pays" (country). At the beginning of the film it is through the experience of Pays (the viewer is told he is one of the ex-prisoners held at the POW camp in Buchenwald) that one learns of the painful contradictions in the so-called return journey to native Senegal when Pays notices that their camp is fenced in with barbed wire. This scene, filled with emotion, shows Pays, dumbfounded, as he becomes immersed in old memories. Touching the barbed wire with his fingers, Sembene's camera lingers on the man for a time, focusing tightly on his fingers as they feel the wires, trembling in disbelief. One of his friends, the commanding sergeant, pacifies him, picking up some sand and sprinkling it on his fingers as he reminds him that they are in their

Ousmane Sembene, Thierno Faty Sow: Camp de Thiaroye; *Senegal, 1987.*
Nwachukwu Ukadike Collection.

native Senegal and not in Buchenwald. On one hand, Sembene is asking
whether there is any difference between the POW camp in Germany
and the camp at Thiaroye. On the other hand, Pays's muteness represents what might be seen in today's reality as symbolizing the political
inertia, economic impotence, and dependency that has become a part
of Africa. After watching *Camp de Thiaroye,* one is sadly made aware
that France's domination of its former colonies continues unabated.
Considering that France is also one of the owners of the International
Monetary Fund (IMF) which, together with Africa's own mismanagement, is milking Africa dry, one cannot but question Senegal's apish
loyalty in the aftermath of the 1991 U.S.-led war against Iraq.[55]

Sembene vividly captures Senegal's tragic alliance with France
through the recalcitrant attitudes of its colonial officers. Toward the
end of the film there is a massacre scene in which the Senegalese soldiers, who had hoped that they had secured the trust of the French
commander for better treatment, are attacked. This scene is carefully
staged in the usual Sembenean fashion of meticulous attention to detail.
It all happens in a night scene that is beautifully lit until gun salvos
punctuate the natural serenity of the sequence. In a long shot we see

the movement of lights in the distance. This movement is caught by Pays, who tries, to no avail, to alert his compatriots to the impending attack. Pays, whom his friends know is mentally deranged as a result of the war, is not taken seriously, and they joke that he is once again having a nightmare about the German concentration camp. As a column of tanks and artillery move nearer, Sembene holds his camera in a static position while witnessing what is to happen. When the attackers release an unprecedented inferno upon the camp, the camera shows only close-ups of the tanks' guns as they fire endlessly; however, the long shots focused on the camp remain unchanged. This enables the viewer to see the Senegalese soldiers as they run for cover. The camp is burned to the ground—heightening the emotional impact that grips the spectators, who at this point are forced to place themselves in their midst. The music that runs through this sequence is carefully chosen for impact. The next scene, which takes place five hours later, is accomplished with a smooth camera pan seeking out the dead bodies. Reminiscent of Sanjine's *Courage of the People,* the mass burial that follows is shot in medium close-up, followed by a long shot as more bodies draped in white are thrown into a mass grave.

The French officers show no remorse or concern for their atrocities. In the scene that follows the burial, one French officer is heard telling another that the colonial minister and the government support their actions. The other asks when the new African recruits are going to be sent to France. Sembene cuts to a huge ship anchored at the dock as the recruits embark, leaving their families behind. If we read this sequence backwards in Hondo's terms, it is very significant in the sense that it mirrors present realities, which is to say that if Africa continues to depend on its former colonizers, independence will remain an illusion.

Both films illuminate African history with utmost clarity without being overtly didactic. In the same way Hondo emphasizes African history through precolonial and colonial images, Sembene alerts African audiences to a united search for autonomous identity. *Sarraounia* and *Camp de Thiaroye* are probably the most violent of African films, but as James Leahy rightly points out, "Nowhere else is violence indulged for its own sake. Colonial conquest was violent and cruel."[56]

Like *Sarrounia* and *Camp de Thiaroye, Heritage . . . Africa* by Ghana's Kwaw Ansah invokes historical characters and draws upon important cultural traditions to make profound statements about colonialism and Africa's struggle for freedom. This film is also among African films that, from conception to finish, are distinguished by high levels of imagination and professionalism. The script is expertly conceived; there are marvelous performances by professional and nonprofessional actors alike, splendid characterizations, and good directing. Together with in-depth composition, superb editing and an intense sound track, the film highlights its own reflexivity and creates a spell-binding and suspenseful mood that is both entertaining and emotionally captivating.

Ansah's *Heritage* tells the story of an African called Kwesi Atta Bosomefi.[57] From his rise through the scholarly and religious education of the colonial era to his subsequent elevation in the colonial administration to becoming an African district commissioner (a rarity), his identity and his name change with his values. Kwesi Atta Bosomefi becomes Quincy Arthur Bosomfield. Bosomfield aligns himself with his British "counterparts," thereby immersing himself in an atmosphere created by the "elite" educated blacks with similar affectations. Thus he abandons all that has real meaning to him and adopts a new culture. There is a series of humiliating encounters between himself and his estranged wife, his mother, and the jailed but unrepentant Kwame Akroma, all dealing with the system he has helped build; these are peppered with vivid recollections of his past; and, finally, through the experience of a frightening and revealing dream, Bosomfield sets his foot firmly on the path to discovering his heritage.

Heritage indicts not only the educated Africans who deny their cultural heritage and slavishly imitate the British way of life but also the acculturation that typifies colonial whitewashing of the people's mentality. Ansah succinctly presents this problem right from the beginning of the film when a church scene sets the mood in what is definitely an ironic sequence structured to demonstrate Christian missionaries' involvement in the acculturation and colonizing process. As worshipers gather in the church, an English priest begins to preach while his African assistant interprets and translates for the non-English-speaking members of the congregation. Seated in the audience are men in European-cut three-piece suits and women in both traditional and European-style dresses and hats. The camera focuses on a fashionably dressed little boy, Archiebold, sitting next to his father, Quincy Bosomfield. As he doses off, his father nudges him awake, suggesting he go outside for fresh air. A tracking shot shows young Bosomfield walking out of the church as the priest continues a sermon on compassion toward the less fortunate:

> Let us take the mentally ill or the destitute, for example, who wander about the street and pick crumbs from the refuse bins and ask ourselves how many were born that way. Or could it be that some of these people were the very teachers who taught you and I in the class yesterday to make us rich and prominent men today? Just cast your minds back and ask yourselves if that man you met this morning or last Tuesday afternoon collecting food from the streets . . . could it have been the same man who yesterday was good enough to be your . . .

As the sentence is abruptly interrupted, the priest looks toward the rear of the church. The worshipers turn their heads to see what is going on. When the camera changes angles, it captures a shabbily dressed woman with a bowl of fruit on her head (an example of the kind of woman the priest has just described). She walks down the aisle toward the altar and sits in a pew. Some worshipers who cannot bear her stench move further away. When the priest refuses to continue, the church wardens forcibly carry the woman out amidst her shouts of "Leave me alone, I have come to pray." Amplified organ music fills the void until the priest, looking up, makes the sign of the cross saying, "Let us pray," as they carry the woman out. "Great and manifold for the blessings which almighty God the Father of all mercies has bestowed upon the people of England when first he sent his Majesty's Royal persons to rule and reign over his subjects. Amen." "Amen," repeats the congregation. The disturbing aspect of this sequence is not only that the priest fails to practice what he preaches, but by refusing to aid the mentally unstable woman the concluding sermon confirms that Christianity has imposed hegemonic values in order to promote Western norms.

Heritage introduces many other sequences intended to show how Africa's cultural systems collide and disintegrate in the face of colonialism and missionary intervention. In the next scene, Ansah cuts to a highly orchestrated frantic dance sequence, the sort misinterpreted by missionaries and colonial administrators as a "fetish dance." Archiebold, who has left the church, is in the midst of people watching the dancers. A distraught and furious Bosomfield is caught by the camera as he pulls his son out of the crowd, holding him by the waistband. He beats Archiebold and takes him to be disciplined by a church clergyman claiming, "A Christian child must not watch a fetish dance." The poor boy, humiliated in the presence of his schoolmates by a second beating, is mercilessly caned—almost naked—his underwear drenched in blood. For a Westerner, beating a little boy in such a manner constitutes barbarity and cruelty, but according to Ansah, such was the regular practice in the colonial school he attended.[58]

As Edward H. Berman notes, "Recent studies have confirmed that missionaries disseminated education neither for its own sake nor to enable Africans to challenge colonial rule."[59] Of the methods used to fracture traditional societies, I can only present here a few well-documented accounts from notable Africans of their missionary education. For Kenya's Oginga Odinga, the missionaries were not only interested in disseminating the gospels of the Bible—they also tried to use the Word of God in order to judge African traditions. An African who followed his people's customs was condemned as heathen and anti-

Christian.[60] Similarly, Nigeria's Mbonu Ojike, reflecting upon school days (in the 1920s) when the missionaries induced pupils to imitate their Western culture in every facet of life, notes that "every good Christian must take a Western name at Baptism." This brainwashing was so perfectly organized that "I mocked my father's religion as 'heathen,' thinking his inferior to the white man's."[61] Achebe's account epitomizes indigenous concern to reverse the oppressive mechanism (in print and in media) responsible for colonialist disinformation. In *Things Fall Apart,* Achebe casts Mr. Kiaga as the African missionary who rejoices when Okonkwo, the son of a traditionalist, abandons his father's house for the missionary compound by exclaiming, "Blessed is he who forsakes his father and mother for my sake."[62] This is in no way a simplistic critique of Christianity's contradiction. It rather proves, as in the tradition of African film practice, that history needs to be rewritten from indigenous perspectives to inform us that overzealous missionaries were never perturbed when they, in Berman's words, "set son against father in direct violation of the fifth commandment."[63]

If brutally beating Archiebold is atavistic, as the scene suggests, this is because Ansah wants to substantiate the critique he makes of colonial subjugation and the undermining of a people's culture. Archiebold becomes infected with tetanus owing to his wounds, and when he lapses into a coma, his mother, Theresa, sends his sister, Penelope, to ask Bosomfield to come home immediately. Bosomfield says he is too busy in the office and instructs his wife to give Archiebold some tablets of APC (headache and cold tablets). The boy eventually dies, and it is the same English priest who officiates at his burial. This sets off a series of problems for Bosomfield; his wife abandons him, calling him a slave for neglecting his own family in order to satisfy the imperial crown.

The narrative unfolds with Bosomfield becoming a more and more restless man, his loyalty to the colonial British turning to one of self-denial and destruction, a necessary procedure that he must undergo in order to recognize his true identity. For example, after Bosomfield's wife leaves him, he is seen at his house socializing in the company of his elite friends. When his mother arrives unannounced, instead of welcoming her into the house, he meets her by the doorstep and offers her a kitchen stool to sit on behind the house, making her look like a servant so that she won't tarnish his image. He must have boasted that he was born with a silver spoon in his mouth. This insensitive attitude, which shows how Bosomfield's psyche has been brainwashed, illustrates the difference between traditionalist and assimilationist cultures. In the film, Bosomfield discards his traditional name, Kwesi Atta Bosomefi. We only know that he is Kwesi because that is what his mother calls him. According to Ansah, his name had meaning: Kwesi means

"Sunday born"; Atta means "a twin"; and Bosomefi means "an illustrious ancestor has been reborn."

After the guests are gone, Bosomfield meets his sleeping mother and asks her into the house. She is happy to see her son occupy a house in an exclusively white colonial officers' quarters (he is accepted because he has assimilated), but at the same time she is concerned about their culture. She bestows a traditional honor on him, handing over a five-hundred-year-old heirloom, an ancestral casket that has been passed on to sons from generation to generation.

Moments after his mother leaves, Bosomfield takes the casket, the container of his family spirit, to his boss, the colonial governor, telling him that it is a special gift which, of course, the governor accepts, acknowledging that it is of an "exquisite craftsmanship and an interesting piece of art." The governor in turn sends the casket to England. Clearly, Bosomfield's action is one of betrayal and misplaced trust. In this action lies a political commentary by the filmmaker reminding the viewer of Africa's many elite sons who have betrayed their fellow citizens after they ascended to their country's leadership, working only to advance the interests of the former colonial masters.

In a highly emotion-charged sequence, after being informed about the loss of the family heirloom, Bosomfield's mother reprimands her son, giving him a lesson on traditional culture, dignity, and self-affirmation, along with one about his imminent doom. Alexandra Duah's performance here and throughout the film is outstanding; through effective handling of cinematic conventions, this scene, with an intricate series of flashbacks, is very enlightening and captures the mood of growing up in the 1960s and attending a colonial elementary school. A long shot shows Bosomfield coming to visit his mother, meeting her, and sitting down to a family tête-à-tête, which soon develops into a lesson for a neophyte.

> *Mother:* Welcome my beloved son.
>
> *Bosomfield:* How are you madam?
>
> *Mother:* By the grace of God I am well.
> Have some water Kwesi.

(Bosomfield lifts a bowl of water. As he opens his mouth to drink, his mother stops him to remember tradition—to pour libation to the ancestors.)

> *Mother:* Remember the forefathers.
> Welcome my son.
> I trust you are taking care of the ancestral heirloom?
> It will forever remain your source of strength and pride.
>
> *Bosomfield:* I gave it to the Governor, my boss.

Kwaw P. Ansah: Heritage . . . Africa; *Ghana, 1988.* Courtesy of Kwaw P. Ansah.

(In disbelief, heartbroken.)

> *Mother:*   You have wounded my soul.
> You have broken my soul.
> You have broken your ancestral link.
> What happened to all the classroom education?
> Where is the common sense?
> Even your illiterate twin sister would have understood this simple message.
> You will never be free if you don't retrieve the heirloom.
> The ancestors will forever haunt you.

A series of dissolves connects images of young Bosomfield growing up, highlighting memorable shots of his mother taking him to school and caring for him. One of the shots is particularly worth mentioning: the young Bosomfield is holding his hand over his head trying to touch his ear. That is how the colonial administrators determined if a child was "big" enough to go to school. If the fingers failed to reach the ear, the child had not reached school age.

From all appearances, *Heritage* is indebted to the Fanonian theory of the "native intellectuals." They are those who are likely to move first into a "blind alley" before going "into the common paths of real life"; that is, after having "proved that he has assimilated the culture of the occupying power," but not without expressing "distress and difficulty," the native intellectual decides "to make an inventory of bad habits drawn from the colonial world" before turning himself "into an awakener of the people."[64] The major achievement of *Heritage* lies in its commitment to what Teshome Gabriel calls "social art." In what amounts to sincere, deep-felt respect toward treatment of theme, character, and situation, Ansah constructs a provocative, authentic, and reflective analysis of Africa beyond sociocultural parameters. In this structure we find projected an optimistic view of Africa which suggests the possibility of a radical transformation.

As in Fanon's thesis, Bosomfield, after going through numerous problematic relationships, reaches the stage at which he begins to question his loyalties. After his son dies, he witnesses the death of another child whom he tries to save by taking him to an all-white hospital. Here he discovers the destructive impact of colonial policies that bar Africans from medical attention even at the point of death. Other problems, compounded by the demands of African nationalist movements abound. As Nii K. Bentsi-Enchill puts it,

> Beside him stand his British colleagues who expect him to stand firm. Behind Bosomfield is the rising tide of his own conscience, first awoken by his mother's warning that until he retrieves the brass casket he shall have no rest, and spurred on by the new perception of the poverty and repression that his compatriots endure.[65]

In the end, Bosomfield is a changed man, although it is already too late. As he is seen struggling to retrieve the heirloom in the last sequence, his demise is imminent, but he dies after common sense prevails—after he denounces the colonial system and secures his own heritage.

Sarraounia, Camp de Thiaroye, and *Heritage . . . Africa* are African films par excellence. All of them critically examine African issues from an African perspective, and since they were made there has been a general antagonism toward them simply because they dramatized the truth.[66] The makers of these films have proven that, through careful planning, good films can be made in Africa without resorting to clichés. The knowledge that is derived from this practice is pan-African in its spirit of recovery and in its retrieval and recontextualization of Africa's past within Africa's present.

6

Conclusion

Whither African Cinema?

This study has focused on the diversity of the black African film experience, from governmental inaction or commitment to establishing well-organized national film industries, to independent filmmakers' relentless efforts to promote growth and the search for an autonomous film language.

Contemporary black African film practice emerged out of the excitement of nation-building and a quest for the revivification of Africa's lost cultural heritage and identity, a quest that has inspired innovative and creative diversification in the cinema and throughout the arts. Sub-Saharan cinema's importance can be ascribed to its commitment to the pan-African spirit—the goal of portraying Africa from an African perspective, which has inspired individuals far beyond the continent's geographical boundaries. With this, the cinema embarked upon its own project of complete decolonization following the example of an already flourishing liberationist literature channeled to this same purpose.

In countries still under colonial domination, such as Angola, Guinea-Bissau, and Mozambique, the cinema was one of the weapons in the war for liberation and an instigator of revolutionary transformation of conciousness. After the war and the achievement of independence, it became an ideological tool for national development and cultural growth. However, the majority of new nations struggling to organize soon discovered that political freedom was no guarantee of economic independence. Aspiring black African filmmakers, similarly, were confronted with the lack of the necessary infrastructure to implement the formation of national film industries, or with bureaucratic red tape and the obstacles created by political inertia. This situation could have been averted or remedied if there had been a coordinated inter-African cooperation on the part of all the governments rather than their acting as impediments to adequate production and systematic distribution and exhibition. Such an undertaking would have been directed to ensure coproduction between states and the establishment of distribution cartels to serve the entire continent, or at least the sub-Saharan region on a regular basis. At a national level, the creation of a national film fund based on revenue accrued from taxes levied on ticket sales, government subsidy in the form of relaxation of taxes on the importation of film equipment, facilitation of foreign exchange approvals, and perhaps more important, the development of a local infrastructure for the renovation of existing theaters and the building of new ones are ways of sustaining a burgeoning film industry. (Burkina Faso is an exception in this respect.) These concerns have been neglected in sub-Saharan Africa, and this neglect, in tandem with the absence of material resources, has hindered the careers of ambitious young filmmakers and the growth of individual film industries.

The results of indigenous filmmakers' indefatigable efforts to engage African governments in the establishment of national film industries have not been encouraging. Evident here is a lack of dynamic cultural policies for overseeing their establishment, resulting in a dearth of indigenous productions. Too often, films exhibited in African countries have been foreign-made while foreign multinationals, interested neither in investing in African film initiatives nor in the exhibition of local productions, have virtually monopolized distribution and exhibition to the detriment of indigenous production. While some countries, such as Guinea and Burkina Faso, did manage to nationalize the film business, similar attempts in the rest of black Africa were not supported by policies linking all aspects of production which could activate undisturbed growth. The inability of many African filmmakers to triumph over material scarcity and economic domination has its roots in both the colonial past and the neocolonial present.

The Present Situation

With the exceptions of Angola, Mozambique, and to some extent Burkina Faso, where there exists systematic state funding of film production, the establishment of national film industries by African governments is still not a priority. As already stated, black African cinema as we know it today is largely independently produced under conditions of hardship extreme. Because their work is not regulated, in almost all cases filmmakers are auteurs involved out of necessity in all phases of production, from conception to finish, distribution to exhibition. Also, film-related equipment and film stock were harder to come by in the 1980s than they were in the 1960s and 1970s, and filmmakers continue to travel overseas for postproduction work. But even this inconvenience was drastically curtailed in the late 1980s owing to foreign exchange restrictions in virtually all independent African countries.

The situation in Africa regarding foreign exchange is precarious and distressful to filmmakers. With over thirty African countries, according to United Nations statistics, mortgaging their economies to the IMF, devaluation of currency (the number one IMF economic stipulation to all recipient Third World debtors) has virtually converted many African currencies to worthless paper or merely fancy bills with photographs of heads of state. For instance, before Ghana embarked on the restructuring of its economy following the IMF's recovery plan, the exchange rate for the cedi, the country's currency, had degenerated from C2.75/$1 in 1983 to C389/$1 in December 1991.

Under this regulation it would not seem financially viable for any filmmaker to attempt to make a film in Ghana. But, in fact, films are still made there (as indicated in chapter 3, Ghanaian feature film production received a boost in the 1980s) and in other African countries strapped by the foreign exchange crunch. In most cases, the majority of filmmakers now rely heavily on coproduction with foreign countries—a strategy that dominated 1980s film practice in black Africa. This strategy has increasingly come under attack from critics who charge that the system strengthens France's economic, political, and sociocultural recolonization of black African film initiatives. On the positive side, however, coproduction appears to be the powerhouse sustaining black African film practice. (Exceptions can be made for Nigerian filmmakers who depend mainly on locally generated funds for their production—Africa's largest yearly output—but these films are intended only for local consumption and most of them are ideologically bankrupt and not known outside the country.)[1]

In this vein, it would seem as though black African filmmakers lack the environment for the production of serious films with accountability toward continental reality. In fact, the reverse is the case. Films like Ousmane Sembene's *Black Girl* (1963), made with funds from the French Ministry of Coopération, and Med Hondo's *Sarraounia* (1986), made with funds partly from France and Burkina Faso, were both severely critical of French imperialism in Africa, although the latter, despite its credibility and artistic sophistication, was "assassinated," to use Hondo's label, by French distributors, for the film's intense ridicule of colonial French forces. Accordingly, Souleymane Cissé's film *Finye*, independently produced with the assistance of Mali's military, which supplied the equipment, was ironically severe in its criticism of the country's military dictatorship but was not prohibited, an unusual demonstration of maturity, to the surprise of everyone. Similarly, Cameroon's *Les Coopérants,* by Arthur Si Bita, partly funded by the government, was devastatingly critical of corruption among that government's functionaries.

There is no doubt that corruption and economic weakness are the biggest contributors to Africa's underdevelopment. Along with problems such as drought, famine, disease, and interstate and intraethnic strife, which can be considered secondary contributors to the draining of resources, the cinema, as an industry, is relegated to the bottom of the list of government priorities.

Africa has emerged from what Clyde Taylor calls "existential distress."[2] Considering the paroxysms of agony for Africa's three hundred million people taken away from their communities as slaves, followed by colonialism and now neocolonialism, this description is accurate. Today, black African states, with the exception of South Africa, are theoretically and politically free, but the majority of the countries are still dependent on their former colonial masters who, by virtue of their economic and technological might, have devised the means to dominate the former colonies even after independence. Added to the general administrative inefficiencies prevailing in neocolonial Africa is the gradual economic deterioration from the first years of independence to the chaos of the 1980s. In essence, colonialism meant de-Africanization and robbery of the continent's wealth, while neocolonialism transformed this state of affairs into indirect domination, the installation of capitalist greed and even worse forms of corruption, which have left government treasuries wanting. Serving only to facilitate the already parasitic African economies, as in the rest of the Third World, these nations have become economically too feeble to control their own affairs without foreign meddling, let alone to have any dominant voice on major world issues. African states, to borrow Edward Said's remark concerning Arab states, which despite their oil wealth, are unable to transform their states to First World industrial status, "have adopted a supine even cringing obeisant attitude"[3] toward the predatory Western industrial giants who after milking them dry give them aid-with-strings-attached in return.

In chapter 2 I noted the effort of the Reagan administration to send a team of "operational experts" (OPEX) to Liberia to straighten out the finances of that country—largely U.S. aid—marred by official corruption. Seventeen financial experts went to Liberia, endowed with sweeping powers to control government expenditures. Press reports indicated mixed feelings toward this operation; while some Liberians

saw this American presence as an "exceptional surrender of control to
an outside power,"[4] many wanted them to stay, citing "administrative
improvements achieved by the group, such as bringing payments of
civil service salaries up to date"[5] and the restoration of Liberia's international credibility. However, Liberian officials devised means to by-
pass OPEX, and within a short time the country was plunged into civil
war. West African peace-keeping forces (ECOMOG) intervened and
succeeded to broker a cease-fire agreement, but proved incompetent
in saving President Samuel Doe's life. Liberia's example is indicative
of the retrogressive economic news of the whole of Africa, where corruption is something as old as the continent itself. For the cinema,
already immersed in the conflict encompassing both skill and material
resources, it is also an undeniable fact that its growth or decline,
progress or failure, is tied to the political, economic, cultural, and psychological realities of this struggling continent.

In spite of the aforementioned predicament, black African cinema
is far from extinct. A handsome display of works varying in scope and
diverse in creativity has emerged from individual energies out of the
concern to decolonize and reassert African identity. It is out of this
political and societal reality that black African film practice emerged
as a questioning cinema, a schema that it uses to explain itself to itself
and to the outside world and to examine the colonial past and the oppressive mechanisms of the neocolonial present. With the latter, African cinema has become highly critical, at the same time using the imperatives embedded in traditional culture (oral tradition) to define its own
aesthetic preferences with which it chooses to address issues concerning African transformation.

The Question of Aesthetics

Black African cinema has often been misconstrued, especially in Western analysis, as constituting a single entity rather than a plurality of
works reflecting the various states and federations of culture within
which they are produced. The fact that there is no one African cinema
means that there can be no universal aesthetics.

This wide array of cultural references on which black Africa's film
practice is based explains the richness of black African film aesthetics,
and is also the basis for the discrepancies in understanding or misunder-
standing of African cinema by, say, the Western audience, or by those
who have been inundated with the Western cinematic tradition. But
African filmmakers have also used African representational forms
based on indigenous cultural sources to facilitate the understanding and
appreciation of its various art forms, and thus, the cultural, historical,

social, and political knowledge of Africa. Moreover, the formulation of an indigenous film practice sensitive to particular cultural contexts strengthens the African position, especially the argument that film should be comprehended outside the culture from which it is made. An example would be the English- and French-language films shown in the colonies where they are understood by African and Third World citizens who can neither speak nor write English. This observation stems from the encouraging writings on African cinema in film magazines and in the news media and in the staging of African film festivals in Europe and the United States. Since the images may be misinterpreted and the aesthetic implications misconstrued, these films, it must be remembered, were made with Africans in mind. But the interest shown in trying to understand them is the most provocative aspect. That people are beginning to know why the films are the way they are is an indication that the world is relating to positive[6] African images from real perspectives as opposed to the "dark continent" portrayals in Hollywood movies where the chimpanzees are more intelligent than the natives.

One of the first goals of the pioneers of African cinema was to create filmic works that were not only for Africans but also by Africans. While the motivational force centers on cinematic examination of Africa in totality, filmmakers assumed the responsibility of creating a new Africa out of the old, which had been victimized by colonial, racist, and Hollywood caricatures of its image, and for the first time fought back, with vehement force, to reassert Africa's lost identity. To effect the restoration of African pride and dignity it was no longer possible to sit on the fence and gaze nostalgically after lost traditional values. If the effort to recapture these values is to be based on the power of the image, truth, and knowledge, it must be confronted and examined from indigenous perspectives and rendered in styles that must not be hidden under egregious imitations of an alien film culture.

To infuse authenticity and believability into this cinematic struggle, elements evolving as derivatives and elaborations of the oral tradition are indispensable. As the master coordinators of this new vision, black African filmmakers have formulated their strategy under the auspices of two conventions—the dominant cinematic tradition and the "living tradition" of the oral storyteller. As Walter Benjamin observes, "The storyteller takes what he tells from experience—his own or that reported by others. And he in turn makes it the experience of those who are listening to the tale."[7]

In the first decade or so of black African cinema, a vigorous attempt was made to give didacticism preference over entertainment. Films stressing educational content with emphasis on the African condition have given the African audience an undistorted insight into aspects of African history—precolonial, colonial, and contemporary. This reeducation strategy is aimed at transforming society by reestablishing confidence and belief in a traditional heritage that colonial ideology had almost eradicated and by helping catalyze support for the refurbishment of a new and genuine Africa.

This quest for autonomy was matched in rigor by compelling experimentation based on cultural parallels or codes that deliberately transgress dominant patterns of signification, but with unstable economies, political upheavals, and what might be termed helplessness. This creative independence was no longer to be approached with dogmatic principles. If the 1960s and 1970s were the most apparent manifestation of this feeling, the 1980s undoubtedly provided a more conciliatory rendering. For instance, Ousmane Sembene, a champion of the didactic tradition, while acknowledging that "cinema is a cultural industry," does believe that profitability ensures entrepreneurial growth. Implying that the success of the African film industry is not only to be measured by a romantic patina of imitative art as opposed to culturally inspired artistic innovation and philosophy, he argues for finding "people and organizations who can effectively distribute African films."[8] Regarding this perennial problem of distribution and exhibition in black African film practice, filmmakers are striving for cinema as an industry by envisaging an entertainment function for films, eschewing the heavy-handed didacticism of the 1960s and 1970s.

Many of the films produced under this new strategy still remain within the overall prerogatives of the black African production "code," maintaining "the sincerity, dedication, and commitment that draws their works into the considerations of art and social thought."[9] While films like *Black Girl, Xala, Soleil O, Baara,* and *Harvest: 3,000 Years* are highly didactic and are placed first in the service of addressing the African audience, such films as *Yaaba, Love Brewed in the African Pot, La vie est belle, Visages de femmes,* and *Les coopérants* are among the new African films that address African issues while also exhibiting concern for viewers outside the continent.

The concern to internationalize black African cinema to accommodate outside viewership for wider coverage and financial recuperation is also being defined in the structure of new African films. For example, while the question of which language to use in films is still hotly debated, an emphasis on image over heavy-handed dialogue is becoming increasingly acceptable. The multiplicity of African languages and dialects coupled with the high cost of dubbing in various languages resulted in the breakdown of this language barrier, enabling films to cut across boundaries. This strategy worked well in many African films and seems to be the norm since it has been emulated by African filmmakers. Contrary to internalizing black African cinema, however, there is also the urge for externalization, which, with the incoming second wave of African filmmakers of the 1980s, ushered in what I have described as digressionary trends. Within this diversification is a "quasi-democratization" of experimental interludes, with structures exemplified by such films as *Yaaba, Bal poussière, Yeelen, Finzan,* and *La vie est belle,* each in its own way confronting the traditional paradigms—for example, structures exemplified by such films as *Heritage . . . Africa, Sarraounia,* and *Camp de Thiaroye,* all of which were made in the late 1980s.

Africa may not be the most conducive place for film production, but through hard work and dedication filmmakers have proven that this continent, which was once a filmic cul-de-sac, when given the right opportunity, now produces some of the world's finest films, responsive to the genuine needs and aspirations of its people. Technically, many of the films display aesthetic and cultural range, sophistication, and emotional affinity with African concerns and the black communities of the diaspora. In congruence with the role of communal art in traditional African contexts, African filmmakers have reexamined Western tools of production. If this art is to become viably independent, it must continue to question the tools of production. Thus, black African cinema assumes autonomy; here is an art for communal enlightenment analogous to the griot's role within the oral tradition. The communal role of art in traditional Africa has always recognized the historical, political, social, and economic factors of the people's development. It is, therefore, interesting to note that while the language of cinema has been defined primarily in the West, oral tradition has served the African user of the motion picture apparatus as an inevitable additive with which to define African cinematographic language, a language at once innovative, accessible, and deconstructive.

Notes

Introduction

1. Inasmuch as "anglophone" and "francophone" and "lusophone" are uncomfortable terms deriving from the Berlin Conference of 1884, which saw the division of Africa into the languages of the European powers, African countries, as colonies and even today as neocolonies, are still defined in terms of the languages of the former colonizers: English-speaking (anglophone), French-speaking (francophone), or Portuguese-speaking (lusophone).

2. Amilcar Cabral, *Return to the Source: Selected Speeches* (New York: Monthly Review Press, 1974); Frantz Fanon, *The Wretched of the Earth* (New York: Grove Press, 1968) and *Black Skin, White Masks* (New York: Grove, 1967); and Kwame Nkrumah, *Consciencism: Philosophy and the Ideology for Decolonization and Development* (New York: Monthly Review Press, 1964).

3. L. Adele Jinadu, "Some African Theorists of Culture and Modernization: Fanon, Cabral, and Some Others," *African Studies Review* 21, no. 1 (April 1978):125.

4. I am indebted to Yusuf Grillo, whose ideas on the classification of African art inspired this discussion on the plurality of black African cinema. See his article "What Is Contemporary African Art?" in *Africa Notes* (Special number on Nigerian Antiquities), Ibadan, 1972, 22–27.

5. Teshome Gabriel, *Third Cinema in the Third World: The Aesthetics of Liberation* (Ann Arbor: Research Press, 1982), 3.

6. Clyde Taylor, "Africa, the Last Cinema," in *Journey Across Three Continents: Film and Lecture Series,* ed. Renee Tajima (New York: Third World Newsreel, 1985), 53.

7. Jinadu, "Some African Theorists of Culture and Modernization," 121–137.

8. My analysis draws on Ngugi's theory of "the quest for relevance" in *Decolonizing the Mind: The Politics of Language in African Literature* (London: James Currey; Nairobi: Heinemann, 1986), 87–108, as it relates to the teaching of critical approaches to literature in schools and colleges. Applied to cinema, the demogogic nature of African films reminds us that film has a universal language and therefore the way in which this cinema is presented to the African populace must be critically examined.

9. Ali Mazrui, *The Africans: A Triple Heritage* (Boston: Little, Brown and Company, 1986), 18.

10. Edward Berman, "African Responses to Christian Missionary Education," *African Studies Review* no. 3 (December 1974), 527–540.

11. The following are some other books and works on African cinema worth noting. *Les cinémas africains en 1972,* by Guy Hennebelle, ed., which was published in the second decade of the birth of African cinema and, like Vierya's book, does not cover recent developments. *Cinéastes d'Afrique noire,* by Guy Hennebelle and Catherine Ruelle, eds., lists the names of black African film practitioners but does not provide a detailed analysis of their films. *Cinéma Africain et décolonisation* (1976), by Ferid Boughedir, a doctoral dissertation (also written in the second decade of African cinema), deserves praise for its enthusiastic and historical positioning of African cinema. Besides delineating important historical aspects, Boughedir's theory of the "thematic and aesthetic concerns" of African cinema (which the author elaborates upon) is a valuable research source that is bound to influence future "up-to-date" comprehensive studies of this cinema. *African Film: The Context of Production* (1982), by Angela Martin, ed., provides very useful information on filmmakers and discusses the themes of black African cinema with an in-depth bibliography. This book is a useful dossier and reference on black African cinema. *African Cinema: The Background and the Economic Context of Production,* an unpublished Ph.D. dissertation by Manthia Diawara, like the *Cinéastes d'Afrique noire* series, extends the discussion of African production histories (although not of the films themselves), but unlike those in the series it offers more detail and insight into the economies of film production in Africa south of the Sahara.

Chapter 1

1. Ngugi wa Thiong'o, *Homecoming: Essays on African and Caribbean Literature, Culture and Politics* (London: Heinemann, 1972), 3–21.

2. The impact of modern changes upon traditional culture has been dealt with by Africanists. See for instance, Reverend John Mbiti, "African Oral Literature," in *FESTAC '77* (Lagos and London: The International Festival Committee and African Journal Limited, 1977), 96–97, and the works of A. Hampaté Bâ, Joseph Ki-Zerbo, and Ali Mazrui.

3. See Frantz Fanon, *The Wretched of the Earth* (New York: Grove Press, 1968), especially the chapter "On National Culture," 206–248.

4. In *Sankofa,* Niangoran-Bouah has shown that the Akan people used a writing system, arguing that Akan or Ashanti gold weights are actually a kind

of encyclopedia used to preserve in miniature the objects and ideas of their culture. See W. R. Johnson, "The Ancient Akan Script: A Review of *Sankofa*," in *Blacks in Science: Ancient and Modern* (New Brunswick: Transaction Books, 1984), ed. Ivan Van Sertima, 197–207.

5. Ngugi wa Thiong'o, *Decolonizing the Mind: The Politics of Language in African Literature* (Nairobi and London: James Currey and Heinemann, 1986), 23.

6. I am indebted to Molefi Kete Asante for this definition. See his book *The Afrocentric Idea* (Philadelphia: Temple University Press, 1987) for a discussion of African-American "orature" and its context.

7. Harold Scheub, "A Review of African Oral Traditions and Literature," *African Studies Review* 28, no. 213 (June–September 1985):1.

8. Ngugi, *Decolonizing the Mind*, 10.

9. The level of sophistication brought to the execution of oral storytelling dispels as erroneous the notion propagated by European colonialists that the structure of cinema was too complex for the African mind to comprehend. See L. Van Bever, *Le cinéma pour africains* (Bruxelles: G. Van Campenhout, 1952), 6. See also Elyseo Taylor, "Film and Social Change," *American Behavioral Scientist* 17 (January–February 1974): 430–431. Assuming this were true, it was not because Africans failed to understand the structure of films. Early African experience with the motion picture is commensurate with that of the European initial reaction: Europeans did not understand the cinema at first exposure. For instance, in 1895 when the Lumière brothers held the first public showing of motion pictures projected on a screen at the Grand Café in Paris, the scene of *L'arrivée d'un train en gare de Ciotat* in which a train enters the station frightened the spectators so much that many members of the audience were said to have taken cover beneath their seats. Additionally, in another Lumière film spectators misconstrued optical illusion for magic and miracle when a rather innocuous scene of workmen knocking down a wall was projected in reverse to show a wall rise up from the dust and stand as it once did (this was clearly a demonstration of cinematic possibilities).

10. See Ruth Finnegan, *Oral Literature in Africa* (London: Oxford Press, 1970); Isidore Okpewho, *The Epic in Africa: Toward a Poetics of the Oral Performance* (New York: Columbia University Press, 1979); C. Bird, "Bambara Oral Prose and Verse Narratives," in *African Folklore*, ed. R. M. Dorson (New York: Doubleday, 1972). See also the works of J. Vansina, Kofi Anyidoho, and Sunday Anozie.

11. Hampaté Bâ, "The Living Tradition," in *General History of Africa*, vol. 1, *Methodology and African Prehistory*, ed. Joseph Ki-Zerbo (Berkeley: University of California Press, 1981), 168.

12. Ngugi, *Decolonizing the Mind*, 36.

13. Fredric Jameson, "Third World Literature in the Era of Multinational Capitalism," *Social Text* no. 15 (Fall 1986):69.

14. The ethnic diversity of Africa created its numerous languages, approximately "750 tribal tongues, fifty of which are spoken by one million or more people. . . . Nigeria has 250 ethnic groups, which speak more than a hundred

different languages—in Zaire there are seventy-five." David Lamb, *The Africans* (New York: Random House, 1982), 14, 299.

15. Paul Radin, ed., *African Folktales and Sculpture* (New York: Bollingen Foundation, 1952), 4. While Radin contends that these "gifted individuals do not live in a vacuum, nor are they interested in art for art's sake" (p. 7), Reverend John Mbiti sheds more light on why such a level of sophistication is a part of traditional development: "In traditional life, artists were not paid with perhaps special exceptions of people who received honor or high positions in society, but the majority simply created for the sake of satisfying their creative urge. Many of the oral works have no known authors—oral literature belongs to the whole ethnic group or nation, being the product of its daughters and sons. There are no copyrights" (p. 96).

16. Fanon, *The Wretched of the Earth*, 241.

17. Ivan Van Sertima, ed., *Blacks in Science: Ancient and Modern* (New Brunswick, N.J.: Transaction Books, 1984), 7–26.

18. Fanon, *The Wretched of the Earth*, 211.

19. Van Sertima, *Blacks in Science*, 8.

20. Fanon, *The Wretched of the Earth*, 210.

21. Jorge Robelo's speech, "The Use of Cinema as an Instrument of Cultural Domination," is a biting criticism of the imperialist use of the cinema for propaganda and dissemination of its ideologies. See reprint of that speech in Angela Martin, ed., *African Films: The Context of Production* (London: British Film Institute, 1982), 4.

22. For the "special" films made for Africans during the colonial periods and the reason behind the making of such films, see L. A. Notcutt and G. C. Latham, eds., *The African and the Cinema* (London: The Edinburgh House Press, 1937).

23. Peter Mwaura, *Communications Policies in Kenya* (Paris: UNESCO, 1980), 35. The author remarks on how, for over sixty years, the Europeans consistently discredited the African culture.

24. Walter Rodney, *How Europe Underdeveloped Africa* (Washington, D.C.: Howard University Press, 1982), 238 ff.

25. For the discussion of the implications and contradictions of colonial exploitation associated with the search for raw materials in Africa, see Ali Mazrui, *The Africans: A Triple Heritage* (Boston: Little, Brown and Company, 1986), 160–161.

26. When the missionaries arrived, and for their mission to succeed, they took upon themselves the burden of transcribing many of Africa's numerous languages in order to promote literacy in both African and European languages. But their ultimate aim was to magnify the impact of their evangelizing effort. If converts could read and interpret the Bible and spread the divine message, there was every likelihood of reaching the as yet unconverted. Colonial governments, in areas occupied by the British, French, and Belgians, also took some initiative in providing Africans with skills not offered by a missionary education, such as training African administrators and civil servants, the handpicked few who received vocational training, and others such as the police. It was

the pressure for self-rule that later forced colonial governments to substitute a wider government-funded education than the missionaries had provided.

27. Edward B. Horatio-Jones, "Historical Review of the Cinema in West Africa and the Black World and Its Implication for a Film Industry in Nigeria," in *The Development and Growth of the Film Industry in Nigeria*, ed. Alfred Opubor and Onuora E. Nwuneli (Lagos and New York: Third Press International, 1979), 74.

28. Jean Rouch, "The Awakening African Cinema," *UNESCO Courier* no. 3 (March 1962):10.

29. Jean-René Debrix, "Le cinéma africain," in *Afrique Contemporaine* no. 38/39 (July–October 1968):7.

30. Horatio-Jones, "Historical Review of the Cinema," 74.

31. See Hannes Kamphausen, "Cinema in Africa—A Survey," *Cineaste* 5, no. 2 (Spring 1972):29.

32. See "Colonialism and the Cinema: Africa Through the Eyes of Westerners," *Young Cinema and Theatre* no. 3 (1973):20.

33. *Young Cinema and Theatre*, 20.

34. Emilie de Brigard, "The History of Ethnographic Film," in *Principles of Visual Anthropology*, ed. Paul Hockings (The Hague: Mouton, 1975), 18.

35. Mary Lea Bandy, ed., *Rediscovering French Film* (New York: Museum of Modern Art, 1983), 19.

36. Justice Thaddeus Owens, cited in Thomas Morgan, "Weekends Jail for Synagogue Fire," *New York Times*, 2 March 1989, B3.

37. See Jacob M. Landau, *Studies in the Arab Theatre and Cinema* (Philadelphia: University of Pennsylvania Press, 1958), 158.

38. Landau, *Studies in the Arab Theatre and Cinema*, 159.

39. Landau, *Studies in the Arab Theatre and Cinema*, 159.

40. Mazrui, *The Africans: A Triple Heritage*, 32.

41. Ngugi, *Decolonizing the Mind*, 16.

42. Asia, South America, Greenland, and the Middle East were among the regions of the world negatively portrayed in the motion picture. But with sub-Saharan Africa, the situation worsened when its people began to be portrayed, as Jean Rouch described it, as "wild creatures whose behavior was intended to provoke laughter" (Jean Rouch, "The Awakening African Cinema," 10). But regarding the films Rouch made (almost all of them in Africa), his career has been described as one of "inveterate amateurism" and "incurable dilettantism" (Emilie de Brigard, "The History of Ethnographic Film," 28).

43. David S. Wiley, *Africa on Film and Videotape 1960–1981* (East Lansing, Michigan: African Studies Center, Michigan State University), ix–x.

44. Robert Stam and Louise Spence, "Colonialism, Racism and Representation," *Screen* 24, no. 2 (March–April 1983):6.

45. Daniel Leab, *From Sambo to Superspade: The Black Experience in Motion Pictures* (Boston: Houghton Mifflin Company, 1975), 20.

46. J. Koyinde Vaughan, "Africa and the Cinema," in *An African Treasury*, ed. Langston Hughes (New York: Crown Publishers, 1960), 85.

47. Robert Stam and Louise Spence, "Colonialism, Racism and Represen-

tation," 4. For a discussion of racism in cinema, see Robert Stam et. al, "Racism in the Cinema: Proposal for a Methodological Model of Investigation," *Critical Arts* 2, no. 4 (March 1983):6–12.

48. This paper, "The Teaching of African Literature in Schools," published by the Kenya Literature Bureau, was first presented at a 1973 conference on the teaching of African literature, held in Nairobi, Kenya, and now in Akivaga and Gachukiah. This information is provided by Ngugi wa Thiong'o, *Decolonizing the Mind,* 18.

49. Also cited in Ngugi, *Decolonizing the Mind,* 18.

50. Walter Lippmann, in his book, *Public Opinion,* as quoted in Jack G. Shaheen's article, "The Hollywood Arab (1984–1986)," *Journal of Popular Film and Television* 14, no. 4 (Winter 1987):148.

51. Joseph Boskin, "Denials: The Media View of Dark Skins and the City," in *Small Voices and Great Trumpets,* ed. Bernard Rubin (New York: Praeger, 1980), 141.

52. Shaheen, "The Hollywood Arab," 148.

53. Donald Bogle's *Toms, Coons, Mulattoes, Mammies and Bucks* (New York: Bantam, 1974), Thomas Cripp's *Slow Fade to Black* (New York: Oxford University Press, 1977), and Daniel Leab's *From Sambo to Black* (Boston: Houghton Mifflin Company, 1977) deal with stereotyping of black Americans. Richard Maynard's *Africa on Film: Myth and Reality* (Rochelle Park, New Jersey: Hayden Books, 1974), David S. Wiley's *Africa on Film and Videotape 1960–1981* (East Lansing: African Studies Center, Michigan State University, 1982), and Francoise Pfaff's "Hollywood's Image of Africa" *Commonwealth* 5 (1981–1982):97–116, denounce the pernicious falsification of African history and culture, while Robert Stam's "Slow Fade to Afro: The Black Presence in Brazilian Cinema," *Film Quarterly* (Winter 1982–83):16–31, offers insight into a wide variety of black roles.

54. Eric Williams, *A History of the People of Trinidad and Tobago* (London: Praeger, 1964), 32. Also cited in Ngugi, *Decolonizing the Mind,* 18.

55. Williams, *A History of the People of Trinidad and Tobago,* 31, and Ngugi, *Decolonizing the Mind,* 18.

56. See Carl Jung, *Psychological Types: Collected Works,* vol. 6 (New York: Harcourt, Brace and Co. 1921). For a detailed account of Jung's racism, see Farhad Dalal, "The Racism of Jung," *Race and Class* 29, no. 3 (Winter 1988):1–22.

57. George Hegel, *The Philosophy of History* (New York: Dover 1956), 91–99, as quoted in Ngugi, *Decolonizing the Mind,* 32.

58. Ngugi, *Decolonizing the Mind,* 18. Wa Thiong'o also attacks other references Hegel made about Africa in the introduction to his lectures in *The Philosophy of History* as particularly distorted and hopelessly disparaging: "Hegel gives history, philosophy, rational expression and legitimacy to every conceivable European racist myth about Africa. Africa is even denied her own geography where it does not correspond to the myth. Thus, Egypt is not part of Africa; and North Africa is part of Europe. Africa proper is the special home of ravenous beasts, snakes of all kinds. The African is not part of humanity."

Only slavery to Europe can raise him, possibly to the lower ranks of humanity. Slavery is good for Africa'' (31–32).

59. Hugh Honour's *The Image of the Black in Western Art,* vol. 4, *From the American Revolution to World War I* (Freibourg: Office du Livre, 1989), is invaluable in this aspect of black representation. See also Albert Boime's review of this book in the *New York Times Book Review,* 2 April 1989, 14–15.

60. S. Kunitz and H. Haycraft, eds., *Twentieth Century Authors* (New York: H. W. Wilson and Co., 1966), 227.

61. For the treatment of blacks in the animated cartoon, see Irene Kotlarz's article "The Birth of a Notion," *Screen* 24, no. 2 (March–April 1983):21–29.

62. Kotlarz, "The Birth of a Notion," 24.

63. Vaughan, "Africa and the Cinema," in *African Treasury,* ed. Langston Hughes (New York: Crown Publishers, 1960), 86.

64. From the plot of *Tarzan of the Apes* in Gabe Essoe, *Tarzan of the Movies* (New York: Citadel Press, 1968), 5.

65. Vaughan, "Africa and the Cinema," 87.

66. See Harold D. Weaver, Jr., "Black Filmmakers in Africa and America," *Sightlines* 4 (Spring 1976):7.

67. Vaughan, "Africa and the Cinema," 87.

68. Terry Bishop, "Filmmaking in Udi," *The Spectator,* 1 April 1949, 431.

69. Terry Bishop, the producer of *Daybreak in Udi,* later admitted that before his film crew arrived at Udi, there were already "ambitious development projects [which] had produced maternity homes, schools, co-operative shops, village halls, water supply schemes, a network of roads and many other forms of village development, all provided by voluntary labor and all started in the first instance on the initiative of the people themselves" (*The Spectator,* 1 April 1949, 431). See also Rosaleen Smyth, "Movies and Mandarins: The Official Film and British Colonial Africa," in *British Cinema History,* ed. James Curran and Vincent Porter (Totowa, N.J.: Barnes and Noble, 1983), for excellent discussions of this subject.

70. *New York Times,* 28 January 1918, 13.

71. Felix-Louis Regnault, 1931, quoted in de Brigard, "The History of Ethnographic Film," 15.

72. Cited in de Brigard, "The History of Ethnographic Film," 15.

73. Vaughan, "Africa and the Cinema," 92.

74. Vaughan, "Africa and the Cinema," 94.

75. de Brigard, "The History of Ethnographic Film," 21.

76. See Martin Johnson, *Congorilla: Adventures with Pygmies and Gorillas in Africa* (New York: Brewer, Warren, and Putnam, 1931), for a personal account of an expedition to Africa.

77. Erik Barnouw, *Documentary: A History of Non-Fiction Film* (London: Oxford University Press, 1974), 50–51.

78. *La croisière noire* is one of the films of that period listed by Rouch as a serious venture that portrayed Africa in a positive light. See Rouch, "The Awakening African Cinema," 10.

79. Similarly, for fear of a popular uprising against colonial rule, the British

reedited American films shown in Africa, where black Americans played roles—no matter how menial those roles were. They were worried that African blacks, seeing how black Americans were "integrated" into America's labor force (for example, participating in such a highly technical and "superior" art such as the cinema), might start asking questions about their own African environment.

80. As translated in *Young Cinema and Theatre* no. 3 (1973):23.

81. Pfaff, "Hollywood's Image of Africa," 6.

82. Pfaff, "Hollywood's Image of Africa," 6.

83. J. R. Rayfield, "The Use of Films in Teaching About Africa," *Film Library Quarterly* 17, nos. 2, 3 and 4 (1984):41.

84. Pierre Haffner, "Jean Rouch jugé par six cinéastes d'afrique noire," *Cinémaction* no. 17 (1982):70.

85. Guy Hennebelle, "Un nouveau cinéaste Nigérien: Oumarous Ganda de moi, un noir à Cabascado," *L' Afrique littéraire et artistique* no. 4 (1968):71.

86. Haffner, "Jean Rouch," 63–64.

87. Mick Eaton, ed., *Anthropology—Reality—Cinema* (London: British Film Institute Dossier, 1979), 6.

88. Teshome H. Gabriel, *Third Cinema in the Third World: The Aesthetics of Liberation* (Ann Arbor, Michigan: Research Press, 1982), 77.

89. Gabriel, *Third Cinema,* 77.

90. Quoted in Vincent Canby, "Documentaries: Limitless Eyes Recording Civilization," *New York Times,* 3 November 1985, 19.

91. *Young Cinema and Theatre,* 24.

92. Mazrui, *The Africans,* 65. For Mazrui's discussion of "The Culture of Hunters," see also "Africa's Identity: The Indigenous Personality," 63–66.

93. Mazrui, *The Africans,* 66.

94. For a fuller discussion of *Lorang's Way,* see my article "Representing Native Kenya on Film: *Lorang's Way* and the Turkana People," *UFAHAMU* 17, no. 1 (Fall 1988):3–14.

95. Quoted in de Brigard, "The History of Ethnographic Film," 30.

96. In her interview in *Camera Obscura,* Trinh T. Minh-ha tried to convince readers that all the technical flaws in both films were meant to function as innovations in documentary filmmaking. I am very surprised that such a supposedly feminist magazine did not question her proclivity for photographing naked breasts. (See Constance Penley and Andrew Ross, "Interview with Trinh T. Minh-ha," *Camera Obscura* no. 13/14 (Spring–Summer 1985):87–111.

97. For example, my paper, which was to be published in *Journal Film*'s special issue dealing with a 1989 ethnographic conference, was cancelled at the last minute because ethnographic filmmakers and their sympathizers, whose work I cited in the paper, threatened to boycott the conference if it was published.

98. Caryn James, "Sophisticated Silliness: *The Gods Must Be Crazy," New York Times,* 14 June 1987, H34.

99. Eaton, *Anthropology—Reality—Cinema,* 10.

100. Cited in Renée Shafransky, "The White Man's Burden Is Himself,"

Village Voice, 17 July 1984, 53. For an excellent and in-depth analysis, see Peter Davis's review of *The Gods Must Be Crazy* in *Cineaste* 14, no. 1 (1985): 51–53.

Chapter 2

1. See "Africa, the Last Cinema," in *Journey Across Three Continents,* ed. Renee Tajima (New York: Third World Newsreel, 1985), 50–58.

2. Walter Rodney, *How Europe Underdeveloped Africa* (Washington, D.C.: Howard University Press, 1982), 14.

3. Rodney, *How Europe Underdeveloped Africa,* 14.

4. See "The Persistence of Psychological and Structural Dependence After Colonialism," in *Decolonization and Dependency: Problems of Development of African Societies,* ed. Aguibou Y. Yansane (Westport, Conn.: Greenwood Press, 1980), 73.

5. Gerard Chaliand's introduction, "The Dimensions of Development," in *Revolution in the Third World* (Harmondsworth, England: Penguin Books, 1978), details aspects of colonial exploitation of Third World countries.

6. Elliot P. Skinner, "Strangers in West African Societies," *Africa* 33 (October 1963):307–320.

7. Pierre Roitfeld, *Afrique noire francophone* (Paris: Unifrance Film, 1980).

8. Ferid Boughedir, "Cinéma Africain et décolonization: (Ph.D. diss. Université de la Sorbonne Nouvelle, Paris, 1976), also cited in Angela Martin, ed., *African Films: The Context of Production,* dossier no. 6 (London: British Film Institute, 1982), 36.

9. Thomas Guback, *The International Film Industries: Western Europe and America Since 1945* (Bloomington: Indiana University Press, 1969), 100.

10. Boughedir, "Cinéma Africain et décolonization," cited in Angela Martin, *African Films,* 40.

11. Edward B. Horatio-Jones, "Historical Review of the Cinema in West Africa," in *The Development and Growth of the Film Industry in Nigeria,* ed. Onuora E. Nwuneli and Alfred E. Opubor (Lagos and New York: Third Press International, 1979), 82. See, also, the cover story, "Asians in Africa," *African Concord* no. 161 (8 October 1987):7–13.

12. Quoted by T. Killick, *Development Economics in Action* (London: Heinemann, 1978), 34.

13. D. K. Fieldhouse, *Black Africa 1945–80: Economic Decolonization and Arrested Development* (London: Allen and Unwin, 1986), 94.

14. See, for example, Ali Mazrui, *The Africans: A Triple Heritage* (Boston: Little, Brown and Company, 1986). I would also recommend that the reader see the nine-part television series "The Africans," jointly produced by the BBC and PBS, which was launched with this volume.

15. When the theaters were renamed "Bendel Theaters," everyone thought they belonged to the then Bendel State Government.

16. See John W. Forje's discussion of "Technological Change and the Development of Africa," *Présence Africaine* no. 143 (3d Quarter 1987):127.

17. General Samuel K. Doe was assassinated in September 1990. For an

account of Liberia's internal turmoil, see Blaine Harden, *Africa: Dispatches from a Fragile Continent* (Boston: Houghton Mifflin, 1990), 217–248.

18. James Brooke, "U.S. Will Oversee Liberian Finances," *New York Times*, 26 April 1987, L11.

19. Paul Biya, the president of the Republic of Cameroon, has proposed a new African development philosophy called "communal liberalism" which, he says, has principles to include the concern for efficiency as well as "the sense of solidarity and the respect for the human personality." See *Communal Liberalism*, English edition (London: Macmillan Publishers Ltd., 1987).

20. Horatio-Jones, "Historical Review of the Cinema in West Africa," 82.

21. One of the ways the newly independent African governments explained their development projects to the predominantly illiterate peasant communities was through mobile cinemas. These shows also provided some villagers with their first experience with motion pictures.

22. The view expressed in most standard history books and articles dealing with black African cinema is that the only significant cinema began with Ousmane Sembene's *Borom Sarret*. Other films are seldom discussed, nor accorded their status, either for their obscurity or because they have been regarded as amateurish or too experimental to consider. We will note here that *Aouré* (1962) received an award at the Saint-Cast Festival in France as well as a bronze medal for short films at the 1962 Cannes Film Festival.

23. This operation came into effect when the French government arranged with the four major newsreel production companies in France—Les Actualités Françaises, Écair Journal, Gaumont Actualités, and Pathé Magazine—to create a fifth that would subsidize the production of the newsreels, educational films, and documentaries, as well as help the newly independent francophone countries to develop their own audiovisual media.

24. A policy change was adopted in the late 1940s in recognition of Africa's role in defending France in World War II, when the Ministry of Colonies in the French cabinet was renamed the Ministry of Overseas France. Ironically, it was also during this same period (1944) that the French colonial authorities massacred the Senegalese infantrymen awaiting repatriation at Camp de Thiaroye (the title of Sembene's film) after they had fought for France during the bloody confrontations against the Axis.

25. Bernard Magubane, "A Critical Look at Indices Used in the Study of Social Change in Colonial Africa," *Current Anthropology* 12, no. 45 (October–December 1971):419–443.

26. Although scripts were censored and politically explosive ones rejected, anticolonialist films such as *La noire de, Soleil O,* and others, whose productions could not be easily suppressed, could be manipulated through distribution. The Coopération could choose to control the impact of these films by buying the rights to distribute them only in French cultural centers in Africa (or not distribute them at all).

27. See Hannes Kamphausen, "Cinema in Africa: A Survey," *Cinéaste* 5, no. 2 (Spring 1972):31.

28. Harold D. Weaver, "Filmmakers Have a Great Responsibility to Our People—An Interview with Ousmane Sembene," *Cinéaste* 6, no. 1 (1973):30.

29. Howard Schissel, "Portrait of Sembene," *West Africa*, 18 July 1983, 1665.

30. Cited in the blurb on back page of Ousmane Sembene's *God's Bits of Wood* (New York: Doubleday, 1962).

31. Schissel, "Portrait of Sembene," 1665.

32. François Sourou Okioh, "Problems of African Cinema," *Young Cinema and Theatre* no. 3 (1982):25–26.

33. Okioh, "Problems of African Cinema," 25–26.

34. From Roy Armes's original article written for publication in the 1986 *International Film Guide*.

35. The destruction of the growth of Côte d'Ivoire cinema came from the government's inability to control the operations of COMACICO and SECMA and its inability to put forward a policy that could revive the operations of SIC.

36. Jean Rouch, and some of the masters of Canadian documentary such as Norman Maclaren, Michael Brault, and Claude Jutra, made films for Niger. Rouch also made films for Mali and Côte d'Ivoire, and Joris Ivens made the educational film *Demain à Nanguila* (Tomorrow in Nanguîla, 1960) in Mali.

37. Cited in Martin, ed., *African Films*, 86.

38. Ousmane Sembene, *Tribal Scars* (London: Heinemann, 1974).

39. Henry Morgenthau, "On Films and Filmmakers," *Africa Report* (May–June 1969):71–72.

40. *International Film Guide* (London), annually since 1964. Surveys of production: For Niger, 1972–1974 (Roy Armes).

41. Françoise Pfaff, "Films of Med Hondo: An African Filmmaker in Paris," *Jump Cut* 31 (1986):44.

42. Pfaff, "Films of Med Hondo," 44.

43. See Tajima, ed., "Africa, the Last Cinema," 54.

44. Pfaff, "Films of Med Hondo," 44.

45. See *L.A. Weekly*, 17–23 August 1984, 43.

46. See *New York Times* review of 15 March 1973, sec. 3, 55.

47. Roy Armes, *Third World Filmmaking and the West* (Berkeley: University of California Press, 1987), 215.

48. Boughedir, "Cinéma Africain et décolonization," 43.

49. In *Mandabi* there are allusions to polygamy, although this is not the central issue. In fact, it was presented as a traditional way of life, though the treatment of women is prone to be misconstrued as relegating them to second-class status.

50. Sembene initially preferred black and white filmstock, fearing the sensationalism that color would bring to his type of study, but he was vetoed by the French producer who financed the film.

51. Rather than letting Sembene portray Africa accordingly, the producer wanted to interject sexual and erotic scenes. Production eventually stopped and their differences were settled in court.

52. See Okey Onyejekwe, "Decolonization and Recolonization in Africa: The Trend for the '80s," *Journal of African Studies* (Fall 1984):27.

53. G. M. Perry and Patrick McGilligan, "Ousmane Sembene: An Interview," *Film Quarterly* 26 (Summer 1973):37.

54. Burkina Faso's contribution to the development of African cinema during this period is unparalleled and unprecedented. A small country of about 3.5 million people with only a few theaters and no significant movie-making record, Burkina Faso took the lead in black Africa and nationalized its theaters. It was this maverick endeavor that made it possible to show African films with ease during the Second African Film Festival held in Ouagadougou, the capital city, in theaters formerly controlled by foreigners.

55. In Julius Lester, "Mandabi: Confronting Africa," *Evergreen Review* no. 78 (May 1970):58.

56. I refer the reader to Françoise Pfaff's excellent study of *Mandabi* in *The Cinema of Ousmane Sembene,* 127–140.

57. Marie Claire Le Roy, "Africa's Film Festivals," *Africa Report* (April 1970):27–28.

58. This would follow the same pattern of development as that of the French government, whose assistance led to the establishment of television production centers in the former colonies, supervised by ministries of information, which, in turn, created film production departments, as in the cases of Senegal and Côte d'Ivoire the Ivory Coast discussed earlier.

59. Guy Hennebelle and Catherine Ruelle, quoted in Angela Martin, ed., *African Films: The Context of Production,* 62.

60. See Guy Flatley's interview with Sembene, "Senegal Is Senegal, Not Harlem," *New York Times,* 2 November 1969, 17.

61. For "The History of the Fédération Panafricaine des Cinéastes," see Guy Hennebelle, "La charte d'Charte d'Alger du Cinéma Africain," *L'Afrique littéraire et artistique* (special issue) no. 49 (3d Quarter 1978); also see Manthia Diawara, "African Cinema," 67–91.

62. Herbert Mbukeni Mnguni, "African Intellectuals and the Development of African Political Thought in the Twentieth Century," *Présence Africaine* no. 143 (3d Quarter 1987):113–121, is an invaluable source for our discussion of this subject.

63. The structure and political aims of pan-Africanism can be found in scholarly works of Adekunle Ajala, *Pan-Africanism: Evolution, Progress and Prospects* (New York: St. Martin's Press, 1973); J. Ayodele Langley, *Pan-Africanism and Nationalism in West Africa 1900–1945* (London: Oxford University Press, 1982); and P. Olisanwule Esedebe, *Pan-Africanism: The Idea and Movement 1776–1963* (Washington, D.C.: Howard University Press, 1982); also cited in Mnguni, "African Intellectuals," 115.

64. Chinua Achebe, *The Trouble with Nigeria* (Enugu, Nigeria: Fourth Dimension Publishing Co., 1983), 11.

65. Frantz Fanon, *The Wretched of the Earth,* 221–223.

66. Herbert Mbukeni Mnguni, "African Intellectuals," 115.

67. For example, Senghor's negritude philosophy, considered historically untenable in many ways, has been criticized by many of Africa's prolific writers and intellectuals such as Nigeria's Wole Soyinka, the 1986 Nobel Laureate for literature, Kenya's Ngugi wa Thiong'o, and South Africa's Ezekiel Mphahlele. See also Herbert Mbukeni Mnguni, "African Intellectuals," 115.

68. Fanon, *The Wretched of the Earth*, 223.

69. Antonio Gramsci, *Selections From the Prison Notebooks* (New York: International Publishers, 1971), ed. and trans. Quintin Hoare and Geoffrey Nowell Smith.

70. Mnguni, "African Intellectuals," 115.

71. Boughedir, "Cinéma Africain et décolonization," 79.

72. When their creative pursuit was threatened by the French Ministry of Coopération, which financed their films, for refusing to follow the French way of making movies, and when their films risked being banned by African leaders because they criticized their lack of direction and ineffective leadership, both filmmakers (who eschewed personal wealth at a time when African elites were beginning to put their personal coffers first before their political virtues) relentlessly pursued the themes they hoped would open the eyes of the people to Africa's problems.

73. Teshome H. Gabriel, *Third Cinema in the Third World: The Aesthetics of Liberation* (Ann Arbor: University of Michigan Research Press, 1982), 7.

74. Ousmane Sembene, *God's Bits of Wood* (London: Heinemann, 1970), 57–58.

75. Med Hondo, "What Is Cinema for Us," *Jump Cut* no. 31 (1986):47.

76. Frantz Fanon, *Toward the African Revolution* (Harmondsworth, U.K.: Penguin, 1970), 114.

77. In concurrence with Ntongela Masilela's reference to this point in "Interconnections: The African and Afro-American Cinema," *The Independent* (January–February 1988), *Emitai, Ceddo, Camp de Thiaroye, Harvest: 3,000, West Indies*, and *Sarraounia* would fall in the latter category. See also Mnguni, "African Intellectuals," 118.

78. As quoted by Paul Nursey-Bray, "Race and Nation: Ideology in the Thought of Frantz Fanon," *Journal of Modern African Studies* 18, no. 1 (March 1980):141. See also Fanon, *The Wretched of the Earth*, 157.

79. In this case, Med Hondo and Haile Gerima (both considered filmmakers in exile) fall into this category by virtue of their film work.

80. First published in *Revista civilização brasiliera* no. 3 (July 1965): n.p.; and in *Afterimage* no. 1 (April 1970):13–14.

81. First published in *Tricontinental* no. 13 (October 1969): n.p. Also in Bill Nichols, ed., *Movies and Methods* (Berkeley: University of California Press, 1976), 44–56; Michael Chanan, ed., *Twenty-Five Years of New Latin American Cinema* (London: British Film Institute/Channel Four Television, 1983), 17–27.

82. Published as "Por un cine imperfecto," *Cine Cubano* no. 66/67 (1970). Also in Bill Nichols, ed., *Movies and Methods*, 28–33.

83. Chanan, ed., *Twenty-Five Years of New Latin American Cinema*, 17.

84. Chanan, ed., *Twenty-Five Years of New Latin American Cinema*, 18.

85. Chanan, ed., *Twenty-Five Years of New Latin American Cinema*, 24.

86. Quoted in Paul Willemen, "The Third Cinema Question: Notes and Reflections," *Framework* no. 34 (1987):14.

87. Willeman, "The Third Cinema Question," 14.

88. Chanan, ed., *Twenty-Five Years of New Latin American Cinema*, 31–32.

89. Chanan, ed., *Twenty-Five Years of New Latin American Cinema*, 33.

90. Robert C. Allen and Douglas Gomery, *Film History, Theory and Practice* (New York: Alfred A. Knopf, 1985), 82.

91. Allen and Gomery, *Film History*, 82.

92. Fanon, *The Wretched of the Earth*, 85.

93. See, for instance, Henry Bienen, "State and Revolution: The Work of Amilcar Cabral," *The Journal of Modern African Studies* 15, no. 4 (December 1977):555–568.

94. Paul Nursey-Bray, "Race and Nation," 135.

95. See G. M. Perry and Patrick McGilligan. "Ousmane Sembene," 40. As quoted in Gabriel, *Third Cinema in the Third World*, 22.

96. Gabriel, *Third Cinema in the Third World*, 22.

97. Perry and McGilligan, "Ousmane Sembene," 40.

98. Pfaff, "Films of Med Hondo," 45.

99. Gabriel, *Third Cinema in the Third World*, 27.

100. On his technique of dragging out and oversimplifying scenes, Sembene stated that the "African public would not believe, for example, that a film character seen going into a shower and [emerging] fully dressed [in the next scene] has actually taken a shower" (Carrie Dailey Moore, "Social Realism in the Works of Sembene Ousmane" [Ph.D. dissertation, Indiana University, 1973], 145). In a rather hagiographical defense of Sembene's position, Carrie Moore (now Carrie Sembene) has written, "Elliptical sequences, which have become a normal part of our American film viewing, disorient the African public. It is this concern with the film reading illiteracy of the African public which explains to some extent the slower pace of African films and the didacticism of [most] of Sembene's films" ("Social Realism in the Works of Sembene Ousmane," 145). To my mind, Sembene's view is aligned with pronouncements made by the pioneers of the British Colonial Film Unit (which Sembene and many other Africans condemned for being too paternalistic and racist) who, in 1935, established the Bantu Film Experiment in East Africa, created to "educate" the Africans. They rejected such commercial films as Charlie Chaplin's, which were thought to be technically too sophisticated for the African mind. Films recommended were those whose scenes were uncut, with action and pace deliberately slowed down and uncomplicated, simplified narratives. (See L. A. Notcutt and G. C. Latham, eds., *The African and the Cinema* [London: The Edinburgh House Press, 1937].) On the choice of seeing the simplified narrative structure of films made by the British CFU and the dominant commercial entertainment film, J. Koyinde Vaughan stated in 1957 that, in spite of the so-called complicated technical conventions of the latter, African audiences preferred those films because the former bored them to death (*Présence Africaine* no. 14/15 [June–September 1957]:218). See also "The Mobile Cinema in the Villages," *Colonial Cinema* (March 1945):12, where an unidentified African writer from the Gold Coast (Ghana), commenting on the reception of British colonial films by Africans, wrote, "No village audience is satisfied until, at the end, they see some comic film, such as *Charlie the Rascal*. I often wonder if Charlie Chaplin knows how many ardent fans he has in the Gold

Coast." Moore's assertion is not wholly true either. Before the coming of African cinema, American, Chinese, Indian, and Italian films were seen by Africans of different classes. When I saw John Wayne's westerns, I understood them. I liked the fast cut of the chase sequences. As kids, when the movie was over, we reenacted the scenes. We enjoyed it. On the contrary, Gerima's *Harvest: 3,000* is slow-paced and yet its coherent editing makes it interesting in the same way Sembene's improved editing and camera work made *Xala* or *Ceddo* distinctive. From this writer's filmmaking experience, it is reasonable to state unequivocally that Sembene's early mistakes are only a necessary path an apprentice has to walk before attaining maturity.

101. Pfaff, "Films of Med Hondo," 45.

102. Pfaff, "Films of Med Hondo," 45.

103. Pfaff, "Films of Med Hondo," 45.

104. Behind Hondo's arsenal of devices is a barrage of images. Here we experience a compression of past and present historical circumstances through montage of variable camera speed, creating rhymes and rhythms. Clearly this analytical strategy is inseparable from his dialectical reasoning and temperament.

105. André Bazin, in *What Is Cinema?* vol. 1, trans. Hugh Gray (Berkeley: University of California Press, 1967), 35–36, notes that in long-duration shots the audience's identification with the image more closely approximates a sense of reality and results in a "more active mental attitude on the part of the spectator and a more positive contribution on his part to the action in progress."

106. William F. Van Wert, "Ideology in the Third World Cinema: A Study of Sembene Ousmane and Glauber Rocha," *Quarterly Review of Film Studies* 4, no. 2 (Spring 1979):209.

Chapter 3

1. For example, movies were brainwashing youth into regarding everything Western as superior to anything African; thus concerned people felt a need to call for African cinema that would portray African realities in the best light.

2. Cited in Niyi Osundare, "A Grand Escape into Metaphysics," *West Africa,* 12 May 1980, 827.

3. This type of free cinema was not only popular in the anglophone states but also in some francophone states, and it was first used by the British colonial government to explain the war to villagers, to encourage them to practice thrift, and to help the war effort. See *Colonial Cinema* (March 1945):11–14, and William Sellers, "Mobile Cinema Shows in Africa," *Colonial Review* (March 1955):13–14.

4. Stanley Meisler, "Look-Reads," *Africa Report* (May/June 1969):80. All other discussions on this subject stem from this article.

5. Meisler, "Look-Reads," 83.

6. Stephen Holden, "The Dark Side of Peter Pan," *New York Times,* 13 September 1987, H36.

7. Joseph Odindo, "African Nations Struggle to Make Television Their Own," *New York Times,* 28 December 1986, E3.

8. Joseph Odindo, "African Nations Struggle," E3.

9. Olawale Awodija, "How America Colonizes Nigeria Via the Media," *Sunday Times* (Lagos), 10 October 1982, 5.

10. *Présence Africaine* no. 144 (4th Quarter, 1987):59–72.

11. N. Frank Ukadike, "Theatre on the Screen: A Filmmaker's View on Nigerian Television," *Nigerian Theatre Journal* 2, no. 1/2 (1985):191–197.

12. Ajoa Yeboah-Afari, "From Apologies to Praises," *West Africa*, 2 March 1988, 783.

13. Nanabanyin Dadson, "TV's Most Wanted Men," *West Africa*, 2 March 1988, 782.

14. Dadson, "TV's Most Wanted Men," 782.

15. Michael Raeburn, "Entretien avec Sam Aryetey," *L'Afrique littéraire et artistique* no. 49 (1978):19, 63.

16. Paulin Soumanou Vieyra, *Le cinéma Africain: Des origines à 1973* (Paris: Présence Africaine, 1975), 103.

17. Odindo, "African Nations Struggle," E3.

18. Odindo, "African Nations Struggle," E3.

19. Cited in Manthia Diawara, "Film in Anglophone Africa: A Brief Survey," in *Blackframes: Critical Perspectives on Black Independent Cinema*, ed. Mbye B. Cham and Claire Andrade-Watkins (Cambridge, Mass.: MIT Press, 1988), 38.

20. Iyabo Aina, "Twenty-five Years of Television Broadcasting in Nigeria," *Television Journal* (Lagos) no. 4 (April—June 1984):20–24.

21. Aina, "Twenty-five Years of Television Broadcasting in Nigeria," 23.

22. Ukadike, "Theatre on the Screen," 194–195.

23. This quota system is an "unequal opportunity employer" because it allows for disproportionate distribution of federal jobs, scholarships, and so on. These positions are not filled by merit. For instance, states with a high literacy rate will have candidates dumped in favor of lesser qualified candidates from states with a low literacy rate.

24. Iyabo Aina, "Face to Face with Lola Fanikayode," *Television Journal* (Lagos) no. 4 (April—June 1984):27. Since 1984, a lot has changed economically. Retail shelves are now full, but implementation of the Structural Adjustment Program (SAP) by the federal government has catapulted prices of commodities to astronomical heights well beyond the reach of the poor.

25. British-sponsored negotiations that worked out independence schedule for Zimbabwe in 1979.

26. The General Certificate of Education examination is a prerequisite for admission to Nigerian universities.

27. James Brooke, "30 Million Nigerians Are Laughing, at Themselves," *New York Times*, 24 July 1987, A4.

28. Françoise Balogun, *The Cinema in Nigeria* (Enugu, Nigeria: Delta Publications, 1987), 22. See my review of this book in *UFAHAMU* 17, no. 1 (Fall 1988):77–80.

29. Jibrin Aminu, "Television and the Nigerian Society," paper presented at the NTA Symposium in Kaduna on 29 March 1983 and published in *The Guardian* (Nigeria), 24 April 1983, 12.

30. Kyalo Mativo, "Resolving the Cultural Dilemma of the African Film," *UFAHAMU* 13, no. 1 (Fall 1983):139.

31. Ukadike, "Theatre on the Screen," 191.

32. Jesse Jackson, "What We Have Won," *Mother Jones* 13, no. 4 (July–August 1988):22.

33. From Sembene's films to the newer African films, almost all filmmakers adhere to this practice.

34. "Zimbabwe Has Much to Offer Foreign Filmmakers," *Images,* supplement to the *Financial Gazette,* 5 February 1988, 27 (by anonymous correspondent).

35. "The Future Is Limited Only by Finance," 25.

36. "The Future Is Limited Only by Finance," 25. I think the author meant Godwin Mawuru (not Mauro), the director of *Neria* (1990).

37. "The Future Is Limited Only by Finance," 26.

38. Under the present arrangement—that is, the Structural Adjustment Program (SAP)—the Nigerian naira holder has seen his or her wallet "sapped" by the power of hard currencies, as wages have not risen to balance commodity prices, which have increased by as much as ten times the dollar or pound rate.

39. David Lamb, *The Africans* (New York: Random House, 1982), 284.

40. Stanley Meisler, "The Nigerian Which Is Not at War," *Africa Report,* January 1970, 17.

41. Ali Mazrui, *The Africans: A Triple Heritage* (Boston: Little, Brown and Company, 1986), 181.

42. Mazrui, *The Africans,* 181.

43. See the review, "Film: *Love Brewed* . . . on Middle-Class Ghana," *New York Times,* 25 April 1981, 11.

44. Mbye-Baboucar Cham, "Film Production in West Africa: 1979–1981," *Présence Africaine* 124 (4th Quarter 1982):174.

45. Françoise Pfaff, *Twenty-five Black African Filmmakers* (Westport, Conn.: Greenwood Press, 1988), 13.

46. Pfaff, *Twenty-five Black African Filmmakers,* 13.

47. *Juju* was reviewed in *West Africa,* 22–29 December 1986, 2649, as *Nana Akoto.*

48. Nii K. Bentsi-Enchill, "Bad Climate for Creativity," *West Africa,* 20 May 1988, 957.

49. From an interview with the author at the twelfth FESPACO in Ouagadougou, March 1991.

50. In a similar circumstance, the prolific Mauritanian filmmaker Med Hondo turned down a $2.5 million offer from an American film producer because this financier wanted him to use a famous African-American actor instead of a less popular West Indian actor.

51. Lindsay Barrett, "The Image of Nigeria's Culture," *West Africa,* 26 October 1987, 2118.

52. Barrett, "The Image of Nigeria's Culture," 2118.

53. Chinua Achebe, *The Trouble with Nigeria* (Enugu, Nigeria: Fourth Dimension Publishing Co., 1983), 19.

54. James Brooke, "In Lagos, Economic Dream Is Now Nightmare," *New York Times,* 14 August 1988, A15.

55. Emmanuel Hart's review of *Son of Africa* appeared in the *Daily Times* (Nigeria), 2 September 1970, 13; cited in Balogun, *The Cinema in Nigeria,* 50; also in Osundare, "A Grand Escape," 827.

56. See also Bayo Martin's "Son of Africa: A Giant Step," *Daily Times* (Nigeria), 24 June 1970; cited in Balogun, *The Cinema in Nigeria,* 50.

57. See Balogun, *The Cinema in Nigeria,* 55; Barrett, "The Image of Nigeria's Culture," 2118.

58. *New Nigerian,* 3 June 1971, as quoted in Balogun, *The Cinema in Nigeria,* 105.

59. From the transcript of the recording of Soyinka's presentation at the 1979 seminar, "Film Industry and Its Relationship to Cultural Identity in Nigeria." See Alfred E. Opubor and Onuora E. Nwuneli, eds., *The Development and Growth of the Film Industry in Nigeria* (Lagos and New York: Third Press International, 1979), 97.

60. The synopsis as provided by the American distributor of the film.

61. See Pfaff, *Twenty-five Black African Filmmakers,* 20.

62. Balogun, *The Cinema in Nigeria,* 62.

63. Barrett, "The Image of Nigeria's Culture," 2118.

64. For the history of the Yoruba traveling theater, see Joel Adedeji, "Alarinjo: The Traditional Yoruba Traveling Theatre," in *Theatre in Africa,* ed. Oyin Ogunba and Abiola Irele (Ibadan: Ibadan University Press, 1978), 27–51.

65. Adedeji, "Alarinjo," 32.

66. Balogun, *The Cinema in Nigeria,* 62–63.

67. Balogun, *The Cinema in Nigeria,* 65.

68. Balogun, *The Cinema in Nigeria,* 65.

69. The reason for this, one-sided as it seems, can be gathered from Balogun's *The Cinema in Nigeria.*

70. Balogun, *The Cinema in Nigeria,* 66.

71. See the article, "From Glitter to Gore in the Film World," *West Africa,* 7 December 1981, 2907.

72. I credit Lindsay Barrett, "The Image of Nigeria's Culture," for some of the names of the artists.

73. Randall F. Grass, "Fela Anikulapo-Kuti: The Art of an Afrobeat Rebel," *Drama Review* 30, no. 1 (Spring 1986):135.

74. Fela's music is as controversial as the musician himself. This popular musician once said, "My campaign is to force an international acceptance of the African product and my weapon is my talent" (Ndubusi Okwechime, "Fela's Parisian Treat: Musical Show or Soldiering for Africa?" *Daily Times* [Nigeria], 18 June 1983, 7). Since he launched his "rebellious" music, Fela's dream for Africa is to encourage a situation in which its people do not have to "ape and make caricatures of others' invention," an Africa that "does not remain the underdog." According to him, only this way can Africa succeed on its own and contribute to the ongoing race of technological development. For Fela, the crusade for African identity must start from oneself and then transform one's

profession. Although this enigmatic African superstar studied at the London School of Music and has played for international communities, on returning to Nigeria, Fela discovered the concept of a liberated African society which moved him in a new direction. Randall F. Grass, summing up the electrifying impact of Fela's music, notes that in postcolonial Nigeria, "which was foundering in waves of corruption, sweeping social change, and war," the message of this brand of music was "immediate and profound. Suddenly the urban masses—as well as progressive intellectuals and respective students—had a spokesperson, a catalyst for mounting challenges. Like traditional musicians, Fela was a lightning rod for the concerns of society, but unlike them he adopted a confrontational posture. Where traditional musicians might admonish a chief or clan member with oblique satire, Fela would make naked accusations and blunt calls to action" (Grass, "Fela Anikulapo-Kuti," 136). Although not everyone approves of Fela's radicalism, his unorthodox attitude toward women, his practice of polygamy, and the smoking of hashish, they do agree, after watching him play or listening to his music, that it is full of substance; it opens listeners' minds to a new vision of African society. Fela's music is inspirational as well as exemplary.

75. Grass, "Fela Anikulapo-Kuti," 137.

76. Grass, "Fela Anikulapo-Kuti," 137.

77. Niyi Osundare, "The King of Laughter," *West Africa,* 12 July 1982, 1821.

78. Osundare, "The Poverty of Nigerian Films," *Nigerian Tribune,* 26 October 1983, 7.

79. Falusi Fola, "Search for Acceptable Format in the Film Industry," *National Concord,* 19 November 1983, 37.

80. Nii K. Bentsi-Enchill, "Money, Power and Cinema," *West Africa,* 16 August 1982, 2093.

81. Bentsi-Enchill, "Money, Power and Cinema," 2093–2094.

82. Bentsi-Enchill, "Money, Power and Cinema," 2094.

83. Eseoghene Barrett, "Worthwhile Effort in Film Making," *Daily Times* (Nigeria), 21 June 1976, 26.

84. See "*The Mask* Is a Very Rough Film," *West Africa,* 11 August 1980, 1487–1488.

85. "Following in 007's Footsteps," *West Africa,* 3 November 1980, 2178–2179.

86. "*The Mask* Is a Very Rough Film," 1488.

87. Ugbomah to the author, 26 April 1992.

88. Charles R. Larson attributes the imitation of Hollywood models as one of the reasons why *Things Fall Apart* received a mixed audience reception despite the fact that "it is a first-rate movie about Africa—in many ways technically superior to the films of Ousmane Sembene" ("The Film Version of Achebe's *Things Fall Apart,*" *Africana Journal* 13, no. 1/4 [1982]:104–110).

89. Ugbomah detailed the problems of making films in Nigeria in "Conversation with Eddie Ugbomah," *The Guardian* (Nigeria), 19 October 1983, 11.

90. Mbye-Baboucar Cham, "Film Production in West Africa: 1979–1981,"

in John D. H. Downing, ed., *Film and Politics in the Third World* (New York: Autonomedia, 1987), 13–29.

Chapter 4

1. See chapter 3, where much of this issue has been discussed with respect to anglophone film practice.

2. Roy Armes, *Third World Filmmaking and the West* (Berkeley: University of California Press, 1987), 288.

3. See Françoise Pfaff, *The Cinema of Ousmane Sembene: A Pioneer of African Film* (Westport, Conn.: Greenwood Press, 1984), 142.

4. Pierre Haffner as quoted in Françoise Pfaff, *Twenty-five Black African Filmmakers* (Westport, Conn.: Greenwood Press, 1988), 233.

5. Quoted in Pfaff, *Twenty-five Black African Filmmakers*, 5.

6. As in the flier distributed by Collective for Living Cinema, New York. For Ferid Boughedir's review of *Touki-Bouki*, see "Le cinéma africain à quin-zeans," *Filméchange* no. 4 (Fall 1978):75–80.

7. See chapter 2 for *Soleil O*'s unorthodox strategy regarding continuity.

8. *Viktor Shklovsky*, "Art as Technique," in *Russian Formalist Criticism: Four Essays*, ed. Lee Lemon and Marion Reis (Lincoln: University of Nebraska Press, 1965), 3–24.

9. Boughedir, "Le cinéma africain," 77.

10. See Angela Martin, ed., *African Films: The Context of Production* (British Film Institute dossier no. 6, 1982), 69.

11. Cited in Pfaff, *Twenty-five Black African Filmmakers*, 219.

12. Pfaff, *Twenty-five Black African Filmmakers*, 220.

13. Safi Faye is still the only prominent independent African woman filmmaker forcefully pursuing her career. Therese Sita Bella of Cameroon did make a half-hour documentary, *Tam tam à Paris* (African drums in Paris) in 1963, and Efua Sutherland made a docudrama, *Araba: The Village Story*, produced by the American Broadcasting Corporation and shot in Ghana in 1967; both have since stopped making films. Women filmmakers whose films have had limited impact in film festivals include Kenya's Jane Lusabe, *Wakessa at Crossroads*; Tanzania's Sigue Endresen, *Women of Hope*, an award-winning film; and at the Washington, D.C. Film Fest of May 1988, *From Sunup* (1985), by Flora Shelling, a twenty-eight-minute short, which lacked directional competence and technical know-how. However, there are many women engaged in television production in Africa.

14. Kwame Nkrumah, *Class Struggle in Africa* (New York: International Publishers, 1970), 14.

15. Annette Michelson, "Dr. Crass and Mr. Clair," *October* 11 (Winter 1979):17.

16. Jay Leyda, *Kino: A History of the Russian and Soviet Film* (New York: Collier Books, 1973), 251–252.

17. Clyde Taylor, "The Screen Scene," *The Black Collegian* 9, no. 5 (May–June 1979):95.

18. Kwame Nkrumah in *Class Struggle In Africa*, 30–35, offers an explana-

tion of the historical origins and associations of this term in his chapter on "Elitism."

19. Noureddine Ghali, "An Interview with Sembene Ousmane," in *Film and Politics in the Third World,* ed. John D. H. Downing (New York: Autonomedia, 1987), 44.

20. Mohammadu Marwa, a Cameroonian otherwise known as Maitatsine, was elevated to the status of a prophet and has a large following in Nigeria. He died at the hands of the authorities in Kano, northern Nigeria, in 1980 during one of the Moslem-inspired riots that ravaged the territory.

21. This point is also discussed in chapter 3.

22. *Jeune Cinéma,* December–January 1976–77, 3, quoted in Pfaff, *Twenty-five Black African Filmmakers,* 281.

23. Pfaff, *Twenty-five Black African Filmmakers,* 278.

24. Also referred to as the Second FEPACI Congress of Algiers.

25. Roland Barthes, *Image—Music—Text* (London: Fontana, 1977).

26. Cited in Manthia Diawara, "African Cinema: The Background and the Economic Context of Production" (Ph.D. diss., Indiana University, 1984), 77.

27. Pfaff, *Twenty-five Black African Filmmakers,* 72.

28. Guy Hennebelle, "*Muna Moto,*" *Ecran* 76, no. 49 (15 July 1976):57.

29. "Africa Seek Europe?" *Sequence* 4, no. 1 (Winter 1978):25. (Contributed by the journal's "Roving Correspondent.")

30. Clyde Taylor, "Africa, the Last Cinema," in *Journey Across Three Continents,* ed. Renee Tajima (New York: Third World Newsreel, 1985), 55.

31. Armes, *Third World Filmmakers,* 223.

32. Segun Oyekunle, "Africans in Hollywood," *West Africa,* 28 November 1983, 2728.

33. Pfaff, *The Cinema of Ousmane Sembene,* 140.

34. Frantz Fanon, *The Wretched of the Earth* (New York: Grove Press, 1968), 149–152.

35. For a discussion of repetition of shots, see Teshome H. Gabriel, *Third Cinema in the Third World: Aesthetics of Liberation* (Ann Arbor: University of Michigan Research Press, 1982).

36. Taylor, "Africa, the Last Cinema," 55.

37. Gerima to the author, December 1986.

38. Gabriel, *Third Cinema in the Third World,* 27.

39. Armes, *Third World Filmmaking,* 216.

40. In Martin, ed., *African Films,* 100.

41. Pat Aufderheide, interview with Med Hondo in *Black Film Review* 3, no. 3 (Summer 1987):10.

42. In Roy Armes's original manuscript, "Black African Cinema in the Eighties," which was published in *Screen* 26, no. 3/4 (May–August 1985): 60–73.

43. From *Finye*'s production kit.

44. The military even helped Cissé with equipment, offering him whatever help he needed to get the film completed. This is contrary to Eddie Ugbomah's case in Nigeria, where the military would not allow him to use their equipment.

Ugbomah spent thousands of dollars to design his own military uniforms and fake guns used in *The Death of a Black President*.

45. "Film Festival Host," *West Africa*, 23 March 1987, 558.

46. See "New Perspectives in African Cinema: An Interview with Cheick Oumar Sissoko," *Film Quarterly* (Winter 1987–88):43–45.

47. Sankara was speaking at the Tenth FESPACO, happily referring to a Malian film that had won an award the previous evening. Mali and Burkina Faso were once enemies.

48. This information, together with that of *Desebagato*, was offered in the report of the Tenth FESPACO, which opened in Ouagadougou on 21 February 1987. See Manny Shirazi, "Film Festival Host," *West Africa*, 23 March 1987, 558.

49. For instance, Ngugi wa Thiong'o, *Decolonizing the Mind: The Politics of Language in African Literature* (London: James Currey; Nairobi: Heinemann, 1986); A. Hampaté Bâ, "The Living Tradition," and J. Vansina, "Oral Tradition and its Methodology," both in *General History of Africa: Methodology and African Prehistory*, ed. J. Ki-Zerbo (Berkeley: University of California Press, 1981), 166–203 and 142–165 respectively.

50. In his 1964 speech "The African Writer and the English Language," now in Achebe's collection of essays *Morning Yet on Creation Day* (London: Heinemann, 1975), 62.

51. In *Decolonizing the Mind*, Ngugi wa Thiong'o makes his position clear. See "A Statement," xiv, and especially chapter 1, "The Language of African Literature," 4–33.

52. See Ngugi, *Decolonizing the Mind*, 19.

53. For fuller discussion of technology and image reproduction, see Jean-Louis Baudry's "Ideological Effects of the Basic Cinematographic Apparatus," *Film Quarterly* 28 (Winter 1974–75):39–47.

54. Mbye Cham, "Ousmane Sembene and the Aesthetics of African Oral Traditions," *Africana Journal* 13 (1982):24–40.

55. Pfaff, *The Cinema of Ousmane Sembene*.

56. Manthia Diawara, "Oral Literature and African Film: Narratology in *Wend Kuuni*," *Présence Africaine* no. 142 (2d Quarter 1987):36–49. Also "Popular Culture and Oral Traditions in African Film," *Film Quarterly* (Spring 1988):6–14.

57. Gabriel, *Third Cinema in the Third World*, 27.

58. See Isidore Okpewho's discussion of this genre in *The Epic in Africa: Toward a Poetics of the Oral Performance* (New York: Columbia University Press, 1979).

59. From Production Press Kit, *Jom*.

60. From Production Press Kit, *Jom*.

61. Pfaff, *Twenty-five Black African Filmmakers*, 229.

62. Francis Bebey, *African Music: A People's Art*, trans. Josephine Bennett (Westport, Conn.: Lawrence Hill and Company), 24.

63. As in oral tradition, the storyteller's ability to manipulate for didactic purposes the conventions of his art form (see chapter 1) is exemplified in *Jom* by the character of the griot who implores his people to reflect on their problems.

64. J. Hoberman, "It's a Mod, Mod World," *Village Voice*, 17 February 1987, 67.

65. The sequence is very interesting and the political message is point blank. Samb-Makharam's cross-cutting reveals the maid oppressors gorgeously dressed, sitting and listening as the griot and the dancer chastise them.

66. Quoted in Pfaff, *The Cinema of Ousmane Sembene*, 173.

67. Pfaff, *The Cinema of Ousmane Sembene*, 174.

68. Diawara, "Oral Literature and African Film," 40.

69. Diawara, "Oral Literature and African Film," 40.

70. Diawara, "Oral Literature and African Film," 40.

71. E. H. Gombrich, *The Story of Art* (Oxford: Phaidon, 1978).

72. See Jean-Louis Baudry, "Ideological Effects of the Basic Cinematographic Apparatus," 40.

73. Segun Oyekunle, "Films for the Future," *West Africa*, 21 March 1983, 726.

74. Diawara, "Oral Literature and African Film," 43.

75. In Ki-Zerbo, ed., *General History of Africa*, 168.

76. Pfaff, *Twenty-five Black African Filmmakers*, 97.

77. J. Hoberman, "It's a Mod, Mod World," 67.

78. Typical of a native Sunday, when everybody takes the day off to rest, men in their mid-twenties to thirties gather around two other men playing the game of *isha*. A popular West African game variedly named *okwe* (Igbo), *ayo* (Yoruba), *wouré* (Bambara), *oware* (Akan), and so on, *isha* is usually played by two people, sometimes up to four; playing pieces (nuts or pebbles) are moved around twelve holes. At such a gathering, new and old stories are told and this particular one concerns Brou and the close friendship between his wife and his brother. Here is the dramatization of a typical gossip scene:

Brou:	What were you saying about Kouassi and N'Guéssan?
First Player:	They're forever holding hands. Quite intimately.
Brou:	What are you getting at?
First Player:	If I were the husband I wouldn't like it.
Second Player:	(Cuts in and asks) What exactly are you saying?
First Player:	Nothing, it is your business.

(The second Player here interrupts the gossip flow by introducing a story to emphasize the gossip narrative. At this time, the camera focuses tightly on Brou's face—worried and looking at the Second Player as he talks.)

Second Player: That reminds me of a story. When I was at Adieke a guy called Leon had a wife called Maya and a niece called Denise.

(Here, the camera pans fast to the First Player, still in close-up, as he giggles briefly.)

Everytime you saw him, he was with his niece. So,

for us she was his niece. One day, surprise!! Mr. Leon married his niece!

First Player: That's what seeing Kouassi and her makes you think?

(At this point, the camera pans back to Brou.)

     Brou: You disgust me. It is disgusting to talk like that.

(Brou stands up and the camera pans to his face.)

So you're saying I should beat my wife or else quarrel with Kouassi? Did I ask you to keep an eye on her? What's it to do with you? I don't like what you're getting at. Not one bit.

(It was only now, during this heated argument, that the camera zoomed out to include all participants.)

First Player: Don't be angry, I'll keep my mouth shut.

Second Player: We didn't mean to upset you. We're just warning you. Take it easy.

The point of this dramatization is that, through gossiping, the men conclude that they should perform their civic responsibility by letting Brou know what was happening.

79. As above, young girls reenact stories and spread some hidden village secrets.

80. Bebey, *African Music,* 14.

81. Bebey, *African Music,* 92.

82. In his production notes, Segun Oyekunle stated that *Parcel Post* is an "experimentation in filmic style which seeks to marry the African oral traditional style, music and dance, African symbols and images with the appropriate elements of the filmic medium to reflect the African ways of seeing and the African experience." This is exactly symptomatic of the intentional reshuffling of form and content within the parameters of oral performance and its cultural offshoots. Some of them are highly visible in the narrative structure where the three parallel tracks mentioned by Oyekunle form a synthesis: the use of the griot who chats, sings, and drums the elliptical commentary of the tripartite conundrum on which the film is based (Nigerian husband, American wife, Nigerian wife); and indigenous language (Yoruba), English, and the pidgin Africanized English of southern Nigeria. All of these, which worked very well in this film, Oyekunle emphasizes as microcosmic to his future film practice.

83. Bebey, *African Music,* 92.

84. Cited in Pfaff, *Twenty-five Black African Filmmakers,* 98.

85. Hoberman, "It's a Mod, Mod, World," 67.

86. In Joseph Okpaku, ed., *New African Literature and the Arts* (New York: Thomas Y. Crowell Co., 1966), 13–23.

87. Okpaku, ed., *New African Literature,* 20.

88. Laura Mulvey, "Visual Pleasure and Narrative Cinema," *Screen* 16, no. 3 (Autumn 1975):6–18.

89. "Filmmaking and Politics in Cuba: The Cuban Experience," *American Behavioral Scientist* 17, no. 3 (January–February 1974):368.

90. See, for example, Keyan Tomaselli, *The Cinema of Apartheid* (New York: Smyrna/Lakeview Press, 1988); Thelma Gutsche, *The History and Social Significance of Motion Pictures in South Africa, 1895–1940* (Capetown: Howard Timmins, 1972); Harriet Gavshon, "The Levels of Intervention in Films Made for African Audiences in South Africa," *Critical Arts* 2, no. 4 (1983); Ntongela Masilela, "*Comeback Africa* and South African Film History," *Jump Cut* no. 36 (1991):61–65.

91. Its exhibition place was the 57th Street Playhouse. After many months it extended to other American cities and to home video. For the analysis of this film and its political intent, see chapter 1.

92. Keyan Tomaselli, cited in Jo-Anne Collinge, "Under Fire," *American Film* 11 (November 1985):38.

93. See the prospects for film production in Kenya and Zimbabwe discussed in chapter 3.

94. See the entry on Nana Mahomo in Pfaff, *Twenty-five Black African Filmmakers,* 195–204.

95. "A Critique of *Last Grave at Dimbaza,*" *Film Library Quarterly* 9, no. 1 (1976):15.

96. See Clyde Taylor, "Film Reborn in Mozambique," *Jump Cut* no. 28 (1983):30–31. Also Ruy Duarte Carvalho's philosophy and that of documentary film in Angola is clearly stated in *O camarada e o camera* (Luanda: INALD, 1984). Published articles and interviews are also available in *Cine Cubano.*

97. Alan Rosenthal, ed., *New Challenges for Documentary* (Berkeley: University of California Press, 1988), 542.

98. Ron Hallis, "Movie Magic in Mozambique," *Cinema Canada* no. 62 (February 1980):19.

99. See John Stone, "Images of a Liberation Struggle: The Film as Document," *Africa Today* 20, no. 1 (Winter 1973):85–92.

100. Stone, "Images of a Liberation Struggle," 85–92.

101. For a detailed explanation, see Amilcar Cabral, "Identity and Dignity in the National Liberation Struggle," *Africa Today* 19, no. 4 (Fall 1972):39–42.

102. Amilcar Cabral, *Return to the Source: Selected Speeches* (New York: Monthly Review Press, 1973), 54.

103. Taylor, "Film Reborn," 30.

104. "Media in Southern Africa" (a CTV Report), *Screen Digest* (January 1978):9–14.

105. See, for example, Pfaff, *Twenty-five Black African Filmmakers,* 212–214.

106. From "A Short History of the Mozambique Movies" by Fernando Duarte. Translated for this writing by Andrew Bryant, from *Celuloide,* supplement of November 1979, 13–16.

107. Hallis, "Movie Magic," 19.

108. This interpretation is provided by Victor Bachy, "Panoramique sur les cinémas Sud-sahariens," *Cinémaction* no. 26 (Special Issue: "Cinémas noirs d'Afrique," 1982):42.

109. Duarte, "A Short History of the Mozambique Movies," 13–16.

110. Teshome H. Gabriel, *Third Cinema in the Third World: Aesthetics of Liberation* (Ann Arbor: University of Michigan Research Press, 1982), 36.

111. Rosenthal, ed., *New Challenges for Documentary,* 543.

112. James Brooke, "Angola Turning to the West to Equip Its Military," *New York Times,* 23 December 1987, 5.

113. Ironically, Savimbi is from Ovimbundu.

114. For a recent profile of Jonas Savimbi, his CIA and South African connections, see *African Concord* 2, no. 18 (August 1988):11–15.

115. See Michael Maren, "U.S. Callousness and Mozambique Massacres," *New York Times,* 22 August 1987, 27; Alain Louyot, "A Journey to the Extremes of Horror: One of the Most Appalling Tragedies in Modern History," *World Press Review* 35 (September 1988):21.

116. "Soviet-Style Underdevelopment," *The Economist,* reprinted in *World Press Review* 35 (April 1988):47.

Chapter 5

1. For the motivations and affectations of this ethnographic paradigm, see my article, "Framing FESPACO: Pan-African Film in Context," *Afterimage* 19, no. 4 (November 1991):6–9.

2. Ntongela Masilela, "Interconnections: The African and Afro American Cinemas," *The Independent* 11 (January–February 1988):14–17.

3. For example, *Yeelen* can be read as a critique of traditionalist culture (the Komo cult) since Mali is 90 percent Islamic and Cissé, the filmmaker, is Muslim. However, skilled in obsfucation, the film evades this primary source of influence.

4. Masilela, "Interconnections," 14–17.

5. John A. A. Ayoade, "The Culture Debate in Africa," *The Black Scholar* 20 (Summer-Fall 1989):2–7, illuminates and synthesizes recent discourses on the subject.

6. Tony Gittens's article is published in *Black Cinema Aesthetics: Issues in Independent Black Filmmaking,* ed. Gladstone Yearwood (Athens, Ohio: Center for Afro-American Studies, 1982), 115–120.

7. Captain Thomas Sankara, cited in J. R. Rayfield, "FESPACO 1987: African Cinema and Cultural Identity," paper presented at meetings of Canadian Association for African Studies, Edmonton, May 1987, 11.

8. Sékou Touré, "A Dialectical Approach to Culture," *The Black Scholar* 1 (November 1969):13.

9. Touré, "A Dialectical Approach to Culture," 23.

10. Touré, "A Dialectical Approach to Culture," 13.

11. See, for example, Françoise Pfaff's article "The Films of Gaston Kaboré and Idrissa Ouedraogo as Anthropological Sources," in *The Society for Visual Anthropology Review* (Spring 1990):50–59. Other references to this article are from the author's original copy, which she kindly made available to me before it was published; therefore, page numbers are omitted in subsequent citations.

12. See note 3.

13. Malian dialect specific to cinema, see Amadou Hampaté Bâ, "Le dit du cinèma Africain," in *UNESCO Catalogue: Films ethnographiques sur l'Afrique noire*. Paris: UNESCO, 1967.

14. Kwame Anthony Appiah, "Is Post- in Postmodernism the Post- in Post-colonial?" *Critical Inquiry* 17 (Winter 1991):342.

15. Kate Ezra, *Human Ideal in African Art: Bamana Figurative Sculpture* (Washington, D.C.: National Museum of African Art, 1986):15. Quoted in Rachel Hoffman, review of *Yeelen* in *African Arts* 22 (February 1989):100.

16. Cited in Hoffman, "Yeelen," 100.

17. See Cissé's interview, "Souleymane Cissé's Light on Africa," *Black Film Review* 4, no. 4 (Fall 1988):12.

18. Amie Williams, review of *Zan Boko, African Arts* 23, no. 2 (April 1990): 93.

19. See, for example, Gilbert Adair, "The Artificial Eye: *Yeelen*," *Sight and Sound* 57, no. 4 (Autumn 1988):284.

20. In the catalogue "Library of Africa Cinema," a project of California Newsreel, distributor of *Yeelen*.

21. Abdoul Dragoss's article in the 1991 FESPACO catalogue, "Environment: An issue which needs to be addressed by African Cinema," draws attention to the significance of the 'cosmic tree.'"

22. Cissé's interview in *Black Film Review*, 15.

23. Appiah, "Is Post- in Postmodernism the Post- in Postcolonial?" *Critical Inquiry* 17 (Winter 1991):346.

24. Apiah, "Is Post- in Postmodernism," 346.

25. The problem of exhibition is still a persistent one, and the sector is still foreign-dominated. Since films produced in the francophone region during the pioneering years were financed by the French government, France also controlled the rights to distribute them. Some of the films were considered too political to be promoted in their home countries.

26. Pfaff, "The Films of Gaston Kaboré."

27. "Feature Films as Cultural Document," in *Principles of Visual Anthropology*, ed. Paul Hockings (The Hague and Paris: Mouton, 1975), 231–251, as quoted in Pfaff, "The Films of Gaston Kaboré."

28. D. Yung, *Variety*, 16 November 1988, 23.

29. As in the process of using still photographs on screen to identify dictators or people who were responsible for unjust punishments on the society, *Courage of the People, Hour of the Furnaces*, and *Battle of Chile* are some of the films that employ this strategy.

30. Pfaff, "The Films of Gaston Kaboré."

31. Françoise Lionnet, "Dissymmetry Embodied: Feminism, Universalism and the Practice of Excision," *Passages Issue* 1, no. 1 (1991):2.

32. N. Frank Ukadike, "Framing FESPACO," 6–9.

33. Blaine Harden, *Africa: Dispatches from a Fragile Continent* (New York: W. W. Norton and Company, 1990), 18.

34. Abdou Diouf, in Olayinde Koso-Thomas, *The Circumcision of Women: A Strategy of Eradication* (London: Zed, 1987), 27. Also quoted in Lionnet, "Dissymmetry Embodied," 3.

35. See Pat Aufderheide's interview with Cheick Oumar Sissoko in *Black Film Review* 6, no. 2 (Winter 1991):4.

36. Rouch's influence on African filmmakers is already discussed in a previous chapter. He contributed to the training of African filmmakers, including Sissoko. Rouch's numerous films about Africa are menacingly degrading (see chapter 1).

37. *Finzan* is distributed by California Newsreel. This description is contained in their catalogue *Library of African Cinema*, 9.

38. Françoise Pfaff, "Africa Through African Eyes: An Interview with Idrissa Ouedraogo," *Black Film Review* 4 (Winter 1987–88): 11–12, 15.

39. Some of the information here was presented in my review of *Yaaba*, coauthored with Richard Porton in *Film Quarterly* 44, no. 3 (Spring 1991): 54–57.

40. William Fisher provides valuable information on Kinshasha's boisterous musical life, stating that Claud Cadiou's French Côte d'Ivoire coproduction *La vie platinée* (1984), a highly successful film "showcasing guitarist Zanzibar and his group 'Les Têtes Brûlées,'" initiated the musical comedy genre. See "Ouagadougou: A Beacon for African Culture," *Sight and Sound* 58 (Summer 1989):172.

41. From an interview with the author in New York City in 1986.

42. See "Cinema Is a Weapon," interview of Haile Gerima by Kwame Karikari in *West Africa*, 24–30 July 1989, 1210.

43. Kwame Karikari, "Cinema Is a Weapon," 1210.

44. V. Y. Mudimbe, *The Invention of Africa: Gnosis, Philosophy, and the Order of Knowledge* (Bloomington: Indiana University Press, 1988), 182.

45. Randal Johnson, *Cinema Novo X 5* (Austin: University of Texas Press, 1984), 49.

46. The "greatest crimes against humanity" here referred to include forms of oppression reminiscent of colonialism, slavery, holocaust (of the Jews), pogroms, wanton massacres (of Iraqi's and the Kurds under the guise of "New World Order").

47. Med Hondo, in an interview with Amir Emery, *New African* 17 (April 1988):39.

48. Margaret A. Novicki and Daphne Topouzis, "Ousmane Sembene: Africa's Premier Cineaste," *Africa Report* 35 (November-December 1990):67.

49. Med Hondo, in an interview with Amir Emery, *New African* (April 1988):41.

50. Jonathan Rutherford, "A Place Called Home: Identity and the Cultural Politics of Difference," in Jonathan Rutherford, ed., *Identity: Community, Culture, Difference* (London: Lawrence and Wishart, 1990), 11.

51. Joan R. Rayfield, "FESPACO 1987: African Cinema and Cultural Identity," paper presented at Canadian African Studies Association annual meeting, Edmonton (7–10 May 1987), 6.

52. Rayfield, "FESPACO 1987," 6.

53. From an interview conducted by this author in San Francisco at San Francisco State University, 1990.

54. G. Williams, *The Expansion of Europe in the XVIIIth Century: Overseas Rivalry, Discovery and Exploitation* (New York: Walker and Company, 1967), 17–30. Quoted in Mudimbe, *The Invention of Africa*, 16–17.

55. Senegal apishly sent troops to the Gulf when it was certain they had no technology to offer Saudi Arabia or the Gulf oil states after the war. It stood to lose everything as opposed to Western countries, which went to safeguard their economic interests. Senegal lost ninety-nine soldiers in an air crash when they were returning home—a number far surpassing casualties of Britain or France, for example.

56. James Leahy, *Monthly Film Bulletin* 55 (January 1988), 9.

57. All quotations in the film's synopsis are adapted, with some adjustments, from Kwah Ansah's production notes.

58. From an interview with the author in Ouagadougou, Burkina Faso, February 1991.

59. Edward Berman, "African Responses to Christian Mission Education," *African Studies Review* no. 3 (December 1974):527.

60. Oginga Odinga, *Not Yet Uhuru* (New York: Hill and Wang 1967), 42. (Footnotes 60 to 62 are cited in Edward Berman, "African Responses," 532.)

61. Mbonu Ojike, *My Africa* (New York: J. Day Company, 1946), 55.

62. Chinua Achebe, *Things Fall Apart* (New York: Oblonsky, 1957), 180.

63. Berman, "African Responses," 532.

64. For the discussion of "Native Intellectuals," see the chapter "On National Culture" in Fanon, *The Wretched of the Earth* (New York: Grove Press, 1968). The quotation is from pages 220–223.

65. See "Black People's Burden," *West Africa,* 30 May 1988, 956.

66. All three films have been suppressed. For example, for political reasons *Sarraounia* was prematurely withdrawn from five out of eighty theaters in France originally scheduled to show it. *Camp de Thiaroye* was not selected for the Cannes Film Festival, and *Heritage . . . Africa* has not received wide screenings outside Africa. Yet films like *Finzan, Yaaba,* and *Tilai* have been widely distributed.

Chapter 6

1. Ola Balogun's films have been shown at various times at London film festivals, and *Alawada* films have been screened for the Yoruba communities in England.

2. Clyde Taylor, "Africa, the Last Cinema," in *Journey Across Three Continents: Film and Lecture Series*, ed. Renee Tajima (New York: Third World Newsreel, 1985), 50.

3. Edward Said, "Spurious Scholarship and the Palestinian Question," *Race and Class* 29 (1988): 24–40.

4. See "Row Over U.S. Aid," *Africa Concord,* 30 September 1988, 15.

5. James Brooke, "Mission to Liberia Evidently Fails," *New York Times,* 5 December 1988, D6.

6. This applies to good and bad things about Africa portrayed in films reflecting the people's history.

7. Walter Benjamin, *Illuminations,* trans. Harry Zohn (Glasgow: William Collins Sons and Co., 1973), 87.

8. See "Film Festival Host," *West Africa,* 23 March 1987, 559.

9. Taylor, "Africa, the Last Cinema," 51.

Selected Bibliography

Achebe, Chinua. *The Trouble with Nigeria*. Enugu, Nigeria: Fourth Dimension Publishing Company, Ltd., 1983.

———. *Morning Yet on Creation Day*. Garden City, New York: Anchor, 1976.

Adedeji, Joel Adeyinka. "Alaringo: The Traditional Yoruba Travelling Theatre." In *Theatre in Africa*, ed. Oyin Ogunba and Abiola Irele. Ibadan, Nigeria: Ibadan University Press, 1978.

Adelusi, Dare. "The Poverty of Nigerian Films." An interview with Niyi Osundare. *Nigerian Tribune*, 26 and 29 October 1983.

"African Cinema Seeks a New Language: Sembene Ousmane, Writer and Film Director (Senegal)," *Young Cinema and Theatre* (Prague) no. 3 (1983): 26–28.

"African Dossier: Hondo, Gerima, Sembene." *Framework* no. 7/8 (Spring 1978):20–37.

Ahmad, Aijaz. "Jameson's Rhetoric of Otherness and the 'National Allegory.' " *Social Text* no. 17 (Spring 1987):3–25.

Aig-Imoukhuede, Frank. "Ten Years of African Cinema." *Présence Africaine* 34 (2d Quarter 1971):331–338.

———. "The Film and Television in Nigeria." *Présence Africaine* 30 (2d Quarter 1966):89–93.

Ajala, Adekunle. *Pan-Africanism: Evolution, Progress and Prospects*. New York: St. Martin's Press, 1973.

Allen, Robert C., and Douglas Gomery. *Film History, Theory, and Practice*. New York: Alfred A. Knopf, 1985.

Alpers, Edward A. "The Role of Culture in the Liberation of Mozambique." *UFAHAMU* 12, no. 3 (1983):143–190.

Althusser, Louis. *Lenin and Philosophy and Other Essays*. New York: Monthly Review Press, 1971.

Amin, Samir. *Accumulation on a World Scale.* New York: Monthly Review Press, 1974.

Anderson, Samantha, trans. *Thomas Sankara Speaks: The Burkina Faso Revolution 1983-1987.* New York: Pathfinder Press, 1988.

Anozie, Sunday O. *Structural Models and African Poetics: Towards a Pragmatic Theory of Literature.* London: Routledge and Kegan Paul, 1981.

Armes, Roy. "Black African Cinema in the Eighties." *Screen* 26, no. 3/4 (May–August 1985):60–73.

———. "Carthage Film Festival." *New African* no. 207 (December 1984):34.

———. *Third World Filmmaking and the West.* Berkeley: University of California Press, 1987.

Asante, Molefi Kete. *The Afrocentric Idea.* Philadelphia: Temple University Press, 1987.

Awed, Ibrahim M., Hussein M. Adam, and Lionel Ngakane, eds. *Pan-African Cinema . . . Which Way Ahead?* Proceedings of the First Mogadishu Pan-African Film Symposium. Mogadishu, Somalia: Mogpafis Management Committee, 1983.

Awoonor, Kofi. *The Breast of the Earth: A Survey of the History, Culture and Literature of Africa South of the Sahara.* Garden City, New York: Anchor Books, 1976.

Bâ, Amadou Hampaté. "The Living Tradition." In *General History of Africa,* vol. 1, *Methodology and African Prehistory,* ed. Joseph Ki-Zerbo. Paris: UNESCO, 1981.

Bachmann, Gideon. "In Search of Self-Definition: Arab and African Films at the Carthage Film Festival." *Film Quarterly* 26, no. 3 (1973):48–51.

Bachy, Victor. *Le cinéma au Mali.* Brussels: OCIC/L'Harmattan, 1983.

———. "Le cinéma du Cameroun." *Le revue du cinéma, Image et son* no. 351 (June 1980):87–94.

———. *Le cinéma en Côte d'Ivoire.* Brussels: OCIC/L'Harmattan, 1983.

———. "Le cinéma en république populaire du Congo." *Le révue du cinéma, Image et son* no. 341 (July 1979):44–46.

———. *La Haute-Volta et le cinéma.* Brussels: OCIC/L'Harmattan, 1983.

Bakhtin, Mikhail M. *The Dialogic Imagination.* Translated by Caryl Emerson and Michael Holquist. Austin: University of Texas Press, 1981.

———. *Problems of Dostoevsky's Poetics.* Translated by Caryl Emerson. Minneapolis: University of Minnesota Press, 1974.

Balázs, Béla. *Theory of Film.* London: Dennis Debson, 1953.

Balogun, Françoise. *The Cinema in Nigeria.* Enugu, Nigeria: Delta Publications Ltd., 1987.

Balogun, Ola. "Decoding the Message of African Sculpture." *The UNESCO Courier,* May 1977, 12–16.

Barnouw, Erik. *Documentary: A History of the Non-Fiction Film.* London: Oxford University Press, 1974.

Barret, Lindsay. "The Image of Nigeria's Culture." *West Africa,* 26 October 1987, 2117–2120.

Barthes, Roland. *Image, Music, Text.* London: Fontana Books, 1977.

Baudry, Jean-Louis. "Ideological Effects of the Basic Cinematographic Apparatus." *Film Quarterly* 28, no. 2 (Winter 1974–75):39–47.

Bazin, André. *What Is Cinema?* Translated by Hugh Gray. Berkeley: University of California Press, 1967.

Bebey, Francis. *African Music: A People's Art.* Translated by Josephine Bennett. Westport, Conn.: Lawrence Hill and Company, 1987.

Benjamin, Walter. *Illuminations.* London: Fontana Books, 1973.

Bentsi-Enchill, Nii K. "Money, Power and Cinema." *West Africa,* 16 August 1982, 2093–2094.

Berman, Edward. "African Responses to Christian Missionary Education." *African Studies Review* 17, no. 3 (December 1974):527–540.

Bienen, Henry. "State and Revolution: The Work of Amilcar Cabral." *Journal of Modern African Studies* 15, no. 4 (December 1977):555–568.

Bogle, Donald. *Toms, Coons, Mulattoes, Mammies and Bucks.* New York: Bantam, 1974.

Boughedir, Ferid. "Cinéma Africain et décolonisation." Ph.D. dissertation, Université de la Sorbonne Nouvelle, Paris, 1976.

———. *Le cinéma Africain de A à Z.* Brussels: OCIC, 1987.

———. "A Cinema Fighting for Its Liberation." In *Journey Across Three Continents,* ed. Renee Tajima, 22–25. New York: Third World Newsreel, 1985.

Brecht, Bertolt. *Brecht on Theater.* New York: Hill and Wang, 1964.

Burch, Noel. *Theory of Film Practice.* Translated by Helen R. Lane. New York: Praeger Publishers, 1973.

Cabral, Amilcar. "Identity and Dignity in the National Liberation Struggle." *Africa Today* 19, no. 4 (Fall 1972):39–42.

———. *National Liberation and Culture.* Translated by Maureen Webster. Syracuse: Syracuse University Program of Eastern African Studies, 1970.

———. *Return to the Source: Selected Speeches.* New York: Monthly Review Press, 1972.

Caughie, John, ed. *Theories of Authorship.* London: Routledge and Kegan Paul, 1981.

Césaire, Aimé. *Discourse on Colonialism.* New York: Monthly Review Press, 1972.

Chaliand, Gérard. *Revolution in the Third World.* Translated by Diana Johnstone. Harmondsworth, England: Penguin, 1978.

Cham, Mbye Baboucar. "Art and Ideology in the Work of Sembene Ousmane and Haile Gerima." *Présence Africaine* 129 (1st Quarter 1984):79–91.

———. "Film Production in West Africa: 1979–1981." *Présence Africaine* (4th Quarter 1982):168–187.

———. "Ousmane Sembene and the Aesthetics of African Oral Traditions." *Africana Journal* 13, no. 1/4 (1982):24–40.

Cham, Mbye Baboucar, and Claire Andrade-Watkins, eds. *Blackframes: Critical Perspectives on Black Independent Cinema.* Cambridge: The MIT Press, 1988.

Cheriaa, Tahar. "Policies, Politics and Films in the Arab and African Countries." *Young Cinema and Theatre* (Prague) no. 4 (1971):27–33.

Cinémaction no. 17 (1981). Special issue on "Cinéma du Maghreb."

Cinémaction no. 26 (1982). Special issue on "Cinéma noirs d'Afrique."

Clark, Ebun. *Hubert Ogunde: The Making of Nigerian Theatre.* London: Oxford University Press, 1979.

Coad, Malcolm. "Ousmane Sembene and *Ceddo.*" *Index on Censorship* 10, no. 4 (1981):32–33.

Cripps, Thomas. *Slow Fade to Black.* New York: Oxford University Press, 1977.

Crowdus, Gary, and Udayan Gupta. "A Luta Continua: An Interview with Robert Van Lierop." *Cineaste* 9, no. 1 (September 1978):26–31.

Cyr, Helen W. *A Filmography of the Third World.* Metuchen, N. J.: Scarecrow Press, 1976.

———. *A Filmography of the Third World (1976–1983).* Metuchen, N.J.: Scarecrow Press, 1985.

Dadson, Nanabanyin. "Production and Co-Production." *West Africa,* 22–29 December 1986, 2649–2650.

Davidson, Basil. *Africa in Modern History.* Harmondsworth, England: Penguin, 1978.

———. *The African Past.* Harmondsworth, England: Penguin, 1966.

———. *The Africans: An Entry into Cultural History.* Harmondsworth, England: Penguin, 1973.

de Brigard, Emilie. "The History of Ethnographic Film." In *Principles of Visual Anthropology,* ed. Paul Hockings. The Hague: Mouton, 1975.

Debrix, Jean-René. "Le cinéma Africain." *Afrique Contemporaine,* no. 38/39 (July–October 1968):7–12.

Diack, Moktar. "Emitai or Africa Arisen." *Young Cinema and Theatre* (Prague) no. 4 (1972):22–29.

Diakete, Madubuko. "Film and Cultural Signification: Reconsidering Minority and Third World Films." *Journal of the University Film Association* 30, no. 3 (Summer 1978):19–23.

Diawara, Manthia. "African Cinema: The Background and the Economic Context of Production." Ph.D. dissertation, University of Indiana, 1985.

———. "Oral Literature and African Film: Narratology in *Wend Kuuni.*" *Présence Africaine* no. 142 (2d Quarter 1987):36–49.

Downing, John D. H., ed. *Film and Politics in the Third World.* New York: Autonomedia, 1987.

Dubois, W. E. B. *The Souls of Black Folk.* Chicago: A. C. McClung and Co., 1903.

Eagleton, Terry. *Criticism and Ideology.* London: Verso, 1978.

———. *Marxism and Literary Criticism.* Berkeley: University of California Press, 1976.

Eaton, Mick, ed. *Anthropology, Reality, Cinema.* London: British Film Institute, 1979.

Eisenstein, Sergei. *The Film Sense.* Translated and edited by Jay Leyda. London: Harcourt Brace Jovanovich, 1970.

Emmanuel, Arghiri. *Unequal Exchange.* New York: Monthly Review Press, 1972.

————. "White Settler Colonialism and the Myth of Investment Imperialism." *New Left Review* no. 73 (May–June 1972):35–37.

Esedebe, P. Olisanwule. *Pan-Africanism: The Idea and Movement 1776–1963*. Washington, D.C.: Howard University Press, 1982.

Fanon, Frantz. *A Dying Colonialism*. Translated by Haakon Chevalier. New York: Grove Press, 1967.

————. *Black Skin, White Masks*. New York: Grove Press, 1967.

————. *Toward the African Revolution*. Harmondsworth, 1970.

————. *The Wretched of the Earth*. New York: Grove Press, 1968.

Fieldhouse, D. K. *Black Africa 1945–80: Economic Decolonization and Arrested Development*. London: Allen and Unwin, 1986.

Fisher, Lucy. "*Xala:* A Study in Black Humour." *Millenium Film Journal* no. 7/9 (Winter–Fall 1980):165–72.

Fletcher, Angus. *Allegory—The Theory of Symbolic Mode*. Ithaca: Cornell University Press, 1970.

Fola, Falusi. "Search for Acceptable Format in the Film Industry." *National Concord,* 19 November 1983, 10.

Fontenot, Chester, Jr. "Frantz Fanon: The Revolutionary." *First World* 2, no. 3 (1979):24–28.

Forje, John W. "Technological Change and the Development of Africa." *Présence Africaine* no. 143 (3d Quarter 1987):122–141.

Foucault, Michel. *Discipline and Punish*. Translated by Alan Sheridan. New York: Vintage Books, 1979.

François, Pierre. "Class Struggles in Mali." *Review of African Political Economy* no. 24 (May–August 1982):22–38.

Frank, Andre Gunder. *Capitalism and Underdevelopment in Latin America*. Harmondsworth, England: Penguin, 1971.

Gabriel, Teshome. "Teaching Third World Cinema." *Screen* 24, no. 2 (March–April 1983):60–64.

————. *Third Cinema in the Third World: The Aesthetics of Liberation*. Ann Arbor: University of Michigan Research Press, 1982.

Garcia-Espinosa, Julio. "For an Imperfect Cinema." *Afterimage* no. 3 (Summer 1971):54–67.

————. "In Search of the Lost Cinema." In *Latin American Filmmakers and the Third Cinema,* ed. Zuzana M. Pick. Ottawa: Carleton University Press, 1978.

————. "Meditations on Imperfect Cinema . . . Fifteen Years Later." *Screen* 26, no. 3/4 (1985):93–94.

Ghali, Noureddine. "An Interview with Sembene Ousmane." In *Film and Politics in the Third World,* ed. John D. H. Downing, 41–54. New York: Autonomedia, 1987.

Gilliam, Angela. "African Cinema as New Literature." In *Journey Across Three Continents,* ed. Renee Tajima, 37–40. New York: Third World Newsreel, 1985.

Gombrich, E. H. *The Story of Art*. Oxford: Phaidon, 1978.

Graham, Yao. "Ghana: The IMF's African Success Story?" *Race and Class* 3, no. 29 (Winter 1988):41–52.

Gramsci, Antonio. *Prison Notebooks*. Translated by Quintin Hoare and Geoffrey Nowell Smith. New York: International Publishers, 1983.

———. *Selections from Political Writings 1910–1920*. Translated by John Mathews. New York: International Publishers, 1977.

Grass, Randall F. "Fela Anikulapo-Kuti: The Art of an Afrobeat Rebel." *Drama Review* 30, no. 1 (Spring 1986):132–149.

Grillo, Yusuf A. "Science and Technology and the Purpose of Art." *Leonardo* 24 (1991):503–504.

Guback, Thomas H. *The International Film Industries, Western Europe and America Since 1945*. Bloomington: Indiana University Press, 1969.

Gutsche, Thelma. *The History and Social Significance of Motion Pictures in South Africa*. Cape Town: Howard Timmis, 1972.

Haffner, Pierre. *Essai sur les fondements du cinéma Africain*. Abidjan-Dakar: Les Nouvelles Editions Africaines, 1978.

Hall, Susan. "African Women on Film." *Africa Report* (January–February 1971):15–17.

Hallis, Ron. "Movie Magic in Mozambique." *Cinema Canada* no. 62 (February 1980):18–24.

Hennebelle, Guy. "The Adventure of Political Cinema." *Cineaste* 10, no. 2 (Spring 1980):20–25.

———. "Les cinémas africains en 1972." *L'Afrique littéraire et artistique* no. 20 (1st Quarter 1972) (special issue).

———. "Socially Committed or Exotic." *Young Cinema and Theatre* 3 (1970): 24–33.

———. "Des cinémas d'Afrique noire depuis 1960." *Recherge, Pedagogie et Culture* no. 17/18 (May–August 1975):3–6.

——— ed. "Le Tiers Monde en films." *Cinémaction Tricontinental*, January 1982 (special issue).

Hennebelle, Guy, and Catherine Ruelle. "Cinéastes d'Afrique noire." *L'Afrique littéraire et artistique* 49 (3d Quarter 1978) (special issue).

Hernandez, Andres R. "Filmmaking and Politics in Cuba: The Cuban Experience." *American Behavioral Scientist* 17 (January–February 1974): 360–392.

Hoberman, J. "It's a Mod, Mod World." *Village Voice*, 17 February 1987, 67.

Holden, Stephen. "The Dark Side of Peter Pan." *New York Times*, 13 September 1987, H36.

Hondo, Med. "Med Hondo." *Framework* no. 7/8 (Spring 1978):28–30.

Honour, Hugh. *The Image of the Black in Western Art: From the American Revolution to World War I*. Houston: Menil Foundation, 1989.

Horatio-Jones, Edward B. "Historical Review of the Cinema in West Africa and the Black World and Its Implication for a Film Industry in Nigeria." In *The Development and Growth of the Film Industry in Nigeria*, ed. Alfred Opubor and Onuora E. Nwuneli, 74–88. Lagos and New York: Third Press International, 1979.

Ibeabuchi, Aloysius. "Why Local Films Are Not Popular with African Audiences." *Daily Times* (Lagos), 7 January 1984.

Iliffe, John. *The Emergence of African Capitalism*. London: Macmillan, 1979.

Iloegbunam, Chuks. "Conversations with Eddie Ugbomah." *The Guardian* (Lagos), 19 October 1983, 11.

Irele, Abiola. *The African Experience in Literature and Ideology*. London: Heinemann, 1981.

Iyam, David Uru. "The Silent Revolutionaries: Ousmane Sembene's *Emitai, Xala* and *Ceddo*." *African Studies Review* 29, no. 4 (December 1986):79–87.

Jameson, Fredric. *The Political Unconscious: Narrative as a Socially Symbolic Art*. Ithaca: Cornell University Press, 1981.

————. "Third World Literature in the Era of Multinational Capitalism." *Social Text* no. 15 (Fall 1986):65–88.

Jinadu, L. Adele. *Fanon: In Search of the African Revolution*. Enugu, Nigeria: Fourth Dimension Publishers, 1980.

————. "Some African Theorists of Cultures and Modernization: Fanon, Cabral, and Some Others." *African Studies Review* 21, no. 1 (April 1978): 121–137.

Johnson, Randal, and Robert Stam. *Brazilian Cinema*. London: Associated University Press, 1982.

Journées Cinématographiques de Carthage: Bilan et Perspectives. Tunis: Ministère des Affaires Culturelles, 1984.

Kamphausen, Hannes. "Cinema in Africa, A Survey." *Cineaste* 5, no. 2 (Spring 1972):28–41.

Killick, Tony. *Development Economics in Action: A Study of Economic Policies in Ghana*. London: Heinemann, 1978.

Ki-Zerbo, Joseph, ed. *General History of Africa, vol. 1, Methodology and African Prehistory*. Berkeley: University of California Press, 1981.

Lamb, David. *The Africans*. New York: Random House, 1982.

Landy, Marsha. "Politics and Style in *Black Girl*." *Jump Cut* no. 27 (July 1982):23–25.

Langley, Ayodele J. *Pan-Africanism and Nationalism in West Africa 1900–1945: A Study in Ideology and Social Classes*. Oxford: Clarendon Press, 1973.

Larson, Charles R. "The Film Version of Achebe's *Things Fall Apart*." *Africana Journal* 13, no. 1/4 (1982):104–110.

Leyda, Jay. *Kino: A History of the Russian and Soviet Film*. New York: Collier Books, 1973.

Lester, Julius. "Mandabi: Confronting Africa." *Evergreen Review* 14, no. 78 (May 1970):55–58; 85–89.

McBean, James Roy. *Film and Revolution*. Bloomington: Indiana University Press, 1975.

MacCabe, Colin, et al. *Godard: Images, Sounds, Politics*. Bloomington: Indiana University Press, 1980.

Magai, Lena. *Dimba Nengue*. Trenton: African World Press, Inc., 1988.

Magubane, Bernard. "A Critical Look at Indices Used in the Study of Social Change in Colonial Africa." *Current Anthropology* 12 (October–December 1971):419–447.

Martin, Angela, ed. *African Films: The Context of Production,* dossier no. 6. London: British Film Institute, 1982.

———. "Four West African Filmmakers." *Framework* no. 11 (Autumn 1979): 16–21.

Martin, Guy. "Fanon's Relevance to Contemporary Political Thought." *UFA-HAMU* 4, no. 3 (Winter 1974):11–34.

Masilela, Ntongela. "Come Back Africa and South African Film History." *Jump Cut* no. 36 (1991):61–65.

Mativo, Kyalo. "Resolving the Cultural Dilemma of the African Film." *UFA-HAMU* 13, no. 1 (Fall 1983):134–147.

Mativo, Wilson. "Cultural Dilemma of the African Film." *UFAHAMU* 1, no. 3 (Winter 1971):64–68.

Maynard, Richard A. *Africa on Film: Myth and Reality.* Rochelle Park, N.J.: Hayden Books, 1974.

Mazrui, Ali. *The African Condition: A Political Diagnosis.* London: Heine-mann, 1980.

———. *The Africans: A Triple Heritage.* Boston: Little, Brown and Company, 1986.

Meisler, Stanley. "Look-Reads." *Africa Report* (May–June 1969):80–83.

Memmi, Albert. *Dominated Man.* Boston: Beacon Press, 1968.

———. *The Colonizer and the Colonized.* Boston: Beacon Press, 1967.

Metz, Christian. *Language and Cinema.* The Hague: Mouton, 1974.

———. *The Imaginary Signifier.* Translated by Celia Britton, Annwyl Williams, Ben Brewster, and Alfred Guzzetti. Bloomington: Indiana University Press, 1982.

Michelson, Annette. "Dr. Crass and Mr. Clair." *October* 11 (Winter 1979): 31–53.

Minot, Gilbert. "Toward the African Cinema." *UFAHAMU* 12, no. 2 (1983): 37–43.

Minter, William. *Portuguese Africa and the West.* Harmondsworth, England: Penguin, 1972.

Mitry, Jean. *Dictionnaire du cinéma.* Paris: Larousse, 1963.

Mnguni, Herbert Mbukeni. "African Intellectuals and the Development of African Political Thought in the Twentieth Century." *Présence Africaine* no. 143 (3d Quarter 1987):113–121.

Moore, Carrie D. *Evolution of an African Artist: Social Realism in the Works of Ousmane Sembene.* Ph.D. dissertation, Indiana University, 1973.

Morgenthau, Henry. "On Films and Filmmakers." *Africa Report* (May–June 1969):71–75.

Mulvey, Laura. "Visual Pleasure and Narrative Cinema." *Screen* 16, no. 3 (Autumn 1975):6–18.

Mwaura, Peter. *Communication Policies in Kenya.* Paris: UNESCO, 1980.

Ngakane, Lionel. "Cinema and the Liberation of People." *Africa* no. 164 (April 1985):88–89.

———. "The Cinema in South Africa." *Présence Africaine* no. 80 (4th Quarter 1971):131–133.

Ngugi wa Thiong'o. *Decolonizing the Mind: The Politics of Language in African Literature*. Nairobi and London: James Currey and Heinemann, 1986.

————. *Homecoming: Essays on African and Caribbean Literature, Culture and Politics*. London: Heinemann, 1972.

Niane, Djibril. *Sundiata: An Epic of Old Mali*. London: Longmans, 1965.

Nichols, Bill, ed. *Ideology and the Image*. Bloomington: Indiana University Press, 1981.

————. *Movies and Methods*. Berkeley: University of California Press, 1976.

Nkrumah, Kwame. *Class Struggle in Africa*. New York: International Publishers, 1970.

————. *Consciencism: Philosophy and the Ideology for Decolonization and Development*. New York: Monthly Review Press, 1964.

————. *Neo-Colonialism: The Last Stage of Imperialism*. London: Heinemann, 1965.

Notcutt, L. A., and G. C. Latham, eds. *The African and the Cinema*. London: The Edinburgh House Press, 1937.

Nursey-Bray, Paul. "Race and Nation: Ideology in the Thought of Frantz Fanon." *Journal of Modern African Studies* 18, no. 1 (March 1980):135–142.

Ogunba, Oyin, and Abiola Irele, eds. *Theater in Africa*. Ibadan, Nigeria: Ibadan University Press, 1978.

Okioh, François Sourou. "Problems of African Cinema." *Young Cinema and Theatre* (Prague) no. 3 (1982):24–30.

Okpaku, Joseph. "African Critical Standards for African Literature and the Arts." In *New African Literature and the Arts*, vol. 1, ed. Joseph Okpaku, 13–23. New York: Crowell, 1966.

Okwechime, Ndubusi. "Fela's Parisian Treat: Musical Show or Soldiering for Africa?" *Daily Times* (Nigeria), 18 June 1983, 7.

Opubor, Alfred E., and Onuora E. Nwuneli, eds. *The Development and Growth of the Film Industry in Nigeria*. Lagos: Third Press International, 1979.

Ostor, Akos. "Cinema and Society in India and Senegal: The Films of Satyajit Ray and Ousmane Sembene." *Cinewave* (Calcutta) no. 7 (October 1984–March 1985):8–18.

Osundare, Niyi. "A Grand Escape into Metaphysics." *West Africa*, 12 May 1980, 826–828.

————. "Following in 007's Footsteps." *West Africa*, 3 November 1980, 2178–2179.

————. "The King of Laughter." *West Africa*, 12 July 1982, 1821.

Otten, Rik. *Le cinéma dans les pays des grands lacs Zaire, Rwanda, Burundi*. Brussels and Paris: OCIC and L'Harmattan, 1984.

Oyekunle, Segun. "The Promises of Mogadishu." *West Africa*, 19 December 1983, 2938–2940.

Paquet, André. "The FESPACO of Ouagadougou—Towards Unity in African Cinema." *Cineaste* 6, no. 1 (1973):36–38.

————. "Toward an Arab and African Cinema: The 1974 Carthage Film Festival." *Cineaste* 7, no. 1 (1974):119–126.

Pearson, Lyle. "Four Years of African Film." *Film Quarterly* 26, no. 3 (Spring 1973):42–47.

Perry, G. M., and Patrick McGilligan. "Ousmane Sembene: An Interview." *Film Quarterly* 26, no. 3 (Summer 1973):36–42.

Pfaff, Françoise. *The Cinema of Ousmane Sembene: A Pioneer of African Film.* Westport, Conn.: Greenwood Press, 1984.

———. "Films of Med Hondo: An African Filmmaker in Paris." *Jump Cut* no. 31 (1986):44–46.

———. "Researching Africa on Film." *Jump Cut* no. 31 (1986):50, 57.

———. "Three Faces of Africa: Women in *Xala.*" *Jump Cut* no. 27 (1982): 27–31.

———. *Twenty-five Black African Filmmakers: A Critical Study with Filmography and Bio-Bibliography.* Westport, Conn.: Greenwood Press, 1988.

Pines, Jim, and Paul Willemen, eds. *Questions of Third Cinema.* London: British Film Institute 1989.

Poitier, Sidney. *This Life.* New York: Knopf, 1980.

Radin, Paul. *African Folktales and Sculpture.* New York: Bollingen Foundation, Inc., 1952.

Rayfield, J. R. "The Use of Films in Teaching about Africa." *Film Library Quarterly* 17, no. 2 (1984):34–52.

Relich, Mario. "Films of Struggle." *West Africa,* 13 August 1984, 1632–1633.

———. "From Glitter to Gore in the Film World." *West Africa,* 7 December 1981, 2907–2910.

Robinson, Cedric. "Domination and Imitation: *Xala* and the Emergence of the Black Bourgeoisie." *Race and Class* 22, no. 2 (1980):147–158.

Rodney, Walter. *How Europe Underdeveloped Africa.* Washington, D.C.: Howard University Press, 1982.

Rouch, Jean. "Le cinéma africain." *Les lettres françaises,* 21 September 1961, 1–6.

Rubin, Bernard, ed. *Small Voices and Great Trumpets.* New York: Praeger, 1980.

Sadoul, Georges. *Histoire du cinema mondial.* 9th ed. Paris: Flammarion, 1972.

———, ed. *The Cinema in the Arab Countries*: Beirut: Interarab Center for Cinema and Television/UNESCO, 1966.

Said, Edward W. *Orientalism.* New York: Vintage, 1978.

———. *The Question of Palestine.* New York: Vintage, 1979.

———. *The World, the Text, and the Critic.* Cambridge: Harvard University Press, 1983.

Sanjinés, Jorge, and the Ukamau Group. *Theory and Practice of a Cinema with the People.* Translated by Richard Scaaf. Willimantic, Conn.: Curbstone Press, 1989.

Sartre, Jean-Paul. *Search for a Method.* Translated by Hazel Barnes. New York: Random House, 1968.

Scheub, Harold. "A Review of African Oral Traditions and Literature." *African Studies Review* 28, no. 2/3 (June–September 1985):1–15.

Schissel, Howard. "Sembene Ousmane: Filmmaker." *West Africa,* 18 July 1983, 1665–1666.

Schmidt, Nancy J. *Sub-Saharan African Films and Filmmakers: A Preliminary*

Bibliography. Bloomington: Indiana University Press and Indiana University African Studies Program, 1986.

Screen (London) 26, no. 3/4 (1985). Special issue on "Other Cinemas, Other Criticisms."

Screen Reader 1: Cinema/Ideology/Politics. London: The Society for Education in Film and Television, 1977.

Segy, Ladislas. *Masks of Black Africa*. New York: Dover Publications, 1976.

Sembene, Ousmane. *Le docker noir*. Paris: Nouvelles Editions Debresse, 1956.

———. *Les bouts de bois de Dieu*. Paris: Amiot-Dupont, 1960. Published in English as *God's Bits of Wood*. New York: Doubleday, 1962; London: Heinemann, 1970.

———. *Voltaique*. Paris: *Présence Africaine*, 1962. Published in English as *Tribal Scars and Other Stories*. London: Heinemann, 1973.

———. *Vehi Ciosane ou Blanche Genése, Suivi du Mandat*. Paris: *Présence Africaine*, 1965. Published in English as *The Money Order, White Genesis*. London: Heinemann, 1972.

———. *Xala*. Paris: *Présence Africaine*, 1973. Published in English as *Xala*. Westport, Conn.: Lawrence Hill and Co, 1980.

———. *Le dernier de l'empire*. 2 vols. Paris: L'Harmattan 1981. Published in English as *The Last of the Empire*. London: Heinemann, 1983.

"Seminar on the Role of the African Filmmaker in Rousing an Awareness of Black Civilization, Ouagadougou, 8–13 April 1974." *Présence Africaine* no. 90 (2d Quarter 1974):3–204.

Senghor, Blaise. "Prerequisites for a Truly African Cinema." *Présence Africaine* no. 49 (1st Quarter 1964):101–107.

Sevastakis, Michael. "Neither Gangsters nor Dead Kings: Ousmane Sembene's Five Fantastic Films." *Film Library Quarterly* 6, no. 3 (1973):13–48.

Shklovsky, Viktor. "Art as Technique." In *Russian Formalist Criticism: Four Essays*, ed. Lee Lemon and Marion Reis, 3–24. Lincoln: University of Nebraska Press, 1965.

Smyth, Rosaleen. "The British Colonial Film Unit and Sub-Saharan Africa—1939–1945." *Historical Journal of Film, Radio and Television* 8, no. 3 (1988).

———. "Movies and Mandarins: The Official Film and British Colonial Africa." In *British Cinema History*, ed. James Curran and Vincent Porter, 129–143. Totowa, N.J.: Barnes and Noble Books, 1983.

Solanas, Fernando E., and Octavio Gettino. "Towards a Third Cinema." In *Movies and Methods*, ed. Bill Nichols. Berkeley: University of California Press, 1976.

Spass, Lieve. "Female Domestic Labour and Third World Politics in *La Noire de*...." *Jump Cut* no. 27 (July 1982):26–27.

Stam, Robert, and Louise Spence, "Colonialism, Racism, and Representation." *Screen* 24, no. 2 (March–April 1983):2–20.

Stone, John. "Images of a Liberation Struggle: The Film as Document." *Africa Today* 20, no. 1 (Winter 1973):85–92.

Tajima, Renee, ed. *Journey Across Three Continents: Film and Lecture Series*. New York: Third World Newsreel, 1985.

Taylor, Clyde. "Africa, the Last Cinema." In *Journey Across Three Continents: Film and Lecture Series,* ed. Renee Tajima, 50–58. New York: Third World Newsreel, 1985.

———. "Black Spirit in South Africa." *The Black Collegian* (September–October 1985):43–44.

———. "FESPACO '85 Was a Dream Come True." *Black Film Review* 1, no. 4 (1985):6–9.

———. "We Don't Need Another Hero: Anti-Theses on Aesthetics." In *Blackframes: Critical Perspectives on Black Independent Cinema,* ed. Mbye B. Cham and Claire Andrade-Watkins, 80–85. Cambridge: The MIT Press, 1988.

Taylor, Elyseo. "Film and Social Change." *American Behavioral Scientist* 22, no. 3 (January–February 1979):424–438.

Tomaselli, Kenyan. *The Cinema of Apartheid.* New York: Smyrna Press, 1988.

———. "Racism in South African Cinema." *Cineaste* 13, no. 1 (1983):12–15.

Traoré, Mahama. "Cinema in Africa Must Be a School." *Cineaste* 6, no. 1 (1973):32–35.

Turvey, Gerry. "*Xala* and the Curse of Neocolonialism." *Screen* 26, no. 3/4 (1985):75–87.

Ukadike, N. Frank. "A Filmmaker's View on Nigerian Television." *Nigerian Theatre Journal,* no. 2 (1985):191–197.

———. "Depictions of Africa in Documentary Film." *Black Film Review* 4, no. 1 (Winter 1987/88):13–15.

———. "Framing FESPACO: Pan-African Cinema in Context." *Afterimage* 19, no. 4 (November 1991):6–9.

Van Sertima, Ivan. *Blacks in Science: Ancient and Modern.* New Brunswick, N. J.: Transaction Books, 1983.

Vansina, J. *Oral Tradition as History.* Madison: University of Wisconsin Press, 1985.

Van Wert, William. "Ideology in the Third World Cinema: A Study of Sembene Ousmane and Glauber Rocha." *Quarterly Review of Film Studies* 4, no. 2 (Spring 1979):207–226.

Vaughan, J. Koyinde. "Africa and the Cinema." In *An African Treasury,* ed. Langston Hughes. New York: Crown Publishers, 1960.

Vieyra, Paulin Soumanou. *Le cinéma Africain des origines à 1973.* Paris: *Présence Africaine,* 1975.

———. *Le cinéma au Sénégal.* Brussels and Paris: OCIC/L'Harmattan, 1983.

———. "Propos sur le cinéma Africain." *Présence Africaine* 22 (1958): 106–117.

———. *Ousmane Sembene cinéaste.* Paris: *Présence Africaine,* 1972.

Wallerstein, Immanuel. *The Modern World System.* New York: Academic Press, 1974.

Weaver, Harold D., Jr. "Black Filmmakers in Africa and America." *Sightlines* 5 (Spring 1976):7–12.

———. "Filmmakers Have a Great Responsibility to Our People: An Interview with Ousmane Sembene." *Cineaste* 6, no. 1 (1973):27–31.

———. "The Politics of African Cinema." In *Black Cinema Aesthetics,* ed. Gladstone L. Yearwood. Athens: Ohio University Center for Afro-American Studies, 1982.

Wiley, David S. *Africa on Film and Video Tape 1960–1981.* East Lansing: African Studies Center, Michigan State University, 1982.

Williams, Eric Eustace. *History of the People of Trinidad and Tobago.* New York: Praeger, 1964.

Williams, Raymond. *Marxism and Literature.* Oxford: Oxford University Press, 1977.

———. *Television: Technology and Cultural Form.* London: Fontana/Collins, 1974.

Yansane, Aguibou Y., ed. *Decolonization and Dependency: Problems of Development of African Societies.* Westport, Conn.: Greenwood Press, 1980.

"Zimbabwe Has Much to Offer Foreign Filmmakers." *Financial Gazette* (Harare, Zimbabwe), 5 February 1988, *Images* (supplement), 27.

Index

357

Breinigsville, PA USA
16 December 2009
229340BV00001B/44/A